Jon E. Lewis is a writer on military affairs and history. His many
previous books include the bestselling *The Mammoth Book of the
Edge*, *The Mammoth Book of Polar Journeys*, *The Mammoth Book
of True War Stories*, *World War II: The Autobiography*, *The Mammoth
Book of Combat*, *Voices from D-Day*, *A Brief History of the First
World War*, *SAS: The Autobiography*, *The Mammoth Book of Covert
Ops*, *The Mammoth Book of Vietnam*, *Spitfire: The Autobiography*,
Voices from the Holocaust and *A Brief History of the First World War*.

Recent Mammoth titles

The Mammoth Book of Undercover Cops
The Mammoth Book of Antarctic Journeys
The Mammoth Book of Muhammad Ali
The Mammoth Book of Best British Crime 10
The Mammoth Book of Conspiracies
The Mammoth Book of Lost Symbols
The Mammoth Book of Body Horror
The Mammoth Book of Steampunk
The Mammoth Book of New CSI
The Mammoth Book of Gangs
The Mammoth Book of One-Liners
The Mammoth Book of Ghost Romance
The Mammoth Book of Best New SF 25
The Mammoth Book of Horror 24
The Mammoth Book of Slasher Movies
The Mammoth Book of Street Art
The Mammoth Book of Ghost Stories by Women
The Mammoth Book of Best New Erotica 12
The Mammoth Book of Unexplained Phenomena
The Mammoth Book of Futuristic Romance
The Mammoth Book of Best British Crime 11
The Mammoth Book of Combat
The Mammoth Book of Erotic Quickies
The Mammoth Book of Dark Magic
The Mammoth Book of Zombies
The Mammoth Book of The Lost Chronicles of Sherlock Holmes
The Mammoth Book of SF Stories by Women

The Mammoth Book of

SPECIAL FORCES
TRAINING

Edited by JON E. LEWIS

RUNNING PRESS
PHILADELPHIA · LONDON

ROBINSON
First published in Great Britain in 2015 by Robinson

A CIP catalogue record for this book
is available from the British Library.

ISBN 978-1-47211-087-9 (paperback)
ISBN 978-1-47211-178-4 (ebook)

Typeset in Plantin by Hewer Text UK Ltd, Edinburgh
Printed and bound in Great Britain by CPI Group (UK) Ltd, Croydon, CR0 4YY

Robinson
is an imprint of
Constable & Robinson Ltd
100 Victoria Embankment
London EC4Y 0DY
An Hachette UK Company

www.hachette.co.uk
www.constablerobinson.com

First published in the United States in 2014 by Running Press Book Publishers,
A Member of the Perseus Books Group

Books published by Running Press are available at special discounts for bulk
purchases in the United States by corporations, institutions and other organizations.

For more information, please contact the Special Markets Department at the
Perseus Books Group, 2300 Chestnut Street, Suite 200, Philadelphia, PA 19103,
or call (800) 810-4145, ext. 5000, or email special.markets@perseusbooks.com.

US ISBN: 978-0-7624-5233-0

US Library of Congress Control Number: 2014943439

9 8 7 6 5 4 3 2 1

Digit on the right indicates the number of this printing

Running Press Book Publishers
2300 Chestnut Street
Philadelphia, PA 19103-4371
Visit us on the web!
www.runningpress.com

CONTENTS

Introduction   1

PART 1: SPECIAL FORCES UNITS
The SAS   7
US Navy SEALs   48
US Green Berets   60
Sayret Maktal   64

PART II: SELECTION
Special Air Service   73
Special Boat Service (SBS)   77
Green Berets   78
US Navy Seals   79

PART III: TRAINING
Fitness   85
Combat Skills and Techniques   108
Booby Traps   144
Weaponry   167
Medical Skills   173

PART IV: SURVIVAL
The Basics   211
The Desert   305
The Jungle   327
The Arctic   334

PART V: MISSIONS
Landings and Raids on Enemy Territory   395
Evasion, Capture & Escape   425

Hijack & Hostage Rescue   470

APPENDIX:
SPECIAL FORCES UNITS OF THE WORLD   485

Sources and Acknowledgements   527
Bibliography   529

INTRODUCTION

"Special Operations are defined as operations conducted by specially trained, equipped and organized Department of Defense forces against strategic or tactical targets in pursuit of national military, political, economic or psychological objectives. These operations may be conducted during periods of peace or hostilities. They may support conventional operations, or they may be undertaken independently when the use of conventional forces ... is inappropriate."

United States Operations Command,
A Special Operations Primer, 1996

When all is said and done, the brutal business of war comes in only two forms. There is the formalized engagement between large regular formations, with their strict uniforms and stricter hierarchies. And then there is the shadowy mission of the irregular, small-scale unit, with its unorthodox tactics and its unusual weapons. The Special Forces.

There have been unconventional forces since the fires of war were first stoked. After all, what did Odysseus do but use "specially trained, equipped and organized" forces to gain entry into Troy by concealing them inside the Wooden Horse? Think, too, of Rogers' Rangers from the French and Indian War of 1756, the British agents who played "the Great Game" in central Asia against the Russians in the early nineteenth century and John Singleton Mosby's Confederate Cavalry Raiders from the Civil War.

Modern special forces date back to the First World War, and the attempts by the Allies and the central powers to break the military deadlock on the Western Front. One stratagem of the Allies was to raise an irregular Arab army under Colonel T.E. Lawrence: this was to foment trouble against the Turks and so draw off Central Power resources from the main show. The Germans, meanwhile, sought to break through the Allied trenches on the Western Front by creating and training special *Stosstruppen*. These "shock troops" caused mayhem during the Michael Offensive of 1918 until Allied might overcame them.

The Germans might have lost the Great War, but they saw clearly that the future of warfare lay with hard-hitting mobile formations, be they of men or machinery. Hitler liked Special Forces because they could be wrapped with the aura of the "superman" so beloved of Nazi philosophy. It was no coincidence, then, that the Second World War opened with a German Special Forces operation – a simulated attack on the German frontier that provided the Führer with the pretext to invade Poland. No surprise either, that the 1940 German invasion of the Low Countries included a dazzling airborne assault on the Belgian fortress of Eben Emael by the Koch Assault Detachment that still causes military historians to gape.

Whereas the Germans had become revolutionaries in warfare, the military establishments of the major Allied powers had long been overtaken by a glacial conservatism. The result: in 1939 the major Allied nations were entirely bereft of Special Forces. Despite the late start, Special Forces soon proliferated amongst the Second World War Allies, both because the complexity of modern warfare made specialization an inevitability, and, with no early prospect of a major offensive against the Germans or Japanese, because morale-boosting raids by a small elite were too much of a temptation. Moreover, the sheer scale of the frontline – stretching around Europe, North Africa and the Far East – simply invited clandestine "behind the lines" missions of reconnaissance and sabotage.

The other allure of Special Forces was that, for a relatively small commitment of men and means, they might achieve a big, even strategically important result. In North Africa the SAS, which began with seventy soldiers, destroyed 300 Axis aircraft on the ground in North Africa. And it is this understanding by the SAS's founder, David Stirling, that Special Forces could play a strategic role in war, and not just be a mob for a particular job, that makes the SAS absolutely the prototype of the modern Special Force. That, plus the SAS's tough selection process, the quality of its training, and its ethos: Who Dares Wins.

Despite the success of Special Forces in the Second World War, with peace in 1945 Special Forces were shut down almost everywhere. Why? The top brass had long been distrustful of Special Forces because they were too independent and too prone to creaming off the best personnel and kit from regular formations. "Expensive, wasteful and unnecessary" was the complaint of Field Marshal Slim. So Special Forces were disbanded.

Yet the face of war after 1945 was not the titanic clash of arms between the Soviet Bloc and the West expected by the general staffs, but a rash of savage little wars in colonial places: Malaysia, Oman, Vietnam, Algeria, the Congo ... In these wars, conventional forces were often of little use. Who better to fight guerrillas than highly trained, cherry-picked, superbly equipped "guerrillas" of the Special Forces? There was a further stimulus to the rebirth of the Special Forces: the spread of terrorism from the 1950s onwards, particularly that emanating from the Middle East. Indeed, with the decline in Communist meddling in the Third World, the main burden of the Special Forces' mission has become anti- and counter-terrorism. "Counter-Terrorism" speeded up exponentially after 1972, when Palestinian terrorists attacked Israeli athletes at the Munich Olympic Games.

Fighting "shadow wars" in ex-colonial countries and counter-terrorist operations does not exhaust the capability of contemporary Special Forces. VIP protection, intelligence gathering, reconnaissance, training forces from foreign nations, even humanitarian assistance, have all fallen into the Special Forces' brief. In short, Special Forces have come to have utility across the whole range of conflict, which is why they are the favourites of politicians. Special Forces enable politicians to secure their designs with risk to few compatriots. Electorates like it – the sight of body bags being flown home, as in Vietnam and the recent war in Iraq, is a distinct vote loser.

The enthusiasm of politicians for Special Forces has ensured that they have escaped the financial cutbacks suffered by conventional military services. Indeed, since the end of the Cold War most special units have seen their budgets grow. So too their responsibilities. "Send for the SAS", or "Send for the SEALs", has become almost a knee-jerk response by the politicos at the first whiff of trouble. You are never going to be short of work as a Special Forces soldier.

While you are reading this, Special Forces are in action somewhere in the world. It takes a special kind of person to be a Special Forces soldier. All Special Forces have stringent selection processes, after which those few who qualify are subjected to gruelling training regimes intended to turn them into killers who are also able to master many military trades, and survive in some of the most hostile places on earth.

This book tells you what you need to know about the UK and the US's Special Forces, their history, their training, and the skills you will be expected to master.

PART I

SPECIAL FORCES UNITS

THE SAS

Of all unlikely places, the Special Air Service – destined to become the world's most famous Special Forces unit – was conceived in a hospital bed in Egypt. Injured in 1941 while undertaking some unofficial parachute training, David Stirling, a twenty-six-year-old subaltern in No. 8 (Guards) Commando, used his enforced sojourn in 15th Scottish Military Hospital in Cairo to conjure a scheme for hit-and-run operations against the Germans in the North African desert.

On his release from hospital in July, Stirling decided to take his idea to the top. To present the plan through the usual channels would only mean it getting buried in what Stirling thought of as "fossilized shit" – bureaucracy, in other, politer words. Although generals are not, by and large, in the habit of granting interviews to second-lieutenants, Stirling hobbled on crutches to General Headquarters Middle East in Cairo's leafy Tonbalat Street; after failing to show a pass at the security barrier, he went around the corner, jumped over the fence and careered inside the building, the warden's bellowed alarms close behind. Up on the third floor, Stirling found his way into the office of Major General Neil Ritchie, Claude Auchinleck's Deputy Chief of Staff. Stirling breathlessly apologized to the surprised Ritchie for the somewhat unconventional nature of his call, but insisted that he had something of "great operational importance" to show him. He then pulled out the pencilled memo on small-scale desert raiding he had prepared in hospital. "He [Ritchie] was very courteous," Stirling remembered years later, "and he settled down to read it. About halfway through, he got very engrossed, and had forgotten the rather irregular way it had been presented." It was Stirling's turn to be surprised. Looking up, Ritchie said matter-of-factly, "I think this may be the sort of plan we are looking for. I will discuss it with the Commander-in-Chief and let you know our decision in the next day or so." The Commander-in-Chief was General Claude Auchinleck, new to his post and under immense pressure from Churchill to mount offensive operations. Stirling's plan was a gift for Auchinleck: it required few resources, it was original, and it dovetailed neatly with Churchill's own love of commandos. Stirling's memo went under the cumbersome title of "Case for the retention of a limited number of special service troops, for employment as parachutists", but there was nothing ungainly about its concept; on the contrary, Stirling understood that in wartime small can be beautifully lethal. The unit Stirling proposed was to operate behind enemy lines and attack vulnerable targets such as supply lines and airfields at night. What is more, the raids were to be carried out by groups of five to ten men, rather than the hundreds of a standard commando force, the very numbers of which made them susceptible to detection by the enemy. Since these special service commandos were to be inserted by air, they had greater range than seaborne troops and did not require costly (and reluctant) Royal Navy support.

While Auchinleck pondered Stirling's memo, Ritchie looked into David Stirling's background. He was pleased and displeased in equal measure by what he found. On graduation from the Guards' depot at Pirbright, David Stirling had been classed as an "irresponsible and unremarkable soldier". He was dismissive of authority. He overslept so much he was nicknamed "the Great Sloth". In Egypt his partying had become legendary, and he had more than once revived himself from hangovers by inhaling oxygen begged from nurses at the 15th Scottish Military Hospital.

But it wasn't all bad. Born in 1915, Stirling came from "good stock": he was the youngest son of Brigadier Archibald Stirling of Keir; his mother was the daughter of the 16th Baron Lovat. After Ampleforth and three years at Cambridge, Stirling had enthusi-astically joined the Scots Guards, before transferring to No. 8 Commando. Like many a commando officer, he was recruited over a pink gin at White's Club by Lieutenant-Colonel Bob Laycock, 8 Commando's Commanding Officer. As part of the "Layforce" brigade, No. 8 Commando had been dispatched to

North Africa, where its seaborne raids had been embarrassing wash-outs. On the disbandment of Layforce, Stirling had jumped – literally – at the chance of joining an unofficial parachute training session organized by another officer in No. 8 Commando. Many people over the years mistook Stirling's diffidence, abetted by the slight stoop common to the very tall (Stirling was six feet six inches) for a lack of ambition: on the contrary, Stirling possessed a core of steely resolve. (Churchill, who met Stirling later in the war, borrowed an apposite line from *Don Juan* for his pen portrait of the SAS leader as "the mildest manner'd man that ever scuttled ship or cut a throat".) This inner determination was the reason why Stirling participated in the impromptu parachute jumping trials at Fuka: he wanted to get on with the war. Unfortunately, the aircraft used, a lumbering Valencia biplane, was not equipped for parachuting and the men had secured the static lines which opened the silk canopies to seat legs. Stirling's parachute caught on the door and snagged; he descended far too rapidly and hit the ground so hard that he was temporarily paralysed from the waist down. Thus he had ended up as a bed patient in the Scottish Military Hospital.

Three days after his meeting with Ritchie, Stirling was back at Middle East Headquarters, this time with a pass. Auchinleck saw him in person. Stirling was given permission to recruit a force of sixty officers and men. The unit was to be called "L Detachment, SAS Brigade". The "SAS" stood for "Special Air Service", a force that was wholly imaginary and whose nomenclature was devised by Brigadier Dudley Clarke, a staff Intelligence officer, to convince the Germans that Britain had a large airborne force in North Africa. To mark his new appointment as the Commanding Officer of L Detachment, Stirling was promoted to captain. There were two particular officers Stirling wanted for his outfit. The first was John "Jock" Lewes, whom Stirling found at Tobruk, where he was leading raids on the Axis lines. British by birth, Lewes had been brought up in Australia, and was an Oxford rowing "blue" who had led his university eight to a historic win over Cambridge. It had been Lewes who had organized the parachute jump at Fuka during which Stirling had crashed. Lewes's influence on the formation of the SAS was paramount: on a visit to Stirling in hospital, Lewes had voiced proposals and queries which had done much to further the embryonic idea of a desert raiding force circling around in Stirling's head.

When Stirling asked Lewes to become the first recruit of "L Detachment", however, Lewes refused point blank. He did not trust Stirling's commitment. But Stirling, as everyone agreed, could be very persuasive. Besides, he was displaying more grit than Lewes had seen in the party boy hitherto. After a month of cajoling, Lewes agreed to join. So did Captain R. B. "Paddy" Mayne. Before the war, Mayne had been a rugby player of international rank, capped six times for Ireland and once for the British Lions. He was also a useful boxer and had reached the final of the British Universities' Championship heavyweight division. Unfortunately, when taken by drink Mayne was not too fussy whom he fought: in June 1941 he'd been returned to unit from 11 Commando for attacking his commanding officer. However, Paddy Mayne was much more than a six-feet-six-inch drinker and brawler. A former law student, he had a "Dr Jekyll" side, and was sensitive, literate, modest and painfully shy. Unquestionably he was brave: he'd won a Mention in Dispatches for his baptismal combat – 1 Commando's raid on the Litani River in Syria. He would end up as one of the four most decorated British officers of the Second World War, with a Distinguished Service Order (DSO) and three Bars. Nevertheless, before accepting Mayne into L Detachment, Stirling extricated a promise that he would not attack his new commanding officer.

Like Lewes and Mayne, most of the rest of the officers and men of L Detachment, who would later be known as "the Originals", were volunteers recruited from commandos beached at the Infantry Base Depot at Geneifa following the disbandment of Layforce. Selection was based on Stirling's personal impression of the men at brief interviews. He also told them that if they failed to make the grade in training they would have to return to their units.

By August 1941, Stirling had established a base at Kabrit, 100 miles south of Cairo in the Canal Zone. Equipment was conspicuous by its absence, due to the parsimony of Q Branch. Arriving by truck at Kabrit, Johnny Cooper, recruited from No. 8 Commando, found only two medium-sized marquees and three 180-lb tents piled up in the middle of the strip of bare desert allocated to us. No camp, none of the usual facilities, not even a flagpole. A wooden sign bearing the words "L Detachment – SAS" was the sole clue that this was base camp.

Being, in his own words, a "cheekie laddie", Stirling had a plan to secure the necessary equipment to complete the camp, which was to "borrow" it from a New Zealand camp down the road. Thus the first – and highly unofficial – attack of L Detachment was a night raid on the camp of 2nd New Zealand Division. L Detachment's one and only three-ton truck was filled up with anything useful that could be found, including tents and a piano for the sergeants' mess. The next day, L Detachment boasted one of the smartest and most luxuriously furnished British camps in the Canal Zone.

Training then began in earnest. From the outset, Stirling insisted on a high standard of discipline, equal to that of the Brigade of Guards. In his opening address to L Detachment on 4 September, he told the men: "We can't afford to piss about disciplining anyone who is not a hundred per cent devoted to having a crack at the Hun." L Detachment required a special discipline: self-discipline. Stirling told the L Detachment volunteers that control of self was expected at all times, even on leave: "Get this quite clear. In the SAS, all toughness is reserved exclusively for the enemy." In return, the usual Army "bullshit" of parades and saluting officers every time they loomed into sight was to be dropped. This informal style was to become a hallmark of the SAS. Stirling expected personal initiative, independence and modesty. Any "passengers" would be returned to their units.

David Stirling also demanded the utmost physical fitness, but it was Jock Lewes who translated the master's ideas into practicalities. The early L Detachment training devised by Lewes was in essence commando training adapted to desert conditions, especially those encountered at night. The emphasis was on navigation, weapons training, demolition training and punishing physical training sessions. Endurance marches became marathons of up to thirty miles a night, carrying packs crammed with sand or bricks.

Everyone joining the SAS had to be a parachutist, since Stirling envisaged insertion by air for his force. No parachute-training instructors were available (the only British parachute-training schools extant were at Ringway, near Manchester, and Delhi, in India), so the SAS under Jock Lewes developed its own parachute-training techniques. These involved jumping from ever higher scaffold towers and from the tailboard of a 112-pound Bedford truck moving at thirty miles per hour across the desert. More than half "the Originals" of L Detachment sustained injuries launching themselves off the back of the Bedford. After this very basic parachute training, the L Detachment recruits made their first live drop, from a Bristol Bombay aircraft. There were no reserve parachutes. Two men, Ken Warburton and Joseph Duffy, died when the snap-links connecting the strops on their parachutes to the static rail in the Bombay twisted apart. Consequently, when they jumped they were no longer attached to the aircraft – and there was nothing to pull the canopies out. Afterwards, 'Original' Bob Bennett recalled:

> We went to bed with as many cigarettes as possible, and smoked until morning. Next morning, every man (led by Stirling himself) jumped; no one backed out. It was then that I realized that I was with a great bunch of chaps.

The drop on the morning of 17 October was a key moment in SAS history. Stirling displayed leadership; he took the men through the doubt and the darkness.

To replace the faulty clips on the Bombay had been straightforward; however, another engineering problem facing L Detachment proved harder to solve. What bomb should the patrols carry to blow up German aircraft? The bomb had to be small enough to be easily transportable but powerful enough to do the job of destruction. Most SAS men infiltrating on foot from a drop zone could only be expected to carry two of the widely available five-pound charges, which would only inflict superficial damage. Once again it was Jock Lewes to the rescue. After weeks of experiments in a small hut at Kabrit, Lewes invented the requisite device, henceforth known as the "Lewes bomb". A mixture of plastic explosive, thermite and aluminium turnings rolled in engine oil, the device was sticky and could quickly be placed onto the side of an aircraft. Just a pound of "Lewes bomb" could annihilate an aircraft, meaning that each trooper could carry the means of dispatching ten.

By the end of August, L Detachment was ready for its final exercise, a dummy attack on the large RAF base at Heliopolis, outside Cairo. Stirling had been bluntly told by an RAF group captain that his plan to sabotage German aircraft on the ground was far-fetched. So far-fetched, indeed, that he bet Stirling £10 that L Detachment could not infiltrate the Heliopolis base and place labels representing bombs on the parked aircraft. Now, Stirling decided, it was time to pay up. The entire orbat (order of battle) of L Detachment, six officers and fifty-five men, trekked ninety miles across the desert from Kabrit over four days, on four pints of water each, and carrying weights to simulate Lewes bombs. Although the RAF knew the SAS were coming, and even set up air patrols, Stirling and his men successfully infiltrated the base on the fourth night and adorned the parked aircraft with sticky labels marked "BOMB". Stirling collected his £10.

The first operational raid by the SAS, Squatter, was planned for the night of 17 November 1941. Five parties were to be dropped from Bristol Bombays, to attack Axis fighter and bomber strips at Gazala and Timimi. The drop zones were about twelve miles from the objective, and the teams were to spend a day in a lying-up position observing their targets before a night attack with Lewes bombs, to be detonated by time-delay pencils. After the attack, the teams were to rendezvous south of the Trig al'Abd track with a motor patrol of the Long Range Desert Group (LRDG). Reconnaissance behind enemy lines was the stock-in-trade of the LRDG, which had been founded by Major Ralph Bagnold, an amateur pre-war explorer of the Sahara. Stirling's attack had a purpose beyond the destruction of enemy aircraft: it was designed to divert enemy attention on the eve of Operation Crusader, Auchinleck's offensive to push Rommel out of Cyrenaica in North Africa. The same evening would see No. 11

Commando attack Rommel's house in Beda Littoria (now Al Baydá), a commando raid that, like so many previous, was a seamless disaster resulting in the loss of thirty men for no gain whatsoever: the house raided had never even been used by Rommel.

Not that Stirling's debut raid garnered a better result, though. Following a Met Office forecast of thirty-knot winds and rain in the target area, Stirling toyed with cancelling the Squatter mission, since airborne operations in anything above fifteen knots invariably ended in the scattering and injuring of the parachutists. On further thought, though, he had decided to go ahead, believing that a cancellation would affect L Detachment's bubbling-over morale. Moreover, in his sales talk on behalf of his intended parachute force, Stirling had promised general headquarters that the unique quality of his unit was that "the weather would not restrict their operations to the same extent that it had done in the case of seaborne special service troops". To Stirling's relief, the officers of L Detachment, assembled ready to go at Baggush airfield, backed his decision to go ahead. So did the enlisted men. "We'll go because we've got to," Stirling told them. Any man who wanted to could leave. No one did.

Of the fifty-four SAS men who jumped out into the windswept night of 16 November, only twenty-one made the rendezvous with the LRDG. The plane carrying Lieutenant Charles Bonington's stick (team of parachutists) was hit by flak, after which an Me-109 fighter delivered the *coup de grâce*; all the SAS men aboard were injured, one fatally. Meanwhile, Lieutenant Eoin McGonigal had been killed on landing, and when his stick set out towards the rendezvous they were captured by an Italian patrol. Nearly every man in Stirling's, Mayne's and Lewes's sticks suffered concussion, sprains or broken bones; Mayne's troop sergeant, Jock Cheyne, broke his back. Since all their gear had been dropped separately, even the walking able found themselves lacking bombs and fuses. What fuses were recovered were then wrecked by driving rain, the storm of 16 and 17 November 1941 being one of the worst of the war in the Western Desert. Demoralized, the survivors trekked to the rendezvous not through blistering heat, as they had expected, but through mud and floods. Stirling and Bob Tait were among the last to arrive. Waiting for them on the Trig al'Abd was Captain David Lloyd Owen of the LRDG's Y patrol:

> One very interesting thing arose from my meeting with David Stirling that morning. David told me all about the operation and that it had been a total failure. He was a remarkable man. He never gave in to failure and was determined to make the next operation a success. I turned over in my mind, "Why the hell do this ridiculous parachuting, why didn't they let us take them to where they wanted to go? We could take them like a taxi to do the job. We could push off while they did their task, and then pick them up at an agreed rendezvous."

The LRDG had just got themselves a job as Stirling's taxi company.

Although Stirling thought his L Detachment SAS might be killed off as a result of Squatter's failure, no-one at general headquarters seemed to care much. General headquarters had bigger problems on its mind than the loss of thirty-four parachutists: Rommel was making his famous "dash to the wire" and a counter-thrust was needed. It would help the counter-thrust if the Axis aircraft at Tamet, Sirte, Aghayala and Agedabia aerodromes were destroyed. Stirling was given another chance and he took it with both hands. This time there was to be no parachute drop: the SAS were to be taxied to the target by the LRDG.

On 8 December, Stirling, Mayne and eleven other SAS men departed their temporary headquarters at Jalo oasis accompanied by the LRDG's Rhodesian patrol under the command of Captain Gus Holliman. Stirling and Mayne were set to raid Sirte and Tamet airfields, which were about 350 miles from Jalo, on the night of 14 December. At the same time, Jock Lewes was to lead a section in an attack on Aghayla. A fourth SAS patrol, comprising four men under Lieutenant Bill Fraser, was to raid Agedabia a week later. Sitting aboard the LRDG's stripped-down Ford trucks, the SAS men were overcome by the vastness of the Sahara. There was no sign of life, and Stirling found the brooding solitude like being on the high seas. Courtesy of dead-on navigation by the LRDG's Corporal Mike Sadler, the SAS were just forty miles south of Sirte by noon on 11 December. Then their luck changed: an Italian Ghibli spotter plane appeared out of the haze to strafe and bomb them. Holliman ordered the patrol to make for cover in a thorn scrub two miles back, and there they lay as two more Ghiblis came hunting, but failed to see the patrol. The element of surprise, the *sine qua non* of the SAS, was lost. Even so, Stirling was determined to press on, and the obliging LRDG dropped the SAS off not at the agreed twenty miles from Sirte, but a mere three miles. Knowing that a reception committee was likely to be waiting, Stirling chose not to risk his whole section but to instead infiltrate the airfield with just one companion, Sergeant Jimmy Brough. The rest of the team, under Mayne, was sent to a satellite airfield five miles away at Wadi Tamet. Unfortunately, during their recce of the airfield Stirling and Brough stumbled over two Italian sentries, one of whom began firing off bullets, causing the SAS men to sprint away into the desert night. Next day, as they lay up near the base, Stirling and Brough watched in bitter frustration as one Italian Caproni bomber after another flew away. Alerted and suspicious, the Italians were evacuating the airfield.

At nightfall, Stirling and Brough tramped in silence to the rendezvous with the LRDG. Once again, an SAS operation had been a wash-out. Stirling knew that unless Mayne and Lewes triumphed, the disbandment of the SAS was likely. Mayne's attack was to take place at 11 p.m.: the hour came and went, unlit by explosions, and then there was a great *whumph* and a bolt of flame in the west, followed by explosion upon explosion. The SAS was in the sabotage business. Stirling and Brough almost danced with delight. Jock Lewes had not enjoyed good hunting, but when Bill Fraser's party reached their rendezvous they reported the most astounding success of all. They had blown up thirty-seven aircraft at Agedabia aerodrome. In this week-long sequence of raids, the SAS had accounted for no less than sixty-one enemy aircraft destroyed, together with petrol, stores and transport.

His tail up, Stirling could not wait to have another go at the enemy. On the presumption that the enemy would not expect another attack so soon, Stirling and Mayne set off from their Jalo desert base on Christmas Day 1941 to revisit Tamet and Sirte.

Their second attack was a mirror image of the first. Mayne destroyed twenty-seven aircraft at Tamet; Stirling was unable to reach the airfield because of the crush of German armour and vehicles around it. He was fortunate to escape with his life: an Italian guard tried to shoot him, only to discover he had a faulty round in the barrel of his rifle. Meanwhile, Fraser and Lewes were taken by Lieutenant Morris's LRDG patrol to raid airstrips at Nofilia and Ras Lanuf. At the latter location, Mussolini had built a grandiose triumphal arch to commemorate his African conquests; to the Tommies it looked similar to the arch at the end of Oxford Street, and "Marble Arch" it became known to one and all throughout the British Army. Lewes had a difficult time at Nofilia when a bomb he was placing on an aircraft exploded prematurely. Withdrawing under heavy fire, he and his party were picked up by their LRDG escort, only to come under attack by Messerschmitts and Stukas in the open desert. Jock Lewes was killed, the survivors scattered.

The death of Lewes was a heavy blow to Stirling, as there was no one else on whom he so heavily relied. There was more bad news: Captain Fraser's patrol was missing – but to this episode, at least, there was a happy ending. On finding the Marble Arch strip bereft of aircraft, Fraser and his section had waited for Morris's LRDG patrol. When, after six days, Morris failed to arrive, the SAS men decided to walk the 200 burning miles to Jalo. Their walk, which took eight days, was the first of several epic peregrinations in the SAS annals, to rank alongside that of Trooper Jack Sillito the following year (again, 200 miles in eight days, drinking his own urine for hydration). Fraser's walk and the unit's bag of nearly ninety aircraft in a month were an emphatic vindication of Stirling's concept of small-scale raiding by a volunteer elite.

It was Stirling's gift as a leader to see the big picture, and where the SAS fitted into it. He was also, due to his social background and boundless confidence, possessed of friends in the highest places. Both attributes came together in early January 1942, when Stirling sought a personal interview with Auchinleck, the Commander-in-Chief, during which he proposed that L Detachment should switch from striking airfields to ports. Although the Crusader offensive had pushed Rommel westwards, the Afrika Korps remained a potent force, not least because it continued to receive supplies of Panzer tanks through the coastal harbours. Stirling pointed out to Auchinleck that Bouerat would become the likely main supply harbour for the Afrika Korps, and that the fuel dumps there could and should be blown up. Auchinleck agreed. When Stirling asked for men for L Detachment, Auchinleck gave him permission to recruit a further six officers and thirty to forty men, some of whom could be drawn from the Special Boat Section of No. 8 Commando. For good measure, Auchinleck promoted Stirling to major.

There was one final thing: Stirling's enemies in general head-quarters (the kind of literal-minded men who considered irregular forces a diversion from the "real" war) had bluntly informed him that L Detachment, because it was a temporary unit, could not have its own badge. Nonetheless, Stirling brashly wore SAS wings and cap badge to meet the Commander-in-Chief. Stirling had calculated correctly: Auchinleck liked and approved of the badge. The SAS badge was more than a mark of an elite unit – it was a debt Stirling felt he owed Lewes, who had been instrumental in its design. The so-called "Winged Dagger" was modelled by Bob Tait on King Arthur's sword Excalibur, while the wings were probably taken from an ibis on a fresco in Shepheard's Hotel in Cairo. The colours of the wings, Oxford blue and Cambridge blue, were selected because Lewes had rowed for Oxford, and Tom Langton, another early L-Detachment officer, for Cambridge. It was Stirling himself who came up with the motto "Who Dares Wins". The badge was worn on berets, which at first were white, but changed, when these attracted wolf whistles, to a sand colour, which they still are.

On the way back to Jalo, Stirling came across fifty French parachutists at Alexandria who, after some vigorous appeals to the Free French commander in Cairo, General Catroux, Stirling annexed for the SAS. He also recruited Captain Bill Cumper of the Royal Engineers, a Cockney explosives expert who would take on the vacancy of demolitions instructor left open by Lewes's death. But Cumper could not take on the whole gamut of training the SAS recruits who were now so numerous the camp at Kabrit was overflowing with them; that mantle, Stirling resolved, should be taken by Paddy Mayne. Sitting in his tent, Stirling explained his thinking to Mayne, who accepted with bad grace verging on insubordination. He would only "do his best", and then only on a temporary basis. Mayne even hinted that Stirling was green-eyed about his success in blowing up aircraft, and pinning him to a desk was a way of stealing the glory.

With a moody Mayne left sulking in Kabrit, on 17 January Stirling launched a raid on Bouerat from Jalo. Taxiing the SAS team out was the Guards patrol of the LRDG, led by Captain Anthony Hunter. As on previous missions, Stirling seemed chained to ill luck. On the sixth day out, the patrol was strafed and bombed in the Wadi Tamrit, with the loss of the radio truck and three men. Then Stirling instructed the two Special Boat Section men in the party to assemble their folbot (a type of collapsible canoe) before the final approach, the plan being for the SBS men to paddle out and set limpet mines on ships in the harbour. As their 1,680-pound Ford truck neared Bouerat, it lurched down a pothole and the folbot shattered. Not that it mattered: there were no ships in the port. Instead, Stirling had to satisfy himself with detonating petrol bowsers and the wireless station.

Picked up by a LRDG truck driven by Corporal "Flash" Gibson, Stirling and his crew rode around, stopping to plant bombs on parked trucks. They then made off to the main rendez-vous. Mounted on the back of the Ford V-8 truck was a novelty – a Vickers K aircraft-type machine-gun, whose .303-inch barrels could spew out bullets at 1,200 rounds per minute. Johnny Cooper was the man with his finger on the trigger:

As we motored at speed along the track, we suddenly noticed flashing lights up ahead of us and a few isolated shots whizzed through the air. Whether they were warning shots or the enemy clearing their guns we did not know, but as our truck accelerated down a slight incline it became painfully obvious that an ambush had been set up ... I slipped off the safety catch and let fly with a devastating mixture of tracer and incendiary, amazed at the firepower of the Vickers. At the same time, Reg [Seekings] opened up with his Thompson, and we ploughed through the ambush, completely outgunning and demoralizing the Italians.

Gibson, with great presence of mind, switched on the head-lamps and roared away at about 40 mph, driving with absolute efficiency and coolness to extricate us from a difficult position.

Gibson was awarded the Military Medal (MM) for the operation, and Johnny Cooper the Distinguished Conduct Medal. The Vickers K, fired for the first time in action by the SAS, became the unit's weapon of choice for the rest of the war.

Aside from the constant struggle with Middle East Headquarters to preserve, let alone expand, L Detachment, Stirling threw himself into the planning of another raid – one which tested the soundness of his strategic vision. This raid was intended to assist in the battle of Malta. Perched in the middle of the Mediterranean, British-controlled Malta posed a mortal threat to Rommel's line of supply back to Italy. Consequently, the Axis forces were trying to bomb and blockade the island into submission. Announcing that the loss of Malta would be "a disaster of the first magnitude to the British Empire, and probably fatal in the long run to the defence of the Nile Valley," Churchill decreed that two supply convoys must get through in the June "dark-phase". Since these convoys would almost certainly be attacked by Axis aircraft operating from Cyrenaica and Crete, Stirling proposed that L Detachment mount a synchronized attack on Axis aerodromes in these locations on 13 and 14 June 1942. Fortunately for L Detachment, its ranks had been modestly enlarged by the annexation of the Special Interrogation Group. This had been formed by Captain Buck and consisted of German-speaking Jews and a couple of Afrika Korps deserters, all of whom were prepared to masquerade in German uniform, knowing all too well their fate if caught.

The various L Detachment teams who were to carry out the raids in North Africa gathered at Siwa, before being escorted to within striking distance of their targets by the LRDG. Stirling, accompanied by his familiars, Cooper and Seekings, headed for Benina aerodrome. For once, Stirling had good hunting. Bombs planted, the SAS men sneaked away to watch what Cooper remembered as a "fantastic fireworks display". He found it difficult to believe that just three men and the contents of their knapsacks had wrought such destruction.

In what was destined to be the last phase of the SAS's war in the Western Desert, the SAS were charged with four tasks, all intended to aid and abet Montgomery's offensive against Tripoli in January 1943. One party was to operate west of Tripoli to facilitate the 8th Army's advance; another was to reconnoitre the defensive Mareth Line with a view to discovering a way around it; a third operation consisted of raiding the enemy's supply lines between Gabès and Sfax; lastly, Colonel Stirling would lead a patrol as far north as northern Tunisia, where it would cut the Sousse railway line. Stirling also intended to link up with his brother, Bill, who had formed the 2nd SAS Regiment, which was advancing eastwards as part of the 1st Army, following the Torch landings in Algeria in November. The link-up with Bill Stirling had more than fraternal importance: David Stirling intended to build the SAS (which some wags now said stood for "Stirling and Stirling") up to Brigade strength.

David Stirling set out for northern Tunisia on 10 January. After successfully completing his reconnaissance of the Mareth flank, he sped towards Sousse. Rommel's position was deteriorating, and haste in knocking out his communication lines seemed sensible. Instead of taking the slower, safer route south of Chott el Djerid salt marsh, Stirling, with five jeeps and fourteen men, headed for the Gabes gap. Stirling was captured by a German parachute battalion.

Following Stirling's capture 1 SAS was placed under the command of Major Paddy Mayne and renamed the Special Raiding Squadron (SRS), while 2 SAS continued to be commanded by Lieutenant Colonel Bill Stirling. Both units functioned independently of each other. Meanwhile, the SBS was unshackled from a brief marriage to the SAS and rebranded the Special Boat Squadron and placed in the care of Major the Earl Jellicoe.

Reorganization was all well and good, but what was the British Army to do with the abundance of Special Forces at its disposal now the war in North Africa was all but over? In truth, there was no place else for the SAS but the Mediterranean. Direct cross-channel attack on Nazi-occupied France was more than a year away, and the Far East campaign had its own Special Forces in Orde Wingate's "Chindits". Accordingly, the SRS and 2 SAS were warned for action in the forthcoming invasion of Sicily (to be followed by the invasion of Italy proper), where they were used wantonly as assault troops rather than Special Forces. Not until early September 1943 and Operation Speedwell was the SAS used strategically. To stop the flow of German troops down Italy following Mussolini's surrender, SAS parachutists were tasked with derailing trains by blowing up railway tunnels. For the size of the force dropped – thirteen men – the Speedwell operation achieved a significant result, and Bill Stirling pressed Supreme Allied headquarters in Italy to action more such deep behind-the-lines sabotage by SAS units. For the most part, Bill Stirling's pleadings fell on deaf ears, beginning a disillusionment with the top brass that would see his eventual resignation as 2 SAS's commanding officer. Even if not deployed to its best advantage, however, the SRS/SAS contributed substantially to the campaign in Italy in 1943, with detachments taking part in significant battles at Taranto and Termoli.

The SRS was withdrawn from Italy in Autumn 1943, but detachments of 2 SAS continued to operate in Italy until the end of the war in Europe. The Regiment's most effective actions in the twilight of the Italian campaign tended to be those jointly undertaken with the partisans, as with 3 Squadron's Tombola operation. Newly raised, mainly from volunteers from the 1st and 6th Airborne Divisions, 3 Squadron was commanded by Roy Farran, now promoted to major. The idea behind Tombola was to insert a well-equipped SAS party into the enemy-held province of Emilia-Romagna, where it would co-operate with partisan brigades ("Commando Unico") in operations against the German defensive position to the south known as the Gothic Line. The centrepiece of Tombola was an attack on the German corps headquarters at Albinea in the Po Valley. One notable feature of Tombola, and similar operations in Italy, was that junior non-commissioned officers and private soldiers were put in charge of partisan teams. "It was extraordinary," Farran wrote, "how successful the British common soldiers were as detachment commanders." In this respect Tombola and its counterparts anticipated 22 SAS operations in Oman in the 1960s, when the Regiment fought alongside tribal levies.

Tombola aside, Italy was a minor theatre for 2 SAS from mid-1944, since, alongside the SRS, it was preparing for the main invasion of Europe: the D-Day landings. Both 2 SAS and SRS became part of SAS Brigade commanded by Brigadier R.W. McLeod, under Lieutenant General Frederick Browning's 1st Airborne Corps. To the undisguised irritation of the SAS, "Boy" Browning made them exchange their sand-coloured berets for the red ones of Airborne. There were other changes. The SRS reverted to its former name of 1 SAS, and expanded to regimental strength. Paddy Mayne remained as commanding officer. The remainder of the Brigade comprised two French parachute battalions, 3 and 4 SAS (also known as *2ème* and *3ème Regiment de Chausseurs Parachutistes*), a Belgian squadron, and F Squadron GHQ Liaison Regiment (Phantom). Almost inevitably, there was an argument as to how the SAS Brigade, of some 2,500 troops, should be used. Despite two full years of SAS activity, most "top brass" continued to be blind to the proper employment of the SAS as saboteurs behind the main battle area. It was at this juncture that the exasperated Bill Stirling resigned his command. He was replaced by Lieutenant Colonel Brian Franks, a founder member of No. 8 Commando. Eventually, there was an outbreak of wisdom and Bill Stirling's concepts were adopted. In brief, it was decided that the SAS Brigade would carry out three types of operation during the invasion of France. First, the SAS would identify targets for the RAF, as well as sabotaging such targets themselves. Second, the SAS would train the French Resistance, to enable the Resistance to help delay the flow of German reinforcements to the front. Third, the SAS would undertake offensive patrols deep behind the lines in armoured jeeps. Any SAS men caught would most likely be executed: Hitler had decreed that 'these men are dangerous' and needed to be "ruthlessly exterminated". Hitler's notorious "Commando Order", however, did little to put off recruits to the expanding SAS.

On 5 June 1945, the eve of D-Day, the first SAS patrols were dropped into France. By the time of the German surrender 11 months later, SAS Brigade had completed more than 50 operations in northwest Europe. Operation Houndsworth was typical of the early offensive patrols of its mission in France. Over three months, 153 jeep-raiding troops from A 1 SAS Squadron (with some 2 SAS and Maquis) made twenty-two railcuts on the Dijon–Paris line, derailed six trains, destroyed seventy vehicles and caused more than 200 enemy casualties. A dramatic validation of the Regiment's motto, "Who Dares Wins", was Major Roy Farran. His squadron of sixty men and twenty-three jeeps was loaded onto Dakota airfield on 19 August 1944 and flown to Rennes airfield, from where they slipped through the frontline. So began Farran's remarkable Jeep operation Wallace, which covered more distance behind the lines than any other 2 SAS mission of the war. The party drove 200 miles through enemy lines in four days, joining the base set up by the earlier Operation Hardy near Chatillon, north of Dijon. His operation, ending on September 17, resulted in 500 enemy casualties, the destruction of ninety-five vehicles, a train and 100,000 gallons of petrol. On the way back through France, Farran's squadron took illicit leave in Paris. Operation Wallace brought him a DSO.

The SAS became the victim of the success it had helped deliver: the removal of the Germans from France left little for the SAS to do. Field Marshal Model, one of Hitler's ablest soldiers, had stabilized the front in north-west Europe, roughly along the Rhine, and operations in Germany behind the lines were not quite unthinkable (indeed, they were entertained) but were eventually ruled out as being suicidal. So far in Europe the SAS had worked in arenas where some support could be expected from the locals; in Hitler's *Deutschland* that would not be the case.

Throughout the winter of 1944–45 the SAS became preoccupied with finding a role for itself. One squadron, as we have seen, was detached under Major Farran for Operation Tombola in Italy; otherwise the SAS had to wait until fluidity came to the north-west front in March 1945 to re-join the fighting. At that point the SAS Brigade, now under control of "Mad Mike" Calvert, was employed by the 21st Army Group for reconnaissance ahead of its drive into the heartland of Germany. Once again, this was not "traditional" SAS work. As they probed into

Germany, SAS units encountered fanatical, if sporadic, resistance from Hitler Youth, the Wehrmacht, the SS, the *Volkssturm* (Home Guard) – anybody, indeed, the Nazi authorities could place in the Allies' way. SAS troopers were amongst the first to enter Belsen death camp: that L Detachment stalwart, Johnny Cooper, who had been commissioned in the field, recalled:

> Once inside we realized the vast size of the camp, and I will never forget my first sight of the inmates. Ostensibly they were living human beings, but to me, the men, women and even children were just walking skeletons.

Then the war in Europe was over. The SAS was ordered to disband. On the morning of 8 October 1945, 1 SAS paraded at its Hylands Park barracks in Chelmsford for the last time. On the same day that 1 SAS was disbanded, 2 SAS took its farewell parade at its Colchester HQ. The French and the Belgian regiments had already been returned to their respective countries.

Officially, on 8 October 1945 the SAS founded by Stirling, Lewes and Mayne ceased to exist; in actuality, it remained alive. Just. A team of SAS men, including L Detachment Original Bob Bennett, were attached to the Military Reparations Committee in Greece, where they proudly sported their winged-dagger badge. Brian Franks, still pained and outraged by the murder of SAS soldiers during behind-the-lines operations in Occupied Europe, organized a team to investigate the crimes and bring those responsible to justice. This became the SAS War Crimes Team, which operated for four years and successfully identified several Nazi perpetrators. Beyond these two small SAS remnants, the regiment's veterans kept in personal contact. Johnny Cooper was invited by David Stirling, long since released from Colditz, to lunch at White's in London. Stirling, thought Cooper, "looked none the worse" for his stay at Hitler's pleasure. Also in attendance were George Jellicoe, Fitzroy Maclean and Randolph Churchill. Such social occasions were pleasant chances to air memories. They were also opportunities for ex-SAS men to plan the regiment's rise anew. Eventually, lobbying of the War Office by SAS veterans, chiefly Mike Calvert and Brian Franks, brought its reward, and in 1947 an SAS unit was formed within the Territorial Army. It was attached to a former officers' training unit, the Artists' Rifles, to become 21 (Artists) TA, based at Duke's Road, Euston. The commanding officer was Lieutenant Colonel Brian Franks, 2 SAS's sometime commander during the Second World War.

Wartime SAS soldiers flocked to the new TA SAS, so many, indeed, that Johnny Cooper found the first training camp "a splendid reunion". This TA SAS unit, which still exists and is complemented by another TA SAS unit, 23 SAS, provided many of the volunteers for a long-range patrol Franks raised for Korea, where the first major war since 1945 was being fought between the Communist North and the UN-backed South. Before Franks' Jeep patrol could be sent to Korea, though, the UN commander, General MacArthur, decided he had no use for it.

What was McArthur's loss was Britain's gain. A Communist insurrection – known as "the Emergency" for insurance-claim purposes – had broken out in the British dominion of Malaya. From hide-outs in the jungle, Communist Terrorists ("CTs"), led by Chin Peng of the Malayan Races Liberation Army (MRLA), were murdering British rubber-plantation owners and their families. The Commander-in-Chief Far East, Sir John Harding, summoned Mike Calvert to Malaya and asked him to find ways of dealing with the CT campaign. Before becoming commanding officer of the SAS Brigade during the Second World War, Calvert had commanded 77 Chindit Brigade. Mad Mike, along with Freddie Spencer Chapman, soldier and author of the memoir *The Jungle is Neutral*, was as close to an expert jungle fighter as the British possessed. Looking at the situation in Malaya, Calvert realized that the Emergency required the British to have a Special Force that would 'live, move, and have its heart in the jungle' just as the enemy did. His proposal for a new unit, the Malayan Scouts (SAS), was accepted. For personnel for the unit, Calvert milked three sources: A Squadron was formed from 100 volunteers in the British Army already in the Far East; B Squadron was comprised of soldiers from 1 SAS, primarily those who had put up their hands for the Korean job; and C Squadron was made up of Rhodesian volunteers.

Unfortunately, while B Squadron – thoroughly marinated in SAS philosophy, discipline and training either by war service or Brian Franks' Duke's Road regime – was the right SAS stuff, the Rhodesians were keen but under-trained. But the real headache was A Squadron, who, save for a few good apples, were poseurs and party animals. It did not help that Calvert himself was keen on wild drinking parties. So notorious was A Squadron's indiscipline that the Malayan Scouts were almost disbanded. Instead, Calvert was sent home with a convenient (and fictitious) kidney illness, and Lieutenant Colonel John Sloane was brought in as commanding officer. A straight-backed, by-the-book officer from the Argyll and Sutherland Highlanders, 'Tod' Sloane unsentimentally returned to unit misfits and implemented proper admin. He was ably assisted in his makeover of the Mayalan Scouts by John Woodhouse and Clarence "Dare" Newell, men who were both to become legendary figures in SAS history. To make the regiment more attractive to volunteers, its name was changed from the Malayan Scouts – which, after all, suggested members would only serve in Malaya – to "22 SAS".

And yet, for all Calvert's waywardness he was, more than Sloane, Woodhouse and Newell, the architect of the modern SAS. Quite aside from creating a unit to bear the appellation "Special Air Service", Calvert proposed that the SAS should work in three- or four-man patrols; that it should win over local tribes by kindness, notably by setting up medical clinics (what later became known as "hearts and minds"); and that it should establish long-term counter-guerrilla bases deep in the jungle. All three of these principles still shape the modern SAS.

The men of the 22 SAS Regiment underwent an experience in Malaya that their successors down the decades would empathize with: fighting in appalling conditions. Johnny Cooper, who had transferred to 22 SAS as 8 Troop's commander (thus becoming, by his reckoning, the oldest lieutenant in the Army, at twenty-nine years of age), was dismayed by the rain. "If there was no great downpour after three or four days, it was reckoned a drought." Sores festered, clothes and boots rotted in the damp, and fevers such as Weil's disease abounded. By the end of a patrol, a soldier would on average have lost ten pounds. Despite the hardships, however, patrols stayed out in the jungle for longer and longer periods, as the regiment's jungle education grew.

By 1956, the regiment was up to a strength of 560 men and making a real contribution towards containing the Emergency: its tally of communist terrorists killed was eighty-nine. Captured Communist terrorists confessed that the SAS patrols, even when failing to make contact with the enemy, were so disruptive as to render guerrilla warfare all but impossible. Four years later, the Emergency was over. The leaders of the MRLA had fled to Thailand, and the murders of civilians had almost ceased. After its eight years in Malaya, the regiment had, despite an inauspicious start, become a highly professional unit. In 1957, in recognition, 22 SAS was placed in the order of battle of the British Army, and as a result was able to re-adopt both the beige beret and the winged-dagger badge. For all this, the future of the regiment was far from assured: the whispers from Whitehall were that 22 SAS would be disbanded when it was finally pulled out of Malaya.

History, however, was on the side of the SAS. In the death agony of empire there came other small wars. Malaya was not a one-off; it was part of an historic trend. Even as the SAS was mopping up in Malaya, another little war in a British-dominated corner of the world was beginning. The next job was far from the green jungles of Malaya: it was on the Green Mountain, the Jebel Akhdar, in Oman.

In 1954 a rebellion against Oman's autocratic (but pro-British) Sultan, led by Ghalib, the Imam of Oman, and his brother Talib, threatened to destabilize the country and interrupt the oil supply to Great Britain. With understandable *realpolitik*, if questionable morality, the British government determined to back the Sultan. An RAF bombing campaign against the rebel stronghold on the Jebel Akhdar failed. An infantry assault on it failed. A plan to drop the Parachute Regiment was cancelled, because the Prime Minister thought the committing of a world-famous regiment overemphasized the importance of the situation. And so the shadow SAS was given the job nobody else could or should do. Lieutenant Colonel Anthony Deane-Drummond, the commander of 22 SAS, was given fifteen days to round up D Squadron from

Malaya and deploy it in Oman, where it did what no other military force had done in a thousand years: it captured the Jebel Akhdar. More than that, the Jebel Akhdar assault had secured the future of the SAS. As Peter de la Billière, a troop commander and later CO of 22 SAS wrote, Oman, more so than Malaya, was a turning point in the history of the SAS:

> We had shown that we were a flexible force capable of adapting quickly to new conditions. We had demonstrated that a small number of men could be flown into a trouble spot rapidly and discreetly, and operate in a remote area without publicity – a capability much valued by the Conservative government of the day. Above all, we had proved that the quality of the people in the SAS was high indeed, and that a few men of such calibre could achieve results out of all proportion to their numbers.

The SAS would return to Oman a decade later, to counter an insurgency by Communists in Dhofar. But first, the drums of war summoned the regiment back to the jungles of the Far East.

From 1963 to 1966, Borneo was the scene of a bloody conflict between Malaya and Indonesia, both of which claimed ownership of the mountainous island. To counter the infiltration of guerrillas from the Indonesian side of the island (Kalimantan) into the northern Malaysian side, the British – Malaya's former imperial masters – organized a border guard of Malaysian, British and Commonwealth troops. A main constituent in this guard was 22 SAS. For the most part, SAS effort in Borneo consisted of the insertion of four-man patrols into the jungle, often for weeks at a time, gathering intelligence and implementing "hearts and minds" programmes. As the "Confrontation" wore on, however, the Indonesians began committing units of their army to the frontier war, and in response the SAS stepped up its activity with offensive patrols into Indonesia itself. Codenamed Claret, these operations were top secret. The codename was apposite: much blood was spilled.

Then it was back to the desert, to Oman, where on the morning of 19 July 1972 there occurred one of the most storied SAS actions. In the fishing port of Mirbat, Oman, a nine-man SAS detachment known as "BATT" (British Army Training Team) slept in a small mud-and-brick building, save for three troopers who were awake talking and keeping guard. In command of the detachment was twenty-seven-year-old Captain Mike Kealy of B Squadron, known as 'baby Rupert' because of his inexperience. As the smear of light on the eastern horizon grew brighter, 250 Communist guerrillas, known as *adoo*, stole to within 400 yards of the SAS "BATT house" and opened fire with mortars, machine guns and small arms. For six hours the SAS team held off the adoo, until reinforcements arrived in the shape of G Squadron. There were two regimental fatalities incurred during 22 SAS's hardest test, trooper Tobin and Corporal Labalaba. For this loss the SAS took the lives of more than thirty-nine adoo. Tragically, Mike Kealy died of hypothermia during an exercise on the Brecon Beacons in 1972.

As the 1970s wore on, the SAS increased its urban counter-terrorist capability, although the regiment's first brush with such work lay in the backstreets of Aden in the previous decade, when it was tasked with eliminating Yemeni insurgents. Thereafter, SAS Counter-Revolutionary Warfare (CRW) work had evolved through sheer Darwinian necessity. Oman aside, the regiment was desperately short of work in the early 1970s – so short, indeed, that training the bodyguards of foreign VIPs became a major strand of regimental activity. In the same period, the camp of 22 SAS, now based after a period of itinerancy at Bradbury Lines (later christened Stirling Lines), next to the River Wye in Hereford, saw the construction of a special house to train marksmen in the skills of shooting gunmen in the confines of a room without hitting VIPs or hostages. Formally called the Close-Quarter Battle House (CQB), the building is more usually known as the "Killing House".

One significant spur to the development of CRW work came in September 1972, when Palestinian terrorists from the 'Black September' group seized the dormitory occupied by Israeli athletes at the Olympic Games. The West German government allowed the gunmen and hostages safe passage out of the country, but as the group moved through Munich airport the German security forces opened fire. In the wild gun battle that followed they mistakenly killed all the hostages. Alarmed by their incapacity to deal with terrorism, European governments began developing elite anti-terrorist units. The British government was no exception. Following a direct request from the Director of Military Operations in September 1972, the new commanding officer of 22 SAS, Lieutenant Colonel Peter de la Billière, reorganized the CRW cell into 'Op Pagoda'. In charge of Pagoda was Captain Andrew Massey, who selected twenty troopers from all sabre squadrons for special CRW (sometimes CT, for Counter-Terrorist) training. The Pagoda team was put on constant standby. Later, the Pagoda role became rotated through the squadrons, so every trooper in the Regiment had a turn, and the team was issued with black overalls and Ingram sub-machine-guns. However, following their observation of the successful German GSG9 storming of a hijacked aircraft at Mogadishu airport in 1977, SAS Major Alistair Morrison and Sergeant Barry Davies recommended adopting the GSG9's main firearm, the Heckler & Koch MP5A2. Tests confirmed its superiority over the American Ingram sub-machine-gun, and the 650 rpm, 2 kg Heckler was adopted by the Pagoda troop.

The Pagoda team's first major call to action came in 1975, when an IRA active-service unit machine-gunned a restaurant in Mayfair, London, and then took hostages in a flat in Balcombe Street. On hearing on the radio that an SAS team was preparing to storm the flat, the IRA gunmen surrendered without a fight. The Balcombe Street siege ended without bloodshed, but it ignited a bloodbath of violence in Northern Ireland, starting with the "Kingsmill Massacre" in which IRA terrorists pulled Protestant line-workers from a bus and mowed down ten of them in the road with machine-gun fire. On 7 January 1976, Prime Minister Harold Wilson publicly committed the SAS to patrol the "bandit country" of South Armagh.

Northern Ireland would never be a happy hunting ground for the SAS. The orthodox regiments of the Army already assigned to the province were suspicious and resentful – after all, SAS deployment suggested that they had failed – and there was little possibility of implementing the SAS's by now stock "hearts and

minds" campaign. Aside from patrolling, the SAS men in
Northern Ireland set up covert observation posts and established
a new undercover spying squad known as the Army Surveillance
Unit (later 14 Intelligence Company). The regiment did not limit
itself to these prescribed and lawful activities. In March 1976 a
Provisional IRA (PIRA) gunman and bomber, Sean McKenna,
was abducted from his home in southern Ireland by masked men,
almost certainly SAS, holding Browning 9 mm pistols, and was
taken over the border to Bessbrook RUC station.

Unfortunately, SAS soldiers in Northern Ireland – eventually
organized in Ulster Troop – took a steady toll of the innocent. By
the end of 1978 the SAS was known to have killed at least ten
people in Northern Ireland, of whom three were guiltless and
one, a PIRA quartermaster called Patrick Duffy, was shot twelve
times in the back. The slaughtered innocents included a sixteen-
year-old boy, John Boyle, exploring a churchyard where the IRA
had cached arms, and a Belfast Protestant pedestrian, William
Hanna, in an incident in which the Army's rules of engagement in
Ulster – by which soldiers could only open fire if they believed a
person was about to fire, endanger life and if there was no other
means of stopping them – were ignored. Even the SAS's greatest
ever blow against PIRA – the killing of eight PIRA terrorists as
they attacked the police station at Loughgall in 1987 – was marred
by the shooting of two villagers driving by, one of whom died.
And if SAS black ops against PIRA were controversial, they were
also deadly dangerous for the regiment's troopers, with at least
two KIA.

Until 1980, the SAS waged war in the shadows. In that year it
hit the headlines around the world.

At 11.25 a.m. on the morning of Wednesday 30 April, the tran-
quillity of Prince's Gate, in London's leafy Kensington district,
had been shattered as six gunmen wearing shemaghs over their
faces sprayed the outside of No. 16 with machine-gun fire and
stormed through the entrance. The leading gunman made straight
for an astonished police constable standing in the foyer, Trevor
Lock of the Diplomatic Protection Group, while the rest, shouting and waving their machine pistols, rounded up the other occupants of the building. The gunmen were members of Mohieddin

al Nasser Martyr Group, an Arab group seeking the liberation of Khuzestan from Ayatollah Khomeini's Iran. No. 16 was the Iranian Embassy in Britain. Just after 2.35 p.m. Salim, the head Arab gunman, laid out his demands by telephone: autonomy and human rights for the people of Khuzestan, and the release of ninety-one Arab prisoners held in Iranian jails. If his demands were not met he would blow up the Embassy, hostages and all, at noon the following day. The siege of Prince's Gate had begun.

The SAS, meanwhile, had been alerted about the siege within minutes of its start, Dusty Gray, an ex-SAS sergeant, now a Metropolitan Police dog handler, having telephoned the Officers' Mess at Bradbury Lines, to warn that its assistance would probably be required at the Iranian Embassy. That night SAS troopers left for London in Range Rovers, arriving at a holding area in Regent's Park Barracks in the early hours of Thursday morning. The official authority from the Ministry of Defence arrived at Bradbury Lines to approve the move some hours after they had already left.

Over the next few days the Metropolitan Police continued their "softly, softly" negotiating approach, while trying to determine exactly how many hostages were in the embassy and where they were located. Scotland Yard's technical squad, C7, installed microphones in the chimney and walls of No. 16, covering the noise by faking Gas Board repairs at neighbouring Ennismore Gardens. Gradually it became clear that there were about twenty-five hostages (at the end of the siege, the exact count was twenty-six), most of them Iranian Embassy staff.

Inside the SAS holding area a scale model of the embassy had been constructed to familiarize the SAS troopers with the layout of the building they would assault if the police negotiations were to break down. The breakdown came at 1.45 p.m. on Bank Holiday Monday, 5 May, when the distinct sound of three shots was heard from inside the embassy. The news of the shooting was immediately forwarded to the SAS teams waiting at their holding area. They would be used after all. Operation Nimrod – the relief of the Iranian Embassy – was on. At 6.50 p.m., with tension mounting, the gunmen announced their demands again, with the codicil that a hostage would be shot every forty-five minutes until their demands were met. Another burst of shots was heard. The door of the embassy opened, and a body was flung down the steps. (The body belonged to the Press Attaché shot earlier in the day. The new burst of shots was a scare tactic.) The police phoned into the embassy's first floor, where the telephone link with the gunmen was situated. They seemed to cave in to Salim's demands, assuring him that they were not tricking him, and that a bus would be arriving in minutes to take the gunmen to Heathrow Airport, from where they would fly to the Middle East. But by talking on the phone Salim had signalled his whereabouts to the SAS teams who had taken up their start position on the roof, and in the two buildings either side of No. 16, the Ethiopian Embassy and the Royal College of Physicians. At around this time, formal responsibility – via a handwritten note – passed from the Metropolitan Police to the SAS.

Suddenly, as the world watched Prince's Gate on TV, black-clad men wearing respirators appeared on the front balconies and placed "frame charges" against the armoured-glass window. There was an enormous explosion. The time was exactly 7.23 p.m. At the back of the building and on the roof, the assault teams heard the order "Go. Go. Go." Less than twelve minutes had elapsed since the body of the Press Attaché had appeared on the Embassy steps. The assault on the building came from three sides, with the main assault from the rear, where three pairs of troopers abseiled down from the roof. One of the first party accidentally swung his foot through an upper storey window, thereby alerting Salim to their line of assault. The pair dropped to the ground and prepared to fight their way in, while another pair landed on the balcony, broke the window and threw in stun grenades. A third pair also abseiled down, but one of them became entangled in the ropes, which meant that the rear assault could not use frame charges to blow-in the bullet-proof glass. Instead, a call sign in the garden from a rear troop in the garden sledge-hammered the French windows open, with the troopers swarming into the building on the ground floor. They "negotiated" a gunman in the front hall, cleared the cellars, and then raced upstairs to the second floor and the telex room, where the male hostages were being held by three gunmen. Meanwhile the pair who had come in through the rear first floor balcony encountered PC Lock grappling with Salim, the head gunman, who had been about to fire at an SAS trooper at the window, and shot the gunman dead.

Almost simultaneously with the rear assault, the frontal assault group stormed over the balcony on the first floor, lobbing in stun grenades through the window broken by their frame charges. Amid gushing smoke they entered and also moved towards the telex room. Another SAS team broke into the building through the plaster division left after the bricks had been removed from wall with the Ethiopian Embassy. Outside, at the front, the SAS shot CS gas cartridges into an upstairs room where one of the gunmen was believed to be hiding. This room caught fire, the flames spreading quickly to other rooms. (The trooper caught in the abseil rope suffered burns at this point, but was then cut free and re-joined the assault.) The SAS converged at the telex room as planned. The gunmen had started shooting the hostages. The Assistant Press Attaché was shot and killed and the Chargé d'Affaires wounded before the SAS broke in. By then the gunmen were lying on the floor, trying in the smoke and noise to pass themselves off as hostages. What then happened is the subject of some dispute, but the outcome was that the SAS shot two of the gunmen dead. Afterwards, some of the hostages said that the gunmen tried to give themselves up, but were killed anyway. In the event, only one gunman escaped with his life, the one guarding the women in Room 9. The women refused to identify him as a terrorist, and he was handed over to the police.

After a brief assembly at No. 14 for emotional congratulations from the Home Secretary, William Whitelaw, the SAS teams sped away in rented Avis vans. Behind them the Embassy was a blaze of fire and smoke. The breaking of the siege had taken just seventeen minutes. Of the twenty hostages in the building at the time of the SAS assault, nineteen were brought out alive. The SAS suffered no casualties. Although mistakes were made in the assault (part of the main assault went in via a room which contained no gunmen and was blocked off from the rest of the embassy), the speed, daring, and adaptability of the SAS proved the regiment an elite amongst the counter-revolutionary forces of the world.

The next major business of the regiment lay south. The Falkland Islands, specks of land almost lost in the vastness of the South Atlantic, had become a British possession in 1833, but Argentina had always disputed the ownership of what it called the Malvinas, and on 2 April 1982 the leader of the nation's military junta, General Galtieri, decided to back that claim with a full-scale invasion of the islands. Immediately on hearing the news of the invasion, the Director of the SAS Group, Brigadier Peter de la Billière, and the commander of 22 SAS, Lieutenant Colonel Mike Rose, put the regiment on standby and lobbied hard for a role in the military campaign for the islands' recovery.

The first task for the SAS was the liberation of South Georgia, 870 miles south-east of the main Falklands group. The execution of Operation Paraquet (soon corrupted to Operation Paraquat, after the branded weedkiller) fell to D Squadron, alongside a patrol from M Company, 42 Royal Marine Commando ("The Mighty Munch"), and a section of the SBS – some 235 men in all. To the roar of supporting gunfire from HMS *Antrim* and HMS *Plymouth*, an SAS composite troop and two composite RM/SBS troops landed in the vicinity of Grytviken. Screened from the settlement by a small mountain, the SAS struck out for the port. Some elephant seals were mistaken for Argentine troops and shot up, and a suspected enemy position was promptly demolished by a Milan missile; the stronghold, alas, turned out to be a piece of scrap iron. These hazards negotiated, the SAS team ascended to the top of Brown Mountain to see the wooden buildings of the port below festooned with white flags. The garrison surrendered without a shot being fired. Next day, the whole of South Georgia was once again in British hands.

Meanwhile, G Squadron and other elements from 22 SAS engaged in some old-style 'eyeball' reconnaissance of Argentine positions on the Falklands. On more than one occasion SAS and SBS patrols ran into each other and opened fire, one such 'blue-on-blue' incident ending tragically with the death of SBS Sergeant "Kiwi" Hunt. Despite such setbacks, the recce teams achieved conspicuously successful results. One four-man patrol, led by G

Squadron's Captain Aldwin, set up a hide on Beagle Ridge, directly above Port Stanley, in an area heavily patrolled by the enemy, and from it spotted a night dispersal area for helicopters between Mounts Kent and Estancia. When the intelligence was relayed back to the fleet, two Harrier aircraft attacked the site, destroying three enemy helicopters.

Besides reconnaissance, the regiment was tasked with its quintessential activity: offensive raiding behind the lines. An early target was the Argentinian airstrip on Pebble Island, off the northern coast of West Falkland, the base for 1A– 58 Pucara aircraft. A raid by forty-five members of D Squadron (inserted by Commando Helicopter Force Sea King helicopters) destroyed, among other assets, six Pucaras. It was a textbook job. It passed through the thoughts of more than one SAS trooper that night that, swap the South Atlantic for the desert, the Argentinians for the Germans, and the RAF helos for the LRDG taxis, 22 SAS was doing exactly what Stirling, Mayne and Lewes had done forty years before.

Presumably the 'Head Shed' at Stirling Lines felt the daring hand of L Detachment's history on their shoulders when they conjured up Operation Mikado, in which B Squadron would attack Exocet-carrying Super Etendard fighters on Rio Grande airstrip on the Argentine mainland. In one fell swoop by the SAS, ran the thinking, the war would be shortened. Some members of the squadron thought the operation suicidal – the airstrip was defended by 1,300 Argentinian marines and state-of-the-art anti-aircraft guns – and the squadron sergeant major even resigned over the issue. When the squadron's commanding officer, John Moss, showed less than requisite enthusiasm, de la Billière summarily returned him to unit. Even if not a death wish, others in the squadron persisted in considering the Paras better equipped to undertake such a *coup de main*, and eventually Mikado was aborted.

There was, though, plenty of 'old-style' SAS stuff to come. On the night before the main Task Force landings at San Carlos, the SAS mounted a series of diversionary raids. These included the landing of sixty D Squadron men, who then marched for twenty hours to reach the hills north of Darwin and attack the garrison

at Goose Green. To put the wind up the Argentinians they simulated a battalion-sized attack (600 men), raining down a torrent
of LAW anti-tank rockets, Milan missiles, GPMG (General-
Purpose Machine Gun) rounds and tracer into the Argentine
positions. So ferocious was the barrage that the enemy failed to
probe the SAS positions and could only manage desultory return
fire. By mid-morning, the main landings accomplished, the SAS
disengaged from Goose Green, 'tabbing' (only Marines 'yomp')
north to meet up with 2 Para as they made their way inland.

Over the next fortnight SAS patrols continued their recces and
probing missions. At the end of May, D Squadron seized Mount
Kent, forty miles behind enemy lines, and held it for several days
until reinforced by 42 RM Commando. This was despite aggressive – and courageous – patrolling from Argentine Special Forces
in a sequence of sharp nocturnal firefights. Following their relief,
D Squadron was in action again when five teams landed on West
Falkland. The considerable enemy garrisons at Fox Bay and Port
Howard enjoyed excellent radio-direction-finding equipment
and responded vigorously. Meanwhile, to reinforce SAS numbers
in the Falklands, a troop from B Squadron was flown from
Ascension Island in Hercules C-130s; the troop was to join the
Task Force by parachuting into the Atlantic, from which they
would be plucked by Gemini inflatables. But it wasn't to be B
Squadron's war. It was tasked with ambushing the enemy reinforcement of the garrison at Fox Bay, but the enemy failed to turn
up. By now it was becoming clear to all that the war was in its last
days.

There remained one major SAS raid, which was mounted in
East Falkland on the night of 13 June. To take the pressure off 2
Para, who were assaulting Wireless Ridge a few miles west of Port
Stanley, the SAS volunteered to put in a raid to the enemy rear
– from the sea. Two troops from D Squadron, one from G
Squadron and six men from 3 SBS rode into Port Stanley harbour
on high-speed Rigid Raiders with the aim of setting fire to the oil
storage tanks. As troopers from the regiment later conceded, the
raid was more audacious than wise. Searchlights from an
Argentine ship in the harbour caught them as they approached,
and the Argentinians opened up with every available weapon,

including triple-barrelled 20 mm Rheinmetall anti-aircraft cannon depressed to their lowest trajectory. These spewed out a constant stream of metal, which obliged the raiders to rapidly withdraw if they were not to suffer heavy losses.

The SAS campaign to liberate the Falklands had its price. A few days after the attack on Pebble Island, a helicopter cross-decking members of D and G Squadron from HMS *Hermes* to HMS *Intrepid* hit some airborne object, probably a giant petrel or albatross, which was then sucked into the air intake. The Sea King plummeted into the icy water with the loss of twenty SAS troopers and attached specialists, plus one of the aircrew. It was the heaviest loss the regiment had suffered in a single day since the Second World War.

With the end of the Falklands campaign, the SAS returned home to Stirling Lines in Hereford. Although the regiment had won a DSO, three MCs and two MMs, and chalked up some outstanding actions and important recces, the mood was sombre. The recent history of the regiment had been in Black Ops; few, if any, of the SAS had fought against a regular army before, and it was obvious that too many mistakes had been made.

Although Peter de la Billière left the Regiment in the mid-1980s, he harboured an affection for –and appreciation of – 22 SAS, as was amply proved in 1990, when the Iraqi president Saddam Hussein rolled his armour into Kuwait. General "Stormin' Norman" Schwarzkopf, the American in command of the coalition gathered to evict Saddam, was notoriously no friend of Special Forces. Encountering a group of US Special Forces in the Gulf, Schwarzkopf barked: "I remember you guys from Vietnam . . . you couldn't do your job there, and you didn't do your job in Panama. What makes you think you can do your job here?" De la Billière, the one British member of Schwarzkopf's planning staff, CENTCOM, however, knew what British Special Forces at least could do, and by early January 1991 300 badged SAS soldiers, plus fifteen volunteers from the elite reserve team of the part-time Territorial Regiments, 21 and 23 SAS, were in Saudi Arabia. It was the biggest gathering of the unit since the heady days of the Second World War.

For an agonising period, though, it looked as though the unit

would be given no role in Operation Desert Storm, the Allied
offensive to remove the Iraqis from Kuwait. The SAS were gathered like so many racehorses before a race, but not sure if they
would be allowed to run. Schwarzkopf intended to degrade
Saddam's military capability by a huge air campaign, while finishing him off with a completely conventional – if tactically brilliant
– envelopment by infantry and armour.

As the regiment made itself ready at its holding area, the world
was hypnotised by the deadline by which President Bush insisted
Iraq implement United Nations Resolution 660 (Iraqi withdrawal
from Kuwait): midnight on 16 January. Saddam refused to blink
or budge, and the regiment was as surprised as most other people
when hundreds of Allied aircraft and Tomahawk Cruise missiles
began bombarding targets in Iraq just before dawn on 17 January.
Within twenty-four hours the Iraqi air force was all but wiped out
and Saddam's command and communications system heavily
mauled. Allied commanders retired to bed at the end of D-Day
most satisfied.

The only nagging area of Allied doubt was Iraq's Scud surface-
to-surface (SSM) missile capability. Though an outdated technology, a Soviet version of Hitler's V2, the Scud was capable of
carrying nuclear and bio-chemical warheads. It could be fired
from a fixed site or from a mobile launcher. Could Saddam still
fire his Scuds? Would he? On the second night of the air campaign,
Saddam answered all speculations by launching Scuds (all with
conventional warheads) at Saudi Arabia and Israel. The six which
landed in Israel injured no one, but they were political dynamite.
If Israel responded militarily the fragile coalition, which included
several Arab members, would be blown apart. Israel declared
itself to be in a state of war, but frantic diplomacy by the Allies
managed to dissuade Israel from taking immediate punitive
action. Batteries of Patriot ground-to-air missiles were dispatched
to Tel Aviv, Jerusalem and Haifa. The Allies diverted 30% of their
air effort to Scud hunting. But in the expanses of vast Iraqi desert
all too often the air strike arrived to find the Scud fired and the
mobile launcher elusively camouflaged. Previously, the US military had believed that its hi-tech satellite observation system
could detect Scuds before launch. Now it was finding that the

Scuds could be many minutes into flight before being betrayed by the flare from their motors. Asked by the media on 19 January about the Scud menace, the normally upbeat Schwarzkopf was obliged to say that "the picture is unclear", and to grumble that looking for Scuds was like looking for the proverbial needle in the haystack.

If the C-in-C was unclear about what to do, the Scud factor gave 22 SAS an absolutely clear-cut mission. De la Billière signalled that "all SAS effort should be directed against Scuds". That very same day, 19 January, the SAS was rushed 1,500 km from its holding area to an FOB (Forward Operational Base) just inside the Saudi border with western Iraq. The move was made in a non-stop twenty-four-hour airlift by the RAF Special Forces flight. The regiment decided on two principal means of dealing with the Scud menace. It would insert into Iraq covert eight-man static patrols to watch Main Supply Routes (MSRs) and report on the movement of Scud traffic. There would be three such patrols, South, Central and North. When Scud sites and launchers were identified, US F-15 and A-10 airstrikes would be called down to destroy them, directed to the target by the SAS patrol using a tactical air link. (Though the SAS patrols carried laser-designators to "paint" targets for Allied aircraft they only used them infrequently.) Alongside the road watch patrols, there were four columns of heavily armed vehicles, "Pink Panther" Land Rovers and Unimogs, which would penetrate the "Scud Box", an area of western desert near the border with Jordan thought to contain around 14 mobile launchers. As is traditional in the SAS, the decision how to deploy was left to the patrol commanders and reached after democratic discussion.

The South and Central road watch teams were inserted on 21 January, and both found that the eerily flat, feature-less desert offered no possibility of concealment. The South road watch patrol aborted their mission and flew back on their insertion helicopter. The Central team also decided that the terrain was lethal, but before "bugging out" in their Land Rovers and stripped-down motorcycles called down an air strike on two Iraqi radars. After a four-night drive through 140 miles of bitingly cold desert the patrol reached Saudi Arabia. Four men needed treatment for frostbite. Road Watch North, codenamed "Bravo Two Zero", had the most isolated insertion, landed by RAF Chinook 100 miles north-west of Baghdad. The weather was appalling, driving wind and sleet, the worst winter in this part of the Iraqi desert for thirty years. Led by Sergeant Andy McNab (a pseudonym), the patrol took food and water for fourteen days, explosives and ammunition for their 203s (American M16 rifles with 40 mm grenade-launchers attached), Minimi machine guns, grenades, extra clothes, maps, compasses and survival equipment. Each man was carrying 209 lbs of kit. Watching a main supply route, the patrol saw a Scud launch and prepared to send their first situation report ("Sit Rep") to base. In the first of several fruitless efforts, Bravo Two Zero's signaller, Trooper Steven ("Legs") Lane, prepared the radio antenna, encoded Sergeant McNab's message and typed it ready for transmission. There was no answer, and no amount of adjusting the set got a response. On the second day an Iraqi military convoy rumbled across the desert towards the team and sited a battery of low-level anti-aircraft guns only yards from where they were hunkered down. The team got off a brief radio message to HQ: "Enemy triple-A gun now in position immediately to our north". The team was now in grave danger of compromise. In mid-afternoon the compromise came. A young Iraqi goatherd looked down into the patrol's lying-up place (LUP), a shallow wadi, saw the troopers and ran off towards the Iraqi soldiers. Bravo Two Zero rapidly prepared to move, checking equipment and gulping down as much water as possible. They had a "fearsome tab"(march) in front of them. Further frantic attempts to radio base that they were now compromised and request "exfil asap" were to no avail, the HF radio rendered near useless by ionospheric distortion. The men loaded their Bergens and moved quickly westwards. As they cleared the bottom of the wadi they heard tracked vehicles approaching from the rear. They dropped into a depression and turned to face the enemy. An Iraqi Armoured Personnel Carrier (APC) opened fire with a 7.62 machine gun.

With a scream of "Fucking let's do it!" the SAS patrol fired off a fusillade of sixty-six anti-armour rockets, rifle grenades and Minimis. They held off the Iraqis twice; it started to get dark, and the patrol decided to get out of the contact area, moving as fast as they physically could manage with their heavy Bergens. As they cleared a slope the Iraqi Triple-A battery sighted them and opened fire. A 57 mm ack-ack round hit one trooper in the back, ripping open his Bergen. When extracted from it he was found to be uninjured. The rest of the patrol voted to "bin" their Bergens for more speed, and eventually lost their enemy in the gloom. At a rallying point, Sergeant McNab decided to use their four personal short-range TACBE (personal rescue beacons) to get in touch with an orbiting AWACS plane to bring strike aircraft down on the Iraqis. Again there was no reply. McNab did a quick appreciation of their situation. The Iraqis would expect them to make south for Saudi Arabia. Jordan was due west, but was a non-combatant ally of Saddam Hussein. A hundred and twenty kilometres to the north-west was Syria, a member of the anti-Saddam coalition. McNab decided to go for Syria. Moving fast towards the Syrian border, Bravo Two Zero walked fifty miles that night, through driving sleet, pausing to rest only four times. Two troopers were in a parlous state, however. Sergeant Vince Phillips had fractured a leg in the contact with the Iraqis and was finding it difficult to move. Trooper "Stan" was becoming dangerously dehydrated. The sound of aircraft high overhead prompted another call on the TACBE. Finally, they got a response. An American pilot on a bombing mission acknowledged their call. The message was relayed to the British Special Ops HQ in Saudi Arabia. British and American helicopters went into Iraq to search for the patrol, but a specific run to a pre-arranged rendezvous was ruled out as too dangerous.

The stop to use the TACBE proved unlucky. In the swirling, raining darkness, Sergeant Phillips, Corporal Chris Ryan and Trooper Stan carried on walking and became separated from the rest of the patrol. Sergeant McNab and his four companions had no option but to continue on without them, hoping they would meet up later. The rain turned to snow. During rests they huddled together for warmth. In their soaked clothes the wind-chill was starting to kill them. Throughout the night they slowly made their way to the Syrian border. Resting during the next day they decided that, if they were going to make it, they would need to hijack a vehicle, preferably something inconspicuous. Watching by a main road they ignored military trucks. In the gathering darkness of evening they spotted the lights of a single vehicle and flagged it down.

The incident has already entered SAS folklore. Instead of the hoped for 4WD, they found before them a bright yellow New York taxi, proudly sporting chrome bumpers and whitewall tyres. The five SAS men pulled out its amazed occupants and hopped in, putting the heater on high. They made good progress towards the border, their shemaghs pulled up around their faces to conceal their Caucasian identity, until they became confused in the lace-work of roads near the border. Along with other traffic they were stopped by Iraqi soldiers at a vehicle checkpoint. An Iraqi "jundie" (squaddie) knocked on the driver's window to ask for their papers. Trooper Legs Lane shot the Iraqi in the head with his 203. The SAS men leaped out, shot two more soldiers and ran off into the desert.

By now the lights of a town across the border were clearly visible. As they neared the border they again ran into an anti-air-craft battery. Shells and small arms fire landed all around. There were now over 1,500 Iraqi troops looking for them. The SAS men had barely six miles to go, but the moon was bright. An Iraqi patrol found them hiding in a ditch. A running firefight broke out in which the SAS soldiers killed scores of Iraqis, but became separated from each other in the process. Trooper "Mark" was wounded in the elbow and ankle and captured. Another trooper, Robert Consiglio, a Swiss-born former Royal Marine, was hit in the head as he covered the withdrawal of Trooper "Dinger" and Lance-Corporal Lane. Consiglio was the first SAS soldier of the campaign to die from enemy fire. He received a posthumous Military Medal. Lane urged "Dinger" to join him and swim the Euphrates, then in full icy flood. Lane emerged on the far bank in a state of collapse. His companion stayed with him and hid him in a nearby hut. When it became clear that Lane was going to die from hypothermia, "Dinger" attracted the attention of a civilian working nearby. By the time an Iraqi retrieval team got to Lane he was dead. He, too, was awarded a posthumous MM. "Dinger" tried to escape but was captured. Sergeant McNab was discovered the next morning in a drainage culvert. Along with the other SAS men captured alive he suffered a month of imprisonment and torture. The latter was brutally physical and ultimately counter-productive. It only made the SAS men more determined not to talk. Though the Iraqi military imprisoned the men together they failed to even covertly monitor their conversations.

As for the trio missing in the desert, Sergeant Phillips was lost in driving snow on the night of 26 January. His companions, "Stan" and Chris Ryan turned back for him but could not find him. His body was eventually found by Iraqi soldiers and handed to the British authorities at the war's end. Later the next day, Stan went to see if he could hijack some transport. As he approached a parked lorry an Iraqi soldier came out of the house. The Iraqi tried to pull a weapon out. Stan shot him with his 203. Six or seven other Iraqi soldiers came running out. Stan shot three of them but then his gun jammed. The Iraqis did not kill him, only beat him unconscious with their rifle butts. When Stan failed to return to the LUP, Ryan decided to set out on his own. He would be the only man from Bravo Two Zero to escape to safety.

Massively dehydrated, his feet and hands turning septic from cuts, and at one point falling unconscious and breaking his nose, Chris managed to cross the Syrian border into sanctuary on 30 January. He had covered 186 miles, evading hundreds of Iraqi searchers, with only two packets of biscuits for nourishment. During the final two days he was without any water. He had filled his bottles from a small stream. When he came to drink the water his lips and mouth burned instantly. The stream was polluted with chemicals from a nearby uranium processing plant.

After the attempt to deploy the static patrols, 22 SAS effort shifted to the four mobile fighting columns. Drawn from Squadrons A and D, the columns – which contained about a dozen Land Rovers or Unimogs together with motorcycle outriders – were the biggest overland fighting force put into the field by the SAS since 1945. The columns had their own Stinger anti-aircraft and Milan anti-tank missiles, plus .5 Browning machine guns, 7.62 mm general-purpose machine guns and 40 mm grenade launchers. One team found a sledge-hammer most useful. The freebooting columns, soon operating in broad daylight, scored spectacular successes as they sped into the Iraqi desert flying enormous Union flags to identify them to friendly aircraft. An Iraqi deputy commander of a gun battery taken POW proved to have on his person a map giving positions of Iraqi frontline units. On 29 January SAS columns called down F-15E airstrikes on two mobile Scud launchers, plus one fixed site. On 3 February in the Wadi Amij ("Scud Alley") locality, a patrol from D Squadron called down an airstrike on a Scud convoy. Only one airstrike hit the target, so the SAS patrol hit the convoy with wire-guided Milan anti-tank missiles, an inspired last-minute addition to the SAS armoury.

These SAS attacks were the first military actions on the ground in the war except for the minor Iraqi cross-border attack on Khafji, Saudi Arabia, on 29 January. Group 2 from D Squadron called an airstrike on a Scud convoy on 5 February, and on the same day fought two firefights with Iraqi troops. Increasingly, the SAS destroyed Scud and launcher themselves, since some were escaping in the gap between their targeting by the SAS and the arrival of the airstrike. To service the Land Rovers and Unimogs, the SAS organised a supply column ("E Squadron") which formed a temporary workshop deep inside Iraq. Everywhere the SAS teams went they caused mayhem, and not only to the Scuds. Saddam (courtesy of the time when the West regarded him as a friend) had an advanced communications network consisting of buried fibre-optic cables. The weak point in the system was that the signal needed to be boosted at above-ground relay stations. A team from 22 SAS blew up seven of these stations alongside the highway from Baghdad to Amman. When the SAS Land Rovers returned to Saudi Arabia at the end of the war, they had covered an average of 1,500 miles and spent between thirty-six and forty-two days behind the lines. The front wings of the Land Rovers were decorated with scores of silhouettes of "kills", including mobile Scuds and communications towers. The SAS had also provided valuable advice to US Special Forces, operating in a "Scud Box" north of the regiment's.

It is a measure of the success of the SAS that General Norman Schwarzkopf, the "enemy" of Special Forces, praised the regiment's "totally outstanding performance" in the Gulf. No less than thirty-nine awards and honours for bravery and meritorious service were given the regiment for its part in Operation Granby, the Gulf War. There was, of course, a price to be paid for the regiment's achievement. In addition to the three SAS soldiers from Bravo Two Zero who were killed, Trooper David Denbury from A Squadron was killed on 21 February during the ambush of a Scud convoy in north-west Iraq. A sapper attached to the regiment was also killed in action.

David Stirling died on 5 November 1990. That evening his body was laid to rest in a London chapel, with his SAS beret and DSO on top of the coffin, next to his Knight Bachelor. The founder of the SAS missed by only weeks the regiment's deployment as behind-the-lines desert raiders in Iraq, in what turned out to be a glorious reprise of L Detachment's raiding half a century before. Even the 'pinkie' Land Rovers of 22 SAS, festooned with kit and guns and attended by soldiers in shemaghs, were strangely reminiscent of L Detachment's Jeeps and men.

An historic circle had been turned. The SAS had returned to the desert, the place of its birth. But the wheel kept on turning. After a decade of 'Green Ops', from the Falklands to the Gulf, the SAS returned to the shadow war of 'Black Ops', courtesy of the conflagrations in the Balkans and, especially, the invasions of Afghanistan and Iraq. (Afghanistan also saw more conventional operations, such as the celebrated Operation Trent attack by the SAS on an Al-Qaeda opium plant). During a six-year campaign in Iraq as part of 'Task Force Black', the SAS was credited with capturing 3,000 insurgents, and killing 350 to 400. Snatching Al-Qaeda operatives from the backstreets of Baghdad might seem a world away from L Detachment's blowing-up of Luftwaffe planes in the Western Desert, but David Stirling would have appreciated the similarity: both campaigns were for strategic ends and both had decisive impacts. L Detachment severely hampered the operational efficiency of the Afrika Korps; 22 SAS degraded the capability of Al-Qaeda in Iraq.

These virtues have a price, which is sometimes paid in blood. At least nine SAS soldiers died in Iraq, their names joining those on the roll of honour inscribed on the regimental clock at Stirling Lines. The clock has a verse from "The Golden Road to Samarkand" by James Elroy Flecker inscribed on its base:

We are the Pilgrims, master; we shall go
Always a little further: it may be
Beyond that last blue mountain barred with snow
Across that angry or that glimmering sea . . .

Individual pilgrims may have failed to 'beat the clock', but the SAS – the world's most famous and most imitated Special Forces unit – most surely has. The SAS worked in 1941 and it works today. It will work tomorrow.

US NAVY SEALS

"I am directing the Secretary of Defense to expand rapidly and substantially . . . the orientation of existing forces for the conduct of . . . unconventional wars . . . In addition, our Special Forces and unconventional warfare units will be increased and reoriented."

President John F. Kennedy, addressing a joint session of Congress, May 1961.

Taking their name from the elements they are trained to fight in, under, and on – Sea, Air, Land – the US Navy's SEALs have their origins in the Second World War's Underwater Demolition Teams (UDTs), which cleared the lane through German beach defences for the 1944 Allied invasion of Normandy. During the Korean War UDTs prepared the way for the amphibious landings at Inchon. In 1960 a US Navy working group was formed to study how the Navy UDTs could "assist or participate" in covert operations. A year later, the Navy's Unconventional Activities Committee presented a mission statement for a new special ops

"SEAL" unit, and the Chief of Naval Operations declared to his senior commanders, "It is the Navy's intention to provide for the waterborne conduct and support of such guerrilla and counter-guerrilla operations as may be directed in the national interest."

SEALs were also in the Navy's interest; with the administration's favouring of the Army's Green Berets, the Navy needed a role in Special Forces capability. In January 1962 President Kennedy authorized the creation of US Navy SEAL Teams One and Two, with One based on the East Coast of Conus (Continental US) at Coronado, California, and Two at Little Creek, Virginia. Recruited principally from the UDTs, the SEALs were soon deployed in Vietnam, with SEAL Team One personnel entering theatre in March 1962 to train their South Vietnamese counterparts in covert maritime operations. The following month, a SEAL Team One detachment was sent to Vietnam to train Biet Hai Junk Force commandos. From 1962 to 1964, the SEALs primarily trained and advised South Vietnamese commandos in guerrilla operations against sites in North Vietnam as part of Operation Plan 34A and under CIA direction. Because Americans were prohibited from entering into North Vietnam, SEAL Team advisers escorted South Vietnamese naval Special Forces to the 17th parallel, when the South Vietnamese continued northwards on their own.

After the Gulf of Tonkin incident in which North Vietnamese forces allegedly attacked US shipping, America committed directly to the Vietnam War and SEAL Team One activity switched to hands-on covert special ops in the South-East Asia theatre, beginning at Da Nang, before switching to the Rung Sat Special Zone (RSSZ), a 400-square-mile delta between Saigon and the China Sea. This was a Vietcong stronghold. The tasks assigned the SEALs in the brown water war ranged from setting up listening posts to the demolition of VC bunkers. More often than not, the SEALs went out in three-man detachments with the simple order, "Sat Cong". Kill Communists. In the first operations insertion was by Mike boat, a heavily armed riverine craft, but later by Boston Whaler, a fibreglass boat with a shallow draught, or an inflatable boat, or even by submarine. The SEALs'

Vietnam arsenal included the 5.56mm M63A1 Stoner light machine gun – a SEAL favourite, because it could be converted to an assault rifle – the M60 GPMG, the M79 grenade launcher, and the ever-reliable 9 mm "Carl Gustav" sub-machine-gun. For clandestine ops, the SEALs carried the 9 mm Smith and Wesson Mk 22 Model 0 silenced pistol, nicknamed the "hush puppy" because it was originally developed for silencing enemy guard dogs. Combat knives such as the Randall, the Ka-Bar and Gerber were standard. "Tiger stripe" camouflage fatigues were often worn in preference to the usual combat issue – green-leaf-pattern uniform – though many SEALs wore blue denim jeans because these best withstood the mosquitoes. A special combat coat was developed for the use of SEALs, made of camouflaged material, with a built-in flotation chamber, which was designed to carry everything a SEAL would need on a mission. They painted their faces green. The Vietcong called them "green faces" and put a price on their heads.

On 19 August 1966 the SEALs suffered their first combat casualty when twenty-eight-year-old Radarman 2nd Class Billy Machen was killed in the RSSZ while on daylight recce. The point man in the patrol, Machen spotted a VC ambush, which he single-handedly engaged; his action allowed his fellow patrol members to take cover and beat off the VC attack. Machen was posthumously awarded the Silver Star.

VC activity in the region was dramatically reduced by SEAL Team One's operations. So successful was SEAL Team One in the Rung Sat that there was general hollering for SEAL operations. So, platoons were sent to the Mekong Delta, one of the major rice-growing regions of the world. Like RSSZ, the Delta was a hard-core Communist stronghold. It would see some of the toughest fighting of the war. Soon the demand for SEAL missions outstripped SEAL Team One's ability to fulfil them, and elements from SEAL Team Two were deployed to Nam. Yet SEAL "missions" largely continued to be unlike conventional missions, which ran to pre-arranged schedules and agreed objectives. SEALs did their own thing. As one senior naval commander put it, once SEAL platoons were deployed, "The SEALs made up their own operations." The SEALS called it "doing SEAL shit."

The SEALs liked combat. SEAL Team Two Ensign Ron Yaw said:

> Action was our prime motive in life. Every time we went on patrol we wanted contact. As a platoon commander, it was my responsibility to design a situation where that desire would be fulfilled.

At the war's height, eight SEAL platoons were in Vietnam on a continuing rotational basis. SEALs continued to make forays into North Vietnam and Laos, and unofficially into Cambodia, controlled by the Studies and Observations Group.

The SEALs were heavily committed to the controversial "Phoenix Program", which, under the auspices of the CIA and South Vietnamese police, formed Provincial Reconnaissance Units (PRUs) of Vietcong defectors. The PRUs were to lead the SEALs into the Delta, so the SEALs could "capture or kill members of the Vietcong shadow government to weaken its capability to support military operations". The American public came to worry that there was no "capture" element in the programme.

On 18 May 1967, Lieutenant Dick Marcinko of SEAL Team Two led his men in an assault on Ilo Ilo Hon, in what is regarded as the most successful SEAL operation in the Mekong Delta. For leading it, Marcinko was awarded the second of his four Bronze Stars. His citation read:

> The President of the United States of America takes pleasure in presenting a Gold Star in lieu of a Second Award of the Bronze Star Medal with Combat "V" to Ensign Richard Marcinko, United States Navy, for meritorious achievement while serving with friendly foreign forces engaged in armed conflict against Communist insurgents on Ilo Ilo Island, Republic of Vietnam. In the early morning of 18 May 1967, Ensign Marcinko led a seven-man United States Navy SEAL squad on an eleven-and-one-half-hour reconnaissance mission of Ilo Ilo Island which is covered with dense foliage and muddy terrain. After two hours of laborious

movement, a well-concealed, heavily booby-trapped Vietcong first-aid station was discovered. Ensign Marcinko directed his squad in the removal of these booby traps, fully utilizing safety precautions and quietness to avoid alerting the Viet Cong forces. Deploying his squad for maximum coverage, Ensign Marcinko approached the area where three medical huts, two bunkers and a cooking hut were located. Contact with the Vietcong was then made resulting in five Vietcong killed, one Vietcong wounded and four CHICOM rifles captured. Numerous drugs, medical texts, personal notebooks, and documents were captured and cooking utensils, twenty kilos of rice and two sampans were destroyed. The ensuing ambulation to the extraction point was opposed by sniper fire which was ultimately suppressed by mortar fire from a Mike boat directed by Ensign Marcinko. Ensign Marcinko's initiative, foresight, perseverance and courage under fire contributed significantly to the successful reconnaissance patrol without injury to his own forces and were in keeping with the highest traditions of the United States Naval Service. (Ensign Marcinko is authorized to wear the Combat "V".)

The following year Marcinko was awarded the Silver Star.

During the 1968 Tet Offensive, Marcinko ordered his platoon to assist US Army Special Forces at Chau Doc. What began as house-to-house fighting turned into a rescue mission of American nurses and a schoolteacher trapped by the VC in the city's church and hospital. Marcinko's team rescued a nurse called Maggie, bundled her into a jeep, and hightailed it to safety, with one SEAL having to lie protectively on top of her. Marcinko received a Bronze Star for the Chau Doc action. The Vietcong put a bounty on Marcinko's head: "Award of 50,000 piastres to anyone who can kill First Lieutenant Demo Richard Marcinko, a grey-faced killer who has brought death and trouble to the Chau Doc province during the Lunar New Year."

The roll call of SEAL casualties mounted. X-Ray Platoon, SEAL Team One, which arrived in the Delta in October 1970, where it spectacularly disrupted Vietcong operations – capturing more than 100 pounds of documents and destroying numerous enemy rice caches and weapons factories – took 100% casualties, with four platoon men killed. On the unit's last mission, 4 March 1971, the platoon's commander, Lieutenant Mike Collins, was KIA. An investigation later revealed that X-Ray Platoon had been compromised; one of its attached South Vietnamese commandos was a Communist agent. By the time of the withdrawal of the last SEAL platoons from Vietnam in 1971 the SEALs were credited with 580 VC killed. Between 1965 and 1972, there were forty-six SEALs killed in Vietnam. The last SEAL killed was Lieutenant Melvin S. Dry, who had stayed on as an adviser, in an abortive operation to retrieve prisoners of war.

Post-Vietnam, the SEALs went on the round of training Allied troops that is so often the lot of Special Forces in peacetime. In 1980, following the reorganization of the US Counter-Terrorist Units under the Joint Special Operations Command, SEAL Team Six was set up under Marcinko as a special counter-terrorist unit. With the invasion of Grenada in 1983, the SEALs were back in the thick of military action. Elements of both SEAL Team Four and Team Six were involved in Operation Urgent Fury, their main missions being the extraction of Grenada's British Governor-General and the capture of Grenada's only radio station, Radio Free Grenada.

There was trouble from the start. Delays meant that Team Six parachuted into the sea at night in wind gusting at twenty-five knots (the recommended maximum wind speed for parachute insertion is eighteen knots) and four of the eighteen SEALs drowned. After re-grouping, the SEALs split into two teams, with one group proceeding to Government House, where they quickly overcame the police guard, but hostile fire prevented the drop of essential kit, including a satellite phone. Besieged by Soviet BTR-60 armed personnel carriers and Grenadian troops, the SEALS were obliged to use the Governor's land line to call in an AC-130 gunship. Pinned down over night, the SEALs were extracted by a group of Marines next morning. Meanwhile, the

SEALs sent to Radio Free Grenada also encountered problems. After knocking back several assaults by Grenadian and Cuban troops complete with BTR-60 armoured personnel carriers, the SEALs were forced to retreat to the sea, where they hid in the water from patrolling enemy forces. They were later spotted by a reconnaissance plane.

The next major SEAL deployment came with the invasion of Panama, code named Operation Just Cause. Deployed were SEAL Teams Two and Four, Naval Special Warfare Unit 8, and Special Boat Unit 26, and DEVGRU (Naval Special Warfare Development Group), aka SEAL Team Six. The strike on Balboa Harbor by Task Unit Whiskey is notable in SEAL history as the first publicly recorded combat swimmer mission since the Second World War. Four SEALs – Lieutenant Edward S. Coughlin, EN-3 Timothy K. Eppley, ET-1 Randy L. Beausoleil, and PH-2 Chris Dye – attached C4 explosives to the dictator General Noriega's personal gunboat the *Presidente Porras*, destroying it at H-Hour, 0100. During an attack on the Paitilla airfield the SEALs suffered four dead in a firefight with the Panamanian Defence Force, though Noriega's Learjet was successfully immobilized by a 40-mm grenade.

In August 1990 the SEALs were sent across the globe for Operation Desert Shield, to restore the sovereignty of Kuwait. Missions included the securing of Kuwaiti oil platforms in January 1991. On 23 February 1991, a day before the ground offensive, a six-man SEAL team led by Lieutenant Tom Dietz set off along Kuwait's shoreline in Zodiac raiding craft; 500 yards from shore they laid explosives and marker buoys. The explosives were detonated at 0100 hours on 24 February, three hours before the Allied assault across the border from Saudi Arabia. As intended, the explosions and marker buoys fooled the Iraqis into thinking an amphibious operation was under way.

In August 1993 a four man SEAL sniper team was deployed to Mogadishu to work alongside the Delta Force as part of Task Force Ranger in the search for the Somali warlord Mohamed Farrah Aidid. They took part in several operations in support of the CIA and Army, culminating in the 3 October "Battle of Mogadishu" where they were part of the ground convoy raiding the Olympic Hotel. All four SEALs were awarded the Silver Star. Naval Special Warfare units also conducted missions in the Lebanon, Somalia, Haiti and Liberia.

After the 11 September attacks in 2001, Navy SEALs quickly dispatched to the decidedly landlocked Afghanistan, where they had an early success seizing the Taliban Mullah Khirullah Said Wali Khairkhwa following a CIA tip-off. The next phase of SEAL operations in Afghanistan was conducted within Task Force K-Bar, a joint special operations unit of US Special Forces and special forces assets from, among other countries, Germany, Australia, New Zealand and Canada. Task Force K-Bar conducted combat operations in the massive cave complexes at Zhawar Kili, the city of Kandahar, and throughout hundreds of miles of southern and eastern Afghanistan. Over the course of six months Task Force K-Bar conducted more than seventy-five missions, killed or captured over 200 Taliban and Al-Qaeda fighters, and destroyed 500,000 lbs of weapons and ordnance.

Navy SEALs participated extensively in Operation Anaconda, the 2002 attack on al-Qaeda and the Taliban in Afghanistan's Shahi-Kot Valley. SEALs were present at the Battle of Qala-i-Jangi alongside their counterparts from the British Special Boat Service. Chief Petty Officer Stephen Bass was awarded the Navy Cross for his bravery during the battle. Lieutenant Michael P. Murphy was posthumously awarded the Medal of Honor after his four-man team was almost wiped out in a firefight during Operation Red Wings in June 2005. Afghanistan witnessed the SEALs' greatest tragedy when on 6 August 2011 seventeen SEALs were killed when their CH-47 Chinook helicopter was shot down by a Taliban RPG round.

Overlapping with the Afghanistan mission was the deployment to Iraq. On 20 March 2003, as part of a mixed force of US Navy SEALs, Polish GROM and British Royal Marines, the Navy SEALs launched what is the largest single SEAL operation in history. Their targets were the MABOT and KAAOT oil platforms, together with their respective onshore petroleum pumping locks, plus the Al Faw port and refinery. All were secured. Coalition military planners were also concerned that retreating Iraqi forces would destroy the Mukatayin hydroelectric dam north-east of Baghdad in an attempt to slow advancing US troops. A mixed team of SEALs from SEAL Team Five and Polish GROM seized the dam after fast-roping down from helicopters.

The War on Terror took a dramatic turn in 2011, when CIA analysts became convinced they had finally found Osama bin Laden's hide-out. The mission to capture or kill the USA's Enemy Number 1, dubbed by the Defense Department Operation Neptune Spear, naturally fell to the country's elite counter-terrorist unit. Under a moonless Afghan sky, shortly after eleven o'clock on the night of 1 May 2011, two MH-60 Black Hawk helicopters lifted off from Jalalabad Airfield. Inside the aircraft were twenty-three men with hard eyes and long stares from the Red Squadron of DEVGRU, SEAL Team Six. A Pakistani American translator and a Belgian Malinois dog were also aboard. Radio communications were kept to an absolute minimum. The SEALs' destination was a concrete house in the small city of Abbottabad, across the border in Pakistan. Abbottabad, situated north of the Pakistani capital, Islamabad, is in the foothills of the Pir Panjal Range. Founded in 1853 by a British major named James Abbott, the city is home to a prestigious military academy, and in the baking Indian summer the cool climate makes it a popular retreat for city dwellers.

A covert operation into the heart of Pakistan carried the possibility of major diplomatic fall-out – Pakistan was an ally, of sorts, but not the sort the US would want to trust on a mission like this. Why, after all, was bin Laden in Pakistan at all? Was he being hidden and succoured by Islamicists in its government? The sending of the SEALs into Pakistan had required the approval of President Obama personally, and to reassure him and his advisers the team had conducted a night-time dress rehearsal of the raid on a mock-up of bin Laden's house. They were impressed; the President had said "Yes".

According to the information gathered by the CIA, bin Laden was hunkered down in the third floor of a house in a compound just off Kakul Road, a residential street less than a mile from the entrance to the military academy. The plan was simple: the SEALs would drop from the helicopters into the compound, overpower bin Laden's guards, seize or shoot bin Laden, depending on circumstances, and fly the corpse out. Fifteen minutes after take-off, the choppers ducked down into an alpine valley and slipped into Pakistani airspace. They were undetected. Pakistan's principal air detection systems look towards India. Even so, the Black Hawk crews, two pilots and a crewman from the 160th Special Operations Aviation Regiment ("The night Stalkers") had taken no chances. The Black Hawks were modified "Stealth" versions covered with radar-damping "skin". Flying behind them were two Chinooks, which were to land and be kept on standby in a deserted area roughly two-thirds of the way to Abbottabad, with two additional SEAL teams on board of approximately twenty-four DEVGRU operators. These were the "Quick Reaction Force" in case anything went wrong on the main raid.

During the ninety-minute flight, sitting in the strangely calm red-lit interior of the aircraft, the SEALs rehearsed the operation in their minds. They were no strangers to action. Since the commencement of the War on Terror in 2001 they had rotated through Afghanistan, Iraq, the Horn of Africa, and the Yemen. DEVGRU had been into Pakistan before, too, on at least ten occasions, usually into the tribal badlands of Waziristan, where senior Al-Qaeda members liked to hole up. But the SEALs had never been as far into Pakistan as Abbottabad. The helicopters skirted the north of Peshawar, and continued due east. In this time of waiting, the kit hung heavy and even the desert camou-flage uniform seemed a little too tight. Most of the SEALs had plumped for the Heckler & Koch MP7, a few the short-barrelled silenced M4. Vest pockets held a booklet with photographs and physical descriptions of the people suspected of being inside the compound. One of these was Ahmed al-Kuwaiti, an Al-Qaeda courier who would unwittingly lead the CIA to bin Laden's compound. Or maybe not. There was no *absolute* certainty that bin Laden was in the compound. At least the CIA had intimate knowledge of the compound's layout: in the run-up to the raid one of the SEALs, Matt Bissonnette, had asked an intelligence officer about one of the many doors the commandos would have to breach. The answer came back straight away: the door is metal and opens to the outside.

The helicopters arrived above the compound at around 12.55 a.m. The mission plan dictated that the SEALs from the first helicopter would fast-rope to the ground and enter the house from the ground floor. The second helicopter would fly to the northeast corner of the compound and secure the perimeter. As the first helicopter hovered over the compound it experienced "vortex ring state", a phenomenon caused by turbulent air, and its tail caught the compound wall. The chopper lunged dangerously on its side, but the pilot managed to bring the nose down to prevent it tipping over. None of the aircrew or SEALs were seriously injured. The SEALs quickly cleared the chopper and placed explosives against the door of the house. Meanwhile, the other chopper landed outside the compound, and its SEAL team scaled the eighteen-feet-high walls to get inside. Matt Bissonnette, who was in this second SEAL team, and a colleague deployed to an outbuilding where Ahmed al-Kuwaiti, bin Laden's courier, was thought to be residing. The two SEALs pounded on the door with a sledgehammer. A shot was fired out. Bissonnette and his colleague, an Arabic-speaker, fired back. There was a cry and a groan from inside.

Immediately after this exchange of fire, a woman's voice called out from inside the building. The door was unlocked and a woman walked out. Caught in the exchange of fire, the woman had a shoulder wound from a bullet. The SEALs' rules of engagement are precise on the question of unarmed, surrendered women: Bissonnette and his colleague held fire; three children trailed the woman into the courtyard. Taking no chances, the SEALs entered the building in textbook fashion, quick and providing cover for each other. Al-Kuwaiti was on the floor. Bissonette and his colleague "squeezed off several rounds to make sure he was down."

This building cleared, Bissonnette and his colleague joined the first SEAL team, which had now breached the main door of the house. Inside, there was total blackness; CIA operatives had disabled the local power station. Through the green gloom of their night vision goggles the SEALs spotted al-Kuwaiti's brother, Abrar, as he poked his head into a hallway on the first floor. He was shot and staggered backwards. The SEALs, amid shouting and screaming, followed him into a side room. Abrar was shot again. His wife tried to shield him, and she was shot dead too. A massive metal door blocked the access to the two top floors. This was blown apart. As the SEALs climbed the main stairs, bin Laden's twenty-three-year-old son, Khalid, rushed towards them. He was killed as he did so. Bissonnette stepped past the body and saw an AK-47 assault rifle propped nearby. Later, it transpired there was a round in the chamber. Khalid had been prepared to fight; he just never got the chance.

As they climbed to the last and third floor, the SEAL point man saw someone peeking out from the door on the right of the hallway, and immediately popped off a round from his rifle, which was fitted with a silencer. The man fell backward. The SEALs sprinted into the room, through an unlocked gate on the stairs; in the bedroom the SEALs found bin Laden lying on the floor, with two women standing in front of him trying to protect him. One of them, Amal Ahmed Abdul Fatah, screamed at the SEALs in Arabic and looked as if she was about to charge. She was shot in the leg, and pushed out of the way. Bin Laden's twelve-year-old daughter stood in the darkness at the back of the room, screaming. She had been named Safia after a contemporary of the Prophet who had killed a Jew in the hope, bin Laden had once explained, that she would grow up to do the same. With bin Laden writhing on the floor Bissonnette and a colleague applied the *coup de grâce* with bullets to the chest. The SEALs then had to positively identify him. To do this they asked his children. To be doubly sure of the correct ID, they also measured him and took blood samples. The SEAL team leader then radioed, "For God and country – Geronimo, Geronimo, Geronimo ... Geronimo E.K.I.A." Geronimo was the codename for bin Laden. EKIA is Enemy Killed in Action.

There were two weapons on a shelf next to the door, an AKSU rifle and a Makarov pistol. The raid had taken fifteen minutes to reach bin Laden in his top floor bedroom. He did not reach for his weapons, either because he was paralysed by fear or because he was hampered by the design of the house and could not understand what was happening. The house was built in segregated compartments with small windows intended to frustrate observation; on that night, it made it difficult for the inhabitants to see what was going on or liaise with each other.

Bin Laden was dead, yet the mission was not over. The SEALs still had to gather as much intelligence material from the compound as possible and get the body out of Pakistan before local forces were alerted. After restraining the women and children in the compound with plastic ties and handcuffs, the SEALs began a methodical search. The downed helicopter also had to be destroyed. After smashing the cockpit controls, SEALs packed the helicopter with explosives and blew it up. Since the team was reduced to one operational helicopter, one of the two Chinooks held in reserve was dispatched to carry part of the assault team and bin Laden's body out. Thirty-eight minutes after arriving at the compound the SEALs, together with bin Laden's corpse, were on their way to Afghanistan. They were two minutes under schedule.

No country wanted the body, so it was dumped, after the appropriate Muslim rites, in the Arabian Sea.

GREEN BERETS

The US Army's Special Forces originated in 1952 and established a base at Fort Bragg, South Carolina, site of the Army Special Warfare School. America has a rich history of operations by unconventional forces, dating back to the French and Indian wars in the days when the thirteen colonies were still British, and including Rogers' Rangers. who were active during the War of Independence. A vast conglomeration of special operations units mushroomed during the Second World War, among them a new Rangers, Merrill's Marauders, Marine Raiders, Underwater Demolition Teams, the Office of Strategic Services (OSS), and the 1st Special Service Force ("The Devil's Brigade"), but they were quickly disbanded after the war. Interest was revived in the 1950s following the Korean War, and that led to the formation of the Special Forces, the name coming straight from the OSS's term for its operational teams.

They were kept at a relatively low strength of 2,300 personnel, and only grudgingly tolerated by the traditionalists in the Army's high command, who did not like any unit with pretensions to elite status. Army administrators discouraged officers from spending more than one tour with the Special Forces, on the basis that they would lose experience in their basic branch, and thus be unfavourably looked-on when it came to promotion.

With the inauguration of President John F. Kennedy in 1961, though, the fate of the Special Forces changed. Kennedy strongly believed that such units were the best way to counter Communist "wars of liberation"; the motto of the Special Forces was "De Oppresso Liber", Latin for "To Free the Oppressed". As it became chic in Washington DC to support the "Green Berets", so named because of their distinctive headgear which had been approved by the President, their numbers increased by several orders of magnitude. While the original Special Forces mission was to organise guerrilla warfare in enemy-held countries, that role changed as more and more Green Berets were sent to South-East Asia, where they became increasingly involved in counter-insurgency operations.

The Special Forces were among the first Americans in action in Vietnam: the 5th Special Forces Group took over the CIA's border surveillance programme, teaching the fundamentals of reconnaissance and local defence to remote tribes in Laos and the Vietnamese highlands. Operating in small teams with large numbers of native auxiliaries, often only marginally less hostile to the government in Saigon than to the Communists, they ran patrols from border camps to uncover Communist infiltration on the Ho Chi Minh Trail. In more settled parts of Vietnam the Green Berets (soon dubbed "the Sneaky Petes") were assigned as advisers by the US military authorities, to provide anything from advice on personal health and drainage to teaching unarmed combat and demolitions to members of the Civilian Irregular Defence Groups.

Hostage rescue had always been a part of the Green Berets' remit, and in 1970 the unit was tasked with a significant mission to save American lives. US military intelligence had spotted in aerial reconnaissance photographs what appeared to be a prison full of American POWs at Son Tay, some 37 km west of Hanoi. Entrusted with "Operation Ivory Coast", the night-time rescue of the POWs, was Colonel Arthur "Bull" Simons, a highly experienced Special Forces officer. At Fort Bragg, hundreds of Special Forces troopers volunteered, from which Simmons selected 103, mostly from the 6th and 7th Special Forces Groups. To carry out realistic training, a mock-up of the Son Tay compound was built, always to be dismantled during the day so it could not be detected by Soviet satellites. During training Simmons was dismayed to find that even his best marksmen were having trouble getting more than 25 per cent of their shots on target in the dark; this difficulty was solved, however, by going outside the normal Army supply channels to acquire "Singlepoint Nite Sites" for the sharp-shooters' M16s. The assault force was formed into three groups: the compound assault force of fourteen men, who would actually be deposited inside the prison compound by crash landing an HH-3E helicopter. Something of a firearms enthusiast, Simmons kitted his men with the best that Army money could buy: 12-gauge shotguns, 30-round M16 magazines, .45 automatic pistols, CAR-15s, and M-79 grenade launchers.

The weather and moon had to be right for the raid to take place, and conditions were deemed acceptable on the night of 20/21 November. President Nixon personally gave the "Go" order. At about 02.18 on the morning of 21 November, the raid helicopters arrived over Son Tay after a nerve-racking low level flight from Thailand and South Vietnam. As a C-130 flare ship illuminated the area with flares, the HH-53, code-named Apple Three, opened up on the guard towers of Son Tay Prison with its mini-guns, bringing them crashing down. Shortly thereafter, the HH-3E carrying the assault party commanded by Major "Dick" Meadows, known as Banana One, landed inside the prison compound; the whole group pressed against mattresses to cushion them against the crash. It came to rest amid branches, leaves and other debris brought down by its whirling rotors during the crash descent. On landing, "Dick" Meadows rushed out with his bullhorn shouting: "We're Americans. Keep your heads down. We're Americans. This is a rescue. We're here to get you out.

Keep your heads down. Get on the floor. We'll be in your cells in a minute." The remainder of the assault party rushed into action, some men laying down suppressive fire, others streaking for the cellblocks to rescue the prisoners.

A few minutes later the command and security group landed just outside the prison's walls. The Support group led by Simons himself, however, had landed 400 metres off course at what was identified on the raiders' maps as a secondary school, but turned out to be a barracks housing Chinese or Soviet advisers to the NVA (North Vietnamese Army). School or not, Simons and his men proceeded to teach its inmates a lesson. Within minutes of touching down, many of the residents of the barracks had been killed, preventing them from reinforcing the prison compound and taking the other raiders by surprise. Having cleared the area, Simons and his men entered the Son Tay compound proper.

The extraordinary effectiveness of the assault was to little purpose: there were no American prisoners at Son Tay. They had been moved days previously. Yet the raid was not a complete failure: it proved that North Vietnam was vulnerable to attacks even in its heartland, and indirectly led to improvements in the conditions of US POWs in North Vietnam. It should not be forgotten, either, that Simons' party had killed dozens of the enemy, many of them non-Vietnamese, without taking any losses themselves.

Following the end of the war in South-East Asia, the Green Berets suffered under the general malaise afflicting the US armed forces; additionally they suffered from having been often inappropriately committed, leading to unsatisfactory outcomes. After ill-starred roles in Iran (notably Operation Eagle Claw, the failed mission to rescue the fifty-two hostages held in the US Embassy in Tehran), Grenada, El Salvador and at Paitilla airfield during the Panama invasion, the reputation of the Green Berets rose inexorably with the first Gulf War, during which Special Forces reconnaissance teams penetrated deep into Iraq, keeping watch on Iraqi troop movements, hunting Scud launching sites, laser-designating targets for coalition air power, and scouting out routes for the coalition's ground offensive.

In 1997 Special Forces were made a separate branch of the Army, and their orders now come via the US Special Operations

Command, which incorporates all special operations units from all US services. Today's Green Berets retain their training function: Special Forces teams can be found passing on their skills to special operations units around the world. Most recently, they have been organising South American and South-East Asian units as part of the US government's worldwide anti-drugs campaign. Training and guerrilla warfare is not the whole story, of course: Delta Force, the US Army's hostage rescue unit (see p 514), is also part of the Special Forces.

SAYERET MATKAL

Sayeret Matkal (General Staff Reconnaissance Unit) is the principal Special Forces unit of the Israeli Defence Force. Modelled on the British SAS, whose motto and winged dagger insignia was adopted in homage, Sayeret Maktal was formed in 1957 to undertake deep reconnaissance into Arab lands, but was transformed in the 1960s into a counter-terrorist unit. Again like the SAS, the Unit operates an anti-authoritarian philosophy, where many decisions are taken in 'Chinese parliaments'. Lieutenant Moshe "Muki" Betser , a legendary Unit commando, explains:

> The hierarchy in the Unit is very different from anywhere else in the army. It's friendlier, more intimate and thus more candid and open, and this unique atmosphere is best seen during the planning phase of an operation. Rank doesn't count in planning a mission. All that matters is inventiveness and originality. Everyone throws out ideas, in a round-table brainstorming session. Nothing is rejected out of hand, as the best ideas are set aside while more are raised. Eventually, the best idea stands out.

Even by the standards of the world's Special Forces, 'the Unit' is shrouded in secrecy. Current strength is believed to be 200.

Candidates wanting to join the Unit are selected on "Yom Hasayarot" (Commando Day), after which they undertake a six-day evaluation, with successful candidates moving on to a twenty-month continuation training course, consisting of, inter alia, paratroop training, counter-terrorism and advanced infantry training, navigation, culminating in a 120-kilometre forced march across hostile terrain. Successful candidates are received into the Unit at the fortress of Masada, and granted the coveted red beret.

The Unit has conducted some of the most famous missions in Special Forces history. In April 1973, as part of Operation Wrath of God, Israel's counter-attack on the terrorists who had murdered its Olympic athletes in Munich the year before, a Unit team assassinated three PLO leaders in Beirut, and blew a PLO HQ sky-high. As many as 100 Palestinian militants may have perished in all.

Then came the Raid on Entebbe. Just after midday on 27 June 1976, Air France Flight 139 was hijacked en route to Paris by members of the German Baader-Meinhof terrorist gang (aka the Red Army Faction) and the Popular Front for the Liberation of Palestine. Fifteen hours later the skyjacked Airbus, with 258, mostly Israeli, passengers aboard, landed at Entebbe airport in Uganda. There the four hijackers were joined by other Baader-Meinhof and PFLP members. The terrorists were personally welcomed by Uganda's dictator, His Excellency Field Marshal Doctor Idi Amin. For all of his grandiose titles, Amin was a former NCO in the British Army.

On the following day, Wilfried Boese, the terrorists' leader, announced their demands to the waiting world: fifty-three of their comrades held in prisons in Israel, Kenya, West Germany and Switzerland must be released. They also required $5 million in cash. Otherwise, they would start shooting the Israeli hostages, now segregated from the remainder of the passengers in a separate room in the airport's old terminal. Apparently Boese, a German, at least had the decency to look uncomfortable when dividing the Jews from the Gentiles: some of the Israeli passengers were actually Holocaust survivors.

The hostage situation left the Israeli Cabinet of Yitzhak Rabin with an agonizing dilemma: should Israel capitulate to the hijackers' demands or mount a rescue bid? And what rescue bid could possibly succeed over such a long distance in a country that, while not exactly hostile, was not exactly neutral either. Entebbe was no less than 2,500 miles from Sharm-el-Sheikh, the southernmost Israeli airfield. Much of that 2,500 miles was over the airspace of Arab countries, all of whom had the capability of attacking Israeli aircraft. After much agony, the Israeli Cabinet unanimously approved a hostage rescue mission involving C-130 Hercules flying a fifty-strong composite force of Sayeret Maktal and the Israeli paras.

On landing at Entebbe, the first "Hippo" aircraft would disgorge a Sayeret Maktal "break-in crew" who would try to reach the airport terminal before their purpose was discovered. To this end the Unit decided to use subterfuge, and commandeered a white Mercedes from a civilian parking lot in Tel Aviv and repainted it black. As Muki Betser explained to the planners:

> I know the Ugandan soldiers. I trained them. We don't need hundreds of soldiers. Instead we use a Mercedes. Every battalion commander in Uganda rides around in one. A soldier spots a Mercedes, he snaps a salute. They'll see us in the Mercedes with a couple of Land Rovers carrying soldiers and they'll assume a general's about to drive by.

For good measure, the twenty-nine men from the break-in crew would wear leopard-spot fatigues like those worn by Ugandan paratroopers. The break-in crew would drive off the Hercules in the Mercedes and accompanying Land Rovers to the old terminal building, just over a mile away, with their lights on, which would take five minutes. After arriving at the terminal they would free the hostages and secure the building.

Lieutenant-Colonel Yonatan Netanyahu was placed in charge of the Unit's break-in crew. A former paratrooper, and the elder brother of the sometime Israeli Prime Minister, Binyamin Netanyahu, he had been decorated for valour during the Six-Day War. Somehow he managed to combine soldiering with studying philosophy at Harvard. He was also an ardent patriot, prepared to give his life for his country. At seventeen he had written:

> Death does not frighten me, it arouses my curiosity. I do not fear it because I attribute little value to a life without a purpose. And if it is necessary for me to lay down my life in the attainment of the goal I set for it, I will do so willingly.

While Netanyahu was driving to the old terminal, the second Hercules, carrying another Unit team and two Armoured Personnel Carriers, would land and secure the perimeter around the old terminal. Unit troops, paratroopers and air force technicians aboard a third Hercules would seize the new terminal and the refuelling station. An APC would also speed to the adjoining military airfield where eleven MiG fighters were stationed and shoot them up. A final and fourth Hercules would carry medical crews.

Meanwhile, the terrorists at Entebbe had as a gesture of "good will" released all the hostages who were not Israeli or aircrew. One of them was a retired French army officer who was able to give Mossad, the Israeli intelligence agency, critical information about the hostage situation. The hostages were kept under twenty-four hour guard in one room, and the Ugandans were definitely aiding the terrorists, indeed, acting as extra guards. The key moment of opportunity for the rescuers seemed to be just after midnight when the hostages were ordered to lie down and go to sleep. Not only would prone hostages be out of the line of fire, but the guard over them would also be at its minimum, with the majority of the hijackers in the adjoining room. The French army officer was also able to give a complete run-down of the terrorists' armoury.

At 3.30 p.m. on the afternoon of 3 July, the rescue mission took off from Sharm-el-Sheikh on the Red Sea. The task force's route took the international flight path over the Red Sea, mostly flying at a height of no more than thirty metres to avoid radar detection by Egyptian forces. Accompanying the Hercules were Phantom jets, who would provide an escort for part of the journey, and two Boeing 707s. The first Boeing contained additional medical facilities, and would land at Nairobi airport in Kenya, the only East African country vaguely sympathetic to Israel. The other Boeing would act as a command-and-control centre and circle Entebbe during the raid. Near the southern outlet of the Red Sea the C-130s turned and passed south of Djibouti, and thence to Kenya, finally approaching Entebbe from the direction of Lake Victoria. As the lead C-130 approached Entebbe after the eight-hour flight, Yoni Netanyahu, Betser and seven others climbed into the Mercedes, and the rest of the assault squad clambered into the Land Rovers. When the Hercules came to a stop, the flight crews released the blocks holding the vehicles, and the rear door was lowered. Netanyahu shouted "Go!" Muki Betser was second in command:

> The car lunged forward and memories poured into me as we came out of the Hercules and into the fresh night air of Africa right after rain. I felt calm, almost serene, looking out into the darkness as Amitzur drove slowly and steadily, like any convoy of VIPs in the Ugandan army, not too fast to attract attention, not too slow as to cause suspicion. The silence of the night was absolute. Far ahead, the old terminal was but a glow in the dark. I turned to look over my shoulder. Right behind us, the Land Rovers did indeed look like Ugandan troop carriers – though the soldiers' faces were white, not black.

As they neared the terminal they were intercepted by a guard, who opened fire. Abandoning the vehicles, the break-in team sprinted the last fifty yards to the terminal, withering machine-gun fire pouring down at them from the control tower. Inside the terminal all the terrorists were killed, along with one hostage who raised himself from the prone position on the floor and was thought by the Unit to be a terrorist. The assault team then began loading the hostages on to the waiting Hercules, coming under fire from the airport control tower. During this brief firefight Netanyahu was shot in the chest, possibly by a Ugandan sniper. The wound was mortal. Betser took over command of the rescue force and directed light machine-gun and RPG fire at the control tower until the threat was suppressed. Meanwhile, one of the APCs riddled the Ugandan MiG jets with bullets and RPG rounds, while accompanying paratroopers attached explosives to the aircraft for good destructive measure; when the Israeli force came under fire from the control tower, Betser ordered the other APC to take it out. Fifty-three minutes after the first Hercules had touched down on Ugandan soil, all the hostages and IDF men were airborne and on the way home. Since they had been unable to refuel as planned because of the firefight around the control tower, the Israelis refuelled the Hippos by permission in Kenya.

Yoni Netanyahu was the only member of the raiding party to die. All seven of the terrorists were killed. Three hostages died at the airport during the rescue attempt: one was killed because he was close to an armed terrorist; the second died in the terrorists' return fire; the third was the young man who had jumped up. Around fifty Ugandan soldiers also died. The last victims of Entebbe were those who felt Amin's desire for revenge. Dora Bloch, a seventy-five-year-old hostage who, after choking on food, had been taken by the Ugandans to a nearby hospital, was dragged from her bed and murdered by two of Amin's officers. When the dictator heard that the Kenyans had aided the Entebbe rescue he rounded up hundreds of Kenyans living in Uganda and had them shot.

The United Nations Secretary-General Kurt Waldheim described the raid as "a serious violation of the national sovereignty of a United Nations member state", meaning Uganda. In his address to the Council of the UN, Israel's ambassador Chaim Herzog said:

> We come with a simple message to the Council: we are proud of what we have done because we have demonstrated to the world that in a small country, in Israel's circumstances, with which the members of this Council are by now all too familiar, the dignity of man, human life and human freedom constitute the highest values. We are proud not only because we have saved the lives of over a hundred innocent people – men, women and children – but because

of the significance of our act for the cause of human freedom.

Whatever the politics, the Entebbe operation set the military gold standard in post-war hostage rescues. The Mercedes commandeered by the Unit was returned to its owner in Tel Aviv. He insisted that the IDF paint it white again.

PART II

SELECTION

SPECIAL AIR SERVICE

A Special Force is ultimately only as special as the men (and, just occasionally, the women) who make up its ranks. To find and maintain the highest calibre of soldier, virtually all Special Forces have a military course which would-be members must complete to a sufficient standard, and SAS Selection is both the gold standard and the fountainhead in this respect. As Colonel Charles Beckwith, founder of the US's Delta Force, famously commented, "There is the SAS and there is everyone else."

Since the regiment's re-formation in Malaya after the Second World War, Selection training has been based on a course devised in 1953 by Major John Woodhouse. It is designed to enlist only those who have the right qualities: mental and physical toughness, self-reliance and the intelligence to think through problems in any circumstance. The unorthodox, anti-military culture of 22 SAS, together with the size of its basic component, a small four-man patrol, and the isolated nature of commando work, also requires a soldier with a particular character. "Selection", as ex-SAS Regimental Adjutant Major "Dare" Newell has put it,

> is designed rather to find the individualist with a sense of self-discipline than the man who is primarily a good member of a team. For the disciplined individualist will always fit well into a team when teamwork is required, but a man selected for team work is by no means always suitable for work outside the team.

Every wannabe Special Forces soldier will need to have the ability to endure and the will to win. Some of the required toughness will be instilled in training. As Chris Ryan, "The One That Got

Selection

Away", observed after his epic 186-mile walk to freedom in the Gulf War, "In 1991 I was at a peak of physical fitness, and armed with the skills, the endurance, the competitive instinct and the motivation which SAS training had instilled in me." For every 150 applicants to SAS Selection, less than fifteen will be 'badged' into the Regiment. And that 150 is also a fairly select bunch to begin with, men with the belief they can be SAS troopers, and with the levels of fitness that come from regular Army training. Many SAS applicants are from the Parachute Regiment, an elite unit itself.

The selection course for 22 SAS lasts for one month. Although the regiment is based at Credenhill in Herefordshire, with a satellite training facility at Pontrilas, much of selection training takes place on the bleak terrain of the nearby Black Mountains and Brecon Beacons, particularly the 3,000-foot peak called Pen-y-fan. As it is impossible to enter the SAS directly, every volunteer must be serving with a regular British military unit. The only civilians allowed to try for selection are members of the SAS's two part-time Territorial regiments, 21 and 23 SAS. Officers must be between twenty-two and thirty-four, other ranks between nineteen and thirty-four. The selection course is run twice a year, once in summer and once in winter.

For those considering Selection the regiment offers a Special Forces Briefing Course at Credenhill, a weekend 'taster' of SAS life and the rigours of Selection itself. There is also an element of fitness training in the shape of standard British Army Battle Fitness Tests, Combat Fitness tests, circuit training, plus speed and endurance runs: the last is likely to be eight miles, and you will need to be looking at a time inside one hour forty minutes. Don't forget there will be time in the swimming pool (jump from the high board, swimming and treading water in combat uniform) and an IQ test.

Selection proper begins with a three-week build-up period for soldiers (two for officers), to allow each volunteer a chance to get up to the physical standard required. The emphasis is on cross-country speed marches over the nearby mountains in which the distance covered, carrying rifle and pack (Bergen), increases every day. So does the weight of the pack, from 18 kg to 25 kg. As

SAS troopers must all be proficient at navigation, basic tuition in map and compass work is given to those who need it. At the beginning of Selection the marches are done in groups, with a DS (Drill Sergeant; keep up with his leading group), but as the course progresses the candidate works in smaller groups, pairs, or alone. Each man is given a Bergen, a compass and map and a rendezvous (RV) he has to make for. There is a time limit for the march, but the candidate is not told what it is. For much of the march he will have to jog. It is usually raining and his Bergen will get heavier and heavier. When he reaches the RV he is given another one, and so on. To increase his anxiety and to test his ability to deal with the unexpected he might be asked to perform a task at the RV, such as stripping down an unfamiliar weapon. For the navigation and endurance exercises the candidates are usually based at Sennybridge in the Brecon Beacons. Part of the kit issued will be a Silva compass and five 1:50,000 Ordnance Survey maps of the area. It makes sense to have brought the maps and studied them hard previously. It makes even more sense to have done some 'recces' of the Brecon Beacons, Hay, Elan Valley, Black Mountains and Forest of Dean beforehand. The swimming tests catch out many applicants: Selection swimming is likely to include 20 lengths of a 50-metre pool in uniform, including boots. As with all Special Forces selection, the instructors will play psychological games to test reactions of the applicants under stress. These include 'soft cop' routines where the DS will seek to undermine the candidate's motivation by offering sympathy.

By the fourth week, Test Week, the culmination of Selection, the numbers on the course will have dropped significantly. Many will have left of their own accord, while others will have been rejected ("binned" in SAS parlance) or forced to quit through injury. Those who remain are exhausted, their stamina and judgment eroded by twenty-one days of exercises beginning at 4 a.m. and ending at 10.30 p.m. It is now that the selectors subject the candidate to the endurance march, the "Long Drag" or "Fan Dance", a 40-mile land-navigation exercise which has to be completed in 20 hours or less. Because of map-reading errors in the difficult mountainous terrain, most candidates end up marching or jogging considerably more than 40 miles. Only the most determined and fit candidates have made it to this point; even so, a handful of them will now fail here. Some have even died doing the "Long Drag", including the SAS hero of the 1972 Battle of Mirbat, Major Mike Kealy, who re-took the march to test his own fitness after a spell doing administrative work.

Those who pass the endurance march are then gathered in the SAS barracks at Stirling Lines, where they are told the bad news: they are not yet in the SAS. They must now endure, after a mere week's leave, Continuation Training. Continuation Training lasts for around fourteen weeks and tutors the potential recruit in all the SAS patrol skills:

- **Standard operating procedures (SOPs),** including the four-man patrol, insertion methods, contact drills, and the more sophisticated and technological navigation skills such as use of GPS. Recruits will also be introduced to the "Killing House", the building which the SAS use for urban hostage-rescue and counter-terrorist training.
- **Escape & Evasion**
- **Weapons-training, demolitions and reconnaissance.** Recruits are used to the SA80 but during Continuation Training will be tutored in handling the MI6, a 5.56 mm rifle with a muzzle velocity of 1000 mps, together with the Heckler & Koch MP5 sub-machine-gun, the SAS's counter-terrorist workhorse. There will also be training and testing in the use of small arms such as the SAS standard side arm, the 9 mm Sig-Sauer P226, or possibly the Browning Hi-Power. Candidates also get to experiment with "foreign" weapons such as the ubiquitous AK47. Three styles of shooting will be taught during Continuation Training: rapid-response; rapid aimed fire; night firing. Recruits are also introduced to anti-armour and anti-aircraft weaponry, notably the LAW 80 rocket launcher and the MILAN missile system.
- **Signalling.** Each student receives instruction in signalling, a vitally important skill for long- range patrolling. All SAS troopers must achieve British Army Regimental Signaller standard, which includes being able to transmit and receive Morse code at a minimum of eight words a minute. The basic radio set

used is the PRC 319. Recruits will also have to become acquainted with laser designation system, used to call in air and artillery strikes.

• Tuition is given in SAS field medicine techniques.

After these fundamentals, the candidates then go on Combat and Survival training. Some three weeks will be spent on jungle training, usually in Brunei, then a similar period in Britain on Exmoor. Here the prospective troopers learn all aspects of living in hostile environments: laying traps, building shelters, finding food and water. The Combat and Survival phase ends in an Escape and Evasion exercise, where candidates must not only live off the land but also do so for three days while being hunted by the "enemy", usually soldiers from local infantry battalions. At the conclusion of the exercise, candidates are subjected to 24-hour realistic interrogation (the Resistance-to-Interrogation exercise, conducted by the Joint Services Interrogation Unit) of the sort they might face if captured by the enemy. The interrogation includes elements of physical hardship, sensory deprivation, and psychological torture. Any candidate who "breaks" is rejected. After Interrogation recruits undergo up to four weeks of parachute training at No. 1 Parachute Training School at Brize Norton. This is static-line parachuting only. The SAS's celebrated HALO and HAHO advanced free-fall techniques are only taught after acceptance into the unit.

Only at the end of all this testing, and on completion of a basic parachute course, will the volunteer be accepted into the regiment and given the beige SAS beret and cloth badge bearing the famous winged dagger.

SPECIAL BOAT SERVICE (SBS)

The initial stages of selection are similar to those of the SAS. Candidates begin by taking a two-day Special Forces briefing course. Then comes a four-week endurance phase, mostly under-taken in the Brecon Beacons in Wales, culminating in the 25-mile 'Long Drag' march; then comes four weeks of basic Special Forces practices and skills, followed by jungle training, followed by four weeks of combat survival. Whereas at this point SAS candidates are 'badged', SBS hopefuls become probationers and go on to more training – all to do with water. SBS candidates are sent on diving, canoeing, and swimmer courses. Only when this stage is completed are candidates fully members of the service.

GREEN BERETS

Candidates begin with a thirty-day Special Operations Preparation Course at Fort Bragg, which focuses on PT, naviga-tion, and SERE (Survival, Evasion, Resistance and Escape). Applicants are expected to be able to perform, from the get-go, a four-mile march in battle dress uniform (BDU) and boots, carry-ing M-16, load-bearing equipment, and a 45-lb rucksack. The overall average four-mile rucksack march time for graduates is 61 minutes. If candidates pass the Preparation Course, they are permitted to move on to the Special Forces Qualification Course, the first thirteen weeks of which are devoted to individual skills and small unit practices such as sniping and close-quarters combat. Then comes phase two, assessment for Military Occupational Specialities, such as weapons, engineering, medi-cine and communications. All Green Berets are expected to become proficient in a language. In the final phase of selection, recruits are taught operational procedures. The final step before qualification is an exercise in Uwarrie Forest, North Carolina, where candidates must evade capture by an "enemy" as well as organise a guerrilla army.

US NAVY SEALS

"The more you sweat in peace, the less you bleed in war."
Sign over the main doorway of the Phil H. Bucklew Center
for Naval Special Warfare at Coronado.

The selection programme for the US Navy Seals is notoriously
gruelling. The Basic Underwater Demolition/SEAL (BUD/S)
course is some seven months long, beginning with three weeks of
mandatory Indoctrination, where candidates learn the SEAL way
(teamwork, teamwork, teamwork) and are 'acclimed' to the high
levels of mental and physical toughness required for the selection
process, let alone being a qualified SEAL. After 'Indoc' comes
seven weeks of basic conditioning at the Naval Amphibious Base
at Coronado, California, known as The First Phase. This trains,
develops and assesses SEAL recruits in physical conditioning,
water competency, teamwork and mental tenacity. Training
begins at 0530 hours and recruits are put through their paces
until late afternoon. The intake is divided into "boat crews" of six
to eight men, and each crew must carry its IBS (Inflatable Boat,
Small) everywhere except bed; simultaneously, recruits are put
through a physical conditioning course consisting of running,
callisthenics and swimming which becomes progressively harder.
Recruits participate in weekly four-mile timed runs in boots,
obstacle courses, swim distances in the sea of up to two miles
wearing fins, and learn small-boat seamanship. Integral to basic
conditioning is "drown-proofing": recruits enter a nine-foot-
deep pool with their hands and feet tied and bob for five minutes,
float for five minutes, swim a hundred yards, bob for another two
minutes, do some forward and backward flips, dive to the bottom
of the pool and retrieve an object with their teeth, return to the
surface and bob five more times. In another endurance test, "cold
water conditioning", recruits are deluged with water at a chill 65

degrees. After that, recruits are obliged to perform an extreme physical task, such as running a mile and half in boots and wet clothes. Such drills require as standard the carrying of the IBS, and voluntary 'drop-outs' are frequent. Verbal harassment by staff comes with the turf: anyone showing weakness or insufficient spirit is likely to be sent for a dip in the cold surf.

After three weeks, recruits still standing undergo "Hell Week": five and half days during which they are kept cold, wet, hungry and sleep-deprived (four hours is the maximum sleep time allowed per day), and toil continuously. Recruits eat 7,000 calories a day and still lose weight. In this condition, they are forced to spend hours doing inflatable boat drills and obstacle courses, all to the tune of bullet and grenade simulators. BUD/S instructors maintain that selection is 90% about mental strength and only 10% about physical strength. When recruits decide that they are too cold, too sandy, too sore, it is their minds that surrender. The last day of Hell Week is "So Sorry Day", when the exhausted recruits – often suffering wounds and running sores – crawl around mud pits. Classes typically lose 70-80% of their intake. The drop-out rate is higher in winter when it is colder.

Those who have completed Hell Week but cannot continue training because of injury are usually rolled back into the next BUD/S class, or the one before they were forced to drop out. There are many SEALs who have attempted Basic Conditioning two or even three or more times before successfully completing selection. Those who pass Hell Week move onto the eight-week Second Phase of Basic Conditioning, which concentrates on the skills of combat swimming, including scuba-diving (open and closed circuit), alongside intensive PT.

The nine-week Third (Land Warfare) Phase trains and qualifies SEAL recruits in basic weapons, demolition and small-unit tactics. Physical training continues, with distances increased, times lowered. The Third Phase concentrates on land navigation, patrolling techniques, rappelling, explosives, and marksmanship. All recruits must qualify on the M-4 rifle as Marksman and most – some 60% – as Expert. Recruits also spend hours on reconnaissance, a key SEAL task. The final three and a half weeks of the Third Phase are spent on San Clemente Island (in the Pacific opposite San Diego), where recruits apply all the techniques they have acquired during training, and participate in a live-firing Field Training Exercise. Candidates must then attend Military Free-Fall School at Tactical Air Operations (TACAIROPS) school in Otay, outside San Diego, for one week of static-line parachute training, and three weeks of free-fall parachute training.

Still the selection process goes on. Recruits must now go through SEAL Qualification Training, or SQT, a fifteen-week course of advanced training that culminates in three weeks of Extreme Cold-Weather Survival on freezing Kodiak Island in Alaska. After the completion of Cold-Weather Survival Training, they are awarded their trident badge and Navy Enlisted Classification code at Naval Special Warfare Center, Coronado, California. Finally, they are assigned to their teams on a probationary basis for an additional six to twelve months' on-the-job training.

PART III

Training

FITNESS

It almost goes without saying that members of the Special Forces are super-fit. There are swimmers who can swim faster, runners who can sprint faster, and power-lifters who are stronger, but few men can match the Special Forces soldiers as all-rounders. Which is no surprise, because Special Forces aim for 'Total Body Fitness' (TBF). Special Forces soldiers are literally 'fighting fit'.

For 'Total Body Fitness' you need to have the right Body Mass Index, which divides your weight in pounds by your height in yards squared. Depending on your body frame and height, this should be between twenty and twenty-four. There are few iron rules about the morphology of Special Forces soldiers, save this: they are not fat. If you've got a gut, lose it. Exercise, sensibly done, usually does the trick if you also cut down on the calories. How to tell if you are fat? Take off your clothes. Jump up and down. Anything that wobbles is fat.

Then again, Special Forces soldiers are usually not thin, because, as every trooper knows, endurance and survival requires fat as fuel. If the body does not have fat reserves it begins to break down other types of body tissue, which can cause debilitating, even deadly, problems.

Tip: Special Forces soldiers aim to ingest 4,000-5,000 calories a day, about double the recommended average intake – but they will be working it off. Ideally, about 15% of the body of the Special Forces soldier will be fat.

GETTING STARTED: HOW FIT ARE YOU?

The key indicator of how fit you are is your heart rate when you are exercising and when you are at rest. To measure your Resting Heart Rate, perform this simple test just after you have woken up in the morning and before breakfast.

Sit in a chair. Place a clock in front of you where you can see it easily, then place the fingers of one hand on the other wrist, about one centimetre below the base of the thumb, and locate the pulse. (Don't use your thumb as it has a pulse of its own.) Now count off how many beats you can feel in sixty seconds. If it is between thirty and sixty you are very fit. Between sixty and seventy-five is good. Between seventy-five and eighty-five is average. From eighty-six to ninety nine is poor. Above one hundred and you are catastrophically unfit. The faster the heart rate, the more oxygenated blood is pumped to the muscles; in normal circumstances, the slower your heart rate is, the better, as this indicates that the heart is fit and working to full capacity as a pump.

Next, dress in light training gear and do a step test measurement. Step up and down on a step or training bench six to ten inches high for exactly three minutes, ensuring that you get both feet on the bench and stand straight before stepping down. Wait for thirty seconds. After that, count how many beats you can feel in the next thirty seconds. Between thirty-three and thirty-six is excellent. From thirty-seven to forty is good. Forty-one to forty-three is average. Forty-four to forty- seven is OK. Higher than forty-eight, and you really have your work cut out. If your heart rate is not below seventy-five at rest and forty after exercise, you have a great deal of work to do to qualify to be in the Special Forces.

US military training puts a lot of emphasis on muscle power, especially of the upper body. Indeed, the highly developed musculature of the US Special Forces soldier is so distinctive as almost to be a giveaway. British Special Forces aim more for endurance. But whatever the Special Force you have your eye on, you will need TBF. The Selection test for the SAS, never mind an SAS operation, requires troopers to carry over 80 lb on long marches. This is a severe stress on the unprepared, un-toned body. And the inflexible body. Flexibility, much overlooked in training, allows muscles to work more efficiently; watch a pro athlete before a race. He or she will stretch, not just to lessen the risk of injury, but to ensure that the body works to its fullest capability. Applicants for Special Forces are advised to 'discover' all their muscle through cross-training – mixing racket sports, swimming, running, cycling, circuit training, etc.

BEFORE BEGINNING ANY EXERCISE PROGRAMME IT IS WISE TO HAVE A MEDICAL EVALUATION.

BAD HABITS

Every Special Forces unit has some inhuman maverick who can smoke and drink without (visible) negative effect. It's not you. All the scare stories about smoking are true. So don't start, or if you do smoke, stop. Moderate alcohol consumption 'off duty' is fine. (A beer can actually provide useful energy and vitamins.) Other drugs are no-nos. You may well be tested to determine your drug-free status.

BASIC TRAINING

Special Forces fitness trainers recommend that any applicant working on muscle development or flexibility training should put themselves in the care of a qualified instructor. Performing exercises incorrectly can cause injury or build up bad habits.

Over-training is also advised against. Inside a Special Forces unit training is strictly regulated, and at least a day a week is taken off. Fitness develops by the structure of the muscles breaking down, then building itself up again. They cannot do this if they are in constant use.

Before taking any sort of exercise, it is necessary to warm up. Warming up slightly increases the heart rate and prepares the organ for exertion. Warming up also raises the temperature of the muscles and makes them more flexible, which in turn reduces the chances of a torn muscle or ligament.

Good warm up exercises are:

1. Gently rotate your head from side to side, and nod forwards and backwards.
2. Roll the shoulders as if shrugging. Swing both arms forwards in large circles several times, then reverse direction.
3. Place your legs slightly apart, raise your arms level with your shoulders, rotate your torso to the left, then the right. Do this several times. Additionally, to give the trunk a thorough warm-up pretend you are spinning a hula-hoop.
4. For your legs: stand with your feet shoulder-width apart. Bend forward and (try to) touch your toes. Then stand on one leg, lift the other behind you, grasp it and gently pull into your buttock. Swop over and do the other leg.
5. Go for a brisk five-minute walk.

PHYSICAL FITNESS COMPONENTS

The physical fitness components necessary for successful completion of Special Forces selection for the Canadian elite Joint Task Forces 2 [JTF2]' include in order of importance:

Aerobic Power: This is the maximum rate at which your body uses oxygen to fuel the work you are doing.

Aerobic Capacity: This is your ability to work at a reasonably high rate for a prolonged period of time.

Anaerobic Capacity: This is your ability to tolerate the fatigue.

Muscular Strength: This is the ability of your muscles to exert force in specific movements such as climbing or pushing. It is also important in resisting injuries.

Muscular Endurance: This is the ability of your muscles to do repeated contractions against light loads.

Power and Speed (Anaerobic Power): Power is the ability of your muscles to provide acceleration while speed is the ability to maintain a high velocity. They are very important for success in sprinting and jumping activities.

TOTAL BODY FITNESS

Once you have warmed up, you can begin on muscle development. For Total Body Fitness, every muscle group must be developed. Muscles are often connected to each other, and if you develop one without exercising those related to it, you can cause severe problems. A lot of people work on their abdomen because well-defined abs look good on the beach. But if, for instance, you overlook the latissimus dorsi in the middle back and the erectors in the lower back, you may cause yourself back pain. Overdeveloped muscle can contain a lot of scar tissue, which gives no real 'power', and can restrict movement. Arnie Schwarzenegger has a great physique for a movie action hero, but would be unlikely to be able to pass a Special Forces endurance selection test.

In TBF you are looking for two things. First, to enhance your cardio-vascular capability so as to build up endurance, by making your heart, lungs and circulation more effective. This is done by aerobic (with air) exercises, such as running and cycling. Second, by means of power exercises, to build strength and physical toughness. There are two broad types of muscle development exercises, those with weights and those without weights.

Exercises without weights

Push-ups: Familiar to everybody, and can be done just about anywhere. Lie face down, put the palms of your hands flat on the ground underneath your shoulders, tense your back and legs, raise your body up. Keep your back straight. Lock arms, then slowly lower your body down until your nose touches the floor. Repeat. The push-up is the basic unit of any military PT training programme, and builds strength and power. A Special Forces soldier should be able to do at least forty-two full push-ups in two minutes.

Chin-ups: Needs a bar about six feet off the ground. Take a wide grip, palms towards you, and slowly pull up to the bar till your throat is level with it, all the while crossing your feet at the ankles. The descent should be as controlled as the ascent. Repeat.

Sit-ups: A standard in US Navy SEAL, Delta and SAS fitness training. Lie with your back on the floor, knees bent, and with your toes hooked under a bar or with someone holding your feet down. Fold your arms across your chest or clasp your hands behind your head. Raise your torso up and forward so you almost touch your knees.

Crunches: Viewed by some as a better way to abdominal strength than sit-ups (because you can use your back muscles to power you into position in a sit-up, while crunches isolate the abdomen.) Lie flat on the floor with your hands behind your head, then curl up, raising your back from the floor and bringing your knees towards your chest. Make sure the small of the back remains on the floor so your back is not placed under undue tension. Uncurl and lie back ready to start again. This develops the front abdominals only. For more 'rounded' abdominals twist the torso to one side, in a 'cross-over crunch' aiming your shoulder at the opposite knee.

Legs raises: Lie flat on your back with your hands underneath your posterior. Keep your legs straight, your toes pointed as though in ballet, and slowly raise your feet six inches off the ground Then raise to eighteen inches off the ground, hold, gently lower back to six inches. Do not let your feet touch the ground. Do 25-30 per set.

Lunges: Stand up straight and take one long step forward with one leg, bending the knee until the thigh is parallel with the ground. Then step back and repeat with the other leg. Make sure you keep your body upright as bending from the waist lessens the efficacy of the exercise. This strengthens the upper leg and thigh.

Parallel dips: Most easily done with parallel bars in the gym, though heavy furniture may suffice. Take your weight on your straight arms, lower yourself until they are parallel to the ground, then raise yourself up again. The exercise strengthens the shoulders, biceps and triceps.

Training with weights

When it comes to weight training, do not use heavy weights. This will only increase muscle mass and probably make muscles fail to do their job. Use bench-press lighter weights and do lots of 'reps' (repetitions). This will train the muscles to respond speedily – which you need in combat.

You should always divide your training sessions between the four main areas of the body: the legs, the abdominals, the arms and back, and the shoulders and chest. That way you will not run the risk of ending with a structural imbalance in your musculature.

It is necessary to build up slowly when you are using weights. You should exercise for no more than an hour, and take a day off between each session to let your muscles recover. If you feel any intense pain, dizziness or nausea you should stop and, if it persists, consult a doctor. You can join a gym, though most useful exercises can be done at home with a bench and couple of dumb-bells and a bar-bell.

Dumb-bell press: Stand with your back straight, and your feet shoulder-width apart, with an equally weighted dumb bell at each shoulder. Alternately raise each one above your head so that you arm is almost fully extended. Use a weight that allows you to do fifteen in each set.

You can also press with dumb-bells to strengthen the

pectorals, deltoids and biceps in 'lateral raises'. Lie flat on a bench facing upwards, holding the dumb-bells with your arms extended out to the side, but keeping the elbows bent. Lift them until they meet over your chest. Lower them slowly to the starting position and repeat about twenty times.

Squats: Again use dumb-bells whose weight you are comfortable with. Begin by standing up straight with your legs a shoulder-width apart and the bar of the weight across your shoulders. Then bend your knees slowly as low as you can go without falling forward. The weight should be kept over the legs, not the back. Straighten the legs slowly, moving back into the starting position.

Curls: Hold a bar-bell at your waist, with your elbows locked, and your feet apart. Keep your back straight and bring the bar up ('curl') towards your shoulders.

The Good Morning Exercise: Stand up straight, hold a bar across your shoulders and behind your neck. Bend forward from the waist until your torso is horizontal to the floor. Straighten up (gently). Repeat about 10-12 times. And no, I've no idea why it's called 'The Good Morning exercise' either.

Side lateral raise: Stand straight, with your feet shoulder-width apart, and a dumb-bell in each hand down by your waist. Keep your arm straight, your shoulders 'pinched' back and raise as though trying to flap your wings. Do sets of ten plus.

You must also concentrate on your breathing throughout as it is vital to all kinds of exercise. In through the nose, out through the mouth, fill the lungs. Your muscles need oxygen.

RUNNING

Running is a fact of Special Forces life. You are going to be doing a lot of it, not least because it is convenient and unbeatable as means of building up endurance. You need to vary your running routines, and you will also need to practise running with weights in a Bergen. Mix the different styles of running over the course of the week.

The speed run: Each week a potential recruit should practise short fast runs of about thirty minutes. Warm up thoroughly, start sedately and quit if you start to feel short of breath or otherwise uncomfortable. As you get fitter, add a belt (military, with some kit in the pockets).

Endurance run: The endurance run should cover about 90 minutes. To avoid exhaustion, switch between running and speed walking. Over time add a Bergen, then some weight in the Bergen, then more weight. SAS selection requires a 37-mile march with a Bergen carrying at least 55 lbs, plus rifle, plus belt.

How to run

Everybody knows how to run, don't they? Actually, they don't. When running you should let your body fall into a natural rhythm, rather than a forced pace. Lean very slightly forward. Keep your arms and shoulders as loose as possible and *do not clench your fists*, but hold them in a loose claw. Clenched fists are a waste of energy. Keep your elbows in (increases balance, reduces drag), with the elbows making a casual right angle. Swing arms smoothly in time with your legs.

Flex your knees slightly, to aid gravity and reduce the impact of your feet hitting the ground. Likewise, keep your feet near to the ground. Reducing impact on your body by such measures is vital when you are carrying a heavy weight. Athletic coaches disagree about the best way to let your foot hit the ground – whether the heel should hit the ground first or the ball of your foot; long-distance runners land on their heels then roll through onto the toe. This is the technique you should try to adopt if it is not natural to you.

Breathe slowly and evenly, and try to get your breathing into the rhythm of your running. For maximum exchange of oxygen, concentrate on exhaling rather than inhaling.

OTHER FITNESS ACTIVITIES

Swimming: Quite aside from the fact that swimming is part of many Special Forces' selection courses, swimming is an excellent aerobic activity that produces many of the positives of running without the stress on the joints and bones. You don't need to do fancy stuff: the front crawl, the breast stroke and treading water are all that are required. Practise 100-metre fast swims, and treading water for up to ten minutes.

   Circuit training: along with cycling, another sure fire improver of strength and endurance. Circuit training consists of a series of exercises (usually 6-8) that work all parts of the body – trunk, lower-body, core, etc. A sample circuit is: sit-ups, step-ups, squat-thrusts, press-ups, shuttle run, compass-jumps.

   Fartlek: A Special Forces favourite training technique that easily bolts on to your usual routine. Fartlek means 'speed play'. All you do is vary the change of pace in your run – so, for example, you might do half a mile at a trot, then sprint 100 metres at full sprint, then slow down to a jog for a minute, then run at 50% capacity for a mile, then walk for a minute. And so on. Fartlek essentially builds up strength and your aerobic capacity. It's best if you can find a hill to incorporate in the fartlek.

   Martial arts: You're going to be doing unarmed combat as a Special Forces soldier, even during selection. Get some practice in. You won't go far wrong with the old 'hard' favourites, karate, ju jitsu, kick boxing.

HYDRATION

When training it is important to keep your water intake high. You need at least three to five litres of water a day. When running, drink half a pint of water half an hour before you begin and another half a pint for every twenty minutes you are on the road. Dehydration drains energy and impairs your mental facilities. If your urine is dark yellow in colour, then you are not getting enough water.

FUELLING FITNESS

Training is physically demanding. You need to take care over nutrition. To get the greatest return on your training investment, you need the right food for muscle building, for energy, and for health. Here are some guidelines.

Eat a balanced diet. Obvious, but it is the fundamental rule of nutrition.

Carbohydrates for fuel. For your aerobic, anaerobic, speed, and strength work-outs, the fuel required comes from carbo-hydrates. These are stored in muscle in limited amounts (as a compound called glycogen) and when they run out you are unable to continue to perform or train. Carbohydrates come in many food forms and include: grains in cereals, pastas, breads, and rice. These are especially beneficial in the hours prior to exercise, but are also helpful after. Whole grains (brown rice etc.) are best.

Fruits and vegetables. At least seven portions a day. A selec-tion of colours is a good idea: there is little point in eating only seven oranges. Fruit and vegetables provide vitamins, miner-als, fuel, and other nutrients for both health and high performance.

Protein. Protein provides the building-blocks for new muscle and the enzymes which help provide energy. Good sources are fish, poultry, lean beef, shellfish, eggs and cheese.

Avoid sugary snacks. The energy provided leads to a boom-slump and may leave you feeling more tired than before you ingested it. Try dried fruit, bananas or starchy vegetables – these will give you long-term energy. Fruit bars and muesli bars are good, as long as they are not packed with added sugar.

Convenience food. Yes, it is easy to open a packet, and put something in the microwave, and everyone does it. But keep the junk food to a minimum. Junk food tends to have little nutritional value, but is rammed with salt and sugar.

Eat breakfast. What your parents told you is true: it's the most important meal of the day. Try to avoid fried food: grill the bacon, poach the eggs. Have porridge, but hold the sugar and salt; add a banana. If you must fry, use olive oil.

Keep alcohol intake to a minimum. It impairs your mental performance and causes dehydration.

Avoid muscle-building supplements. Some Special Forces training programmes ban them. Everything necessary to the Special Forces diet can be obtained in a balanced diet.

THE US SPECIAL FORCES FITNESS PROGRAM

The US Army's John F. Kennedy Special Warfare Center and School has designed a five-week fitness programme to get Special Forces candidates into the appropriate shape before they arrive at Fort Bragg. Achieving physical fitness is not an overnight process; the body must go through three stages. The programme lays out the stages of physical fitness, as follows:

1. The first is the toughening stage, which lasts about two weeks. During this time the body goes through a soreness and recovery period. When a muscle with poor blood supply (such as a weak muscle) is exercised, the waste products produced by the exercise collect faster than the blood can remove them. This acid waste builds up in the muscle tissue and irritates the nerve in the muscle fibre, causing soreness. As the exercise continues, the body is able to circulate the blood more rapidly through the muscles and remove the waste material, which causes soreness to disappear.

2. The slow improvement stage is the second stage in attaining physical fitness. As the body passes through the toughening stage and continues into the slow improvement stage, the volume of blood circulating in the muscle increases and the body functions more efficiently. In the first few weeks the improvement is rapid, but as a higher level of skill and conditioning is reached, the improvement becomes less noticeable. The body reaches its maximum level of performance between six and ten weeks. The intensity of the program and individual differences account for the variance in time.

3. The sustaining stage is the third stage during which

physical fitness is maintained. It is necessary to continue exercising at approximately the same intensity to retain the condition developed.

The preparatory course says that physical work-outs should be conducted a minimum of four days a week. Work hard one day; ease off the next. A hard and easy work-out concept will allow maximum effort for overloading both the muscle groups and cardio-respiratory system; it will also prevent injury and stagnation in the programme. Prior to each work-out, ten to fifteen minutes should be devoted to performing stretching exercises.

This the programme of hard work-out days: You can determine what to do on the 'easy' days.

WEEK I

Day 1: See what you can do

(a) APFT (Army Physical Fitness Test, which consists of three events: 2 minutes of push-ups, 2 minutes of sit-ups, and a 2-mile run. Scores can range from zero to 100. For a 100% score a 22-26-year-old male recruit would need to do 75 push-ups, 80 sit-ups, and a sub-13-minute run. See http://usarmybasic.com/army-physical-fitness/apft#. U5m4EvldXcw
(b) 100-yard swim.
(c) Forced march cross-country with 30-lb Bergen, aiming for 3 road miles in sub-45 minutes, or 60 minutes if cross-country.

Day 2

(a) Three sets of push-ups in half-minute periods.
(b) 3-mile run at moderate pace, around 8-9 mph.
(c) Rope climb
(d) Forced march with 30 lbs, 5 miles in 1 hour 15 minutes along a road, or 1 hour and 40 minutes cross-country.

Day 3

Repeat the forced march of Day 2.

WEEK II

Day 1
Forced march, but extend distance to 8 miles with 35-lb rucksack in 2 hours (road), or 2 hours 40 minutes (cross country).

Day 2

(a) Three sets of push-ups, pull-ups, sit-ups (maximum repetitions in 35-second periods x 3)
(b) Run 5 miles (moderate 8-9 mph).
(c) Three sets of squats with a 35-lb rucksack (50 each set); don't bend the knee more than 90 degrees.

Day 3

Forced march with a 35-lb rucksack, 10 miles in 3 hours (along a road) or 4 hours (cross-country).

WEEK III

Day 1

(a) Four sets of push-ups, pull-ups and sit-ups (maximum repetitions in 40-second period).
(b) Run 4 miles (fast to moderate 7-8-minute-mile pace.)
(c) Four sets of squats with a 40-lb rucksack.

Day 2

Forced march 12 miles with a 40-lb rucksack in 4 hours (along a road) or 4 hours and 40 minutes (cross-country).

Day 3

(a) Four sets of push-ups, sit-ups, pull-ups (maximum repetitions in 45-second period.)
(b) Run 6 miles (fast to moderate 7-8-minute-mile pace).
(c) Four sets of squats with a 40-lb rucksack.

WEEK IV

Day 1

Forced march 14 miles with a 50-lb rucksack in 4 hours (along a road) or 4 hours and 40 minutes (cross-country).

Day 2

(a) Four sets of push-ups, sit-ups and pull-ups (maximum repetitions in one-minute period).
(b) Run 6 miles (fast to moderate 7-8-minute-mile pace).
(c) Four sets of squats with a 50-lb rucksack.

Day 3

Forced march 18 miles with a 50-lb rucksack in 4 hours and 45 minutes (along a road) or 6 hours (cross- country).

WEEK V

Day 1

(a) Run 3 miles (fast 6-7-minute-mile pace).
(b) 500-metre swim (non-stop, any stroke, but not on your back).

Day 2

APFT. You should be able to achieve a score of at least 240 (minimum of 70 points in any one event). If not, work out harder.

Day 3

Forced march of 18 miles with 50 lb rucksack in 4 hours and 30 minutes (along a road) or 6 hours (cross-country).

Once in shape, stay in shape. If you have met this minimum programme, modify by increasing weight and decreasing target times. But be smart: don't injure yourself.

REMEMBER:
THERE IS A VERY STRONG CORRELATION
BETWEEN A CANDIDATE'S SCORE ON THE APFT
AND GRADUATION FROM THE SPECIAL FORCES
ASSESSMENT AND SELECTION. 78% OF
CANDIDATES WITH AN APFT SCORE OF 276+
PASS THE COURSE; ONLY 31% OF CANDIDATES
WITH A 206-225 SCORE GRADUATE.

ARE YOU READY?

A good test as to whether you are getting close to the fitness standard for Special Forces is where you meet the 'passing-in' standard for the British Royal Marines' Commando course. The Pass In comprises:

> Fifty sit-ups in two minutes
> Five pull-ups using an over-arm grasp
> Jump into a pool from a high board
> Swim 100 metres freestyle
> Tread water for two minutes
> Pass the Basic Fitness Test (with boots)
> Pass the Combat Fitness Test
> Pass the TOET (rifle training test)

The Basic Fitness Test (BFT) is mandatory for every soldier in the British Army twice a year. It consists of two parts, both run over a 1.5-mile course. Part one is a squad run/walk normally done in a group of at least ten men. Part two is another 1.5 miles, often back over the same course, run as best individual effort. The test is done in PT kit and trainers.

Combat Fitness Test (CFT) is normally taken once a year: it is an 8-mile march in full kit and carrying a weapon, and 35 lbs of kit. The cut-off time is one hour and fifty minutes.

MENTAL FITNESS

You can be as fit as fiddle but if you are as thick as a brick you are not going to get into Special Forces. IQ tests are a component of most selection programmes. Luckily your brain, like your body, can be improved. IQ is not static, and can be improved by as many as 15 points in a week. Here are two simple steps to becoming brainier.

First, revise basic maths, using any widely available school text books. It's far from unknown for potential recruits to be given surprise maths tests during selection – often when they are exhausted. So, try solving maths problems when you are dog tired.

Secondly, buy some books of logic puzzles and IQ tests. In truth, there are only so many types of IQ question out there, and you may well recognise the form of those before you on test day. It's called 'the practice effect'. Anyway, doing puzzles improves your mental abilities. Both in training and combat, you need mental dexterity and agility. (IQ tests require, among other things, the exercise of working memory and the ability to process visual information at speed. Both are necessary battlefield skills.) Try and solve problems and answer questions at the end of a long run, and with a deadline – a short one.

All candidates for Special Forces are subject to psychological testing. You will be evaluated as to whether you fit into and understand the ethos of Special Forces. That ethos was never better explained than by David Stirling, the man who founded modern Special Forces, in his "Philosophy of the SAS":

The Philosophy of the SAS

To understand the SAS role it is important first to grasp the essential difference between the function of Airborne Forces and Commandos on the one hand and that of the wartime Special Operations Executive on the other. Airborne Forces and Commandos provided advance elements in achieving tactical objectives and undertook tactically scaled raids, while the SOE was a para-military formation operating mainly out of uniform. In contrast, the SAS has always been a strictly military unit, has always operated in uniform (except occasionally when seeking special information) and has functioned exclusively in the strategic field of operations. Such operations consisted mainly of: firstly, raids in depth behind the enemy lines, attacking HQ nerve centres, landing-grounds, supply lines and so on; and, secondly, the mounting of sustained strategic offensive activity from secret bases within hostile territory and, if the opportunity existed, recruiting, training, arming and co-ordinating local guerrilla elements.

The SAS had to be capable of arriving in the target area by air and, therefore, by parachute; by sea, often by submarine and foldboat; or by land, by foot or Jeep-borne penetration through or around the enemy lines. To ensure surprise the SAS usually arrived in the target area at night and this required a high degree of proficiency, in all the arrival methods adopted for any particular operation.

Strategic operations demand, for the achievement of success, a total exploitation of surprise and of guile – accordingly, a bedrock principle of the Regiment was its organization into modules or sub-units of four men. Each of the four men was trained to a high level of proficiency in the whole range of the SAS capability and, additionally, each man was trained to have at least one special expertise according to his particular aptitude. In carrying out an operation – often in the pitch-dark – each SAS man in each module was exercising his own individual perception and judgement at full strength. The SAS four-man module could be viable as an operational entity on its own, or be combined with as many other modules as an operation might require.

In the early days of the SAS, Middle East HQ sometimes

tended to regard us as a baby Commando capable of "teasing" the enemy deep behind the lines during the quieter periods but available, in the circumstances of a major defensive or offensive confrontation, to undertake essentially tactical tasks immediately behind or on the flank of an aroused enemy. It took some further successful raids to persuade HQ to acknowledge that our role should remain an exclusively strategic one.

In today's SAS the importance of good security is thoroughly instilled into every man. Certain delicate operational roles require the Secret Service to invest in the SAS Command highly classified intelligence necessary for the effective planning of these operations and, just as importantly, for special training. For such intelligence to be entrusted to the SAS, its security disciplines have to be beyond reproach.

As the SAS was operating at a distance of up to 1,000 miles from Army HQ, an exceptionally efficient wireless communication was essential. Frequently we would require interpretation of air photographs of target areas, taken while an SAS unit was already deep in the desert on its way to attack them. An effective communication system became even more important to the SAS in Europe. (Their own dedicated and special communications are still an essential feature of SAS operations.)

Recruitment was a problem, as we had to depend on volunteer recruitment from existing Army units. Not unnaturally, Commanding Officers were reluctant to see their most enterprising individuals transfer to the SAS, but eventually Middle East HQ gave us firm backing and we were usually able to recruit a few volunteers from each of the formations which had undergone general military and desert training. We always aimed to give each new recruit a very testing preliminary course before he was finally accepted for the SAS. Today the SAS is even more ruthless in its recruitment procedures.

Once selected, our training programme for a man was an exhaustive one and was designed to give him thorough self-confidence and, just as importantly, equal confidence in his fellow soldiers' capacity to outclass and outwit the enemy by use of SAS operational techniques.

We kept a careful track record of each man and capitalized

whenever possible on the special aptitude he might display in various skills such as advanced sabotage technique, mechanics, enemy weaponry, night-time navigation and medical knowledge, etc. This register of each man's special skills was vital to make sure that each of our modules of four men was a well-balanced entity. Historical precedents, demonstrating how vital this concept could be to the winning of wars, were ignored and we, therefore, had to start again nearly from scratch. Luckily, the British, for one, now acknowledge the validity of the strategic raid, hence the continuing existence of the SAS regiment. The SAS today fully recognizes its obligation to exploit new ideas and new developments in equipment and, generally, to keep a wide-open mind to innovation and invention.

From the start the SAS regiment has had some firmly held tenets from which we must never depart. They are:

1. The unrelenting pursuit of excellence;
2. Maintaining the highest standards of discipline in all aspects of the daily life of the SAS soldier, from the occasional precision drilling on the parade ground even to his personal turn-out on leave. We always reckoned that a high standard of self-discipline in each soldier was the only effective foundation for Regimental discipline. Commitment to the SAS pursuit of excellence becomes a sham if any single one of the disciplinary standards is allowed to slip;
3. The SAS brooks no sense of class and, particularly, not among the wives. This might sound a bit portentous but it epitomizes the SAS philosophy. The traditional idea of a crack regiment was one officered by the aristocracy and, indeed, these regiments deservedly won great renown for their dependability and their gallantry in wartime and for their parade-ground panache in peacetime. In the SAS we share with the Brigade of Guards a deep respect for quality, but we have an entirely different outlook. We believe, as did the ancient Greeks who originated the word "aristocracy", that every man with the right attitude and talents, regardless of birth and riches, has a capacity in his own lifetime of reaching that status in its true sense; in fact in our SAS

context an individual soldier might prefer to go on serving as an NCO rather than have to leave the Regiment in order to obtain an officer's commission. All ranks in the SAS are of "one company" in which a sense of class is both alien and ludicrous. A visit to the sergeants' mess at SAS HQ in Hereford vividly conveys what I mean;

4. Humility and humour: both these virtues are indispensable in the everyday life of officers and men – particularly so in the case of the SAS which is often regarded as an elite regiment. Without frequent recourse to humour and humility, our special status could cause resentment in other units of the British Army and an unbecoming conceit and big-headedness in our own soldiers.

COMBAT SKILLS AND TECHNIQUES

SPECIAL FORCES PERSONAL PROTECTION

It now costs around £1 million ($1.5 million) to train a Special Forces trooper, so any money spent on keeping him alive is money well spent. The trouble is that such personnel are prone to all types of attacks and aggressive or defensive counter-measures, so it is difficult to decide exactly what to protect an individual against.

The result has been a wide array of protective clothing, with each item proof against something or other, and designed in isolation from everything else. This often means that when all the various items are worn together they do not integrate: NBC respirator face seals may be broken when a helmet is put on, weapons cannot be sighted through respirator lenses, bullet-proof garments interfere with movement and so on.

The IPPS

This integration problem has been overcome by five British companies who have got together and developed a protective outfit that is proof against most threats to Special Forces personnel. It is known as the Integrated Personal Protection System (IPPS) and has been tested by Special Forces. The IPPS is not just a design venture: it has been developed using all manner of practical combat experience, and the result is a superb protective outfit. Starting from the skin outwards, the basis of the IPPS is a set of carbonized viscose "long johns" underwear. The material is light and comfortable to wear but is flame-retardant, as is the main over-garment, a one-piece assault suit also made from carbon-fibre material, in this case Nomex 3. The suit incorporates flame-retardant pads at the elbows and knees, allowing the wearer to crawl safely over hot surfaces such as aircraft engines during hijack hostage rescue missions. Incidentally, the suits are very similar to those being worn by tanker crews currently operating in the Persian Gulf, but theirs are coloured bright orange; the IPPS is usually black.

Armoured vest

Over the flame-retardant garments the IPPS features a bullet-proof waistcoat made of soft fragmentation armour, with a built-in trauma liner to absorb shock. Without this liner internal injuries could occur even if a bullet is stopped by the armour. The soft armour protection is enhanced by inserting curved ceramic plates at the front and back: these can stop .357 Magnum bullets at a range of three metres. A groin panel can be added if required.

The helmet

Further armoured protection is provided by a special helmet known as the AC 100/1, a National Plastics product made from layers of a Kevlar-type material. This can withstand the impact of a 9-mm bullet at close range, and to ensure the wearer's head is not knocked off by the impact, the helmet uses a bullet trauma lining.

An optional fire-retardant leather waistcoat can be worn over the suit and armour protection, and is used to carry special equipment such as an assault axe, stun grenades or rescue knife, all in specially-fitted pockets or leather loops.

Respirator

These days some form of respirator is worn operationally by most Special Forces, so the IPPS uses a specially developed respirator known as the SF10, a variant of the Avon S10 used by the British Army. The SF10 has an internal microphone, but its most prominent features are the outset-darkened eyepieces. These have been incorporated to cut down the flash produced by stun grenades or other bright lights. The SF10 can also be fitted with its own air supply from an air bottle carried in the leather waistcoat or an extra filter canister can be worn.

Communications

The respirator microphone connects into an assault team communications harness known as the CT100, which has a chest or respirator microphone and press-to-talk switches located on the wrist or anywhere handy. The communications system uses electronic earphones designed to cut out sound produced by grenades or gunfire (i.e. high air pressure) but allow all other sounds to be heard normally. The earphones are connected into the communication harness to allow the wearer to listen in to a team command net.

The main feature of the IPPS is that all the components are designed to work together. For instance, the IPPS helmet does not interfere with the respirator seal, and the ear defenders fit under helmet ear lobes that have been designed for just that purpose. The darkened eyepieces permit almost any weapon to be aimed and fired without difficulty, and even though the protective waistcoat can stop most fragments or bullets it still allows complete freedom of movement.

Belt kit

A belt carrying combat or other gear can be worn, and an abseiling harness has been developed for use with the IPPS which provides an indication of the degree of movement available.

CAMOUFLAGE AND CONCEALMENT

Good camouflage and fieldcraft are almost as important as good marksmanship – in fact, a well-camouflaged man who is a poor shot will probably survive longer than the badly concealed sniper. In an escape and evasion operation, camouflage and concealment are paramount. The hunted man will conceal himself and sleep by day, and move by night – and here even the cover of darkness will not negate the importance of camouflage. Personal camouflage (PC) has certain simple rules that will defeat the most obvious sensor on the battlefield – the human eye.

Shape

Your helmet, web equipment, rifle and other kit such as manpack radios have a clear, often square shape – and there are no squares in nature. Break up straight lines by the addition of "scrim" – neutral-coloured strips of cloth in browns and greens. Camouflaged elasticated pack covers exist, and these can be stretched over packs and radios.

Rifles and LMG/GPMGs have a clear shape, and are often black. Though scrim can be used to break up their line, it is not advisable to fix it to the stock – it may slip when you are firing and by shifting your grip cause you to shoot inaccurately. It is better to cover the weapon with camouflaged tape, or even green masking tape (tape is a useful aid to PC – see "Sound").

A discarded vehicle camouflage net is a very useful source of camouflage for PC. It will have nylon scrim that has been treated to give an infra-red reflection similar to vegetation. Fixed to the back of packs and webbing, or in the netting on a helmet, it breaks up shape very well and enhances the chlorophyll-based infra-red camouflage treatment (see also "Silhouette").

Shine

In the old days of brass buckles, soldiers were told these should be allowed to grow dull, or be covered with masking tape. However, most web equipment has plastic or alloy fittings that do not reflect – but there are still shiny surfaces even on a modern battlefield. Binoculars and compass surfaces, even spectacles, can catch the light. There is little that can be done about spectacles, but when using binoculars or a compass make sure that you are well concealed: like radios, they are "signature equipment" and attract attention. Stow binoculars inside your smock, and take care that your map is not opened up and flapping about – a drab map case with the map folded so that it gives the minimum working area is all that is needed. Take care also that the clear cover to the map case does not catch the light.

Shine also includes skin. At night it will catch moonlight and flares, and even black soldiers need to use camouflage cream.

Facial Camouflage

1. *The first coat:* First get rid of all that white shining skin. Mix a small quantity of camouflage cream with spit in your hand and rub it all over your face, neck and ears. This gives a full light coverage of camouflage. Then cover your hands with the cream.
2. *Breaking up the shape:* Now break up the outline and shape of the eyes, nose and mouth. Any pattern that breaks up this familiar format will do; use more if you're going in night patrol. Don't forget your neck and eyes.
3. *Finishing it off:* Fill in the rest of your face with earth, loam and green colours, then spit in your hands and rub them over your face to blur it all together. On the move you will

probably sweat heavily so you must top-up your face-cream as you go along.

Silhouette

Similar in many respects to shape, silhouette includes the outline of the human form and the equipment it is carrying. The shape of the head and shoulders of a man are unmistakeable and an unscrimmed helmet attracts attention. The use of vegetation as garnishing helps break up the silhouette. Thick handfuls of grass tucked into equipment can remove the shape of the shoulders, and garnishing on the helmet breaks the smooth curve of the top and the line of the brim.

Silhouette also includes fieldcraft – however well camouflaged you may be, it is little help if you "skyline" by walking along the top of a hill, or stand against a background of one solid colour.

Smell

Even the most urbanized man will develop a good sense of smell after a few days in the open. He will be able to detect engine smells, cooking, body odour and washing.

Some smells are hard to minimize. Soaps should be scent-free, and activities such as cooking confined to daylight hours when other smells are stronger and the air warmer. One of the greatest giveaways is smoking: both smoke and discarded butts have a unique smell. Rubbish produced by cooking as well as smoking should be carried out from the operational area and only buried as a second choice. Buried objects are often dug up by animals: such refuse can give a good indication of the strength and composition of your patrol or unit as well as its morale. The disciplines of refuse removal are important.

Helmet Camouflage

The new issue Kevlar helmet comes complete with a cover of DPM – standard military camouflage colours – and straps for local camouflage.

- Disguising the shape. Cover the helmet with strips of scrim and cloth
- Adding local camouflage. Insert local vegetation under the elastic.

Sound

You can make a lot of noise while out on patrol. Your boots can squeak; your cleaning kit or magazines may rattle in your ammunition pouches. Even your webbing can creak if it is heavy. Fittings on your weapon may rattle. Radios can have background "mush". Coughing and talking can carry for long distances in the darkness of a clear night. You must become familiar with a "silent routine" in which field signals replace the spoken word, or conversations are conducted in a whisper. Proper stowage of kit, taping of slings and other noisy equipment and a final shakedown before a patrol moves out will reduce noise. If a position is being dug, sentries should be positioned at the limit of noise so that they can see an enemy before he hears the digging.

Colour

Most modern combat uniforms are now in a disruptive pattern camouflage, there may be times when this is less helpful. If you are evading capture and are unarmed, drab civilian outdoor clothing will be less conspicuous if you encounter civilians. The trouble with camouflage-type clothing is that in the wrong environment, like cities, it seems to do the opposite and say, "Hey, look at me!" In fighting in built-up areas a camouflage of greys, browns and dull reds would be better.

The use of sacking and empty sand bags as scrim covers would help here.

Natural vegetation used to garnish helmets and equipment will fade and change colour. Leaves curl up and show their pale under-surfaces. You may have put grass into your helmet band and now find yourself in a dark wood, or be wearing dark green ferns when you are moving across a patch of pale, open grass land. Check and change your camouflage regularly.

The most obvious colour that needs camouflaging is that of human skin, and for that you need camouflage cream. As mentioned, even black or brown skin has a shine to it. A common mistake is to smear paint over the front of the face and to miss the neck, ears and back of the hands. Camouflage cream needs to be renewed as you move and sweat. A simple pattern is to take stripes diagonally across the face – this cuts through the vertical and horizontal lines of the eyes, nose and mouth. Some camouflage creams have two colours, in which case you can use the dark colour to reduce the highlights formed by the bridge of the nose, cheek bones, chin and forehead. The lighter colour is used on areas of shadow.

Association

The enemy may not see you, but he might spot your equipment or trash and associate that with a possible unit on the move. The cans stacked near a vehicle park, perhaps with white tape around them, are likely to be fuel. A cluster of radio antennas shows that a company HQ is on the move or dug in. Antennas can also catch the light and show up as long, hard shadows in an otherwise concealed position. Most antennas can be situated away from the set, so put them on a reverse slope where they are not only invisible to the enemy, but also have some of their signal screened. Failing that, locate them against a building or tree.

Camouflage is a complex and sometimes contradictory skill. There is a reduced TI signature in a building under cover; but buildings attract attention. Hessian should be used on a vehicle among cold buildings; but not in warmer woodland. If you want to remember one rule to camouflage, it is that you should not give the enemy the signal that will make him look twice. To a trained observer the unusual – a flash from a plastic map case, or the smell of cooking – will alert him and he will bring his own senses to bear on the area.

Vehicle camouflage

Good camouflage and concealment is often a trade-off against good fields of fire or good positions for observing enemy movement. Radio communications work better with line-of-

Sight, but sitting on top of a hill is very public. And if you are trying to evade or escape you will need a vantage point for a sentry to observe likely enemy approaches, and may be observed yourself. Assuming that you are part of a group of six to twelve men and that you have a light vehicle like a Land Rover or Jeep, how would you conceal your position while evading capture?

Any vehicle will be under suspicion. If you are moving in convoy, take care to avoid bunching. Vehicles close together are very recognisable from the air, and make easy targets for enemy aircraft. And remember the following points when finding somewhere to position your vehicle.

1. If you are near buildings, for instance on a farm, try to get the vehicle close to a wall or under cover in a barn. A camouflage net will attract the attention of a nearby enemy. Use hessian and local materials to disguise the vehicle.
2. If you park in the country, try to find the shadow of a hedge to disguise the vehicle's hard shape. But remember that in northern and southern latitudes the sun moves, and the shadow of the morning can be the sunlit field of the afternoon.

VEHICLE CAMOUFLAGE CHECKLIST
Site selection: Choose a harbour area away from the edge of the wood, away from tracks and with good cover overhead as well as at ground level. Try to pick a "hull down" or "dead ground" position. Remember to back the vehicle in: you may have to exit fast.

Hessian sacking: All the principles of personal camouflage apply equally to your vehicle. Black hessian destroys the shine from windows, headlights and numberplates and disguises the general shape of the vehicle.

Net poles: A good selection of net poles is essential to hold the camouflage net off the vehicle to disguise its shape. Chicken wire can also be used. You must not cut poles from trees around your position: the cut-off shoots will give you away. Harbouring two vehicles together with nets over both can be helpful in producing a more natural shape. Remember, you cannot afford to leave any equipment lying about; concealment is an ongoing task, as the threat of discovery is ever-present. Plastic bags and uncovered windscreens are asking for trouble.

Camouflage net: Use the surrounding trees as well as the poles. The ideal situation is to create a camouflage "garage" you can drive into and out of without having to remove net, poles etc.

Two-sided net: There are two sides to a camouflage net, with different colour combinations, so use the side that best matches your surroundings. Late evening can be particularly difficult with low sunlight catching the glass fittings of your vehicle. As a short-term precaution cover the windscreen and lights when you stop, not forgetting the reflectors.

If your vehicle is military, it will have been painted with IR reflective paint and you should not cover this with hessian, which will produce a blue-grey colour on any infra-red device the enemy might be using. You should cover the reflective surfaces and then deploy a camouflage net.

A camouflage net should stand clear of the vehicle, partly so you can get in and out, and also to disguise the vehicle's shape. It should stretch far enough to contain any shadow that the vehicle might cast. Ideally, it should also have a "mushroom" on the top: a frame of wire about the size of a domestic saucer. This gives a smooth line when the net is stretched over. Make sure the net will not snag on the vehicle or underbrush or trees, preventing any quick exit you might need to make.

Shell scrapes and track plan: As soon as the position is occupied, a route around the site must be marked by cord and cleared. By using this track plan, disturbance of natural ground is minimized. Shell scrapes must be dug in "stand to" positions.

Siting

Avoid the obvious. If the enemy are looking for you they will sweep the countryside, and if there are not many of them they will concentrate on rivers and woodland, farmhouses, barns, known caves and natural cover. All are on maps, and the first move that an enemy search team will make is to do a map reconnaissance and look at likely locations.

Track plan

A track plan is essential if you are going to stay in the location for any length of time. Trodden grass and footprints will show clearly from the air, and large areas of normally lush undergrowth can be flattened in a way that attracts attention. Vehicle tracks are even more dramatic from the air – bad drivers will carve a path across a field in a way that no farmer would dream of driving. Track planning means attempting to copy the normal routes adopted by animals, farmers or locals. Thus vehicle tracks along the edge of a field and a footpath that might also be used by the inhabitants will pass unnoticed by the enemy.

IR signature

The infra-red band is the most difficult to avoid. Thermal imaging will penetrate cover, and activities like running a vehicle engine to charge batteries or simple tasks like cooking become a major problem, since both will show as a very strong hot point in an otherwise cool terrain. Though a cave may not be ideal if it is on the local map, it will give good thermal screening. Parking the vehicle under cover will also reduce its IR signature – but again remember that barns and farmhouses are very obvious and may attract attention from the air or ground.

Sound and smell

As with personal camouflage, sound and smell are important. If you run your engine to recharge batteries you will make noise and exhaust fumes (and take care that fumes do not blow into the vehicle if the exhaust pipe is blocked by the camouflage). Use a flexible metal extension pipe to reduce the noise. If you are in a convoy, the sound of your vehicles will attract attention and so will your radio traffic.

Personal camouflage

Smell will come from cooking as you prepare your evening meal and the smell of fuel is also distinctive. Spilled fuel and the wrappings from rations are a calling-card for an alert enemy.

Concealing your position

Don't make the mistake of thinking you're safe as long as you have dug your position. A good hide or bunker should be invisible even at close quarters; if you have dug it well and are careful in your movements, it may pass unnoticed. But the enemy can still

spot you if you haven't been careful enough, so keep the following in mind.

- The colour of soil that has been dug from lower than about a
  metre is lighter than the topsoil, and a trench has a strong
  shadow at the bottom. Conceal earth by covering it with turfs;
  and put light-coloured straw at the bottom of the trench to
  reduce some of the shadow. This will also be more
- pleasant to walk on and live in.
- In a tropical environment, cover can grow very quickly, so
  replace plants and creepers around your position and it will
  soon be concealed.
- A simple basha made up with poncho or basha sheet can be
  square, shiny and noisy. Do not put it up until after last light,
  although you can position it flat on the ground before dark.
  Carry a length of old camouflage net; it will break up the shape
  and shine.
- When you are cooking or brewing up keep your opened kit to
  a minimum; you might need to make a quick getaway. Also,
  avoid littering tins and wrappers around the position that may
  catch the light and be seen from a distance.
- It is commonly thought that a hand torch with a red filter does
  not show at night. It does; it's certainly less obvious than a
  white light, and it does not impair night vision, but it shows.
  Do not use a torch at all; by last light you should have set up
  your position so that your kit is packed and you can reach for
  your weapon, webbing and pack without needing one.

NAVIGATION

As a Special Forces soldier, you will be expected to operate in the
most remote and inaccessible regions of the world: this means
being able to navigate with pinpoint accuracy under the most
arduous circumstances. Although you are equipped with the

most up-to-date satellite navigation and communication equipment, you must still be able to operate with the most basic navigational aids: a compass, map, altimeter and watch. You will also find that navigation is central to Special Forces selection.

Forest and jungle navigation

Forest navigation is probably the most difficult, because your visibility is minimal and your path obstructed. If you don't keep an accurate record of your precise location, you will soon get hopelessly lost, particularly in tropical rain forests. Under other navigational circumstances you are able to travel safely as long as you can recognize the prominent landmarks, but when you can only see trees and bushes it is all too easy to wander off-course.

The Hollywood image of a forest navigation is of cutting a trail through the tangled undergrowth with a machete in one hand and a compass in the other. This has nothing to do with reality: the last thing any forest traveller wants to do is to "cut a trail". Most forests are honeycombed with a complex network of unmapped tracks and trails, human and animal. Although they may not seem to lead to your destination, using them will almost certainly make your journey far quicker and easier. If you have a choice of two trails to follow, and if you know precisely where you are, follow the path that points in what is the nearest to the right direction. By recording the bearings and distances between bends in the path, you will be able to plot its course on your map. Continue this process until you are as near to your estimation as the trails will take you. You may now have to march on a direct bearing to your destination, cutting a trail. Better still, you could "aim off" so that you intersect an easily recognisable land feature such as a road, railway or river that will lead directly to your target. If you are using a river, make sure you know which direction the river flows in : it is not always obvious.

Surveying your path

Surveying a path is not difficult. You just need two pieces of information: direction and distance. Direction is obtained by using your compass to sight down the trail to the next bend adjusting your magnetic bearing to a grid bearing, and plotting a line from your known position. To work out distance, you now walk down the trail to the point at which you sighted, counting your paces. When you reach your sighting, compare the pace totals of your team and take an average. This is called "bracketing". An experienced team will already know the relationship of their paces to distance, in varying terrain, having worked this out during training.

Another way of determining distance travelled is to estimate your speed of travel. Speed is distance divided by time. By checking the time it takes you to pass between two identifiable land features and dividing this by the distance you have travelled (taken from the map), you will know your current speed. Update and revise this as often as possible, and make allowances for terrain changes. If, for example your speed is estimated at 4 km/hour and you have been walking at approximately that speed for two and a half hours, you will have travelled 10 km (distance = speed multiplied by time).

The most accurate way to establish your distance is to use both methods. As commander, estimate your speed of travel while two of your team act as pace counters by notching a stick every 50 paces.

Trail cutting

Trail cutting means keeping a straight course. Accuracy is vitally important: if you are 4 degrees off course, after 3 km you can be up to 250 metres off course – more than enough to miss your objective. By cutting two saplings and stripping the bark off them you can improvise two surveying poles. Use these to set your course by, and you should be able to navigate with pinpoint accuracy. Simply set the poles 20 metres apart in line with your intended direction of travel, so that they act as a visual guide for the trail you are cutting. As the trail progresses, leapfrog your rear pole forward, setting it in position by a back bearing to the remaining pole.

Navigating around obstacles

While following a bearing you may come across obstacles such as lakes, swamps, crevasses and ravines. To avoid these there are two techniques that will enable you to maintain your course.

1. **Avoidance by landmark.** If there is an identifiable landmark within easy reach you can walk to it and take a fresh bearing from this point to your objective. If you are confident of your ability to judge distance you can avoid travelling all the way to the landmark.
2. **'Boxing'.** Walking three sides of a box around the obstacle. By counting paces and walking a right-angled box you should be able to resume your correct course.

Alpine navigation

Another field of operations common to the Special Forces soldier is the mountain and Arctic environment. Navigation in these areas follows all the basic rules, but there are other considerations: probably the most hazardous is glacier navigation. Wherever possible, gain high ground before crossing glaciers so that you can scout a route through the ice falls. Glaciers are basically huge rivers of ice. Their rate of flow is determined by their mass and the slope of the underlying rock. They usually consist of two parts: the lower glacier, which is free of snow in the summer and often referred to as the dry glacier, and the upper glacier, covered in snow all year round with the snow packed down to form the glacier ice itself. This is often called a wet glacier.

Crevasse dangers

Although the ice is plastic at its surface, it cracks as it passes over rises in its underlying rock or at the outside of bends it flows around. These cracks are called crevasses. In most cases it is possible to predict where these will occur by studying the contours of your map. "Lurker" crevasses, which occur in predictable locations, are caused by flows in the ice.

The most dangerous part of the glacier is the upper or "wet" glacier as snow can obliterate the crevasses, often forming bridges across them. Whenever you cross "wet" glaciers you should always be roped together.

Flowing water

As a general rule, where you can see water flowing across the surface of the glacier the danger of crevasses is minimal. This is because water will disappear down the first available crack or crevasse; so where you can see the water there can be few cracks.

Fixing your Position

To gain an accurate fix on your position when crossing glaciers, you use a combination of information:

1. First measure the aspect of your position, by taking a bearing at 90 degrees from your position to the direction in which the glacier is moving. By comparing this to the contour lines on your map you should be able to estimate your approximate location.

2. Secondly, take an altitude reading from your altimeter. This will enable you to gain a precise fix on your location. Remember to set your altimeter to the correct height each time you pass a spot height, as its reading will vary with the barometric changes of local weather conditions. If overnight you seem to gain height, it indicates a loss of pressure and therefore that bad weather is imminent. If, on the other hand, you lose height, the pressure indicates imminent good weather.

Navigation without instruments

As the truck brakes hard and your "rookie" guard drops his cigarette, you take the chance to make a bid for freedom, vaulting the tailgate and running like a fox, looking for cover. After an hour you slump into the shade of a yew tree and look back. You can't see any sign of your pursuers, but they're there somewhere. You must put as much ground between them and you as possible. You were in the truck for about two hours, travelling at about 50 mph, so at the worst you're 100 miles behind the lines and probably much less. You could be back at HQ in a week. But your escape map and compass were taken when you were searched! Never fear, there are ways of navigating for which no map or compass is required.

The mental map

No matter what your job is – running the field kitchen or leading the raiding party – make sure you know the geographical features of the location!

1. Where are the major rivers, and in which direction do they flow?
2. What are the local hills called and in which direction do they extend?
3. In which direction do the local railway lines run?
4. Where are your own lines and where are the enemy lines?
5. In which nearby towns or villages are there garrisons of enemy troops?

These are the beginnings of a detailed mental picture that you should build up and constantly update. Using your mental map, you should be able to guess where you are and so decide what direction to head in. Remember that survival navigation is much less accurate than instrument navigation. Instead of a bearing you need a plan, such as "strike NE to the southern hills, following them east to their end, then strike due north to the northern hills and follow them east until I reach a gap where the Blue river runs north west to our lines." If you know where the areas of population are, plan your route to skirt round them. To make even such a basic plan work, you must figure out your bearings. You need to know how the sun, stars, moon and planets act as indicators of direction, and you must practise using them.

The Sun

This is your most obvious indicator of direction, so long as it is not covered by cloud. It rises in the east and sets in the west; this is always true, no matter what hemisphere you are in. Near the Equator, the sun appears to be almost overhead; further north the sun will always be south of you, and further south it will be north of you.

Find out where true north is by measuring the shadow cast by a vertical stick. To do this, find a piece of level ground, preferably bare earth, and put a 30-cm straight stick vertically into the ground. Using a short marker stick, record the end of the shadow cast by the vertical stick. As the sun moves west the shadow will move east. Wait until the shadow has moved a few centimetres and mark its end again. By drawing a line between the two markers you will have a west to east line. If you need a north/south reference, simply draw a line that cuts the west/east line at a right angle.

USING YOUR WATCH TO FIND NORTH

Northern temperate zone
1. Place a small stick in the ground so that it casts a definite shadow.
2. Put your watch on the ground so that the hour hand points along the shadow.
3. Find the point on the watch midway between the hour hand and 12 o'clock. A line from the centre of the face to this point indicates due south.

Southern temperate zone

1. Place the stick in the ground.
2. Put the watch on the ground so that 12 o'clock points along the shadow.
3. A line drawn from the centre of the watch to a point midway between the hour hand and 12 o'clock points north.

NOTE: If your watch is on British Summer Time (Daylight Saving Time) you must take the mid-point of the hour hand and 1 o'clock. You can still use this method with a digital watch: simply draw out the clock face in the dirt with the hands representing the correct time GMT.

USING THE MOON

If you're evading capture you will probably be travelling at night. To obtain your bearings you can use the moon and stars.

In general, the moon can be seen more often than the stars. Unlike the sun, the moon does not physically glow; it just reflects the light of the sun. A new moon occurs when the moon is between the Earth and the sun, with its dark side towards us, and a full moon is when the Earth is between the moon and the sun. Between the new and full moons, we see the moon partially illuminated on one side or the other.

Like the sun, the moon moves in a regular and predictable manner. If the moon rises before the sun sets, the illuminated side is the west. If the moon rises at the same time as the sun sets, it will be a full moon and you will need to know the time to attain the direction. If the moon rises after the sun has set, the illuminated side is the east side.

The moon can also be used to find direction in the northern hemisphere in the following way.

Imagine a line joining the tips of the crescent of the

moon or bisecting the full moon and continuing to the horizon: this line is south. In the southern hemisphere use the same method to find north.

The stars

Gaining an approximate fix on north or south from the stars is an ancient and easy skill. The technique differs between the northern and southern hemispheres.

1. In the northern hemisphere, the star Polaris (the pole star) is your guide to true north. This is because it is never more than 1 degree from the North Celestial Pole. If you are facing the pole star, you are facing true north. To find Polaris, first find the easily recognized constellations "the Plough" or "Cassiopeia" which will guide you to Polaris.

2. In fact, the South Celestial Pole is so devoid of stars it is called the Coal Sack. If you are facing the South Celestial Pole you are facing true south. To find the pole, draw an imaginary line from the Southern Cross (do not confuse this with the "false cross") and another imaginary line at 90 degrees to the two bright stars east of the Southern Cross. The point at which these two lines intersect is a point approximately 5-6 degrees off true south.

FINDING POLARIS

On a clear night in the northern hemisphere, the direction of north is indicated by the North Star. This is not the brightest star in the sky and can be difficult to find. All other stars revolve around the North Star. Or you can find the group of stars known as the "Plough" or Ursa Major, which is usually fairly prominent. A line joining the stars forming the blade of the plough points to the North Star.

THE SOUTH CELESTIAL POLE

In the southern hemisphere you can find the direction of true south by finding the south celestial pole. Unfortunately there are no convenient star markers, and you have to work out the position from the southern cross and two adjacent bright stars.

Cloudy nights

On cloudy nights you may not be able to see enough of the night sky to use these methods. If you can see some stars, choose a bright star that you will be able to observe, unobscured, for some minutes. If it falls, you are looking west; if it rises, you are looking east. If it arcs up to the right you are looking approximately south-east, and if it arcs down to the right you are looking approximately north-west.

Natural landmarks

If you are on the move and in a hurry you will need quicker references. Because the landscape and vegetation is shaped by the local environmental conditions you can gain rough indications of direction by simple observation. However, you will find these indicators to be unreliable guides, and you should never rely upon one indicator alone.

Remember that prevailing weather conditions vary from region to region and are especially unpredictable in hilly or heavily wooded areas. Success in navigation depends on your choice of landmark: lone isolated trees in flat country are the ideal choice. By comparing the results of several differing natural navigation aids – for example, grass tufts, the way a star moves and the moisture of leaf litter at the base of a tree – you should be able to move over unfamiliar country in any direction you want.

1) Wind

Make sure you are aware of the prevailing wind direction in any area in which you are operating. The generally prevailing wind in England is south-westerly (and in north-west Europe north-westerly). Lone trees and isolated new plantations will lean away from the prevailing wind direction. So do tussocks of grass and other forms of upright vegetation such as ferns. Small isolated woods, especially near the coast, have stunted trees on their windward sides. In sandy areas, tails of sand form behind small bushes and plants, pointing directly away from the wind. Sand dunes and snow cornices are gently sloping on their windward side and steep on their lee (sheltered) side.

2) Effect of the Sun on vegetation

The sun also greatly affects vegetation, in particular isolated trees, whose branches should be more numerous and foliated on the sunny side (south in the northern hemisphere and north in the southern hemisphere). Because of this you will also usually find that the decaying vegetation at the base of the trunk is drier on the sunny side: a good night-time guide. The stumps of felled trees will show their growth rings more tightly packed on the sunny side.

Nature's signposts

Remember:

Trees

Isolated trees have more branches with more leaves on the sunnier side of the tree: in the northern hemisphere this means south.

Isolated buildings

On barns in an exposed position, the sunnier side will be drier, with less moss and algae, indicating south in the northern hemisphere.

Tree stumps

The growth rings of the stump will be more tightly packed on the sunnier side, indicating south in the northern hemisphere. The leaf litter will also be drier at the base of the stump on that side.

River crossing

If you are on the run or are operating in wild terrain, you are likely to encounter water obstacles that you may have to cross. They may be fast moving rivers or large marshy areas of clinging, stinking and tiring mud. Each has its dangers, but also its drills for survival. Here we deal with rivers, using techniques from US Army Manual FM21-76.

Finding your crossing-point

A river or stream may be narrow or wide, shallow or deep, slow-moving or fast-moving. It may be rain-fed, snow-fed or ice-fed. Your first step is to find a place where the river is basically safe for crossing, so look for a high place from which you can get a good view and look out for the best crossing-point. If there is no high place, climb a tree.

Check the river carefully for the following features:

1. A level stretch where it breaks into a number of channels. Two or three narrow channels are usually easier to cross than a wide river.
2. Obstacles on the opposite side of the river that might hinder your travel. Try to select the spot from which travel will be the safest and easiest.
3. A ledge of rocks that crosses the river. This often indicates dangerous rapids or canyons.
4. A deep or rapid waterfall or a deep channel. Never attempt to ford a stream directly above or even close to such spots.
5 Rocky places. Avoid these, you can be seriously injured if you fall on rocks. An occasional rock that breaks the current however, may assist you.
6. A shallow bank or sandbar. If possible, select a point

upstream from such a feature so that the current will carry
you to it if you lose your footing.
7. A course across the river that leads downstream, so that you
can cross the current at about a 45-degree angle.

Avoid cold water

Be sure to check the water temperature before trying to cross a
river or water obstacles. If the water is extremely cold and you are
unable to find a shallow fording place, do not attempt to ford it.
Devise other means for crossing; for instance, you might improvise a bridge by felling a tree over the river. Or you might build a
raft large enough to carry both you and your equipment.

Crossing a fast river

If you are going to ford a swift, treacherous stream, remove your
trousers and underpants so that the water will have less grip on
your legs. Keep your shoes on to protect your feet and ankles
from rocks and to give you firmer footing. Tie your trousers and
important articles securely to the top of your pack; if you have to
release it, everything will be easier to find.

Carry your pack well up on your shoulders so that you can
release it quickly if you are swept off your feet. Being unable to
get a pack off quickly enough can drag even the strongest of
swimmers under. Don't worry about the weight of your pack, as
this will help rather than hinder you in fording the stream.

Find a strong pole about 12 cm (5 inches) in diameter and 2
to 2.5 metres (7 to 8 feet) long to help you ford the stream. Grasp
the pole and plant it firmly on your upstream side to break the
current. Plant your feet firmly with each step, and move the pole
forwards, slightly downstream from its previous position, but still
upstream from you. With your next step, place your foot below
the pole. Keep the pole well slanted so that the force of the current
keeps the pole firmly against you.

Crossing as a team

If there are other people with you, cross the stream together. Make sure that everyone has prepared their pack and clothing as above. The heaviest person should be on the downstream end of the pole and the lightest person on the upstream end. This way, the upstream person will break the current, and the people below can move with comparative ease in the eddy formed by him. If the upstream person is temporarily swept off his feet, the others can hold him steady while he regains his footing.

As in all fording, cross the stream so that you will cross the downstream current at a 45-degree angle. Currents too strong for one person to stand against can usually be crossed safely in this manner.

Do not rope your team together in fast-flowing water: the action of the current may hold any fallen member down.

Floating across

If the temperature of a body of water is warm enough for swimming but you are unable to swim, make a flotation device to help you. Some things you can use are:

Trousers: Knot each leg at the bottom and button the fly. With both hands grasp the waistband at the sides and swing the trousers in the air to trap air in each leg. Quickly press the sides of the waistband together and hold it under water so that the air will not escape. You now have water wings to keep you afloat. These have to be re-inflated several times when crossing a wide stretch of water.

Empty containers: Lash together empty tins, petrol cans or boxes and use them as water wings. You should only use this type of flotation in a slow-moving river or stream.

Plastic bags: Air-fill two or more plastic bags and securely tie them together at the mouth.

Poncho: Roll green vegetation tightly inside your poncho so that you have a roll at least 45 cm (18 inches) in diameter. Tie the ends of the roll securely. You can wear it around your waist or across one shoulder and under the opposite arm.

Logs: Use a stranded drift log if one is available, or find a log near the water's edge. Test it before starting to cross, however, as some tree logs, palm for example, will sink even when the wood is dead.

Bulrushes: Gather stalks of bulrushes and tie them in a bundle 25 cm or more in diameter. The many air cells in each stalk cause it to float until it rots. Test the bundle to make sure it will support your weight before attempting to cross.

Two-man rafts

If you are with a companion and each of you has a poncho, you can construct a brush or Australian poncho raft. With this type of raft you can safely float your equipment across a slow-moving stream or river.

Brush raft

The brush raft will support about 115 kg (250 lb) if properly constructed. Use ponchos, fresh green brush, two small saplings and a rope or vines.

1. Tightly tie off the neck of each poncho with the neck draw-string.
2. Attach ropes or vines at the corner and side grommets of each poncho. Be sure they are long enough to cross to and tie with those at the opposite corner or side.
3. Spread one poncho on the ground with the tied-off hood upwards.
4. Pile fresh, green brush (no thick branches) on the poncho until the brush stack is about 45 cm (18 inches) high.
5. Pull the poncho neck drawstring up through the centre of the brush stack.
6. Make an X-frame of two small saplings and place it on top of the brush stack.
7. Tie the X-frame securely in place with the poncho neck drawstring.
8. Pile another 45 cm of brush on top of the X-frame.

9. Compress the brush slightly.
10. Pull the poncho sides up around the brush and, using the ropes or vines attached to the corner and side grommets, tie diagonally from corner to corner and from side to side.
11. Spread the second poncho, tied off hood upwards, next to the brush bundle.
12. Roll the brush bundle onto the centre of the second poncho so that the tied side faces downwards.
13. Tie the second poncho around the brush bundle in the same way as you tied the first poncho around the brush (10).
14. Tie one end of a rope to an empty canteen and the other end to the raft. This will help you to tow it.

Australian poncho raft

If you don't have time to gather brush for a brush raft, you can make an Australian poncho raft. Although more waterproof, this will only float about 25 kg (55 lb) of equipment. Use two ponchos, two 1-metre poles or branches, and ropes, vines, bootlaces or comparable material.

- Tightly tie off the neck of each poncho with the neck drawstring.
- Spread one poncho on the ground with the neck upwards.
- Place and centre the two poles about 45 cm apart on the poncho.
- Place the rucksacks, packs and other equipment between the poles, including items that you want to keep dry, such as boots and outer garments.
- *At this point you will need your companion's help to complete the raft.*
- Snap the poncho sides together.
- Hold the snapped portion of the poncho in the air and roll it tightly down to the equipment.
- Twist each end of the roll to form pigtails in opposite direction.
- Fold the pigtails over the bundle and tie them securely in place using ropes, vines or bootlaces.

- Spread the second poncho on the ground with the tied-off hood upwards. If you need more buoyancy, place some fresh green brush on this poncho.
- Place the equipment bundle, pigtail-side-down, on the centre of the second poncho.
- Wrap the second poncho around the equipment bundle following the same procedure as you used for wrapping the equipment in the first poncho.
- Tie ropes, vines or other binding material around the raft about 30 cm (12 in) from each end of the pigtail.
- Place and secure weapons on top of raft.
- Tie one end of a rope to a canteen and the other end to the raft. This will help you in towing the raft.
- When launching or landing either type of raft take care not to puncture or tear it by dragging it on the ground. Let the raft lie on the water for a few minutes to ensure that it floats before you start to cross the river or stream. If the river is too deep to ford, push the raft in front of you while swimming.

Log raft

This will carry both you and your equipment if you are unable to cross in any other way; if you have an axe and a knife you can build it without rope. A suitable raft for three men would be 3.5 m (12 feet) long and (2 m) 6 feet wide. You can use dry, dead standing trees for logs, but spruce trees that are found in polar and sub-polar regions make the best log rafts.

- Build the raft on two skid logs placed so that they slope downwards to the bank. Smooth the logs with an axe so that the raft logs lie evenly on them.
- Cut four off-set inverted notches, one in the top and one in the bottom of both ends of each log. Make the notches broader at the base than at the outer edge of the log.
- To bind the raft together, drive through each notch a three-sided wooden crosspiece about 30 cm longer than the width of the raft. Connect all the notches on one side of the raft before connecting those on the other.

- Lash the overhanging ends of the two crosspieces together at each end of the raft to give it additional strength. When the raft enters the water, the crosspieces swell binding the logs together tightly.
- If the crosspieces fit too loosely, wedge them with thin pieces of dried wood. These swell when wet, tightening and strengthening the crosspieces.

CROSSING ON A RAFT

REMEMBER: A deep and fast-moving river can be crossed several times using a pendulum action at a bend in the river; this is necessary when several men have to cross. However, remember the following.

- The raft must be canted in the direction of the current.
- The rope from the anchor point must be 7-8 times as long as the width of the river.
- The attachment of the rope to the raft must be adjustable to change the cant of the raft so that it can return to the starting bank.

Flash floods

Beware of rapidly-increased water flows. Flash floods are a common feature in the tropics and can arrive suddenly many miles from any apparent storm. Try to cross steadily but quickly. Heat loss will be substantial, and you could quickly become weak. Once out on the other bank, take your clothes off and wring out as much water as possible. Change into dry kit if you can. Otherwise, put your wet clothing back on – it will soon dry out as your body warms up.

Rapids

Crossing a deep, swift river or rapids is not as dangerous as it looks. If you are swimming across, swim with the current – never fight it – and try to keep your body horizontal to the water. This will reduce the danger of being pulled under.

In fast, shallow rapids, travel on your back, feet first; use your hands as fins alongside your hips to add buoyancy and to fend off submerged rocks. Keep your feet up to avoid getting them bruised or caught by rocks.

In deep rapids, travel on your front, head first; angle towards the shore whenever you can. Breathe between wave troughs. Be careful of backwater eddies and converging currents as they often contain dangerous swirls.

Other water obstacles

You may also face bogs, quagmire, muskeg or quicksand. DO NOT try to walk across: trying to lift your feet while standing upright will make you sink deeper. If you are unable to bypass them you may be able to bridge them using logs, branches or foliage. Another way to cross is to lie face downwards with your arms spread and swim or pull your way across. Be sure to keep your body horizontal.

In swamps, the areas that have vegetation are usually firm enough to support your weight and you should be able to crawl or pull your way through miles of swamp or bog. In open mud or water areas without vegetation, you can swim.

Ropework

Whether you are rigging a camouflage net or tensioning a rope across a chasm, your success or failure – maybe your life – will at some stage depend upon your or a mate's ability to tie a secure knot. How many times have you seen a tangle of cordage, jammed knots, ropes unravelling at their ends? These are the signs of dangerous and sloppy rope-handling. Although you will not be in constant contact with ropes, an understanding of rope and knots is a fundamental requirement of the professional soldier. Assuming you have no specialist equipment available, how do you learn to work efficiently and safely with rope?

Teach yourself knots

There is no substitute for practice. You will find learning easier if you use two two-metre lengths of 5-mm climbing accessory cord, ideally of different colours. You haven't learned a knot until you can consistently tie it behind your back: in a combat situation you may have to tie a life-saving knot, quickly in the dark, and possibly under water, for example while crossing a river.

Basic rope terminology

Handling cordage: Nothing is more frustrating than having to constantly untangle rope or string when you need it in a hurry. Get into the habit of always coiling and hanking rope correctly.

Hanking and coiling: Hanking is the term used to describe the correct method of gathering short lengths of small cordage such as paracord. Wind the cord around the thumb and little finger of one hand in a figure-of-eight fashion, leaving about a metre to spare. Take the coils off your hand and wrap them with the spare length, finishing off with a half-hitch or two pulled tight.

Long lengths of small cordage should be coiled. Coiling is the correct method of gathering rope. Correctly coiled rope should not contain kinks. Before coiling, make sure the working end of the rope (i.e. the end not in your hand) is unattached. As you take on the coils, twist the rope between your thumb and index finger so that perfect coils are formed, without twists or kinks.

Once coiled, double back about a third of a metre of the fixed end, take off the last coil and wrap the coil tightly from the fixed end to the double-back. Pass the working end through the loop formed at the double-back, and pull on the fixed end to lock the whipping tight.

Types of rope

Choose your rope carefully. Each type of rope has its own characteristics and uses; the wrong choice of rope could easily prove fatal – for instance, you should never climb on hemp ropes.

Wherever possible, familiarize yourself with the types and specification of the ropes available.

Hawser-laid ropes

These are the traditional type of rope, normally constructed from three strands. The advantage is that the rope can be easily inspected for wear and tear, but the disadvantage is that it tends to wear more easily than braided ropes, and unless correctly handled tends to kink. More importantly, it does not stretch to absorb the energy of a fall in climbing.

Braided ropes

Often referred to as Kernmantel, (Kern = Core; Mantel = Sheath), these ropes are almost totally made from man-made fibres. The core of the rope is the major load-bearing part, with the sheath acting as a protection from abrasion and other external hazards, and providing, in some cases, comfortable handling. The disadvantage is that it is impossible to detect progressive wear on the core of the rope.

This type of rope has a limited safe lifespan if used for climbing: successive heavy falls will weaken it, so you must know a rope's history before you use it.

Materials

The material the rope is made from is more significant than its method of construction. Rope can be made from natural or man-made fibres; the latter is the most common nowadays.

Natural fibres

Hemp, sisal, cotton etc. are rapidly being replaced by the man-made fibres. The disadvantages of natural ropes are numerous: when wet they lose 30% of their strength and are heavy and difficult to handle; they are prone to mildew and vermin, and are uncomfortable to handle.

They do, however, have one great advantage over man-made fibres: when hot they do not melt, which makes them the best choice in situations of high friction and fire emergencies.

Sea-going vessels still have to have their ships' ladders made from natural ropes, in case of fire. The time gained by having ropes that smoulder rather than melt is a significant safety feature, even though the ropes need replacing more frequently.

The other advantage of a natural rope is its tendency to "sing out" before it breaks – an audible warning that has so often saved Tarzan in the movies. Watch out: the acid from batteries will rot natural rope.

Man-made fibres

In most cases, these are stronger, more durable, lighter and cheaper than natural fibres. However, they are more slippery and require careful attention to knots. The cheapest man-made fibres available are polythene and polypropylene ropes: these are the very smooth orange and blue ropes often seen on lifebelts and building sites. These ropes float (hence their use on lifebelts), but are weak compared with the other man- made fibres. They also tend to suffer more from ultra-violet decay, most noticeable as a lightening and opaque change in their colour, which greatly reduces their strength.

Polyester or terylene is much stronger than polypropylene and is often used by sailors. This is also the material from which modern abseiling and caving ropes are made. Although fine for these specific activities this type of rope should never be used for climbing with, because it is pre-stretched. A fall taken on such a rope would break the climber's back.

Nylon is the man-made fibre used for climbing ropes, due to its ability to absorb shock by stretching. If a climber falls, the force of the fall is taken gradually, thus cushioning the jolt.

Climbing ropes

Climbing ropes come in two main types: half ropes and single ropes. They are marked accordingly. Half ropes need to be used in pairs or doubled, whereas a single rope can be used on its own. Because climbing rope stretches it should not be used for towing or assault pioneering tasks.

Rope strength

To use the full strength of any rope, the load must be taken equally by all the fibres. This only happens when the rope is pulled in a straight line. When a rope is bent, for example over a cliff edge, the fibres on the inside chafe which severely weakens the strength of the rope. If an 11-mm climbing rope passes around a karabiner clip with a 5-mm diameter, the rope strength reduces to 70%.

The strength of a rope depends on its weakest part. When you are constructing rope bridges, lifting weights or carrying out any other assault pioneering tasks, it makes sense to have a rough idea whether the system you have built is going to take the load. The rule for the working strength of dry fibre ropes in hundredweights is given by its circumference in inches squared.

So a safe working load for a new three-inch fibre rope is about 3 x 3 which is 9 hundredweight (500 kg).

Whenever a knot is tied in a rope, bends are introduced, causing weakness; some knots weaken rope more than others.

Tracking

As a soldier, your knowledge of tracking will enhance your awareness, increase your ability to gather intelligence and sharpen your fieldcraft. If you are in command during an extended border operation, a tracking capability will enable you to build an accurate map of the localized enemy movements without having to send out large numbers of patrols.

But for a survivor, tracking skill means food. If you're close to civilisation, man-made obstacles such as fences and irrigation channels force game to pass through bottlenecks, making trapping easy. But in remote sparsely populated areas it is not so simple. You must be able to recognize the trails of local game and be capable of following them from their resting areas to their feeding areas, where trapping is easier.

Good trackers are rare. When they are needed for military purposes, commanders usually employ hunters from the local indigenous population. But this does not mean that Westerners cannot track: some of them are among the world's best trackers. A tracker is a reader of "sign". He takes a few faint pieces of information and, using the process of deduction and comparison with previous experience, puts the puzzle together.

Obstacles to trackers

The more experience the tracker has, the better able he is to do the job. But he must still beware the following:

Lack of confidence: Even the best trackers use intuition, and a tracker must know when to trust a hunch. With lives at stake, lack of confidence can cloud your ability to think straight. Experience is the only solution.

Bad weather: 'Sign' does not last for ever. Wind, rain and fresh snowfall will all obliterate it; many a trail has gone cold because the tracker has not paid enough attention to the weather forecast. With unfavourable weather imminent, short cuts may need to be taken to speed the "follow-up".

Non-track-conscious personnel: By the time trackers are called in to follow the trail, the clues at the proposed start have usually been destroyed by clumsy feet. If you are fortunate enough to work with a team that can recognize "sign" even though they cannot read it, you will have extra pairs of eyes to help you find the vital clues.

Unsympathetic commander: Tracking is a solitary business, requiring great concentration. A tracker must have the trust of the commander and must be able to trust his cover group. Tracking often seems to be painfully slow, but the tracker will be moving as fast as he can: never rush him. The more intelligence he has at his disposal the better, so tell him what is going on; your knowledge of enemy movements may make sense of an otherwise meaningless clue.

Try to allow the tracker time to impart a rudimentary knowledge of tracking to his cover group, and make sure the cover group are all patient men: the tracker has the challenge of the trail to hold his attention, but the cover and support group does not. If they make any noise it is the tracker who is at greatest risk.

Attributes of a tracker

Tracking is mainly a visual skill. Your eyesight, whether you wear glasses or not, must be 20/20. Short-sighted people often seem to make good trackers once their eyesight is corrected. A general ability to observe is not enough for tracking; you have to piece information together, like Sherlock Holmes. You must also be patient, persistent and constantly questioning your own theories, especially if you are "solo tracking". Very often, you will trail your target to within touching distance. To reduce risks, self-defence and close-quarter battle skills are vital.

Although modern equipment plays an important role in the task of tracking, remember that it does not replace your tracking ability; it just makes life easier.

Learning to track

Tracking is not a particularly difficult skill to learn, but it needs dedication and much practice. Once you have learned the basic principles and techniques you can practise in your own time. If you want to reach a high standard, it will help if you have a team-mate who can lay trails for you. Make sure you keep a log: this must include the duration of the track, the time of the day, the ground conditions and the level of difficulty.

BOOBY TRAPS

A booby trap is designed to cause sudden and surprise casualties and to reduce morale by creating fear, uncertainty and suspicion. You will only be able to counter booby traps if you understand how they work, in what circumstances they are employed and what they look like.

Booby traps are used in various terrorist situations but are more likely to be used in a jungle environment than anywhere else, mainly because they are more easily hidden, but also because the materials to make them are readily to hand.

Jungle traps

The jungle guerrilla will be restricted in the operational employment of booby traps only by the extent of his imagination. The range and variety of traps used by the Vietcong was bewildering, and responsible for lowering the morale of government forces in Vietnam. Guerrillas will continue to use booby traps along obvious lines of communication, forcing troops to move cautiously or to deploy engineers and assault pioneers to clear routes – very time-consuming – or to move deeper into the jungle where the going is appreciably more difficult.

The sides of roads, rivers and streams and any track or ridge line are likely targets. When they are on the defensive, guerrillas will use booby traps to protect a bunkered camp, a defended village or a tunnel system. They will be laid in conjunction with obstacles, wire, conventional mines and road blocks to deter any detailed reconnaissance of their position and to give advance warning of an attack. They will also use booby traps to cover their withdrawal.

But, despite the very real and unpleasant threat of booby traps, there is something you can do about them. First, learn all there is to learn about booby traps. Knowledge dispels fear; know your enemy and you're halfway to beating him. Five examples of jungle booby traps are:

1. The barbed spike plate
This is a very common trap. It is easily made and can be placed anywhere, and is difficult to detect before the damage is done. The spikes are often tipped with poison such as human excrement.
2. The punji bear trap
The punji bear trap is a refinement of the basic pit trap to counter the steel plate in the bottom of the issue jungle boot. The trap is concealed under brushwood or leaves on the track. When you walk over the trap, your leg plunges down into the pit, pivoting the boards, which close on your leg

spiking it above the ankle. This arrangement leads to damage to the unprotected area of the calf above the boot.

3. The overhead grenade trap

A grenade is suspended in the overhead foliage. As you trip a wire, the pin is pulled from the grenade suspended above you. You have 3-5 seconds to get out of range of the blast; difficult because the shrapnel from the grenade is likely to travel a great distance due to its height above the ground. It is particularly effective at night. By day, the trip-wire can be removed to allow the enemy or civilians to use the track.

4. The cartridge trap

This trap is easily set up and is very effective. It is buried so that the head of the round is only partly exposed; pressure on the tip sets the round off.

5. Grenade daisy chain

The trip wire is camouflaged across the track and when pulled, the first grenade explodes. This breaks the wire to the second grenade, which has had its pin removed, and releases the lever. The second grenade explodes, breaking the wire to the third grenade and so on.

THE WAY THE ENEMY'S MIND WORKS

A guerrilla will follow some common-sense rules when he is setting up his booby traps.

- He will go to enormous lengths to conceal his device.
- The charge and mechanism will be concealed or made to resemble some harmless object.
- He will usually choose a constricted location where you are channelled into his trap. Any defile or enclosed space such as a room or tunnel is a potential booby-trap site.
- Traps are usually laid in groups, so that when you come across them you are likely to spring at least one of them. There will be dummy booby traps to confuse you; having disarmed an obvious trap, the idea is that you will be sufficiently off your guard to blunder into a second one.

- Guerrillas often place traps on obstacles. The removal of the obstacle, which may be a road block of some kind, sets off the trap. Similarly, traps can be placed on attractive items such as weapons, food or potential souvenirs.
- When you think you have discovered a booby trap and the method of setting it off, beware a second method!

Detecting booby traps

Booby traps are operated by a pull, pressure, release or delay mechanism, or a combination of more than one method. When looking for booby traps, there is no substitute for sharp eyesight and awareness. Among the many things you can look out for are loose dirt or newly filled areas; loose or taut wires; rope, strings or vines or sticks and stones in unnatural-looking positions, providing marker indicators. The foliage may be disturbed or damaged or camouflage may look out of place or have died. Also look out for plastic wrapper materials protruding from the ground, and in particular for any electrical lead wires. And, of course look for irregular tread patterns and footprints on roads and tracks.

Marker indicators may give you the best warning that a booby trap is in the area. Guerrillas have traditionally marked their booby traps to warn their own men and sympathetic locals to avoid the area. The sort of indicators they have used are piles of stones, crossed sticks, broken saplings or marks on the trunks of trees. One specific marker has been a stick balanced in the fork of a tree. This is surprisingly difficult to detect, and has been known to indicate a mine or booby trap some 10-20 metres away.

Another example is knotted tufts of grass: four tufts of knotted grass at each corner of a square indicate a mine or trap within the encompassed area. Another simple but often used indicator is a short piece of bamboo stuck into the ground at 45 degrees and pointing towards the booby trap. Perhaps the hardest example of all to detect is a twig threaded through a leaf to indicate the very close presence of a trap.

Dealing with booby traps

If you are aware of these methods of detection and recognition, you stand a very good chance of avoiding a booby trap. If you detect a booby trap you should ideally call in an expert to deal with it – an engineer or assault pioneer. But sometimes a device has to be neutralized quickly and there are two things you can do to disarm the device – providing you use your common sense.

First, by pulling with a cable and hook from a safe distance and from behind cover you can either set off the device intentionally or disrupt the mechanism. Secondly, you can destroy the device by placing a charge next to it and then detonating it from a safe distance. *But never attempt to disarm a device by hand.*

Avoid the obvious routes

The best way of combatting booby traps is to avoid tracks and roads whenever possible. But if you have to use tracks, avoid setting a pattern; it is unlikely that the guerrillas will be able to booby trap or mine *every* track or road. When using roads look out for:

Rut traps: Keep out of old ruts. The puddles and mud could conceal an excavation under a tarpaulin with a wire anchored on one end with the other attached to a grenade. The grenade can be used as the booster charge to initiate a secondary explosion inside a pot filled with explosive and scrapyard confetti. This type of mine was commonly used by the Vietcong.

Rut grenade traps: Puddles and muddy ruts in the road can be used to disguise a simple pressure plate of wood or wire mesh that, when stepped on or driven over, acts on the two anchored wires attached to the operating rod threaded through the grenade pins.

Locals can be a useful source of information; even if they are not willing to help you directly, their behaviour can provide clues. If they are avoiding an area, it's for a good reason. And if they show signs of anxiety or agitation at the close proximity of troops, this is a sure indicator that something is amiss.

Any future jungle enemy will continue to employ booby traps.

Find out everything you can about his likely booby-trap methods, types and procedures, and understand the disciplines for coping with the threat. If you become "jungle wise", a booby trap is unlikely to surprise you.

Mines and large-scale booby traps

Mines are often deployed as booby traps or combined with other explosives as nasty surprises for the unwary. This is particularly common in counter-insurgency, so it is especially important to take precautions and to understand the sort of devices you may encounter. Most booby traps exploit haste, carelessness or curiosity. By staying alert to the danger, you increase your chances of survival. There are eight general precautionary measures which should be observed at all times.

- Never leave any of your own equipment behind where hostile forces could make use of it. In Vietnam, careless American troops left a trail of valuable equipment behind them. Grenades slipped into webbing by the lever may look good in the movies, but many fell off and were literally handed to the enemy. Similarly, US landing zones were often littered with everything from empty cans (ideal for grenade traps) to rifle magazines, loose rounds and many other items useful to the needy guerrilla. British readers need not be smug: the British Army was guilty of the same thing in the Boer War in South Africa during 1900-1.
- When on the move, maintain proper spacing. Mines have a limited radius of effect, so dispersed formations suffer less damage. Men or vehicles that bunch up are asking for trouble.
- When driving, drivers should follow the tracks of the vehicle in front. If he is safe, then so are you. Conversely, don't drive in old tracks you know nothing about. They are a favourite spot for an anti-tank mine.
- If a unit on foot sustains casualties to mines, approach the wounded with caution: secondary mines or booby traps are often used against those who rush in to assist a mine victim.

- Vehicle floors can be sandbagged and a thick rubber mat over the sandbags will further reduce blast and secondary fragmentation if you detonate a mine. Keep your arms and legs in.
- Mines can be command-detonated – i.e. someone watching from the bushes presses the plunger as you drive past the bomb. This was a favourite IRA ambush technique. One answer is to vary the speed and the spacing of vehicles to make it hard for the terrorist to judge the right moment to set it off.
- Never allow single vehicles out on their own. They are an easy target and very tempting for terrorists/guerrillas who regard small units of troops as a potential source of weapons and equipment.
- Key personnel are an obvious target for command-detonated mines. A conspicuous command vehicle bristling with radio aerials is easily singled out, so do not place all the HQ personnel in the same APC. The same "eggs in one basket" principle applies to medical and other specialists.

COMMAND-DETONATED ROCKET ATTACK

Most rockets, from the 66-mm LAW to single BM-21 rounds, can be fired as booby traps or command-detonated devices. The only way to defend against this type of attack is not to bunch up and not to drive at constant speed. Foot patrols should be used to clear any potential firing points.

Detection and search techniques

Detecting mines and booby traps is hard, slow work which demands careful observation and a great deal of concentration. There are certain areas worth particular attention, and various clues which will help you survive. Once again, get into the habit of thinking: "If I were going to booby-trap this area, where would I lay the trip-wire?" Expect a trap and you may well find it.

Observe the movement of the local people: guerrillas usually aim to single out the security forces in the familiar "battle for the hearts and minds". If the farmer suddenly stops using one particular gate, there could be a very good reason. Gates and places where paths pass through dense undergrowth are favour- ite spots for a booby trap, and don't forget to look above you and to the flanks for grenades or shells in the trees. Entrances to buildings, caves or tunnels require special caution.

Look out for any signs and markings which the enemy may be using to mark his mines – this could be anything from knotted grass to the positioning of stones. If you can learn his signs they will act as signposts in the future.

You have been warned about leaving kit behind for the enemy. Be very cautious if the enemy has been so obliging as to leave weapons or supplies lying about for you. They may well be wired to something nasty. Check all items which would make good souvenirs: they also make good booby traps.

Bridges, drainage ditches, culverts and streams are common sites for mines and booby traps and they should be checked. Beware the crude yet effective 'bridge trap', where the bridge supports or cross-rails have been cut so will collapse under the weight of a soldier or vehicle, leaving him or it to plunge onto concealed punji stakes.

Disarming methods

The first step to surviving the mined battlefield is to detect, recognize and locate mines. Having done this, your safest bet is to bypass the area you know to be dangerous, but in certain circum- stances this will not be possible. In combat you may need to maintain the momentum of an attack. Engineer units will have to destroy mines in place to allow the safe passage of friendly troops and the rest of the mines will be neutralized later by EOD (Explosive Ordnance Disposal) teams.

Making a mine safe means displacing or replacing safeties in the firing assembly and separating the main charge from the detonator. If this is not possible, the mine must be destroyed in place.

A mine can be deliberately detonated if the damage is accept- able and the tactical situation permits. For example, a mine by a roadside can be detonated without much trouble, but if you deliberately explode a powerful enemy mine on a strategically vital road bridge you may have some explaining to do.

Before trying to remove a mine, probe around the main charge with care to locate any anti-handling devices which have to be neutralized. Identify the type of firing mechanism and replace all safety devices. If you have any doubts about neutralising the mine, pull it out with a grapnel or rope from behind cover. Wait at least thirty seconds after extracting it in case it has a delay-action fuse. Only trained specialists should attempt to disarm a mine by hand unless the device and appropriate disarming techniques are well-known.

Non-explosive traps

Not all booby traps are explosive. Improvised traps may take many forms that may seem alien to Western eyes, but such traps are still widely used in the jungle environment for trapping animals such as bush pigs. The Vietcong simply scaled up their traps to deal with a larger prey. These traps are usually covered pits, or work by a tripwire that releases a spear.

With non-explosive traps follow the general principles above, being especially alert for further mines and booby traps near a trap you have found. Also, a trap may be several booby traps together: you find one wire, think you are safe and walk round it straight into the punji pit.

If you bypass a trap, mark it clearly for any following troops. Loose spike-type devices and bear traps which have been sprung should be picked up and disposed of so they cannot be re-used after you have gone. Spike pits should be exposed to view and later dismantled and filled in.

Be particularly careful when clearing or neutralising traps activated by trip-wires. This includes such devices as log or ball maces, angled arrow traps, suspended spikes and bamboo whips. Clear all troops from the area and set off the device from a safe place using a grapnel.

Other traps

Falklands booby trap
Hundreds of booby traps were left in the Falklands by the Argentine forces. These can be divided into two main categories: those that used the M5 grenade and those improvised using available components and explosives. Many booby traps were improvised in the field by military engineers using available components: most used a trip wire to release a spring-loaded striker to fire a detonator. The main charge was normally American-made TNT demolition blocks buried in the ground. Occasionally the TNT blocks would be used to initiate an item of explosive ordnance such as a large artillery shell; one such device was discovered in a culvert near Port Stanley connected to a 1,000 lb-aircraft bomb. Other variations include attaching a short wire to an innocent-looking object such as an ammunition box. This would explode if the item was removed by the victim.

Vietcong and IRA traps
Bamboo bomb: Any tube, such as a bicycle frame or section of bamboo, can be used as a container for explosive. These could be used as booby traps or as grenades packed with metal scrap. The Vietcong packed explosives in growing bamboo on the side of a known patrol route; in the same way the IRA made mines out of cast-iron drain pipes on the sides of houses.

The Coconut mine: Any non-metallic mine will produce fragmentation that will now show up well on an X-ray of the victim. The Vietcong made highly effective IEDs out of hollowed-out coconuts packed with black powder and a detonator. Fragmentation effect was usually enhanced by placing stones and broken glass round the mine.

Anti-vehicle traps: Tank crews can see very little when buttoned up and will therefore drive with hatches open when out of contact. This type of grenade booby trap is designed to injure the crew and any infantry riding on the tank or in trucks or other soft-skinned vehicles. The grenade bodies are tied to the main wire and the pins are tied to stakes driven into the ground. More than

two grenades are usually used; the whole arrangement is camouflaged in the trees lining a road for example.

    Helicopter landing site trap: Where there is a limited number of
helicopter LZs, such as in the jungle or if you get into the habit of
using an LZ more than once, you could find this waiting for you.
The grenades or charges on the poles would usually be hidden in
the trees.

Mines

The war is over and the soldiers have departed. The odd rusting
tank or water-filled crater bears mute witness to years of bitter
fighting, but civilian traffic now passes over rebuilt roads and
bridges. As you pass across a field towards the edge of the village
there is a dull boom from across the track. The plough stops
dead, the ox stands patiently – but the farmer lies in a bloody
heap. The troops may have returned to barracks, but their mines
remain on duty.

    Combat zones and old battlefields the world over are domi-
nated by minefields. Vietnam, Laos and Cambodia remain littered
with mines: the old infiltration routes along the borders were
showered with air dropped mines by the US Air Force and unexploded ordnance in the south continues to inflict casualties.
Afghanistan has been similarly treated by the Soviet forces and
more recently by the opposing sides in the civil war. Throughout
North Africa the desert still conceals lethal leftovers from the
Second World War, and in the western Sahara the Polisario guerrillas and the Moroccan army both sowed new fields. In the
Falklands, tiny plastic anti-personnel mines are moved out of the
marked danger areas by the winter storms and continue to present a serious hazard. You may be lucky and never need to know
how to survive the mined battlefield; but if by accident or design
you find yourself tip-toeing across eggshells in some foreign field,
a knowledge of mines could mean the difference between life and
death.

    A bewildering selection of mines confronts any soldier trying
to learn how to counter them. Different nations manufacture

mines that produce similar effects but are of totally different construction. The only general preparation you can make is to learn how mines are used, how they are constructed and how armies mark minefields and make them safe for themselves.

But if you're on operations against an unexpected opponent, you won't have a chance to become familiar with his mines prior to hostilities. This is what happened to the sappers of the Falklands Task Force, who had little idea of the type of mines used by the Argentinians. In the end, young sappers had to infiltrate booby-trapped minefields and recover examples of live mines.

Mines are being developed with increasing sophistication to keep phase with their primary target – the battle tank – and have an enormous psychological as well as physical impact on an enemy. If you are to survive the mined battlefield, you must appreciate that you are in as much danger from "friendly" devices as you are from your enemy's. Remember, the mine is a double-edged weapon.

The Basic principles

A mine is made up of a fuse, a detonator, a booster (sometimes), a main charge, and a body or case. An initiating action causes the fuse to function and this starts the explosive train, whereby a flame or concussion is caused by electrical or mechanical means and is applied to the detonator. This then sets off the booster, if there is one, or the main charge. A variety of initiating actions can set off the process:

1. Pressure (downward force caused by a man's foot or the wheel or track of a vehicle).
2. Pulling (on a trip-wire attached to the fuse).
3. Tension release (release of tension such as cutting a trip-wire that prevents the fuse from acting).
4. Pressure release (release of pressure that prevents the fuse from acting).
5. Electrical (closing a circuit that activates the fuse).
6 Timer rundown (a pre-set timer arrives at a point that activates the fuse).

Other types of initiating actions include vibrations, magnetic influence, frequency induction and audio frequency.

Types of mine

There are three main types of mine: anti-tank, anti-personnel and chemical. Anti-tank mines, designed to damage or destroy tanks and other vehicles and their occupants, can be blast-type, disabling wheels or tracks; vertical-penetration, attacking the bottom of a vehicle; or horizontal-effect, placed off routes to attack the side of vehicles.

Anti-personnel mines are designed to disable or kill personnel. The blast type have an explosive charge and detonate when stepped on. Fragmentation types contain shrapnel or have a case which fragments when the main charge fires, and are divided into static mines (which detonate in place), bounding mines (which bound into the air and explode several feet above the ground), and horizontal-effect mines (which expel a spray of shrapnel in one direction).

Not all mines are harmful. You may come across phoney mines – dummies planted to make the enemy think they have found a live one, and waste time tackling it or avoiding it.

Handling mines

Like any other explosive material, mines and their fuses must be handled carefully. Most mines have safety devices to stop them going off by accident or prematurely, but as a soldier you may also find yourself having to improvise mines in the field, so get used to taking great care.

Any amount of explosive can be fused and placed as a mine. Grenades and some demolition charges already have fuse wells for installing firing devices; bombs, mortars and artillery shells can be used, and incendiary fuels in containers can be rigged as flame mines. The aspects of handling mines are:

- *Fusing:* This means installing the detonator and fuse assembly.

Fuse wells should be clean and free of foreign matter when the fuse and detonator are put in.

- *Arming*: When the fuse is installed, you arm the mine by removing all safety devices. The mine is then ready to function.
- *Safing*: In general, this is the reverse of arming. If you put the mine in place yourself and kept it in sight the whole time, you can remove it from its hole for safing. If not, attach a long rope or wire, take cover, and pull the mine from the hole. Safing involves checking the sides and bottom of the mine for anti-handling devices and disarming them if found; replacing all pins, clips or other safety devices; turning the arming dial, if there is one, to "Safe" or "Unarmed"; and removing the fuse and, if possible, the detonator.
- *Neutralising*: This means destroying the mine if safing is thought to be too risky, as in the case of improvised mines which will probably be unstable and dangerous. But do not detonate chemical mines: they will contaminate the area.

Anti-handling techniques

There are several devices for preventing someone disabling a mine. Enterprising engineers are apt to booby-trap their mines to make it difficult and dangerous to clear them. Anti-lift or anti-handling devices, when attached to a mine, will detonate it or another charge nearby if the mine is lifted or pulled out of its hole. An anti-disturbance device sets off the explosion if the mine is disturbed or shaken. Shielded, twisted firing wire can be attached to command-detonated mines to defeat enemy ECM. Long-pulse or multi-pulse fuses can defeat tank mine-clearing rollers and explosive mine-clearing charges. Another way of dealing with mine-clearing rollers is to place an unfused anti-tank mine (or explosive charge) in the ground, connected with detonating cord to a pressure fuse of firing device about three metres away. The roller then rolls over the unfused mine and activates the fuse when the tank itself is over the mine or charge.

BE AWARE: ANTI-HANDLING DEVICES

Most anti-tank mines cannot be set off by a man's weight, so unless they are used in conjunction with AP mines, infantry could lift them. *For this reason, many mines will have anti-handling devices fitted to additional detonator wells.*

Slightly more sneaky is the use of a second mine to booby-trap the first, using a pull-firing device. Most anti-tank mines are equipped with extra detonator wells, but the same effect can be achieved with quantities of explosive placed with the mine.

Avoiding mines

The US Army manual on mine warfare says, "Train to prevent panic". This is easy to say but rather harder to achieve. As you stand on a jungle trail with a screaming legless man in front of you, just what do you do? Rushing out of a live minefield is an obvious recipe for disaster, but staying put in combat will probably leave you in a killing ground under heavy fire. There is no guaranteed safe way out of a minefield, but if you know what different mines look like and understand how they work and the correct way of moving to safety, then you are in with a chance.

The only certain way of surviving the mined battlefield is to avoid blundering into a minefield in the first place. Although the famous skull and crossbones sign with "*Achtung Minen*" written above will only be seen in the cinema, well-trained armed forces do mark their minefields. Memorize the signs used by both friend and foe, and make sure you are fully briefed on marking used by an enemy.

NATO minefields are signposted on the friendly side with triangular red markers; the side nearer the enemy is only shown by a single strand of wire about knee high. The area will be fenced with a strand at ankle and waist height with the "Mines" inverted triangle every 20 metres. Minefield safe lanes will only be marked on the friendly side, and maximum use will be made of existing fences, so look at the signs, not at the type of fence.

Marking safe lanes is a tedious and labour-intensive job. The

US Army uses the Hunting Lightweight Marking System, a set of steel-tipped plastic poles and yellow reflective tape. The kit is man-portable and the pins are robust enough to be hammered through tarmac. Unfortunately, not all armies are so diligent: witness the way the Argentinians scattered mines all over the Falkland Islands without even keeping a proper record of their position.

Types of mines

Air-dropped mines

The Soviets mined many guerrilla infiltration routes in Afghanistan with air-dropped devices. Similar mines were used by the US Army in South-East Asia, and they will no doubt continue to be encountered in counter-insurgency campaigns throughout the world. They are quick to lay and highly effective: Italian VS50 mines can be dropped by helicopter at a rate of 2,000 per pass.

They are also the one type of minefield you can escape by rapid withdrawal from the area if you are unfortunate enough to have them dropped on your current position. Most air-dropped mines do not arm themselves for a couple of minutes, but you should make sure your identification is correct before hot-footing it away. Other characteristics of air-dropped mines are:

- Fuses can be delay, pressure or magnetic.
- Anti-tank and anti-personnel mines may be dropped together.
- Most will self-destruct within a few days or even hours, but do not bank on them all self-destructing at the same time. Mines that self-destruct can be useful for security forces, which can then sweep the area in safety after the mines have done their damage.

Soviet liquid mines

One type of scatterable mine introduced by the Soviets in Afghanistan deserves a mention, although its use creates some interesting moral problems. This particular kind are small plastic cells filled with liquid explosives, and are camouflaged or even shaped to look like transistor radios, dolls or other harmless items. They detonate when moved or compressed, and are thought to contain an unstable explosive similar to nitroglycerine, which is safer when frozen. They are yet another good reason to be alert to the presence of booby traps. Stay switched on even when there is no obvious danger.

Soviet anti-personnel mines

Before you launch yourself onto the battlefield you must have a thorough knowledge of Soviet/Russian/Eastern European mines that have been exported worldwide in the last thirty years, many of which have ended up in the hands of terrorists and rogue states.

The PFM-I AP mine/bomblet
Air delivered, plastic and filled with liquid explosive, this has a bulbous, irregularly-shaped body coloured green, sand or arctic white. Any distortion of the body will fire it; this includes light pressure while handling. It does not self-destruct and cannot be neutralized.

The PMD series
This wooden box has a hinged lid, overlapping the sides with a deep groove cut in it above the fuse assembly, and rests on the striker retaining pin. Some have a safety rod locking the lid.

Pressure on the lid forces the winged retaining nut from the striker and fires the mine.

OZM-4
Pressure, command or trip-wire detonated, this bounds 1.5-2.4 metres into the air and explodes showering fragments over a 50-metre diameter.

POMZ-2M
A wooden stake with cast iron fragmentation body, activated by trip-wire, this can be neutralized by securing the striker retaining pin and removing the wire. It is normally laid in clusters of three or four.

PMN

The rubber-covered pressure plate on top of this small plastic mine is secured to the body by a thin metal bank. The mine has a side hole for the firing mechanism and primer charge, opposite which is an initiator adaptor. The mine is armed 15-20 minutes after removing the safety pin.

TM-62

This is a family of anti-tank mines which come in plastic, metal, wood or waterproof cardboard casings and are detonated by 175-600 kg, so a man's weight will not usually set them off. They have a two-second delay, so the tank is well over the mine when it explodes.

TM-46

The commonest mine in Soviet service, this has a metal body and can be laid by hand or machine. It is pressure-plate-activated with an operating force of 210 kg.

TMN-46

Like the TM-46 this is activated by 210 kg pressure and can be fitted with a tilt rod fuse. The important difference is the extra fuse well in the bottom of the mine for booby-trapping.

TMD-B

This is a wooden box mine dating from the Second World War. The top three slats are pressure boards; the middle one is hinged to allow the fuse to be inserted. When armed, the pressure board is held in place with a wooden locking bar.

TMA-3

A Yugoslavian plastic mine with no metallic parts found all over the world, this is blast- and water-resistant. It has three fuse wells, and a fourth in the bottom for booby trapping. Operating weight is 180-350 kg.

MRUD anti-personnel mine

The Yugoslavian equivalent of the Claymore, this fires 650 steel balls over a 60-degree arc with a lethal radius of 50 metres. Activated by trip-wire or remote control, it will not damage tanks but will wreck soft-skin vehicles.

Mine injuries

One of the most widely encountered types of mine is the Soviet PMD series of wooden and anti-personnel mines. Simple to lay and difficult to detect, they are used by guerrilla forces all over the world. They are activated by pressure and were encountered by members of 22 SAS serving in Oman. It was observed that the local "Firqha" – tribesmen fighting for the government and officered by SAS personnel – suffered less damage than the SAS if they stepped on a mine: treading on a PMD generally led to the tribesman losing his toes, but SAS men in DMS or desert boots lost their whole foot at the ankle. British soldiers unfortunate enough to be wearing high-neck boots like the US Corcoran jump boots often lost their leg up to the knee. Mines, like all explosives, will take the line of least resistance.

Unfortunately it is not true to say that you can always minimize injury by swapping your combat boots for a pair of Ho Chi Minh sandals. In the Vietnam War, the tiny American "gravel" anti-personnel mines contained only a very small charge. It was enough to cripple someone wearing light footwear, but a hefty pair of boots would actually reduce the damage. Moral of the tale; find out what mines you may be facing and act accordingly.

Where to expect mines

Mines are frequently positioned in specific locations rather than laid in rows in a field like potatoes. Favourite sites are roads and trails, especially junctions and bottlenecks. They may have been placed to block one route while troops observe another, ready to engage a target with direct fire. In jungle or thick forest the available tracks are screamingly obvious places to choke with mines, forcing the enemy to hack his way noisily through the undergrowth.

Detecting Mines

Mines vary in scale from anti-personnel weapons such as the IJS "gravel" mine, shaped like and little bigger than a teabag, to massive anti-tank mines designed to pierce armour plate and destroy a 60-ton armoured vehicle. The sheer diversity of modern mines rules out any single answer to them. All you can do is to employ as many techniques and procedures as possible. Each one provides a degree of safety; combined, they can significantly weaken a powerful weapon.

Military counter-mine operations consist of detection of individual mines; breaching and clearing minefields; sowing a cleared enemy minefield with your own mines; prevention of enemy mining; and detection of enemy mine-laying. In combat you must make full use of all intelligence-gathering resources to obtain enemy mine information. This will enable you to plan the use of sensors, aggressive counter-mining or other tactics as necessary to defeat his efforts. There are a number of basic rules to surviving the mined battlefield:

Denial of opportunity

Aggressive patrolling prevents the enemy laying his mines. The effects of patrols can be increased with night vision aids and sentry or scout dogs. In addition, sensors can be used on major routes and areas where enemy mining is heavy; sensors can alert quick-reaction forces to move in on the threatened area, or can be used to bring fire on the enemy. However, US forces in Vietnam never really found an answer to local guerrillas mining the roads – the infantry manpower needed for intensive patrolling was seldom available. South African forces were painfully aware how easy it is to mine isolated roads near their borders, and consequently developed mine-resistant vehicles designed to survive anti-tank mines.

Denial of material

The enemy may rely on captured material for this conduct of mine warfare. This is especially true in guerrilla warfare: in

Vietnam, many Vietcong booby traps used captured American ordnance. VC sappers were also known to infiltrate American perimeters protected with Claymore mines and reverse them, so that they exploded in the wrong direction. Strict measures must be taken to deny the enemy all materials that can be used for mine warfare.

Intelligence
There must be a complete system for reporting mine incidents. Analysis of reports may be combined with communication intelligence sources. The purpose is to reveal areas of heavy mining by the enemy as well as the types of mines and firing devices used.

Training
Proper training reduces casualties from mines and booby traps. Intensive unit-level training should be conducted on how the enemy emplaces and camouflages these weapons.

Protective measures
These measures may include the wearing of body armour and helmets by sweep teams, sandbagging the flooring of vehicles and requiring the occupants to keep their arms and legs inside. In the South African Army it was a chargeable offence not to be strapped into your harness when riding in a Buffel-type APC. Soldiers on foot must avoid bunching up at the site of a mine detonation: the enemy may have placed other mines to take advantage of this natural tendency.

Search
Detection of mines is an action performed by soldiers in all phases of combat; search is a more deliberate action taken by single soldiers, teams or small units to locate mines or minefields. Do not wear sunglasses when looking for mines: with them you are less able to detect trip-wires and camouflage.

Be alert for trip-wires in these places:

• on the shoulders of roads at likely ambush sites

- near known or suspected anti-tank or anti-vehicle mines
- across the best route through dense plant growth
- in villages and on roads or paths into them
- in and around likely helicopter landing-sites
- in approaches to enemy positions
- at bridges, fords and ditches
- across rice paddy dikes

Check anything that might conceal a mine or its triggering device:

- mud smears, grass, sticks, dirt
- signs of road repair, for example new covering or paving, ditch and drainage work
- tyre marks, skid marks or ruts

Be alert for signs that might mark or point to hidden mines:

- signs on trees, posts or stakes, or signs painted on the road. Most are small and not easy to spot.
- marks other than signs – for instance, sticks or stones placed in a line, clumps of grass placed at intervals. Look for patterns not present in nature.
- wires leading away from the side of a road: they may be command firing wires.
- odd items in trees, branches or bushes – they may be explosive grenades, mortar rounds or artillery shells; odd features in the ground – for instance, wilting plant camouflage.
- Old ruts in the road are dangerous; stay out of them.
- Watch the civilians. They may know where local mines are, so see where they don't go – for instance, one side of the road or certain buildings.
- Be careful of any equipment left behind by, or belonging to the enemy: it may be booby-trapped.
- Listen for the sound of a delayed-fuse device. If you think you hear one get down – fast.
- Do not use any metal object as a probe; the metal can close the circuit between contacts. Use sharpened wooden sticks.
- When feeling for trip-wires, use a lightweight stick.

- Use scout dog teams to detect booby traps.
- Check all entrances (to buildings, caves, tunnels etc.) for booby traps, and search the approaches and surrounding area for anti-personnel mines.
- If you find an anti-tank mine, inspect by eye and probe for anti-handling devices.
- Remember that the enemy can use command detonated mines. Search and clear road shoulders and surrounding areas before other mine-clearing work. Make sure you cover all potential firing positions and remove any wires and booby traps. Buried firing wires can be exposed and cut by single-toothed rooters running along 10 to 50 metres from the road. Protect the clearing party with security forces.

Probing

Probing is a way of detecting mines by piercing the earth with a sharp but non-metallic object – e.g. a pointed stick. It is slow and hard work, but is probably the most reliable way to find mines.

When probing follow this procedure:

1. Move on your hands and knees or stay prone. Look and feel upward and forward for trip-wires or pressure prongs. Keep your sleeves rolled up and remove watches and rings – your sense of touch must be at its keenest.
2. After looking and feeling the ground, probe every five centimetres across a one-metre frontage. Press the probe gently into the ground at an angle of less than 45 degrees from horizontal. Never push the probe straight down or you may detonate a pressure mine.
3. If the probe won't go in freely, the soil must be picked away with the tip of the probe and the loose earth or stones removed by hand.
4. If you touch a solid object, stop probing, remove the earth by hand and check it out.
5. If you find a mine, remove just enough of the surrounding soil to see what type it is. Then report it.
6. As you probe your way forward, the cleared lane must be

marked for the following troops, and mines you have located must be clearly signposted.

Caution: If you know or suspect the enemy is using magnetically influenced fuses, make sure no-one is carrying anything made of iron or steel in the vicinity of the mines. This means no steel helmets, bayonets, rifles etc.

DETECTION
Remember:

The best way of detecting mines is by direct vision, combined with a knowledge of minelaying methods. On the principle of setting a thief to catch a thief, if you understand how to plant mines properly you will have a much better grasp of mine detection. Sweep teams made up of trained observers, men with electronic detectors, and probers have proved highly effective, but security forces must be deployed to the flanks and rear of sweep teams to avoid ambush. Mine and tunnel dogs have been used with success to detect booby traps, trip wires, unexploded ordnance, punji pits and arms caches, as well as enemy troops. These dogs should be used with other detection systems, not as a single system.

WEAPONRY

Special Forces soldiers are not only trained to use the weapons of their country and its allies, but are also familiarized with the armaments of the enemy. In a firefight, they may need to grab whatever is to hand. The range of armaments available to Special Forces soldiers is vast, and individual troopers may have personal favourites; that said, some arms are perennials among Special Forces soldiers of the West. If you are in the military or a reserve force take every opportunity to familiarize yourself with and practise with these weapons. If you are not yet in the military, read up on them: no-one ever failed selection for knowing too much about arms and military history. Be keen.

Heckler & Koch MP5

The Heckler & Koch machine pistol has been a staple of Special Forces since the GSG-9 Mogadishu rescue in 1977. Firing from a closed bolt, the MP5 is probably the most accurate sub-machine gun in production, which offsets its high-end price tag. It takes a 9 mm parabellum cartridge. Weight: 3 kg. Effective range: 200 m. Manufactured in a number of variants. The US Navy SEALs have a specially manufactured (N) version.

AK-47 Assault Rifle

Selective-fire, gas-operated 7.62 mm assault rifle, first developed in the Soviet Union by Mikhail Kalashnikov in 1947 (hence the "47"). The terrorist's weapon of choice, being available, cheap and ultra-reliable, it fires at 600 rpm on automatic. Indeed, its extraordinary ruggedness means that some Special Forces use it in adverse combat situations, notably "over the beach".

Remington 870 Tactical Shot Gun

A pump-action, 12-bore shotgun, which is the military version of the Remington 870, it comes in a wide range of configurations of different barrel lengths, stocks and manufacturing materials.

M870 shotguns are ideal when used for close-quarters battle (CQB) in urban environments.

Counter-terrorism teams such as 22 SAS and Delta Force assaulters use the M870 as a breaching shotgun. In this configuration, the M870, typically with a 10-inch barrel and with stock removed, is loaded with special breaching rounds which are used to shoot away door hinges and locks.

FN SCAR STD

Assault rifle chambered in 7.62 x 51 mm NATO calibre and fitted with 16-inch barrel as standard; this can be replaced with a short 13 barrel for close-quarter combat in less than five minutes. The rifle is then called SCAR-H CQC.

C8 Carbine SFW (Special Forces Weapon)

Canadian version of the US-made M4 carbine, the Diemaco (now Colt Canada) C8 SFW (Special Forces Weapon), has been used by the SAS since the late nineties, replacing the M16 as the regiment's primary assault rifles. The weapon was used by the regiment during the Operation Barras hostage rescue mission in 2000.

The C8 fires a 5.56 x 45 mm round and uses standard NATO 30-round magazines. The C8 is a versatile weapon capable of being fitted with a variety of scopes and attachments, including an underslung 40 mm grenade launcher. A shortened version (C8 CQB) is used for protection work.

Heckler & Koch G3

The G3 is a 7.62 mm automatic rifle developed in the 1950s by Heckler & Koch with the Spanish state-owned agency Centro de Estudios Tecnicos de Materiales Especiales (CETME). Based on CETME's 7.92 mm LV-50, it was engineered to take the NATO 7.62 mm round. H&K further modified it to fire in both semi-automatic and automatic firing modes. The weapon can be fitted with an optional four-position safety/fire selector that enables a three-round burst mode of fire. The sight is mechanically adjustable for both wind and elevation. The rifled barrel ends with a slotted flash suppressor, which can be used to attach a bayonet. It can also mount a 40 mm HK79 under-barrel grenade launcher.

Heckler & Koch 5.56 mm G36 Assault Rifle

In the early 1990s, Heckler & Koch designed a new assault rifle for the German Army and for export. It came up with the G36 5.56 mm assault rifle, which was adopted by the Bundeswehr, the Spanish Army, police departments around the world, and Special Forces (especially the compact G36 Commando version). It has an operating system similar to the old Armalite AR-18 rifle. A wide variety of firing mode combinations can be produced by installing the appropriate trigger unit: standard options are single-shot, fully automatic fire, two- or three-round bursts in any combination. A folding skeleton butt stock is standard, as are two scopes – a 3.5x telescope sight for accurate shooting at long range with, above it, a second red-dot sight for fast target acquisition at short ranges.

SIG Sauer P226

The Schweizerische Industrie Gesellschaft-Sauer P226 is a full-sized service pistol originally chambered for a 9 mm Luger round. It was designed for the 1984 US trials as a replacement for the M1911A1. The Beretta 92SB-F won on cost, but the P226 performed so well that it was taken up by the US Navy and, when delivered to a higher specification, adopted by the SEALs. It is also used by 22 SAS.

Browning Hi-Power

A pistol with pedigree, being originally commissioned by the French Army from John Moses Browning himself. First produced in Belgium, on the Nazi occupation of that country it was issued to the Wehrmacht as Pistole 640(b); the Hi-Power (sometimes

High Power) has long been popular with covert operations groups such as the SAS.

AW50

The Accuracy International AW50 (L121A1) sniper rifle can, when loaded with appropriate ammunition, become an anti-material weapon capable of neutralizing a variety of hard and soft targets. The penetrating power of the AW50 means it can be used to engage targets hiding behind cover.

M72 66 mm LAW

The M72 Light Anti-Tank Weapon is the portable, one-shot replacement for the bazooka. It comprises a rocket packed inside a launcher that is made up of two tubes, one inside the other, the outer one being both container and firing mechanism. To fire the LAW, the inner tube is telescoped out towards the rear. As the warhead emerges from the tube, fins spring out from the base to stabilize its flight. The launcher is then discarded. The high-explosive anti-tank shell is activated on impact.

FIM-92 Stinger

The American-built FIM-92 Stinger is a shoulder-held anti-aircraft launcher of heat-seeking missiles. It is used widely by Special Forces, conventional and guerrilla forces. The supplying of Stingers to the Afghan Mujahideen in the 1980s enabled them to turn the war against the Soviet occupiers.

M249 5.56 mm Machine Gun

Gas-operated, air-cooled, with a quick-change barrel, allowing the gunner to rapidly replace an overheated or jammed barrel. A folding bipod is attached near the front of the gun. The M249 can be fed from both linked ammo and M4 magazines.

FN Herstal 5.56 mm Minimi Light Machine Gun

The Minimi, developed by the Fabrique Nationale (FN), was originally designed for the 7.62 x 51 mm NATO round, and later redesigned around the 5.56 mm cartridge. However, at the request of USSOCOM, FN has recently revived the more powerful 7.62 mm version in several different configurations.

FN Herstal 7.62mm MAG General-Purpose Machine Gun

MAG stands for Mitrailleuse d'Appui General, or "general-purpose machine gun". Based on earlier Browning designs, the FN MAG is ultra-reliable under all conditions. In a US Army test, it was discovered that it could fire an average of 26,000 rounds before failure. During the assault on Goose Green in the Falklands War, British paratroopers were forced to fire over 8,000 rounds without significant pause to change the barrels. The weapon has three different settings for the rate of fire: 750, 850, and 950 rpm.

Beretta 9 x 19 mm Model 92 Pistol

The Beretta 92 is a series of semi-automatic pistols designed and manufactured by Beretta of Italy from 1972. In 1985, the Beretta 92SB-F was adopted as the standard sidearm of the United States military as the M9; in 2005, the US Marine Corps placed an order with Beretta for 3,480 M9A1 pistols, a new variant with an accessory rail.

SEAL Knife 2000

Properly the SOG S37 SEAL Knife, this tactical knife was subjected to (and passed) one of the most stringent evaluations ever undertaken by the US government, which included sharpness, edge-retention, breaking-limit, not to mention immersion in salt water, petrol and fire. It has a 7-inch serrated blade. Weight: 12.6 ounces.

Glock 17

One of a family of handguns made by Glock GmbH of Austria, this is a 9 mm pistol employed by several Western Special Forces. Has a capacity of 17+ rounds, which is part of its attraction. Delta Force also use the Glock 22, a full-size pistol chambered in .40.

MEDICAL SKILLS

All Special Forces troopers receive a thorough grounding in medical and health skills (and some will go on to become medical specialists). After all, it is the indispensable condition of being a warrior that you can look after yourself and your buddies. Also, since the 1960s, part of the 'hearts and minds' approach of Special Forces has required operatives to give medical and health advice to the people they work amongst.

Field Sanitation

In war, the number of casualties due to enemy action has always been exceeded by the number caused by illness, and similar problems often arise on expeditions and military exercises. Very often this is due to bad hygiene that leads to stomach upsets and diarrhoea. You can avoid illness by taking proper preventive measures. You must be fit to start with, maintain personal hygiene and change into clean clothes as often as possible. Pay attention to food and water, and dispose of waste carefully.

General Health

Before setting out on any form of expedition or training you must be in good general health: if you are suffering from flu or a stomach upset, for example, these are likely to get worse. Also, if you are suffering from or just recovering from an infectious disease you may get worse yourself and will almost certainly pass it on to others. Make sure your teeth and gums are in good condition. Many a soldier on operations or training has had to be evacuated because of dental trouble.

Personal hygiene

1. Keep as clean as possible, paying particular attention to your feet: these must be washed daily and dusted with powder.
2. Clean your teeth regularly. If you don't have a toothbrush and paste use a twig and salted water.
3. Continue to shave every day, even though it's easier not to bother. But avoid after-shave, not just for practical reasons but because it will dry on your skin and make it sore.
4. Change into clean clothes as often as possible, and change your socks every day. Natural fibres such as wool and cotton will breathe and allow sweat to evaporate. If you are out for any length of time you will have to wash your clothes: you can buy traveller's clothes-washing liquid in a tube, which will work in cold water.

Urinal

Dig a pit, fill with stones or gravel and cover, but insert a wide tube or funnel. This sort of pit allows urine to drain quickly into the earth rather than create a foul-smelling swamp in camp. Place some obvious marker on the spot so you can find it at night.

Water

In Britain and the USA you can drink tap water, but this is not necessarily the case in the rest of the world. Even in Europe, although most indoor taps are safe, those in farmyards may not be.

Never assume that river or stream water is safe, even if it looks clear. Any water that you cannot be sure about must be purified by boiling or by adding water-purification tablets. These will be on issue or you can buy them from camping shops.

All water that is used for drinking and cooking should be treated. It is not necessary to purify water for washing, but avoid it if it's obviously polluted.

Field latrines

Shallow trench latrines are one way of dealing with the approximately 350 kg of faeces produced every day by an infantry battalion. This assumes the troops are eating the 24-hour ration pack, which tends to bung you up. If fresh food was available then the quantity would increase. The 5- or 6-metre deep, water-filled medieval-style pit works fine until some idiot pours disinfectant in, killing the bacteria that make the pit work.

HEALTH IN COLD CONDITIONS

Working in a cold climate can cause major health problems. The physical effects of cold cause real difficulties, but in addition the loss of morale caused by the cold can in itself lead to further trouble. Problems with the cold are not confined to the Arctic or mountain regions. They also happen in relatively mild climates, especially when associated with wetness. Exposure causes a substantial number of casualties and even some deaths on exercises in the UK.

Illnesses

Hypothermia

Simply means sub-normal body temperature. It is often called exposure when it happens outside and hypothermia when it affects old people indoors, but it is the same thing. There are a number of factors that may lead to it:

1. *Lack of food:* Food provides the energy for the body to produce heat. To combat cold, the calorific value of the food needs to be increased. Lack of food will lower the ability to cope with cold.
2. *Poor clothing:* In cold weather, you need extra clothing. Multiple layers that trap air are the most effective way of retaining body heat. You lose a lot of heat through your head and feet, so make sure you have proper headgear and footwear.
3. *Dirty clothing:* Wet, damp and dirty clothing is a poor insulator and increases heat loss. Keep your clothes clean, and remove damp or wet clothing during rest periods and dry it out. This applies particularly to footwear: socks must be changed and boots allowed to dry as much as possible.
4. *Alcohol:* Alcohol causes the blood vessels in the skin to dilate which increases heat loss. Alcohol may make you feel warmer, but in reality it has the opposite effect.

The treatment for hypothermia requires the casualty to be warmed slowly. Change any wet clothes and place him in a warm environment in a bed or sleeping bag. It may be necessary for someone else to get in as well to provide gentle heat. Cover his head to reduce heat loss. Moderately hot, sweet drinks will provide energy and gradually raise the temperature. *Do not give alcohol.* Evacuate the casualty as soon as possible.

Snow blindness

This is a temporary blindness caused by direct and reflected light. Snow is a very good reflector and will exacerbate the effects of the sun. The eyes become sensitive to glare, blinking increases, and the eyes begin to water and feel irritable. Sight begins to have a pinkish tinge and eventually the vision is covered by what appears to be a red curtain. At the same time the pain increases, so it can be a very frightening condition. Fortunately, the eyes will recover, given time, if they are covered with pads and rested. It can be avoided altogether by wearing proper sunglasses.

Sunburn
Just as the light effects of the sun on the eyes are increased in snow, so are the tanning effects on exposed skin. You may need to use cream, especially on your lips.

Frostbite
Frostbite is what happens when body tissues freeze, and it is your extremities that are most vulnerable to attack. Unfortunately the onset of frostbite can often go unnoticed until it is too late. The freezing prevents body fluids reaching the affected tissues, and they will eventually die. When this happens they will slowly turn black and drop off, but the damage is done long before this stage is reached. In the early stages the affected parts are cold, firm, numb and marble white. It is essential to recognize frostbite at this stage to avoid lasting damage.

To treat frostbite, use body heat to warm the affected part, while encasing the whole body in a sleeping bag. Hot drinks may be given and the casualty should then be evacuated.

DO NOT:

1. Rub the injured part.
2. Expose the injured part to fire or similar heat.
3. Exercise the injured part.

Frostbite can be prevented if the proper clothing is worn, especially on the hands and feet, which are the parts most at risk.

Immersion foot
Immersion foot, also known as trench foot, is caused by a lack of blood circulation and prolonged exposure to wet conditions. There are three stages:

1. The feet become white, numb and cold.
2. The feet become red, hot and painful.
3. The feet can become swollen, develop cellulitis (a form of inflammation) and eventually gangrene.

Prevention involves various measures:

1. Keep your circulation going by exercise.
2. Do not restrict your circulation with tight trousers or with tight binding round the bottom of trousers.
3. Keep your feet as dry as possible.
4. Change socks daily and use powder on your feet.
5. Keep your feet clean.

Properly cared-for feet should give you little trouble. Should someone exhibit the symptoms of immersion foot:

1. Remove boots and socks and warm and dry the casualty's feet, handling them gently. Do not rub or massage them or expose them to fire.
2. Elevate the feet.
3. Put the casualty into a sleeping bag.
4. Give hot drinks.
5. Give Paracetamol.
6. Evacuate the casualty as a stretcher case.

Health Overseas

A lot of military training is still carried out overseas. Years ago, troops went out by sea, and the long voyage would give them time to acclimatize to the tropical environment. Nowadays, flying out means that you can be deposited in a tropical country without any period of acclimatization. Heat-related illness can be a danger even without exceptionally hot weather. Strenuous training when unfit in warm weather can cause it – and heat exhaustion can kill.

Body temperatures

The body temperature must be maintained close to its norm of about 37'C to stay healthy. In addition to heat from the sun, and reflected heat from the sun, and reflected heat from the ground and surrounding objects, any physical activity produces heat. To maintain the normal body temperature, this heat must be lost. This is done by sweating, which causes heat to be released from the body as it evaporates. In a climate where the temperature is over 30°C a man may lose 10-15 litres of sweat a day, even without exerting himself. This amount of water needs to be replaced.

In addition to the water loss, there will be salt lost in your sweat. If the body is not acclimatized, this loss can be serious and can result in heat cramps. Salt added to food should be sufficient to replace this, but it should not be added to water without medical advice. There is, however, a safe alternative which can be added to your water bottle. This is Dioralyte, a compound of the minerals and salts lost through sweating, commonly used in the rehydration of patients suffering from diarrhoea.

Prevention of heat illness

It is much easier to prevent heat illness than to treat it.

Acclimatization

A period of acclimatization helps the body to adjust to the heat; the main effect is to reduce the salt loss in the sweat to about half its previous levels. The blood vessels on the skin dilate, so increasing the amount of heat loss. This normally takes about three weeks.

Fluid intake

No-one can be trained to do without water; it is dangerous and will make you ill. Obviously, though, your liquid intake does not have to be restricted to pure water. Fruit juices and tea are just as good. Be careful with alcoholic drinks, since alcohol is a diuretic and causes you to pass more fluid as urine than you take in. It is possible to raise your body fluid levels before an arduous exercise by drinking more than normal (but not alcohol) in the 12 to 24 hours before the start of the exercise.

Shelter
Your shelter should be light in colour to reflect the heat, and should allow air to circulate and provide shade.

General health
Your general health is important. Personal hygiene is essential, and you must pay particular attention to your skin and feet. If you're overweight your body will be less able to respond effectively to heat; strenuous physical activity can cause heat illness even in temperate climates for those who are unfit or unused to it.

Heat Illnesses

Sunburn
Sunburn is a form of superficial burn that can be prevented. One day in the sun will not give you a tan, but it could give you serious burns. Wear clothes that cover as much of your skin as possible, and do not spend too much time in the sun; half an hour on the first day is more than enough.

Prickly heat
Some people are more susceptible than others to this irritable condition of the skin. Your skin needs to be kept very clean, but soap can make it worse, so rinse it off thoroughly after washing. Hair must also be regularly washed but well rinsed. Loose clean clothing should be worn, including clean underclothes.

Heat cramps
Heat cramps are caused by a lack of salt. They can happen in any part of your body and can be quite severe, but are easily prevented by ensuring that there is adequate salt in your diet. If they do occur, seek medical advice.

Heat exhaustion

This can happen when you're working hard in relatively high temperatures, and is more likely to happen if you're overweight or unfit. Excessive sweating causes abnormal fluid and salt loss, leading to circulatory failure. This results in

1. Headache, nausea and dizziness.
2. Pale, clammy skin.
3. Weak, rapid pulse progressing to hot, flushed, dry skin and full, bounding pulse.
4. Cramps. The casualty will have the signs of shock plus heat cramps. The body temperature may be normal or slightly raised. If not treated, the casualty may become unconscious.

To treat heat exhaustion lie the casualty down in a cool place. Remove as much of their clothing as possible and give them frequent drinks of water to which salt has been added; half a teaspoon of salt or sodium bicarbonate to a litre. Get them to drink as much as you can and get medical help as soon as possible. In combat, if the casualty is unconscious, insert the rectal drip set to restore the fluid balance, since at least 60% of water is absorbed by the colon.

Heatstroke

Heatstroke is a very serious condition that if not recognized and treated quickly can result in severe brain damage and death. The heat regulating mechanism of the body ceases to work and the temperature keeps on rising. The brain literally cooks. The signs of heatstroke include:

1. Disturbed behaviour
2. Delirium, partial loss of consciousness and coma
3. Tiredness, headache and irritability
4. Nausea and vomiting
5. Reduced or absence of sweating
6. Strong, bounding pulse
7. Hot, flushed and dry skin

The casualty's temperature must be reduced by whatever means are possible. He should be moved into a cool, dry place and have his clothing removed, and then be sponged down with tepid water, or if possible wrapped in a wet sheet. In both cases, fan the body to assist cooling. Give frequent small drinks of water. Get him proper medical help without any delay.

First aid in combat

If you get hit, sort yourself out if you can. Otherwise, whoever gets to you first will help you. In a tactical situation lightly wounded men can carry on fighting after being given first aid, and must be encouraged to do so.

Each section contains a combat medic who is trained in combat first aid; he is, however, primarily a rifleman and may well become a casualty himself. So you must not only know the life-saving techniques, but be practised in their use. There is nothing worse than watching one of your mates die because you don't have the skill or the knowledge to save him. Dealing with a casualty while in contact with the enemy will be covered in the orders issued before every operation. But the following applies in general to various phases of war.

The attack

Once you are across the effective fire line, winning the firefight and fire-and-manoeuvring forward, you cannot afford to stop. If someone gets hit and you are near him there is a strong temptation to go and help, especially if he is making a lot of noise. The result is that more and more people are drawn into casualty handling, less fire goes down on the enemy and his fire gets heavier and more accurate.

As more people get hit, you lose the firefight and the attack fails. Withdrawing from the EFL is as expensive as fighting through, so you might as well remove the source of injury by killing the enemy and let your reserve platoons give first aid as they move up behind you.

Patrols

Casualties incurred on the route out will be left with a guard, if your patrol has sufficient strength, and the standby patrol will be tasked to collect them. If you're on the route back, you take your casualties with you. If you're in contact with the enemy, you must take your casualties back with you as you break contact. If you are going to leave them, you must be 100% sure that they are dead.

Generally recce patrols will not be large enough to take many casualties and go on with the mission. Fighting patrols are intended for combat and are therefore large enough to take casualties.

Defence

If someone in a four-man main battle trench gets hit, one of the others gives first aid while the remaining two continue to fire. If, however, the enemy has closed to within grenade-chucking distance, it's not a good idea for anyone to stop firing.

Do not move around the position to help other trenches unless you have dug communication trenches. Forward slope positions are very difficult to move casualties back from, compared to reverse slope. The best approach is to carry out immediate first aid in situ and make the casualty as comfortable as possible in the shelter bay until rounds stop flying.

Internal security

The terrorist or insurgent uses casualties to create more casualties; he will aim to injure or kill one man or unit to draw the remainder into an ambush, or near command-detonated mines or a sniper. Watch out!

The Four Bs

When carrying out first aid, remember the four Bs – Breathing, Bleeding, Breaks and Burns. Be positive and don't fiddle about.

First of all decide which casualty to treat first. The order of priority of injuries to treat is:

1. Stoppage of breathing
2. Bleeding wounds
3. Broken bones
4. Burns

Remember also that the casualty who is making the most noise is rarely the most seriously injured; don't make the mistake of treating a broken leg while a head injury case quietly dies.

You must deal with breathing first, because if a casualty has an obstructed airway and cannot breathe he will die, however well you treat his other injuries. The human brain starts to suffer permanent damage after about four minutes without oxygen, so you must get a casualty breathing again as quickly as you can.

For all casualties:

1. Assess the tactical situation; do not endanger yourself. If the enemy are still in business continue firing, keep under cover and look out for falling masonry, mines, booby traps etc. If a vehicle is involved, switch off the fuel supply.
2. Assess the casualty; check him out completely and remove him from danger if possible. At least drag him into cover, and give protection if necessary from chemical weapons.
3. Deal with priorities – remember the four Bs.
4. Reassure the casualty, no matter how revolting his injury, and tell him what you are doing while you work on him.
5. Try to keep him warm and dry.
6. Give morphine only for pain.
7. Never leave the casualty alone.
8. Take the casualty's ammo and any specialist equipment he may be carrying.

WHEN YOU COME ACROSS A CASUALTY
1. LOOK
2. LISTEN

3. THINK
4. ACT

The unconscious casualty
You must place an unconscious casualty in such a position that no further harm will come to him. An unattended, unconscious casualty can easily die by choking to death on his own vomit. To keep his airway clear, place him in the recovery position. Tuck his nearside hand under his body and the other over his chest. Cross the far foot over the nearer one. Then, supporting his head with one hand, grasp his clothing on his hip and roll him towards you. Check that his airway remains clear, and make sure that he cannot roll right over onto his front and that his neck stays extended. By placing him in this position his airway will stay clear even if he vomits, and he will not swallow his tongue. Check his pulse every fifteen minutes and examine the rest of his body for obvious injuries. Casevac an unconscious casualty as soon as you can, and never leave him alone.

Remember that anyone with neck or spinal injuries must not be moved, and you will need further assistance.

Breathing

Check his mouth
A casualty with an obstructed airway may have stopped breathing completely, but you are more likely to find him choking. First, look into the casualty's mouth and extract anything obstructing his throat. You must not be squeamish: remove whatever is there, even if it is covered with blood or vomit. Sometimes the tongue can fall back and block the throat. You clear the casualty's airway by extending his neck; with him flat on his back, tilt his head right back. If he doesn't start to breathe then you must resuscitate him; otherwise, treat him as an unconscious casualty.

There are five main causes of an obstructed airway:

1. Suffocation
2. Teeth, including false teeth
3. Swelling of the mouth or throat

4. Blood, water or vomit
5. Bone or tissue injuries

Resuscitation Techniques

CAUTION

These techniques can harm a casualty if improperly performed. The information given here is for familiarisation only and formal training should be obtained before you attempt to use them.

Exhaled Air Resuscitation (EAR)

This is the best way to get a casualty breathing again, and is best learned on the Resusci Anne type of dummy: do not practise on another person. Here are the steps to follow for EAR:

Is he asleep? First, make sure that the casualty is indeed not breathing. This may seem obvious, but there have been cases of people trying to resuscitate someone who is simply asleep. Look carefully at the casualty. Is he/she unconscious? Can you wake him up? If not, is his chest moving?

Do not spend too long making up your mind: every moment is vital. Follow the procedure given here, and make sure the casualty's chest is rising each time you blow. If it isn't, you are not doing it correctly.

1 *Pulse*: Check the casualty's pulse at his carotid artery. If his heart has stopped you will need to perform cardiac compression as well as resuscitation.

2 *Airway*: To perform resuscitation, place the casualty on his back and extend his neck by tilting his head back. Check his airway and remove any obstructions. Loosen any tight clothing around his neck.

3 *Inflate his chest*: Pinch his nose, take a deep breath and breathe hard into his mouth, hard enough to make his chest rise. Then remove your mouth and allow his chest to fall. Repeat every six seconds and continue until he begins to breathe. If EAR is still not working, check that his airway is still clear and that his neck is extended properly.

Don't be squeamish. The most difficult part of EAR is getting started. The casualty may have other injuries; there may be blood and vomit in and around his mouth. He may even be dead. But apart from a quick wipe around his mouth there is no time to be lost; without prompt EAR, the casualty will die.

When the heart stops. If a casualty has stopped breathing his heart may have stopped too. When you first examine the casualty, check his pulse by feeling the side of his windpipe; you should be able to feel the carotid artery at work. This is the best place to check, as a weak pulse is difficult to detect at the wrist.

External Cardiac Compression (ECC)

1 *Check pulse*: Check the casualty's pulse at his carotid artery and if there is no pulse commence ECC. NEVER perform ECC on someone whose heart is still beating.
2 *Position*: Position the casualty as for EAR; neck extended and airway clear. Now find the lower end of the sternum (breastbone).
3 *Your hands*: With both your hands palm down, place one on top of the other with the fingers interlaced. Place the heel of the lower hand three fingers width up from the bottom of the sternum.
4 *Commence compression*: Push down with the weight of your body, pushing the casualty's breastbone towards his spine. Lift your hand to allow the chest to recoil. Repeat 60 times per minute, checking the pulse every fifth push.

WARNING
You must never practise External Cardiac Compression on a real person: it is very dangerous. Never start or continue to give cardiac massage to a casualty whose heart is beating, no matter how faintly.

Combining EAR and ECC
If someone's heart has stopped beating, their breathing will soon cease and you will have to carry out artificial respiration as well as cardiac massage. Ideally, two people should treat the casualty;

one doing EAR and the other ECC. However, you might have to do both on your own until help arrives. If you do, then use fifteen compressions of the heart to two expansions of the chest. Remember to keep the airway clear.

Bleeding

When you've got the casualty breathing again, you can turn your attention to controlling any bleeding – the second most common cause of death from injury. Bleeding may be in the form of a slow ooze from the very smallest of blood vessels, or a much more rapid loss from a major vessel. If it's spurting out, it is coming from an artery and this is very serious. Occasionally, bleeding stops of its own accord, either from retraction of the blood vessels or clotting of the blood, but this is likely only with small or superficial wounds.

First steps

These simple measures will help to control bleeding in most cases. Points 2 and 4 apply to injured limbs. The most important factor in dealing with bleeding is speed! But make sure that you are treating the most serious wound. Check over the whole body and, in the case of gunshot wounds, do not expect the exit hole to be in line with the entry point.

1 *Place the casualty in a comfortable position*: This reduces the blood flow, as his heart will be making less effort to pump blood.
2 *Raise the limb*: This also reduces the bleeding, but think carefully before doing this in case you cause further injury. If in doubt, don't!
3 *Apply pressure to the bleeding wound*: This will often stop the bleeding completely. Place a dressing over the wound and apply pressure with the palm of your hand. Make sure the dressing is big enough, and use a sterile one if available; but any piece of clean material will do. If you can't find a dressing big enough to cover the wound, press it down where the bleeding is worst. If bleeding continues despite pressure,

apply a second dressing on top of the first. Do not lift the first one to see what is happening! You can apply up to three dressings, and none should be removed until the casualty gets to hospital.

4 *Immobilize the limb.*

Pressure Points

Any place where an artery crosses a bone close to the skin is a pressure point: pressure applied at these areas will, in theory, interrupt the blood flow. If the pressure point is between the heart and the bleeding point, you may be able to stop the flow altogether.

In practice, only two pressure points are of much use: the brachial (upper inner arm) and femoral (groin) areas. Direct, firm pressure at these points can be used to stop bleeding in the arms and legs. To carry out the procedure:

1. Place the thumb or fingers over the pressure point.
2. Apply sufficient pressure to stop the blood flow and hence the bleeding.
3. After 15 minutes, slowly release the pressure.
4. If bleeding has stopped dress the wound.
5. If bleeding starts again, repeat the process.

The release of pressure after 15 minutes is essential to allow blood to reach the tissues beyond the pressure point; if this is not done they may be damaged. Resist the temptation to release pressure in under 15 minutes to see how you are getting on, as bleeding will not yet have been controlled.

Internal bleeding

Internal bleeding is harder to deal with. It may have been caused by a severe blow to the abdomen, a crush injury to the chest, or by the blast effects of an explosion. Also, if a bone is broken, especially a large one such as the femur (thigh bone), there will be bleeding in the surrounding tissue.

Internal bleeding can cause any or all of the following symptoms:
1　Pallor
2　Cold, clammy skin
3　Rapid, weak pulse
4　Restlessness and weakness

Treatment is difficult and depends on rapid evacuation to hospital. In the meantime, talk to the casualty and make him as warm and comfortable as you can.

Chest wounds
Chest injuries can be very serious and must be recognized and treated urgently; prompt evacuation to proper medical care is essential. You can treat superficial injuries like any other wound, with a clean dressing, but watch out for these serious problems.

Crush injuries
The casualty may have fractured ribs, often in several places. At the site of the injury the chest wall will no longer be rigid, and breathing becomes difficult as the chest is no longer effective in pumping air in and out of the lungs. Worse, air could be getting moved from one side of the chest and back again rather than up and down the windpipe. The casualty tries to overcome this by taking deeper breaths, which only makes matters worse.

Look for the following symptoms:

1. Abnormal movement of the chest.
2. Painful and difficult breathing.
3. Distress and anxiety.
4. Cyanosis (blueness) of the lips and mouth.
5. Signs of shock.

The aim of the treatment is to stop the abnormal movement of the chest wall. If the casualty is unconscious, you should:

1. Check and clear his airway.
2. Place him in the three-quarters prone position.
3. Place a hand over the injured area to provide support.

4. Place a layer of padding over the area and secure it with a firm, broad bandage.
5. Treat for shock.

If he is conscious, carry out steps 3 and 4 with him sitting upright.

Open chest wounds

If the wound is severe enough there may be a hole in the chest wall. Air will get in and the lung will collapse, and air will go in and out of the hole instead of up and down the windpipe.

Look for the following symptoms:

1. Shallow and difficult breathing.
2. The sound of air being sucked in and out of the chest wall.
3. Bloodstained fluid bubbling from the wound.
4. Cyanosis of the lips and mouth.
5. Signs of shock.

The treatment aims is to prevent the air going in and out of the chest wall. Quite simply, you must plug the hole. Whether the casualty is conscious or unconscious you should:

1. Make sure his airway is clear
2. Seal the hole in his chest by placing a large dressing over the wound and fixing it in place with a firm, broad bandage. Make sure it completely covers the wound, forming a seal.
3. Place the casualty on the injured side to help maintain the seal.
4. Treat for shock.

Bleeding into the chest

Crush or open wounds may be accompanied by bleeding into the chest. It may also happen without obvious external signs of injury, particularly following an explosion when the casualty suffers what is known as blast injury.

You should suspect bleeding into the chest if the casualty:

1. Shows signs of shock.
2. Is coughing up blood.
3. Has difficulty in breathing.

Unfortunately there is very little a first-aider can do to treat internal bleeding into the chest apart from general measures for the treatment of shock. The important thing is to recognize that there is a problem and arrange for urgent evacuation.

Abdominal Wounds

The abdomen, the part of the body between the chest and the pelvis, is often mistakenly referred to as the stomach. The stomach is just one of the contents of the abdomen; other important organs are the bowels, liver, spleen, kidneys and bladder. An abdominal injury may result in severe shock, and the majority of cases will require surgery. As well as injury to internal organs there may be considerable internal bleeding. A further cause of trouble is infection, which is particularly likely if the gut is penetrated or torn.

First aid treatment is very simple. All you can do is make the patient comfortable and cover the wound.

The symptoms of an abdominal wound are usually obvious. Part of the guts may be sticking out. There may be severe bruising to the abdomen or lower chest, back or groin. The injury may be the result of a direct blow, or the casualty may have suffered a blast injury. Other signs are:

1. Pain or tenderness in the abdomen.
2. Vomiting, which may contain blood.
3. Tense abdominal muscles.
4. Shock.

The treatment begins by making the casualty lie down on his back with his knees drawn up. This will help to relax the muscles and ease the strain on the abdomen. If the patient is not suffering too much shock, the head and shoulders may also be raised.

Cover the wound with a clean dressing. If any guts or tissues are sticking out, don't try to push them back in; just leave them as they are and cover with the dressing. Also, don't try to remove the debris from the wound or you will make matters worse.

Do not give the casualty any food or drink, but protect him from further injury and from wind and rain and keep him warm. Arrange for speedy evacuation.

WARNING:
Casualties with abdominal wounds should not be given anything by mouth.

Breaks (Fractures)

After you've dealt with the casualty's breathing and bleeding, the third priority is broken bones. Fractured bones can cause serious injury or death, but can often be successfully treated and a complete recovery achieved. A great deal depends on the first aid you give the casualty before he is evacuated for treatment. Before he can be moved you must immobilize the fracture; the basic principle of splinting is to immobilize the joints above and below the break.

Immobilizing
You must keep the fracture still to prevent the sharp edges of the broken bone moving about. This achieves three things:

1. Stops further damage to tissue, muscle, blood vessels and nerves.
2. Reduces pain and shock.
3. Stops a closed fracture becoming an open one because of bone fragments penetrating the skin.

Rules for splinting
1. Remove watches, rings and garments from the limb, or these may reduce the flow of blood to the hand or foot when the injured part becomes swollen.
2. If the tactical situation allows it, splint the fractured part before moving the casualty and without any change in the

position of the fractured part. If a bone is in an unnatural position or a joint is bent, leave it as it is.

   If circumstances force you to move a casualty with fractures in his lower body before you can apply a splint, tie the injured leg to his other leg. Grasp the casualty beneath his armpits and pull him in a straight line. Do not roll him or move him sideways.

3. Apply the splint so that the joint above the fracture and the joint below the fracture are completely immobilized.
4. Place some padding between the splint and the injured area. This is especially important between the legs, in the armpits and in areas where the splint rests against the bony parts such as the wrist, knee or ankle joint.
5. Bind the splint with bandages in several places above and below the fracture but not so tightly that it interferes with the flow of blood. Do not bandage across the fracture. Tie bandages with a non-slip knot against the splint.

Signs and symptoms
Symptoms of a fracture include pain when slight pressure is applied to the injured area, and sharp pain when the casualty tries to move the area. Do not move him or encourage him to move in order to identify the fracture, because the movement could cause further damage and lead to shock. Other signs are swelling, unnatural movement of the limb, bruising and crepitus (the distinctive sound of fractured bone ends grating together).

Types of fracture
1. *Open fracture*: An open fracture is a break in the bone and in the overlying skin and flesh. The broken bone may have punctured the skin or a bullet may have penetrated the skin and broken the bone.
2. *Closed fracture*: In a closed fracture the bone is broken but the skin remains intact. There may be tissue damage and the area is likely to swell and later bruise. It may only be a sprain, but you should assume the worst and treat it like a fracture.

If you have nothing to construct a splint with, immobilize an injured arm by securing it to the casualty's chest. Slings can be improvised from belts or bits of shirts or blankets. Remember to put some padding between the splint and the injured arm.

Burns

Burns are the last of the four Bs. They are an increasingly common type of injury, particularly in tactical military situations where damage to vehicles often results in fire or explosions. Burns range from the superficial and small to those involving extensive tissue damage. People with extensive deep bums may eventually die from them, but the great majority of fire deaths result from damage to the lungs by smoke and fumes or by the heat of the fire. People who have this sort of damage may have little or nothing in the way of visible breathing. In these cases you should try expired air resuscitation until medical help can be obtained, but unfortunately this is often unsuccessful. However, that's no reason for not trying.

NEVER APPLY BUTTER OR SIMILAR FAT: THIS WILL INSULATE THE AREA AND CAUSE FURTHER DAMAGE.

Types of burn
Burns used to be described as first, second or third degree, but this system is no longer used; burns are now classified as superficial, or deep. Superficial burns will appear red, swollen and tender.

Treatment
If the casualty is on fire your first priority is to extinguish the flames Use water if available, or a blanket to smother the flames. If indoors and the building is not at risk, stay inside. Rushing out would only make the flames worse. If he is not, the first thing to do, as with any injury, is to remove the casualty from the source of danger. Hopefully, someone else will extinguish the fire, while you deal with him.

Wrap the casualty in a heavy material which will not catch fire and lay him on the ground. Then remove any clothing which has been soaked in boiling fluid, but do not remove burnt or charred clothing unless it is continuing to be a source of heat. If clean water is available immerse the burn area to cool it. This reduces further heat damage and reduces the pain.

A burn is a wound like any other, and is treated in the same way – with a clean dressing. Cover the whole area to prevent infection getting in and more fluid leaking out. Burns can cause extensive fluid loss, and this must be reduced as much as possible. Leave any blisters intact; they are performing a useful function in keeping fluid in. They may be removed later in hospital, but it's not a first aid job. Also, do not attempt to remove any burnt skin.

Deep burns will be surrounded by very red skin and be blistered and swollen. In the most serious instances the skin may be pale and waxy and even charred. Even the smallest burn can be very painful, but paradoxically, some large deep burns can be surprisingly pain-free because the nerve endings have been burnt away.

Splints and slings may help to keep the patient comfortable and will therefore reduce pain. Prepare them in the same way as for fractures.

SIX STEPS FOR DEALING WITH BURNS

1. If the casualty's clothing is on fire, lay him down and extinguish the flames with water, a fire bucket or similar heavy material that will cut off the air from the fire.
2. Cool the burn area using clean water or other harmless liquid – for example, milk, beer, etc. It is important to stop the "cooking" effect of the heat: do not apply fat, cream or ointments.
3. Cover the burn with a sterile dressing.
4. Do not break any blisters or remove burnt clothing (unless it is hot).
5. If the casualty has facial burns, make a mask with a

clean dry cloth, and cut holes for nose, mouth and
eyes.
6. Immobilize a badly burned limb as for a fracture.

Field first aid – improvisation

There might come a time when your oppo has been hit and you
haven't got the kit to help him. But most "official" first-aid kit is
unnecessary, so you should not be tempted to burden yourself
with a vast collection of equipment. Every soldier is trained in
first aid. The only pieces of equipment he carries are dressings;
everything else has got to be improvised.

Dressings

A field dressing is a large pad of gauze with a bandage attached;
ideally it should be in a sterile packet, and each soldier should
carry at least three. A lot of dressings that are commercially available are frankly too small; a dressing cannot be too large. If you
cannot find a proper dressing the next best thing is a suitable
gauze pad held in place with a crepe bandage. Failing this, any
clean material will do; clean cotton is best, so use handkerchiefs
or shirts folded to make a pad or torn into strips to make a bandage. If you can't find anything very clean, use the cleanest part up
against the wound and the less clean further away. Remember,
most gunshot wounds are highly contaminated anyway by the
bullet; bits of cloth have been pushed into the wound and dirt
sucked in as the temporary cavity caused by the wound
re-pressurizes.

Splints

Splints can be made from anything that is reasonably rigid –
wooden planks, branches or metal sheeting. Items of military
equipment might be suitable, but if you decide to use your rifle,
pay attention to the tactical situation first. Inflatable splints are
carried by the combat medic.

Leg splints

See illustration for how to apply improvised splints for a fracture of the lower limb or ankle. Note that the knots are against the splints, not the leg.

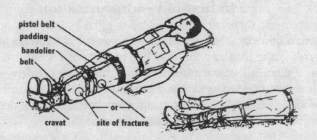

You can use the uninjured leg as a splint for the fracture; pad out the gaps between the legs before you start tying them together. Leave the boots on and tie them together firmly at the base and the top of the boot. There should be no shortage of things to use as strapping; the picture shows just a few ideas. They must be placed as shown and this is the minimum number that will be effective.

Arm splints

The aim of splinting is to immobilize the limb and prevent the break getting any worse. Both diagrams show methods of splinting a broken arm or elbow where the elbow is not bent. Try to pad the splint so that the casualty feels comfortable and immobilize the whole arrangement by strapping it down to the chest.

The binding or cravats should be firm enough to prevent movement, but not so tight that they limit the blood flow. Use a piece of cloth or bandage so that it does not cut in. Remember to immobilize the joint above and below the fracture.

Stretchers

If you need to evacuate a casualty you will need a stretcher. Lightweight rope stretchers, as used in climbing, are ideal and can be carried, one per section. The new issue stretcher is collapsible and can be easily carried in a Bergen.

If you have to improvise, things such as doors and planks are obvious choices, but you may have to make do with branches or rifles. Obviously whatever you use must be as comfortable as possible for those who have to carry it. This becomes increasingly important the further the stretcher has to be carried.

If you do not have a stretcher and haven't time to improvise, you may have to carry the casualty in, for instance, a fireman's lift. There are several ways of making things easier for yourself, particularly in getting the casualty up on to your shoulder.

From the recovery position haul the casualty up onto your knee and balance him there while you change grip to under his armpits. Then heave him on to his feet, leaning against you. Hold out the casualty's right arm and then duck under the arm. Put your head against his chest and your left arm between his legs, holding the right knee in the crook of your elbow, and swing him up onto your shoulders. The higher up you carry him, the easier it is. Hold his right arm and leg together in your left hand, and carry your rifle in your right hand.

Casualty carrying techniques

"Stretcher bearers" always seem to be on hand in the movies, but the truth is that they will always be thin on the ground forward of the company aid post. In most cases you will have to move your own wounded back via platoon headquarters.

Wounded are usually controlled by the platoon sergeant. The lightly-wounded should be given first aid and encouraged to fight on, and the walking wounded should move to the CAP under their own steam if possible.

The rest can roughly be divided into the conscious but immobile, and the completely out-of-it. There is a wide range of carrying techniques to deal with the different categories, so learn and practise them now. In any future European war there will not be sufficient helicopter assets for casualty evacuation.

Types of carry

The drag

This is for conscious or unconscious casualties and requires a good deal of upper-body strength. With the casualty on his back, adopt an all-fours face-to-face position over him, with his arms tied together and looped around your neck. Tie the arms of the casualty around your neck at the elbow to make the task easier. Then only his legs will drag in the dirt. This is a good technique if you are under fire.

The side drag

This, with its variations, is the method you will use when in close contact with the enemy and where cover is limited (when the rounds start flying you will pick it up naturally). With one hand grasp the casualty's shoulder webbing and, with your feet alongside him, lever yourself along on elbow and thigh. You can also try looping your foot through his webbing and dragging him on the end of your boot.

The fireman's lift

This is comfortable to the carrier but hell for the patient. It does tend to make you a large target, and it is difficult to get the unconscious casualty onto your shoulders without help.

The piggy-back

This is really only useful if the casualty is conscious and can use both his arms. It can be quite comfortable if you sit the casualty on your webbing, transferring his weight onto your shoulders.

Webbing carry

This method is best for short distances in place of the fireman's lift for a casualty who can't be doubled over. Hold the casualty on your back, his head next to yours and facing the same way, by grasping his shoulder, or webbing, with your hands close to your neck.

Webbing stretcher

Sit the casualty in his webbing the wrong way feet through the shoulder straps to produce a harness.

The seat

By crossing and linking your arms in this way, you can carry a casualty who is unable to walk. As a third soldier will be needed to carry the wounded man's weapons and kit, it is easy to see how a couple of casualties can paralyse a unit.

The sit

This method provides back support but less of a seat. Two men hold hands so that one hand-grip is below the casualty's knees and the other behind his back, with his arms grasping the carriers' shoulders.

Extracting casualties from vehicles

You should be familiar with most Army MT and AFVs and know the positions of all the hatches, the fire extinguishers and the fuel cut-off.

Casualties in vehicles are often severely injured, with multiple wounds, burns, etc., so practise the techniques now.

Battle casualty evacuation

The first man in the casualty evacuation system is the soldier who has been wounded. The first thing he has to do is to stabilize his injury – in other words, stop the flow of blood, move into a position that prevents his lungs flooding or throat clogging, or simply keep broken limbs supported so that simple fractures don't become compound. Your buddy may also assist if he is nearer than the section medic.

Battle casualty marking

When treating a casualty you can make the medic's job a great deal easier and prevent complications further down the line of casualty evacuation by marking the casualty's forehead with the relevant information. The section medic will label the casualty when preparing him for casevac, but labels can be lost; information on the forehead cannot.

The symbols are:

X   Emergency evacuation necessary.
T   Tourniquet applied, with the date, time and group writ-
      ten underneath.
H   Haemorrhaging.
M   Morphine, with the date and time of the injection writ-
      ten underneath.
C   Gas – contaminated chemical casualty.
XX   Nerve agent poisoning.
R   Radiation sickness.
P   Phosphorous burns.

The section medic will then check the casualty on orders from
the section commander – remember that in contact with the
enemy the medic may himself become a target. Next, the platoon
medic will be brought in to prepare the casualty for evacuation
and, while this is happening, platoon HQ will contact company
HQ with a request for a casualty evacuation.

The company stretcher bearers then evacuate the casualty to
the Company Aid Post. The stretcher bearers will be moving
backwards and forwards between the platoons that are in contact
and the company and, as long as they are not badged up with red
crosses, can also be used to move up ammunition.

They can't do this if they are protected by the Red Cross,
because this organisation is dedicated to humanitarian work and
cannot give material support to the battle – a convention normally
respected by both sides.

In an infantry battalion medics are normally members of the
band (or buglers or pipers) who combine their skills as musicians
with first aid training. The company medic ensures not only that
the casualty goes on his way to the Regimental Aid Post (RAP) in
a stable condition, but also that medical supplies are fed back
down to the section from the RAP.

Shock
Shock is a term that is very often misused and misunderstood.
How often have you heard of people being admitted to hospital
suffering from shock after an accident? In the vast majority of

cases they are suffering from no such thing. What has actually happened is that they have had a nervous reaction to the accident; they are not suffering from shock in the medical sense of the word.

True shock is a major cause of death after injury, and is the reaction of the body to a loss of circulating body fluid, which in most injury cases means a loss of blood. In the case of burns the casualty may lose a substantial amount of fluid from the burn itself.

A casualty suffering from shock will show several of these symptoms:

1. Paleness
2. Cold and clammy skin
3. A fast, weak pulse
4. Rapid, shallow breathing
5. Anxiety
6. Faintness, giddiness and blurred vision
7. Semi-consciousness or unconsciousness

He will also have a low blood pressure, although it is unlikely that you will be able to measure this. These signs are the result of the body's attempt to keep up the blood pressure and so maintain an adequate supply of blood to essential organs such as the brain. Unfortunately, the signs of a purely nervous reaction can be very similar; people can be pale sweating and indeed sometimes unconscious. If in doubt, treat for shock.

There is very little the first-aider can do in the way of treatment: evacuation to proper medical assistance is essential, as the casualty will need intravenous fluids or blood. But while waiting for this, you can take some immediate steps.

1. Lie the casualty down.
2. Make sure his airway is clear.
3. Look for and stop any bleeding.
4. Raise his legs above the level of his head.
5. Support any injured limbs with splinting.
6. Protect the casualty from exposure to wind and rain.
7. NEVER give the casualty alcohol.

8. Reassure the casualty.
9. Raise the casualty's legs so that they are higher than his heart but check his legs for fractures first.
10. Keep the casualty warm. Remember to insulate him from the cold ground; don't just pile a blanket on top.
11. If you are forced to leave the casualty or if he is unconscious, tilt his head to one side so that he will not choke if he vomits.

Battle shock

This is a temporary psychological reaction to the stress of battle which can produce similar symptoms to shock. Heavy casualties or prolonged bombardment can cause physically sound soldiers to become unable to fight effectively. During the First World War "shell shock" was not sufficiently understood, and some victims found themselves charged with cowardice. In fact, if detected early and treated as far forward as possible, battle shock can be overcome. Those most at risk are inexperienced troops or newly-arrived replacements who are not yet "part of the team". However, courage can be a consumable resource, and if a combat veteran exhausts his reserves he too can fall prey to battle shock.

Most people in action will show some signs of fear, so sweating or trembling are not reliable indicators of impending battle shock. Watch for the following symptoms:

1. Physical symptoms without actual injury.
2. Severe restlessness.
3. Overwhelming despair.
4. Panic reaction to sound.
5. Indecision among officers or NCOs.

Casualties from battle shock are best treated forward rather than sent to the rear away from their own unit. Respite from the worst of the battle, sleep, hot drinks and the chance to relive experiences with friends all help repair the psychological damage. Getting a casualty busy with some simple but useful task is also helpful. Avoid medication or alcohol.

Hysteria

A fatal combination of youth, inexperience and poor discipline can lead to some troops becoming hysterical and going berserk. The treatment is:

1. Remove the casualty's weapons and make them safe.
2. Administer diazepam tablet from the cap of the casualty's Combopen. Repeat at 30-minute intervals if necessary.
3. If tactically necessary, administer morphine.
4. Casevac the victim. The stretcher bearers should take the casualty's personal weapon.
5. At all times be calm and reassuring.

Out of the battle

In transit, you must protect casualties from the weather, chemical agents and enemy weapons. Shock can kill, and it can be accelerated by wet and cold. Casualty bags have been produced for work in an NBC environment, but it may be necessary to make repairs to the casualty's NBC suit as an expedient.

The casualty will retain his weapon while he is evacuated, though the section medic will probably have removed and redistributed ammunition and grenades. The weapon will need to be made safe, and you should search for other weapons at an early stage.

Enemy casualties are evacuated in the same way, but they are disarmed when they are captured. Security is the unit responsibility, though a wounded Prisoner of War (POW) is unlikely to wish to escape or cause trouble.

The Regimental Aid Post varies in size depending on the type of battalion, but a typical team comprises a Regimental Medical Officer (RMO) and eight assistants. They will document casualties and dead – the dead are brought in, in the same way as casualties. The usual daily work of the RMO is to treat the battalion sick. From the RAP, the casualty will be evacuated by ambulance to the Dressing Station in the divisional administrative area, where he is treated for further evacuation, or return to his unit. He will not receive any surgery here.

Field surgery
Surgery in the field can be brought forward to the casualty, rather than the man having to make a long journey to the rear. Helicopters have made evacuation fast and reliable, but the turn-around time can be critical. Battle injuries have some uniquely unpleasant features – blast and fragments can produce extensive damage. Though a gunshot wound may be precise, the track of the round after it has entered the body can be unpredictable, and the exit hole can be larger than the entry hole. Dirt, clothing and fragments enter the body with the round, and tissue is damaged by the passage of the round through the body.

The only advantage the field hospital surgeon has is that the casualty is basically a fit man. There is no danger of heart attack, respiratory collapse, or thick layers of subcutaneous fat to be penetrated. Recovery can be fast, with sleep and proper nursing, since a man in his late teens or early twenties is the "ideal" patient. The problems lie in psychological adjustment to permanent disablement or the death of close friends.

Triage and survival
A uniquely grim feature of battlefield surgery is the triage system. Developed by the French in the First World War, triage is the classification of incoming casualties by types. T1 can have his life saved by emergency surgery, T2 can await treatment, T3 has relatively minor injuries and can look after himself: the last type, T4, has serious multiple injuries. In surgical terms T4 may not be worth working on. He may die after surgery, and meanwhile a T1 may slip into a T4 while this operation is under way. A US army surgeon recalled his first encounter with T4 in Vietnam, when he saw an unconscious casualty apparently neglected in the corner of the ward. When he started to work, a colleague told him not to bother. Raising the soldier's head, he showed the young surgeon that half the man's brain was spilling out of his smashed skull.

Educational role
Despite this, it is vital that men should know that when they are asked to put their life on the line, they are backed by an efficient evacuation and treatment system. They will fight more effectively.

The RMO has an important "educational" role within a battalion explaining the system and ensuring that everyone understands basic first aid. The panic and terror that can ensue after a man has been hit will be reduced if he knows what to do and what will be happening to him now that he has become a casualty

PART IV
SURVIVAL

THE BASICS

Survival is not just about when it all goes wrong; survival is about living off the land and operating safely, efficiently and probably covertly in hostile environments – the sort of environments that governments like to send Special Forces.

Shelter

Finding shelter from sun in the desert, or from the freezing cold of the Arctic, is even more important in such places than looking for food or water. Exposure to extremes of heat or cold can kill you in hours, and not just in exotic latitudes. Even "soft" climates like that of the south of England can be deadly on a bad winter's night. You'll discover in this section how to protect yourself from extreme conditions, and how to make yourself comfortable and secure in more friendly environments too.

Choosing a shelter site

You must start to look for somewhere to hide or spend the night at least two hours before it gets dark. This will give you time to find the spot, clear away enough undergrowth or rocks to make a sleeping area, and time to get the material together to make your shelter as well.

There's one more thing you may have to look for in a survival site: protection from enemy forces. Where this is important you have to consider these factors:

1. Concealment from the enemy.
2. Camouflaged escape routes.
3. Ability to signal to friendly forces

And don't forget ordinary things like protection from the elements, insects, rock falls, and wild animals.

A survivor will always look out for certain types of ground, and avoid them by instinct. Flash floods can be upon you in seconds as a result of heavy rain falling miles away. So you must avoid apparently dry gullies in and around the foothills of a mountain range. Avalanches and landslides don't give you a lot of warning, either, so if you're forced to sleep in country that might produce either one, make sure your shelter site will give you protection from anything that might come down from above.

Be wary of river banks, in case the water level rises suddenly. The same applies to the sea shore: make certain you're above the high water mark.

The season of the year has to be considered, too. In winter, you need protection from winds coming out of the north, and a source of fuel for your fire; in the summer, what you need most is a water supply and protection from biting, stinging insects. The ideal shelter in one season might be a completely different spot at another time of year.

Types of shelter

The type of shelter you'll build depends very much on the kind of material you have available. If you have a poncho, a ground-sheet or a parachute, or even a plain sheet of plastic, you're at a very big advantage.

In general, don't make shelters bigger than you need to. This is especially important in winter. A one-man parachute tent, for instance, can be kept just about bearable by the heat from a single candle. If you use it in a snowfall, though, you'll have to keep the weight of snow off it constantly, so that it doesn't all cave in on top of you. The smaller your shelter, the easier this job will be.

The simplest form of shelter is a lean-to made from a poncho, a length of rope and two trees. First of all, make sure that the back of the lean-to will be into the wind. Tie support ropes to two corners of one of the long sides of the poncho. Tie off the neck opening. Secure the two support ropes to two trees at about waist height (lower if concealment is important), and peg out the free side with three short sticks. If there are no trees around, you'll have to cut poles to use instead.

If you are in an unfamiliar environment, begin looking for your shelter site at least two hours before sunset. It is important to know how to construct a variety of different shelters so that you can use whatever is to hand.

Bivi shelter
A poncho can be used to make a two-man shelter known to British soldiers as a "bivi" (short for "bivouac"). In a wooded area, lay the poncho out on the ground to ensure that you have enough room, then clear the ground area of cones, roots, stones, etc. Attach the poncho to four trees by its corners and make sure that it is stretched taut. In a tactical situation it should be no more than 50 cm (20 inches) above the ground. Tie the hood off and tie it to a branch to raise the centre of the poncho so that the rain can run off.

Improvised lean-to
Making the maximum use of available cover, this lean-to is built against a wall on a simple framework of branches.

Poncho lean-to
A poncho tied between two trees makes a quick and easy shelter. Tie a short (10 cm) stick to each rope, about 1 cm from the poncho: this will stop rain water running down the rope into the shelter.

Poncho tent
This is lower than a lean-to and gives protection from the weather on both sides. On the other hand, it has less space and restricts your field of view.

Low silhouette shelter

Positioned no more than 50 cm above the ground, a poncho can make a good shelter, with two or three 'sides' being made from logs, stones or turf.

In a desolate area where there are no trees, lay the poncho on the ground and, using it as a template, trace out its outline. De-turf the area 15 cm (6 inches) or so inside the cut line, and build a low turf wall around the shape of the poncho, leaving one end open. This will be the entrance to the poncho/tent and should be positioned facing the direction of any enemy threat.

Place one 60-cm (2-foot) tent pole at each end and peg down the corners and sides to make the poncho into a tent. The sides should overlap the layers of turf, and the poncho is then again pulled taut and the hood tied off. Do not rest anything against the poncho or it will let in the rain.

If you have a parachute, you can make a very spacious tepee-type tent by lashing three poles -between three and four metres (10 to 12 feet) long – together into a tripod, and then spreading the material over this frame. Extra poles will give more support, but you can just lean these against the first three; there's no need to lash them. You can tie the top of the parachute to the branch of a tree, and then keep the lower edge spread out with pegs. This type of tent doesn't work well if you need to conceal yourself – its height and sharp lines make it very easy to see.

Even if you're on the move all the time, you can still use your parachute to make a rough and ready shelter. Fold the canopy into a triangle and run a line, something over head height, from a tree to the ground, 5 or 6 metres (17 feet) away. Drape the parachute over the line and peg out the sides. If you have a little more time, cut a pole about 5 metres long and use that instead of rope to make the ridge. Cut two shorter poles and use these instead of pegs to keep the sides out.

Tuck the canopy sides around the side poles until the fabric is taut, and then use the extra fabric as a groundsheet. Wedge another pole between the two lower ones to keep the mouth of the bivouac open.

The basha

If you have no man-made materials, you can still make a very effective shelter, a basha, although it will take a great deal longer. Don't try to be too ambitious to start with. Just make a simple lean-to at first; you can always make another side to it later on, if you don't have to keep on the move.

Find two trees that are close together and facing in the right direction – the line between them should be at right angles to the prevailing wind. Cut a straight pole, about 2.5 cm (1 inch) in diameter, and long enough for you to lash to the two trees, one or two metres off the ground. Cut six or eight three-metre poles and lean them against the first one. Weave saplings, vines and twigs through and around the sloping poles. Then cover these with leaves, grass, pine needles or anything else that's to hand, starting at the bottom and working up. Put more of this same material inside to make your bed. A similar basha can be built by supporting the end of the ridge-pole on an A-frame, the other being driven into a bank or hillside.

One advantage of the lean-to made from local materials is that it blends in with its surroundings, and so is far more difficult to detect than one made from a poncho.

Shelter can mean more than just a roof over your head. In swampy or marshy country, for instance, it will be just as important to build a sleeping platform that is well off the ground, so that you can stay dry. Remember that a bed like this will have to bear all your weight. There's no point in trying to make one unless you have really substantial poles available.

Instead of building a platform, you can make a simple hammock out of a poncho, groundsheet or parachute canopy. Trees make better supports than poles that you have to drive into the ground.

Natural shelters

Often you'll find it easier and more rewarding to spend time looking for a natural shelter rather than building one of your own. Look for caves, crevices or rocks on the side of hills away from the wind, fallen trees and large trees with low-hanging branches.

There are some places best avoided. Stay away from low

ground if you can: these areas get cold and damp at night. Thick undergrowth is often infested with insects; check for snakes, scorpions, spiders and other pests. And wherever you settle make sure there's nothing loose about that could fall on you in a storm.

No matter where you find yourself, remember that the effect on your morale of having a place to "come home to", even if it's only a lean-to made out of brush wood, could mean the difference between life and death. Your will to live is what will really keep you alive, and anything that strengthens it is in your favour.

Making Fire

Fire can be your best friend. It keeps you warm and dries your clothes; it cooks your food and purifies your water. But it can be your worst enemy, too. In enemy-held territory it can give away your position quicker than anything else. And a major burn is a dreadful wound, causing massive fluid loss and leaving you open to infection.

Fuel, heat, oxygen

You have to bring three things together to make fire: fuel, heat and oxygen. Take away any one of these, and the fire goes out.

About a fifth of all the air around us is oxygen. All you have to do is make sure that there is free passage of air around – and especially up through – the fire.

Heat – the heat to start the fire – you have to provide. Friction in one form or another is the usual way, but you can use the rays of the sun, and perhaps even electricity, in its place.

Different forms of fuel

You have to provide fuel in three quite different forms – tinder, to catch the spark; kindling, to set the flame; and the fuel itself, to keep the fire going.

Most fuel will not burn when it's wet. The water surrounds it and cuts off the air supply. Non-porous fuels like coal will burn when they are wet, however, and liquid fuels like oil, kerosene and petrol are completely unaffected by water. But in most parts of the world it's wood, vegetable matter or dried animal dung (from herbivores) that you'll be burning, and this you must keep dry. Gathering and storing fuel for the fire is a very good example of how forward thinking pays dividends. But there is always something you can do to make a fire, even if you're shivering to death in a freezing rainstorm and the matches are soaked through.

Look for:

1. A sheltered place to build a fire.
2. Old, dead wood.
3. Kindling.
4. Tinder.

Take these tasks one at a time. Look for a rock overhang on the lee side of a hill or outcrop, or a low fallen branch, or a fallen tree. At this stage you're looking for protection for the fire, not shelter for yourself.

Gathering fuel

Dead wood, as long as it's not actually lying in water, will usually have some dry material in it somewhere, but the best sources are dead timber that's still standing, and dead branches that are still attached to the tree. Look for the bark peeling off.

The main difference between kindling and proper fuel is its size. Remember, the kindling takes up the sparks and glowing embers from the tinder and turns it into flames that will ignite the fuel. Small, bone-dry twigs are the best, but if necessary you can make "fire-sticks" by shaving larger pieces of shallow cuts to feather them. This is a job much better done in advance.

Tinder must be dry. Absolutely, perfectly dry. You should have some already, packed up securely in a water-tight box next to your skin. If not, you'll have to find some. Don't look too far to start with: you won't need very much. Try the lining of your pockets and the seams of your clothes. The lint that collects there makes good tinder, except for wool. Dry bark, shredded into tiny pieces; dead grass, fern and moss; dead pine needles; downy seed heads from thistles and smaller plants – all these make good tinder, as long as the material is dry. The common factor is the size of the individual pieces or fibres. They must be tiny, so that as much of their substance as possible is exposed to the air and to the spark or flame.

The vital spark

If you don't have matches or a lighter that works, there are several alternative ways to start a fire. If you have direct sunlight and a magnifying lens, you can use the glass to focus the sun rays on to the tinder and start it burning that way. But this won't work at night in a rainstorm!

Alternatively, you could use the "flint and steel" method. If you have a so-called "metal match" (a metal strip with tiny flint chips embedded in it), then use that, scraping your knife blade along it to produce a shower of sparks.

Or look for a piece of flint or other very hard stone. Then you can use your knife to strike sparks off it – use the back of the blade. If you have a piece of hacksaw blade, you should use that to save damaging your knife.

Alternative technology

There are two other ways of making fire. The bow and drill and the fire saw both rely on friction between two pieces of wood. You have to make a small part of one of those pieces hot enough to set the tinder going. It is possible – but you'll only need to try it once to become fanatical about carrying matches with you everywhere you go!

Fire bow

Making a fire from the friction of wood upon wood really is a last-ditch alternative. The few aboriginal tribes that still make fire this way spend a very long time selecting exactly the right materials. Nevertheless, in the desert, where it's perfectly dry, it is possible to start a fire in this way.

You'll need:

1. A piece of green hardwood, about a metre (3 feet) long and 2.5 cm (1 inch) in diameter.

2. A piece of dry hardwood, 30 cm long and 1 cm in diameter.
3. A 5 cm hardwood cube, or a shell or a suitable stone.
4. A piece of dry softwood, 2.5 cm thick.
5. A cord for the bow-string.

To make the fire bow:

1. Make the bow loosely using the cord and the long piece of hardwood.
2. Round off one end of the short piece of hardwood, and taper the other slightly.
3. Carve out the centre of the hardwood cube to fit the taper, or find a stone or shell of the right shape.
4. Make a depression in the softwood, close to one edge, and make a groove from it that leads to the edge.
5. Put some tinder next to the end of the groove.
6. Loop the bow-string round the drill, maintain pressure on the top with the cap, and work the bow backwards and forwards to create friction between the hardwood drill and the softwood baseboard. Wood dust will build up in the groove, and the end of the drill will become red-hot and ignite it.

Fire saw
You'll need:

1. A piece of bamboo, 5-8 cm in diameter and 1/2 metre long.
2. A forked stick, to anchor it into the ground.

To make the fire saw:

1. Split the bamboo lengthways.
2. Cut two notches in a straight line across the two exposed edges near to one end.
3. Brace the notched bamboo with the forked stick.
4. Fill the space between the notches with a handful of tinder.
5. Saw in the notches until the tinder ignites.

Fire tongs

1. Make a thong (a strip or string of tough material) using rattan (a sort of tropical vine), leather or very tough cord.
2. Split a dry stick and hold the split open with a small wedge.
3. Run the thong through the split.
4. Place a small wad of tinder in the split.
5. Secure the stick with your foot and run the thong back and forth to create frictional heat. The tinder will eventually ignite.

Vehicle fuel

If you have a vehicle you have another option – use the battery. Rip out some wire and attach a piece to each terminal. Touch the bare ends together and you'll get a spark. If the vehicle is petrol-(gasoline) driven, you can use a tiny amount of the fuel to help the process along, but remember that petrol in its liquid form doesn't burn. You can only set fire to it as a vapour. So, use less than a teaspoonful, soak some rag and make the spark in the air just above the surface. Diesel fuel doesn't work in this way – you need a good-size flame to set it alight at all.

Hints for the firemaker

When you're making a fire under difficult conditions, you must start small and add to it very carefully. If you've been unable to find a site sheltered from the wind, then you must make a wind-break, although it may be simpler to dig a sloping trench and light the fire inside that.

If the ground is very wet, use stones as a base, but make sure that they're not porous. Porous stones can explode: that will not only injure you, but also blow the fire all over the place.

Don't worry about making an elaborate fireplace at this stage. Get the fire alight first.

THE LOG CABIN PILE

This is a very good way of laying a fire. Plenty of air can circulate and it will not collapse until it's well away.

Make a nest of dry grass and the smallest twigs. If you can find a dry bird's or mouse's nest, so much the better. It will have down and fur mixed in with the grass, and probably some dry droppings too – all of them excellent tinder. Put your tinder inside. Arrange dry kindling over it in the shape of a cone, or make a lean-to by pushing a green stick into the ground at an angle of about 30 degrees and build up the kindling along it to make a sort of tent.

Make sure that you've got all the materials you need to hand before attempting to light the fire – you may only get one chance, and at the beginning you'll have to work quickly, adding small amounts of kindling as the fire grows.

Keep the fire going

If you have a choice of different types of wood to use as fuel, use softwood – pine and spruce, for example – as the first load of fuel, but be careful of sparks. These woods contain resin and burn quickly. To keep the fire going, use hardwoods such as oak or beech. They're much longer-lasting.

You can use a mixture of green and dry wood to keep the fire going through the night, but don't just dump wood on it without thinking. Make sure that you keep a good stock of fuel close at hand, and arrange it so that the heat from the fire will help to dry the fuel out. Keep kindling at hand, too, so that you can revive the fire quickly if it looks like dying out.

Improving the fire

How you improve the fire site depends on what you're going to use it for. A fire that you use for smoking food, for instance, isn't much use for anything else. Its purpose is to produce lots of smoke inside an enclosure. You won't be able to cook on it, and it won't give out much warmth.

You can cook on an open fire, but it's not very efficient: it's better to construct a stove of some sort.

The simplest stove needs something like a five-gallon oil drum. Punch holes in one end and in a ring all around the side at the same end. Cut out a panel about two inches above that ring of holes. Punch a large hole in one side of the drum near the other end, to let the smoke out. Place the stove on a ring of stones to allow the air to circulate from underneath.

Now you can transfer some of your fire into the stove, stoke it through the cut-out panel and cook on top. It'll give off enough heat to keep you warm, too, and has the very positive benefit of not showing sparks and flames like an open fire does.

You can achieve much the same effect with a fire pit. Dig a circular pit, and then another smaller one, slantwise, that meets it at the bottom. The slanting hole is for the air to circulate up through the fire, so dig it on the side of the prevailing wind. If you dig it close to the trunk of a tree, the smoke will go up into the foliage and be dispersed, helping to disguise your position.

Reflectors and windbreaks

You can make a fire more effective as a source of warmth by building a firewall across one or two sides, to reflect the heat back towards you. The simplest way is to drive four green-wood stakes into the ground in two pairs, three or four inches apart, with three or four feet between them. Fill up the space with trimmed branches and trunks, but don't bind them together. That way you get a firewall and a stack of dry wood all in one!

Poor conditions

You may have to build your fire in the wet – on snow, or in a swamp, for example. In the snow it's easiest to build a base out of layers of green wood. In swamp or marshland, raise that platform up on four legs.

Don't bother to chop or even break up long pieces of wood for an open fire. Start at one end and feed the log in as it burns, or lay it across the fire and wait until it burns through, then turn the ends in.

Having gone through all the pain of getting your fire going, don't let it go out! Use well-dried hardwood during the day; it produces very little smoke. As the evening approaches, you may want to add green or damp fuel to produce smoke that will drive away insects.

A SIMPLE FIRE CRANE
Use a green-wood pole with a forked notch to hold a container over a fire. Beware of large, naked flames: a burning pole will wreck your meal. Cut a pole, make a small notch where the pole will hang over the centre of the fire. Place one end of the pole on the ground, and support the forked end with an upright stick (2-3 feet high) pushed into the ground, so that the pole lies across the top of the fire.

Alternative fuels

If you have a vehicle, almost every part of it that isn't metal will burn. Mix oil, petrol or diesel with sand in a pit and set fire to it. Rip out the upholstery and the trim and use for fuel. The tyres will burn if you get them hot enough, but stay upwind of the smoke! Hydraulic fluid from the brake and clutch systems is highly flammable, and so is neat anti-freeze. All of this applies to aircraft as much as ground vehicles.

Animal droppings, if they are perfectly dry, are a very good source of fuel: easy to light, slow-burning and almost smokeless.

After a while, looking after your fire will become second nature to you. You'll sense changes in its mood, and be able to change its character to do different jobs.

Water

Water is a basic human need. There is no adequate substitute, and without it you cannot live more than a few days. Within the human body water acts as a stabilizer: it helps to maintain warmth in cold environments, and is vital for staying cool in hot environments. It is also part of the body's mechanism for distributing food and removing waste. As soon as you are cut off from a source of fresh water, you begin to dehydrate. The rate at which you dehydrate depends on a number of factors: the amount of water your body already contains, the clothing you are wearing, the local temperature, how hard you are working, whether you are in shade or sunlight, whether you are smoking and whether you are calm or nervous.

Effects of dehydration

1. Inability to swallow.
2. Failing senses.
3. Breathing difficulty.
4. Thirst.
5. Discomfort.
6. Speech difficulty.
7. Headache.
8. Inability to walk.
9. Dizziness.
10. Nausea.
11. Loss of appetite.
12. Collapse.

You will collapse after losing 12% of your body weight. Heat exhaustion is still a killer on exercises in the UK as well as abroad. You must be able to recognize the signs in your mates; it doesn't have to be a hot day to kill them. If all the danger signs are ignored, sweating will eventually stop and the victim will collapse.

If you allow dehydration to continue, there will come a point when you can no longer search for water. Your first priority is to minimize further dehydration and, having done this, you must find water. (If you are stranded in a desert with little chance of finding water, stay still to prevent further dehydration, and make efforts to signal for rescue.)

Reducing dehydration

- Find shade.
- Move slowly and do not smoke.
- Cover exposed skin to prevent evaporation of sweat.
- Suck a pebble (helps prevent exhalation of moisture through the mouth).

POINTS FOR SURVIVAL

1. Avoid eating until you have secured a source of safe water.
2. Do not ration your water; drink as much as you can when you can.
3. Urine is a good indicator of dehydration. The darker its colour, the more dehydrated you are.
4. Bacteria multiply faster in warm water, so water gathered early in the morning, at its coolest, is safer.

Finding water

You do not have to be in a desert to have difficulty finding water. Forests often offer such poor visibility that, although surrounded by water-loving trees, you cannot spot readily available surface water. (In combat conditions, however, you may have to deliberately avoid obvious sources of water, for fear of ambush.)

So how do you go about finding water? The first thing you do is to remember the following points:

- Water runs downhill, so make for lower country.
- Where there is water, there is usually an abundance of lush vegetation. If possible, learn to recognize the moisture-loving plants in the area. If this vegetation is wilted or dead, it probably indicates chemical pollution.
- Animals need water, too. Observe the habits of the local wildlife: it may lead you to a source of water.
- Grain-and seed-eating birds need water, so observe them too.
- Listen for frogs croaking: they live in water.

• Cliffs often have seepages of water at their base, so look carefully.

Sources of water (assuming no equipment)

Familiarize yourself with the various sources of water and their relative merits.

Dew

Dew is one of the most reliable sources of water for the survivor. It can be collected soon after it has started to form until it evaporates in the morning sunlight. Improvise a mop from an absorbent article of clothing. Drag this through long grass or use it to wipe the condensed moisture from shrubs and rocks. If you do not have a convenient mop, finely teased, non-poisonous inner barks or grasses can be used. When the mop is saturated, wring out the water into a container. Although labour-intensive, this is a very effective way to collect water.

Dew itself is a pure source of water, but when you wipe it off vegetation and rocks you also wipe off bacteria and perhaps parasites. It is therefore best to boil this water before consumption.

Rain and snow

Rainwater is usually the safest source of water in the wilderness. If it rains, make sure you gather as much as you can. But remember, the water is only as pure as your method of collection: if you are in doubt, boil it before consumption. Snow, if it is clean, is probably pure. The major problem with snow is melting it – a time-consuming and labour-intensive process, as you require eight to ten containers of snow to produce one container of water.

Ice

Ice is not pure and should always be boiled before consumption, but is far more economical as a source of water than snow. Icicles are often found hanging from trees and rocks, so may provide you with a ready source of water. Those hanging from trees may be slightly stained brown by the tannin in the bark, but unless they are very heavily stained they will be safe to drink after boiling.

Puddles and hidden water
Rain water is often trapped in depressions in rocks, called kettles, and in puddles. While it may smell foul and be stagnant, it only needs filtering and boiling to make it drinkable. Rain water can also be found trapped in hollows in trees. Unfortunately, this is often so badly polluted with tannin as to be undrinkable. However, if you expect rain you can bale these hollows out and let them fill with fresh rain water; as long as you use the water before it too becomes tannin-stained, you have a handy water tank. Always boil this water before drinking it, and only use water found in non-poisonous trees.

Drinkable saps
For short-term relief of thirst, you may be able to tap the sap of certain trees. The sap of maple, birch and sycamore can be tapped during the early spring (sycamore will produce sap from spring to autumn, depending on local conditions). Sap is quenching but it contains sugar, which if taken in sufficient quantity will hasten dehydration; in fact, the woodland Native Americans still boil maple and birch sap to produce sugar.

Only mature trees should be tapped, and the sap drunk while fresh, as it will ferment if stored. Some plants can also be used to provide water. (See Jungle section for further 'tappable' trees.)

Springs and seepages
Springs are often regarded as foolproof sources of drinking water, but unfortunately this is not true: spring water should be boiled before drinking. Very often, springs are covered with soil and appear as patches of saturated ground supporting lush plant growth. To obtain water from these areas, dig an Indian well (see below).

Ponds
These are principally a feature of farmland, and therefore a

potential source of water for the evading soldier. Such water should always be considered suspect, as at the very least there will be fluke infestation. Keep contact with this water to a minimum, and if used as a source of drinking water, filter and thoroughly boil it before drinking.

Streams, rivers and lakes
Streams are often a tempting source of water, but care should be taken as they are very often polluted by decaying carcasses of animals that have drowned or become caught in boggy ground.

In alpine regions, the clear ice-cold glacial meltwaters carry an invisible hazard: sediment – rock powder scoured from living rock by the awesome power of the glacier. If this is not filtered out, you may get digestive problems.

The further water travels from its source, the more pollutants it picks up. In an age where chemicals are an integral part of farming and land management, rivers and lakes should be avoided as sources of water.

INDIAN WELL

The Indian Well is an easily prepared and efficient method of collecting reasonably good water. Selection of the ground is all important and the water produced requires filtering and boiling. Also, it takes some time to produce clear water, and quality is dependent on soil type. In practice, watch out for sources of contamination, boil very carefully, and add Steritabs.

1. Dig a hole about half a metre deep and half a metre wide. Water will begin to seep into the hole.
2. You can push a stick into the sides of the well to increase seepage of water into the wet.
3. Bale out this water carefully so that you do not stir up the sediment at the bottom of the hole. Repeat this process until the seeping water is fairly clear.
4. After some time, the water at the top of the well will be clear enough to collect. Be careful not to disturb the muddy layer that usually lurks at the bottom.

Purifying water

Now you've found a source of water. Is it safe to drink? The answer seems obvious – assume the water is dirty and purify it – but dehydration is causing you to be uncharacteristically impatient and irritable. You are tired, hungry, lonely and somewhat frightened. Your hands and shins are covered in the scratches you sustained searching what seemed like every patch of vegetation in the last hundred miles. And but for the incessant biting of the mosquitoes you would fall asleep.

You are faced with water that will need filtering and boiling before it is safe to drink, but you have no container and no fire. Surely one little sip won't hurt?

Without the support of modern medicine to fall back on, wilderness survival is all about maintaining good health. The human body is an amazing machine, but it is finely tuned: it only takes one drop of contaminated water to make you ill. Of the many waterborne problems you may develop, the most common is diarrhoea. In a survival situation, diarrhoea may prove fatal. It causes dehydration and makes hygiene very difficult, increasing the risk of further unpleasant infections, and destroys the will to live.

To make your water safe, you will need three things:

* Fire
* A container
* A filter

As a fire will also warm you, drive away the mosquitoes and boost your morale, it is usually best to start this first. Hopefully you will have practised your fire-lighting skill, as this is a bad time to learn!

Improvised water containers

Improvised water containers fall into three categories:

1. *Kettles:* containers that can be used directly over flames
2. *Cauldrons:* cannot be used directly over flames, but can be used for rock boiling

3. *Storage:* containers that should be solely used for carrying
   or storing safe water.

Kettles

Kettles can be made from flammable materials because the water
contained within them prevents their burning. The secret is not to
allow the flames to reach beyond the water level.

In some tropical regions, bamboo can be found with stems
large enough to be turned into kettles. Many other containers can
also be improvised from bamboo, and sometimes fresh drinking
water can be found trapped in the stems.

The woodland Native Americans routinely made kettles from
birch bark while on their travels. Only the outer bark is used. It
should be carefully removed from an unblemished section of the
trunk, and can be made pliable by either soaking or gentle warming by the fire. The brown inside of the bark is the most durable
side, and is used to form the outside of containers, which can be
simply made by folding.

Cauldrons

Cauldrons are made from materials that will hold water but are
not suitable for direct heating; to boil water put heated rocks into
it.

If your local soil is clay, or clay-like enough to contain muddy
water, a ground cauldron can be made. Dig a bowl-shaped
depression in the ground and smooth the inside. Form a raised
rim at the top, to help prevent humus falling into the cauldron.
Make the cauldron one third larger than the amount of water you
intend to boil. This will allow for the water displaced by the heated
rocks. To prevent sediment muddying your water, you will need
to line the pit. For this you can use either some material (for
example, a T-shirt) or large non-poisonous leaves such as dock or
burdock. Take great care to ensure that the lining fits snugly. The
water purified in this type of cauldron will always be a little
muddy, but if you leave it to settle you can skim clear water off of
the top.

Rocks and trees

Water can often be found in depressions in rocks, and the hollows in trees, and these can be turned into ready-made cauldrons. Again, allow for the displacement of the heated rocks by choosing a depression large enough. If possible, it is best to scrape any slime out of these depressions prior to their use. This is especially important when using tree hollows.

Remember, never rock-boil in a poisonous tree.

Skin

If you are able to catch an animal of the size of a rabbit upwards, you will have secured meat as well as two containers good enough to stew it in: if you are careful with the skinning and gutting, both the skin and the stomach can be used as cauldrons.

To use the skin you can leave the fur on or take it off, as you please. To use the stomach it is best turned inside-out. You have a choice when making your skin cauldron. You can line a pit with it, securing it around the rim by stakes, or you can suspend it from a tripod.

Wooden bowls

Bowls and containers can be carved out of wood. While not as quickly constructed as the previous methods, wooden bowls are well within the capabilities of a survivor. If carefully made, they are portable and very durable.

The best method of producing a wooden bowl is to "burn and scrape". To achieve this, make a small depression in the centre of your bowl-to-be and place a couple of glowing coals in this depression. Then by blowing on the coals, ideally through a reed straw, you can use them to char the surrounding wood. When you have charred a patch of wood, scrape it away using a sharp stone, and begin the process again. It does not take long to form a reasonable-sized bowl.

Storage containers

The manufacture of storage containers is a long-term prospect. They can be made from the materials discussed above, and also from clay pottery and tightly-woven basketry.

Filtering

Having secured a container in which to boil your water, you now need a filter to remove the particles of dirt suspended in the water.

The simplest filter that can be improvised uses a pair of ordinary trousers. Simply turn them inside-out, placing one leg inside the other, and tie the leg off at the bottom. Soak the material before use: this helps tighten the weave, making the filter more efficient. Suspend the filter so that you can easily filter it, with the container positioned underneath to collect the clean water that drips out. Such filters can be improved by filling them with charcoal.

Rock boiling

Rock boiling is an easy and effective way to purify water. The rocks must be of a manageable size and weight, and thoroughly dry. (Rocks from stream beds and damp places contain moisture which, when heated, expands, causing the rock to explode. Also, glass-like rocks such as flint and obsidian should be avoided.)

Heat the rocks in your fire, and when hot transfer them to your container with some improvised tongs. Tap off any ash before dropping them in the water. Do not wait to use these skills until you have to: practise is essential to success.

Rules for water

If you have plenty of water, drink more than your habitual amount every day. It'll keep you fit even when your food is in short supply. If you are short of water but have plenty of food, remember that eating will make you thirsty. If you have to ration yourself to less than a quart of water a day, avoid meat, or dry, starchy foods, or those that are highly flavoured. Go for foods with a high carbohydrate content – hard sweets and fruit bars are ideal if you have them. If both food and water are limited, keep work to a minimum. Hunting animals is hard work – another reason to learn how to survive on plants.

Food

Food is more important to you than you probably realize. In a survival situation food is crucial, for every meal you cook affects your level of morale. By making an effort in cooking and presenting your meal, you give your mind something to work on, helping you to retain your identity and self-esteem. It is also more likely that you will make full use of the nutrients in your food, and so remain fit and healthy. During the Second World War many soldiers were stranded on islands in the Philippines. Daily diet became an all-absorbing part of their life, prompting the saying "You've got to have an appetite to survive."

Plants

After two or three days without food, you will actually notice how you lack energy – and your morale will drop, your resistance to disease will diminish, and your hopes of making a quick getaway, if you have to, become mere wishful thinking. The old adage that an army marches on its stomach is especially true for a survivor. Now most of your body's stored energy has been used up in building your shelter and staying warm, finding food is the next priority.

You are probably thinking of hunting and trapping meat. While these are obviously important, few survivors are expert enough to rely on their hunting skills for at least the first three to four days. By that time you should be accustomed to the daily movements of the local wildlife. It is one thing to catch a rabbit on a survival exercise in Yorkshire, but quite another to trap a maned wolf in South America. Don't neglect the major source of food that can't run away from you: edible plants.

Meat or vegetarian?
For a survivor, the relative merits of meat or plant diets are academic. You can eat only what is available to you, and it is quite likely that your diet will be severely imbalanced. But it will keep you alive.

In general, an all-plant diet will do you less harm than an

all-meat diet, although in the Arctic you will need meat, and especially fat, to produce body heat. Ideally, you would combine a meat and plant diet, in much the same way as you would at home. The meat will provide protein to build muscle, while the plants provide carbohydrates and calories for energy, as well as useful starches and sugars. If you are injured, you may not be able to hunt. So try to include nuts and seeds in your diet, so they will help to replace the protein lacking in a meat-free diet.

Many people think that subsisting on plants is like being reduced to an animal scrabbling around popping unmentionable berries and roots into your mouth. In fact, people have died because they were reluctant to eat plants. You should try to live as normal a life as possible, gathering enough plants for a meal, and preparing them carefully. Many of the plants you are eating were once part of mankind's staple diet, the ancestors of the plants we presently cultivate. Be adventurous, and experiment with your resources. A gourmet feast around the campfire is the greatest morale booster in the world!

Is the plant edible?
In answering this question, there is no substitute for knowing the plant. *Only eat a plant that you have positively identified as edible.* Luckily you don't need a degree in botany to recognize edible plants. Many common "weeds" are useful for food. This means that you need to be familiar with relatively few plants to get by. Get a good naturalist's field guide to edible plants and carry it while on training exercises. You can enjoy the benefits of wild edibles at any time. Improve your compo ration diet by complementing it with fresh herbs, or try mixing fresh young hawthorn leaves into your compo minced beef for extra flavour.

SOME EDIBLE PLANTS
(NORTHERN HEMISPHERE)
Hazel Catkins (Corylus avellana)
The pollen has a high food value, as do the hazel nuts.
Wood Sorrel (Oxalis acetosella)
The leaves taste of apple peel but should only be eaten

in small quantities. It is useful for removing the taste of something nasty from your mouth.

Ramsons (Allium ursinum)

The flowering stems of this plant can stand in for spring onion or garlic seasoning. This plant is very widely distributed through Europe but rare in the north. It is found in damp woodlands, often occurring along stream bank.

Cattail (Typhus latifolia)

This is an all-year-round survival feast. The pollen, green flower-head and young stems are all edible. These are best-boiled. The corm or bulb of the plant is high in food value and can be found in winter. The plant is distributed widely in Europe but not in Scotland.

Marjoram (Origanum vulgare)

This aromatic herb is useful for flavouring meat. Marjoram is usually found in rough permanent grassland, hedge banks, scrub and roadsides in dry soils.

Spear Thistle (Cirsium vulgare)

The green parts lose their pickles when boiled and make a tasty soup. The roots are also edible. This is a common weed throughout Europe.

Wild Chamomile (Matricaria recutita)

This makes a very soothing tea. It is a frequent weed of arable crops and waste ground.

Stinging nettle (Urtica dioca)

Cook as green vegetable.

Rosebay willowherb (Chamerion angustifolium)

The young shoots and leaves are edible. It often forms dense stands in areas of felled woodland or waste ground.

Mallow (Malva sylvestris)

The leaves and flowers make a tasty soup. It is usually found in dry, well-drained soil on roadsides, bank and waste ground.

Blackberry (Rubus fruticosus)

All parts of this plant are edible, not just the berries. The dried leaves make an excellent tea.

Red clover (Trifolium pratense)

The flower heads can be added to stews and tea can be made from the leaves. This is a common plant of pastures, meadows and rough grassland, roadside verges and cultivated ground.

White dead nettle (Lamium album)

The dried leaves make a very refreshing tea and the fresh leaves can be added to soups. This is a plant of woodlands, fens, ditches and river and stream sides and is also associated with fire sites and abandoned buildings.

Acorn (Quercus petraea)

Acorns can be roasted and then ground into a passable coffee. However, you do need to spend time leaching them in water to remove some of the bitterness. They can also be ground and leached and used as a flour.

Bracken (pteridium aquilinum)

The fern has coarse compound leaves about a metre long. The young leaves can be boiled and eaten as greens. Limit the amount of bracken you eat as it may contain substances that interfere with enzyme action in your body.

Foxtail grasses (Setaria species)

These are grasses recognized by their narrow cylindrical head containing long hairs. The dense heads of grain drop when ripe. The grains are edible raw, but become less bitter when boiled.

Juniper (Juniperus species)

Junipers are trees or shrubs with very small, scale-like leaves densely crowded around the branches. Each leaf is less than half an inch long. The berries and twigs are edible.

Mulberry (Morus species)

This tree has alternate simple, often lobed, leaves with rough edges. The fruits are blue or black and many-seeded, and can be eaten raw or cooked or dried for later use.

Nodding onion (Allium cernuum)
This is just one example of a great number of wild garlics and onions. The bulbs and young leaves are edible and if you eat enough they will give your body a smell that will repel insects.

Yellow Nutsedge (Cyperus esculentus)
This is a very common plant which has a triangular stem and grass-like leaves. It grows to a height of 8 to 24 inches (20 to 60 cm). Edible tubers of half to one inch (1 to 3 cm) in diameter grow at the end of the roots. They can be eaten raw, boiled or baked. They can also be ground into a coffee substitute.

Pines (Pinus species)
The seeds of all species of pine are edible, as are the young cones which appear in spring and should be boiled or baked. The bark of young twigs is edible, as is the inner bark of thin twigs. It is rich in sugar and vitamins especially when the sap is rising. Pine resin can be used to waterproof articles and made into glue by heating.

Obtaining and preparing edible plants
It is equally important to know how to prepare the plants you find. Each part of a plant requires its own method of preparation.

Underground parts
Edible roots, tubers and bulbs are vital to you, as they are extremely high in stored starch. They are usually best cooked. In winter the roots can often be discovered by searching for the withered stems of the plants.

Removing underground parts from the earth is not always easy. Plants such as first-year burdock have a particularly tenacious root, which requires major excavation before you can get it out. Use a stick to dig a crater around and under the root, and lever it out. If the ground is frozen, thaw it by lighting a fire or putting heated rocks above the poor. Roots can be cooked by steaming, pit baking or boiling.

When learning to recognize edible roots make certain you examine them during the summer, when you can study them attached to identifiable stems. The roots and bulbs of poisonous plants are very often the most deadly parts.

Stems and leaves
The green parts of most edible plants are usually more bitter and fibrous than cultivated vegetables. For this reason you may find that you need to boil them in more than one change of water, but don't overcook them, or you'll destroy their nutrients. The best way to overcome this problem is to include them in a stew.

Try things out
Experiment with your local edible greens to discover which can be cooked like asparagus (the tender young shoots), those best used in stews, and those that make a good tea substitute. Tea substitutes, such as dried bramble leaves, are very important as morale-boosters. Try to build up a stock of them, so that in the dark evenings you can brew up. This will give you confidence in your ability to overcome your difficulties. When picking edible leaves, choose the succulent young leaves just as you would in a market.

Bark: The inner bark of many trees can be used as a source of food, especially, in the high north country: birch, pine, aspen, willows and cottonwoods. The white inner bark is often fibrous, and the best way to prepare it is to dry it and then grind it into flour. In an emergency it becomes more palatable when toasted.

Pollen: Hazel catkins and bulrushes are two of the best sources of pollen. This can be cooked as a form of gruel or, better still, mixed in with other wild flours.

Flowers: The flowers of edible plants are often neglected as a source of food. They can be colourful as part of a wild salad. Many are full of flavour and can be used as seasoning for stews.

Fruits: Besides eating wild fruits raw, you can cook them into warm syrups and sweet fruit drinks. These too are tremendous morale-boosters.

Grain and seed: Seeds and grain can be made into flour. While the process may seem laborious, the results are well worth the effort. First, thresh and winnow the seed to remove the chaff. After this it can be parched on hot stones, if you need to store it for long. Or you can grind it to produce flour. The easiest way to collect the seed in the first place is to beat it off the stem onto a spread tarpaulin or jacket.

Nuts: Nuts contain much protein and can even be used to produce cooking oil. Some nuts, particularly acorns, are too bitter to eat.

Making the most of edible plants

Once you have learnt a bit about edible plants, you will be able to conjure up amazing meals. Make your menus as varied as possible, partly for nutritional reasons (you need a diversity of food-stuffs) but also for the upkeep of morale. Same old, same old food is depressing, while concocting meals occupies the mind in positive ways. Do not forget to use plants as seasoning; wild birds' eggs, for instance, have a strong flavour, so season the meal with herbs, such as wild marjoram, or even wild mushrooms such as the ink-cap or Jew's ear. Served with a side order of ramson stems (the survivor's spring onion) and boiled nettle leaves, this makes a survival meal of Cordon Bleu standard.

Fungi
Poisonous fungi

Before beginning to learn about edible fungi, make sure you are familiar with the features common to the high poisonous *Amanita* family of fungi, with their bulbous base, "volva" or skirt, and white gills. In fact, you should avoid any fungus with white gills. *Amanita phalloides*, the death cap, is one of the most common deadly species of fungi, having all of the above features under a greenish yellow cap. Avoid all *Amanitas*, and all *Iocybes*. Learn to recognize them – they are particularly dangerous families.

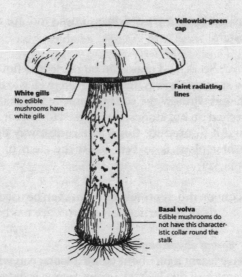

Yellowish-green cap

Faint radiating lines

White gills
No edible mushrooms have white gills

Basal volva
Edible mushrooms do not have this characteristic collar round the stalk

You must also avoid:
Cortinarius speciosissimus
Gyromitra esculenta
Entoloma sinuatum
Pascillus involutus
Agaricus xanthodermus
Agaricus placomyces
Ramaria formosa
Clitocybe rivulosa
Clitocyle dealbata
Lepiota fuscovinacea
Stropharia Hornemannii
Hebeloma crustuliniforme
Boletus satanas
Russula emetica
Scleroderma aurantium

Edible fungi
There are a lot of myths about eating fungi, but if you are a survivor or evader, edible fungi give you a versatile, easily-gathered and tasty source of nourishment. The food value of fungi is high.

They provide valuable fat, carbohydrate and protein in quantities between those of meat and green vegetables. More importantly, they are good stomach fillers, making you feel well fed. This is a big plus in psychological terms. But fungi are an unpredictable source of food, so when you have a chance to gather edible fungi, take it. You can dry and store for future use what you don't eat immediately.

While the vast majority of fungi are harmless, the small proportion that are dangerous can cause serious poisoning, which may be irreversible. *Never experiment with fungi you have not positively identified as edible.* There are many old wives' tales about how to recognize edible fungi, but never follow such rules. If you do not know the fungi, leave them alone.

THE FIELD MUSHROOM
Usually found in meadow or pasture, these are the mushrooms you usually buy in the shops. They can be dried for later use.

THE PARASOL MUSHROOM
A very tasty and large mushroom that grows in woods and pastures. In the early stages of development, before the cap spreads, it can look like a different species to the untrained eye.

The parasol is excellent baked or sliced and added to stews. The delicate top is the best part and has a meaty flavour. Remember, some fungi are toxic if eaten raw. If in doubt, leave well alone. But the parasol (*Macrolepiota procera*) is fine whether raw or cooked.

THE GIANT PUFFBALL
There are several species of puffball or edible boletus; all are more edible when young. They are white or grey when young, becoming yellow or brown with age.

THE SHAGGY INK CAP
The ink cap, which disintegrates progressively into an inky liquid mess, is edible before the rot has set in and is common in mixed woodland.

DRYAD'S SADDLE
This is a large fleshy fungus that, when cooked, has a similar flavour to meat and is very filling.

SPARASSIS CRISPA
This is an edible fungus that usually grows on rotting tree trunks and fallen branches. It is commonly associated with pine.

JEW'S EAR FUNGUS
This is found in mixed woodland throughout the year. It is especially common in autumn and favours elder. It is one of the "jelly" fungi and, although revolting to look at, tastes good.

CHICKEN OF THE WOODS
This fungus usually grows on the sides of trees, has a very tasty chicken flavour and can be eaten raw.

YOU CAN ALSO EAT:
Horn of Plenty *(Craterellus cornucopioides)*
Cep *(Boletus edulis)*
Morel *(Morchella esculenta)*
Oyster mushroom *(Pleurotus ostreatus)*
Chanterelle *(Cantharellus cibarius)*
Wood blewit *(Lepista nuda)*

RECOGNISING EDIBLE FUNGI

The essential feature about fungus is that you must know exactly what you are eating. You cannot take short cuts; there is no general rule on what is and is not edible. Start by learning a few easily-recognized edible species such as those in the suggested list. Once you are confident you can identify these, you can add to your knowledge. Do not experiment: get expert help.

Cooking plants and fungi
Even with those fungi that are safe to eat raw you are better off cooking them, not least because the cooking process is likely to

destroy any bugs lurking on them. Mushrooms are best boiled or fried; roasting on a spit is only going to leave you with dry offerings akin to parchment.

You can boil, fry, parch, bake, steam, roast or broil food in the wild just as you would at home in your kitchen. But you'll probably have to make your own substitute pots and pans and cooker, as few plants take well to being cooked on a spit!

Boiling is one of the best methods, as it gets rid of most harmful substances, while retaining the plant's juices, which contain salts and vital nutrients. Boil, bake or roast roots and tubers. If the sap of the plant contains sugar, dehydrate it by boiling until the water has gone. To leach, crush the food, put it in a container, and pour boiling water through it.

Frying is something you can do on a hot, flat or concave rock if you don't have a frying pan – use the rock just like an ordinary skillet. Parching works well with nuts and grains: put the food on a rock or in a container, and heat until it is scorched.

Baking calls for an oven and a steady, moderate heat, as does steaming. You can bake by using a closed container over a slow fire, or wrapping your food in leaves or clay. But both baking and steaming are best done in a pit when you're surviving in the wild. To bake food, dig a pit and partly fill it with hot coals. Put your food – and some water – in a covered container, and put it in the pit. Cover it with a layer of coals and a thin layer of earth. You can also line your pit with dry stones. Build a fire in the pit then, as it burns down scrape the coals back, put in your container of food, and continue as above. Bake or roast tough, heavy-skinned fruit. Juicy fruit can be eaten raw or boiled.

Steaming works best with shellfish or other foods that need little cooking, such as plantains or green bananas. Wrap the food in large leaves or moss, and put one layer on the coals. Add another layer of moss or leaves, and then another of wrapped food, and so on. When your pit is almost full, push a stick right down through all the layers. Seal the pit with more leaves, or earth, and then remove the stick. Although mushrooms can be steamed you may find they leak 'ink' and discolour any foods in the pit below them.

THE EDIBILITY TEST

1. Do not eat for eight hours before starting the test.
2. During the test period, take nothing by mouth except purified water and the plant part being tested.
3. Sniff the plant to test for strong or acid odours, but bear in mind that smell alone does not indicate that a plant is inedible.
4. Break the plant into its basic components – leaves, stems, roots, buds and flowers – and test only one part at a time.
5. Select a small portion of a single component and prepare it the way you plan to eat it.
6. During the eight hours before you try the plant, test for contact poisoning by placing a piece of the plant part you are testing on the inside of your elbow or wrist. Usually 15 minutes is enough time to allow for reaction.
7. Before putting the prepared plant in your mouth, touch a small portion (a pinch) to the outer surface of your lip to test for burning or itching.
8. If after three minutes there is no reaction on your lip, place the plant part on your tongue, holding it there for 15 minutes.
9. If there is no reaction, thoroughly chew a pinch and hold it in your mouth for 15 minutes. DO NOT SWALLOW.
10. If no burning, itching, numbness, stinging or other irritation occurs during the 15 minutes, swallow the food.
11. Wait eight hours. If you suffer any ill effects during this period, induce vomiting and drink a lot of water.
12. If no ill effects occur, eat half a cup of the same plant part, prepared in the same way. Wait another eight hours. If there are still no ill effects, the plant part as prepared is safe for eating.

CAUTION: Test all parts of the plant for edibility, as some plants have both edible and inedible parts. Don't assume that a part that was edible when cooked can also be eaten raw. If you want to eat it raw, test it raw.

EDIBLE FOOD CALENDAR
(NORTHERN HEMISPHERE)
What to Look Out for When
January–March

Lamb's Lettuce
Laver
Birch (sap)
Bistort (March)
Biting Stonecrop
Bog Myrtle
Brooklime
Chickweed
Chicory (Leaves)
Cleavers
Colt's Foot
Dandelion (leaves)
Dead-Nettles (March)
Docks
Dulse
Fat Hen (March)
Fennel (leaves, March)
Garlic Mustard (March)
Ground Elder
Ground Ivy
Hairy Bittercress
Hawthorn (leaves, March)
Herb Bennet
Horseradish
Jew's Ear
Kelp
Lettuce Laver
Lime (sap)
Morel (March)

Nettle
Primrose (March)
Reedmace (roots January, shoots February-March)
Salad Burnet
Scurvy Grass
Sea Purslane
Shepherd's Purse
Sorrel
Spruce
Stinging Nettle
Sweet Violet
Tansy
Watercress
Wild Garlic
Wild Parsnips
Wintercress
Wood Sorrel

April-June

Alexanders
Balm
Bistort
Biting Stonecrop
Black Mustard
Bog Myrtle
Borage
Brooklime
Broom
Burdock
Carragheen
Chamomile
Chanterelle
Cleavers
Coltsfoot
Comfrey
Coriander
Corn Salad
Cow Parsley
Cowslip

Dandelion
Dead-Nettle
Dulse
Elder (flowers)
Fairy Ring Mushrooms
Fat Hen
Fennel (leaves)
Field Poppy
Garlic Mustard
Giant Puffball
Good King Henry
Gorse
Ground Elder
Ground Ivy
Hairy Bittercress
Hawthorn (leaves)
Herb Bennet
Hogweed
Hops (shoots)
Horseradish
Ivy-Leaved Toadflax
Jew's Ear
Kelp
Lady's Smock
Laver
Lime
Lovage (leaves)
Mallow
Marsh Samphire
Meadowsweet
Morel
Mugwort
Nettles
Nipplewort
Orache
Pignut (June)
Plantain
Primrose

Reedmace (flowers)
Rock Samphire
Rosebay Willowherb
Rosemary
St. George's Mushroom
Salad Burnet
Scurvy Grass
Sea Beet
Sea Kale
Sea Lettuce
Sea Purslane
Shepherd's Purse
Silverweed
Sorrel
Sow Thistle
Spignel (leaves)
Spruce
Sweet Cecily
Sweet Violet
Tansy
Wall Pennywort
Watercress
Wild Cabbage
Wild Celery (Smallage)
Wild Garlic
Wild Strawberry (June)
Wood Avens and Wood Sorrel
Woodruff
Yarrow

July–September

Agrimony
Ash
Balm
Barbery
Beefsteak Mushroom
Bilberry
Black Mustard
Blackberry

Blackcurrant
Blackthorn (sloes, September)
Bog Myrtle
Borage
Brooklime
Bullace (September)
Burdock
Caraway
Carragheen
Cep
Chamomile
Chickweed
Cloudberry
Comfrey (July)
Coriander
Corn Salad
Crab Apple
Cranberry
Crowberry
Dandelion
Dulse
Elder (berries)
Fairy Ring Mushroom
Fat Hen
Fennel
Field Mushroom
Ground Elder
Ground Ivy
Hairy Bittercress
Hawthorn (benies)
Hazel Nuts (September)
Heather
Hen of the Woods
Herb Bennet
Hogweed
Hops (cones)
Horn of Plenty
Horseradish

Hottentot Fig
Jew's Ear
Juniper (September)
Kelp
Laver
Mallow (leaves)
Marjoram
Marsh Samphire
Meadowsweet
Mugwort
Nipplewort
Parasol Mushroom
Pignut (until July)
Poppy
Red Clover
Rowan
Salad Burnet
Sea Beet
Sea Buckthorn
Sea Lettuce
Sea Purslane
Service Tree
Shaggy Cap Mushrooms
Shepherd's Purse
Silverweed
Sloe
Sorrel
Sow Thistle
Spignel (roots and seeds)
Strawberry
Sweet Cecily
Tansy
Wall Pennywort
Watercress
Wild Celery
Wild Cherry
Wild Garlic (bulbs)
Wild Marjoram

Wild Raspberry
Wild Rose (hips)
Wild Strawberry
Wild Thyme
Wintercress
Wood Blewit
Wood Sorrel
Woodruff
Yarrow

October-December

Alexanders (roots)
Barberry
Beech
Beefsteak Mushroom
Biting Stonecrop
Blackberry
Blackthorn (sloes)
Brooklime
Bullace
Cep
Chanterelle
Chickweed
Corn Salad
Cowberry
Crab Apple
Cranberry
Crowberry
Dandelion (roots)
Dulse
Elder
Fairy Ring Mushroom
Fat Hen
Field Mushroom
Fennel (seeds, roots)
Garlic Mustard (roots)
Hairy Cress
Hawthorn
Hazel

Heather
Herb Bennet
Horn of Plenty
Horseradish (roots)
Jew's Ear
Juniper
Kelp
Laver
Lettuce Laver
Lovage (seeds)
Medlar
Oak (acorns)
Oyster Mushroom
Parasol Mushroom
Poppy
Redcurrant
Reedmace (roots)
Rosemary
Rowan
Salad Bumet
Sea Lettuce
Sea Purslane
Service Tree
Shaggy Caps Mushroom
Shepherd's Purse
Silverweed
Sorrel
Spignel (roots)
Sweet Cecily
Sweet Chestnut
Walnut
Watercress
Wild Canot
Wild Rose
Wintercress
Wood Blewit
Yarrow

Seashore Food

The coastline offers the survivor a wide variety of food sources if you know what to look for. The major problem is a psychological one: you may have to eat some fairly unappetising items. The essential precaution is to learn as much as you can about the subject first by familiarising yourself with the food sources the seashore has to offer and trying some of the techniques described below. You will be able to overcome your initial reluctance. Then, if you find yourself in a survival situation near the coast, you have already won half the battle.

Drinking water is always one of the survivor's top priorities. By digging a shallow well just above the high-water level you will be able to collect fresh (if a little brackish) water. Don't dig too deep, or the sea will seep in. This is a good technique to practise next time you visit a beach. If you have a vessel to boil water in, boil sea water and collect the steam in a clean cotton cloth. Squeeze out the cloth and you have distilled, drinkable water. Now it is time to forage for food.

The coastline is abundant with food sources, but there are a few basic rules to remember to avoid food poisoning or contamination from all the waste man so thoughtfully dumps into the sea. The edible items discussed here are all standard.

Tropical beaches are more abundant but so are the dangers. The basic rules are:

1. Don't eat anything too brightly coloured red, yellow or green. It is a natural sign of poison being present.
2. Don't eat any items washed up or away from their natural environment.
3. Avoid anything with a very strong smell.
4. If in doubt, don't eat it.

Shellfish
Only eat shellfish you find alive; dead ones can be used as bait. Bivalve molluscs feed by filtering food particles out of the water. They also filter out and retain bacteria which, in warm weather, multiply and can cause food poisoning to humans. This is

especially true of mussels and oysters, which filter large quantities of water daily and relish the warm, soupy conditions near sewage outlets.

Clams *(Mya arenaria)*
Common in the middle and lower shore, clams look like large mussels and can be up to 10-13 cm (4 inches) across. Wash thoroughly as for cockles and scald for 10 minutes. Remove the meat from the shell and cut syphons off. The remaining meat should then be fried or baked for 30 minutes or boiled until tender.

Cockles *(Cardium edule)*
Widely distributed along British coasts, they are normally found 25-75 mm (¼-¾ inch) beneath the surface of the beach. Wash off the mud and sand and stand in clean water for at least six hours. Drop into a pan of boiling water and simmer for five minutes. Eat on their own or with soup.

Limpets *(Patella vulgata)*
Found on rocks below high water, limpets should be soaked for about six hours then boiled for five minutes. They can be rather tough, but further boiling will tenderize them.

Mussels *(Mytilus edulis)*
Commonest of European shellfish, are delicious, but you must exercise considerable caution when collecting them. They are responsible for most cases of shellfish poisoning. Stand in at least two changes of fresh water and check carefully that each one is alive before cooking. They can be boiled, or baked in ashes.

Scallops *(Pecten maximus)*
These are the classic shells we all recognize; found on the lower shore, they are only uncovered at very low tides. Like clams, they require a lot of cooking. Wash and scald, cut away the white and orange flesh and fry or boil until cooked.

Whelks *(Buccinum undatum)*
Whelks are the largest of the gastropods (coiled shells). They are very meaty, but require a great deal of boiling otherwise you will still be chewing on the same whelk hours later. Like the smaller winkle, they can be found in rock pools and among seaweed.

Winkles *(Littorina littorea)*

You will need a large number of these small, spiral-shaped pointed shells, normally dark grey in colour, for a decent meal. Soak them in fresh water to clear them of sand, then plunge into boiling water for about 10 minutes. Extract the meat with the proverbial winkle pin.

Preparing shellfish

1. Test mussels by sideways pressure: if the animal is alive you will feel some resistance.
2. Other shellfish are tested by forcing the shell open a fraction of an inch. If the animal is alive and well it will shut again quickly once you release the pressure. If it is already open, opens wide with ease or fails to shut again, it is safer to assume the thing is dead and that you should not eat it.
3. Always wash seashore edibles in plenty of fresh water. Shellfish should be left to stand in clean water overnight if possible. Check they are still alive when you come to cook them: a single dead one will contaminate the rest of your meal.
4. Always cook thoroughly to kill naturally present bacteria.

Seaweeds

Most seaweeds are edible raw or cooked, and they form a valuable addition to your diet providing your water supply is adequate, because they tend to make you thirsty. They are found in inshore waters and attached to rocks at low water. In addition to general rules, there are three specific rules concerning seaweed:

- Only eat fresh, healthy specimens. Eat nothing with strong odours or flavour: seaweed should be firm to the touch, not wilted, slimy or fishy-smelling.
- Do not eat thread-like or slender forms. Sea sorrels contain small amounts of sulphuric acid which can severely upset your stomach. They betray their presence by bleaching out other plants nearby. The test, if you are not sure what you've found,

is to crush a little of it in your hand. The released acid will make the plant decay quickly and in 5-10 minutes it will give off an unpleasant odour.

- Inspect seaweed carefully and shake out any small organisms, e.g. tiny crabs.

There are many types of seaweed. Those found in Europe include:

Bladder wrack: Fresh or dry fronds may be used, boiled in soups or stews. It can also be dried to make tea of a sort.

Carragheen (Irish moss): This is found on the rockier Atlantic shores. Tough, feathery and many-branched, it is red/purple to purple/brown. Boil it and eat stewed with fish, meat or other vegetables.

Enteromorpha intestinalis: A mouthful to say but a satisfactory mouthful to eat, this is widely distributed and can be eaten raw or dried and used in soups.

Laver: Found on the Atlantic, Pacific and Mediterranean coasts, this is plentiful around the UK and is eaten in Wales. A thin, leaf-like transparent membrane with fine, wavy flat fronds, it is red, purple and brown in colour. Cut just above the base so you don't kill the plant off. Wash it thoroughly to remove grit, and simmer slowly. It can be eaten like spinach or rolled into balls, dipped in bread crumbs and fried. If survival cuisine is beyond you, you can still eat it raw.

Sea lettuce: Found in the Atlantic and Pacific, this is lettuce-like in appearance and is coloured light to dark green. It may be eaten raw or used as a vegetable.

Shoreline plants
There are a few plants found along the shore which can provide the survivor with quite reasonable food.

Marsh samphire (Salicornia)
This thrives in salty marshlands along the foreshores of Europe and has been described as the next best thing to asparagus. Ready from the longest day in June to the last day of August, the young shoots can be eaten raw in salads or cooked in a little boiling water. Drain and add a little butter and pepper if

you have any. Eat by stripping the soft flesh away from the hard, spiny stems with your teeth. Marsh samphire now appears on some restaurant menus as a delicacy.

Sea arrow grass (Triglochin maritima)

Found near north temperate coasts, salt marshes and grassy foreshore areas, this can be eaten raw but is best added to soups or boiled as a vegetable.

Sea beet (Beta vulgaris)

Also known as wild spinach, this was the ancestor of our beet-root, sugar beet and spinach. The leaves may be picked from spring to autumn. It is full of natural minerals, especially iron and vitamins A and C. Wash the leaves well and remove the thicker stalks before boiling in a very little water. Better still, steam it for about ten minutes.

Sea kale (Crambe maritima)

A cabbage-like plant growing in large clumps with huge, fleshy grey/green leaves, it is found in shingle, sand dunes and along cliffs on north temperate coasts and it was known to the Romans, who preserved it in barrels for long sea journeys. Pick young leaves and white underground shoots from February to May. Boil briefly, chop and boil for a further twenty minutes in changed water. They can also be steamed or baked.

Crustaceans

These are a major food source – but also a common cause of food poisoning, so proceed with caution. Never eat a raw crustacean. Cook them by covering with sand and earth and building a fire over the pile: they will cook in their own juices. A better way is to boil them in water.

Crabs, crayfish, lobsters, shrimps and prawns are found throughout the world and all are edible. They go off quickly, so eat them soon after catching them. Boil some water, insert the crustacean, and eat 20-30 minutes later.

Fish

Fish can often be found in pools at low tide around the bases of rocks and under clumps of weed, and eels and small fish are often left behind by the tide. A great deal of fluid is stored in the flesh and the spine cavity of fish and, surprisingly, this is not salty. Hunting fish in pools is not easy: traps and spears will both work, but only if you have practised first. A maze trap works well for flatfish and others in coastal areas. It should be about 2-2.5 metres (6-8 feet) across with a mouth of 40-50 cm (2 feet). The outer walls of wood or stones should project 60 cm or so into the trap. Avoid small, spiny fish, which are likely to be poisonous. Fish can be boiled, roasted in a fire, baked in clay or cooked on a spit. Prepare them by cutting off the heads, removing the guts and cleaning them out. A very sharp survival knife is an essential item here. Small fish can be eaten whole without cleaning. Never eat a fish with a suspiciously powerful odour, sunken eyes or slimy or flabby skin. If in doubt, prod it with your thumb: if it remains dented, do not eat it. Use it for bait instead.

Common octopus (Octopus vulgaris)
You may be able to spear octopus amongst the rocks, but the better method is to leave out large tin cans or sections of pipe with a few stones secured to the bottom just below the low-tide mark. Octopi will adopt these containers as lairs when they move in at high tide: they will form the stones into a wall at the open end of the tin. The only real problem is getting the octopus out of the tin.

Birds
All sea birds are edible, either raw or cooked, although some may taste a little peculiar. Roasting and baking in clay are good ways of cooking, but boiling is most nutritious as you retain all the juices. Before cooking, a bird should be bled and drawn and the feathers removed, although a small bird can be rolled in clay and baked: the feathers and skin come away when cooked. The livers are particularly good, and the entrails make good bait for fishing. Do not attempt to kill or ear any bird unless you are in a genuine wartime survival situation. All wild birds in the UK are protected by law.

Other food sources
Other possible food sources include sea urchins, sea cucumbers, starfish, razor shells and lug worms. And don't forget that the

seashore will be inhabited by dune-dwelling creatures such as mice, rabbits and lizards: all these can go in the survivor's pot. As in all survival situations, living on the seashore is all about making the maximum use of whatever is available.

Fishing

If you are fortunate enough to be stranded in an area with a lake or river, you have a rich source of food waiting to be gathered. Fish are rich in protein, the brains and skin are rich in fat, and the meat can also be stored long-term. The problem is how to remove the fish from his natural environment to yours.

As someone intent purely on survival, you cannot afford any sporting niceties. The fishing techniques you will need to use are usually outlawed. You must be able to catch your fish in quantity, and as easily as possible. Before you actually start fishing remind yourself of the danger of water, especially in your weakened physical state. Should you fall in, remember the tip of the old salmon fishermen – throw your arms out crucifix-fashion, and try to float down to a shallow pool where you can wade out. If you panic and throw your arms up in the air you will only sink faster. (In crocodile-infested waters try to stay as dry as possible!)

While fish may seem more easily trapped and hunted than other animals, you must bear in mind that you need to catch an awful lot of fish to provide the same volume of food as a medium-sized land animal. At the end of the day, your catch must be big enough to justify the time and effort. This will be largely dependent on how well stocked your river is.

Whether you decide to hunt or trap fish, the time-honoured hunting rules apply. Study the fish in your locality, see where the biggest fish prefer to swim as the position of the sun changes, get to know their habits – especially their feeding habit. Once you have caught a fish, study its stomach contents to find out what it was feeding on. The more you know, the easier your task will be.

Hunting fish
Although hunting fish usually produces a smaller catch than

trapping them, it can be a quick way to a short-term meal, and is ideally suited to survivors on the move. The hunting tools are also simpler and more easily made than trapping gear.

Fish are able to detect unusual disturbances in the water, and can see movement above the water. To avoid alerting them to your presence, always try to minimize your movement and noise. Walk carefully – fish can feel heavy footfalls through the water.

Tickling

Some fish, particularly trout and salmon, will allow you to touch them while in the water. To catch fish like this you need to be actually in the water. The ideal type of stream is wide, and shallow and clear.

Approach your fish slowly and carefully, with your hands already in the water. Once you are close enough to touch the fish, pass your upturned hands under him very gently. You will probably fail the first time you do this, out of sheer astonishment, for the fish seem to nestle against your hands. Once your hands are in position, grab the fish. Bend it in your hands and it won't slip away. In one smooth action, cast it on to the bank. While this technique does require the confidence that comes with practice, it does work, and can be a very effective way to catch fish in the right circumstances.

Torch and blade

At night, fish can be attracted to light. Wade into a shallow stream with a torch made of birch bark, and you should be able to catch the fish attracted by slashing at them with the blunt end of a machete or a thin blade carved of wood. Make certain you hold the torch high in front of you so as to avoid casting your shadow on the water. If the river is too deep to wade into, you can use the same technique from the river bank, using a long spear to catch the fish.

Spear and lure

You can easily make fish spears from available wood, and they can be very effective. They fall into two basic categories – pin and snag. You use the simplest spears to pin the fish to the river bed. They are usually made of a single piece of wood, pronged or split at the point, and crudely barbed. They are very quickly made and very effective. The "snag" or "leister" spears are more complicated to make. They work by snagging the fish on barbs rather than pinning the fish to the bottom. For this reason they are better than pin spears in deep water. You can make these spears with detachable heads attached to the spear shaft by a length of strong cordage. In this way the fish can thrash around without any risk of breaking the spear head.

Spears are best used in conjunction with a suitable lure. Simply carve a small fish-shaped piece of wood, modelled on the local "small fry", and attach it to a long length of cordage. By drawing this along in the water you should be able to attract the attention of a large predatory fish and "lure" it within range of your spear. Because water refracts light you will need to aim slightly below where the target appears to be.

Trapping fish

Methods of trapping fish are more useful to you in the long run as they free you to work on your other important chores. However, the apparatus you need will take longer to make. If you are establishing your survival camp, setting fish traps should be one of your priorities. Your land traps will usually take less effort to set and can be more easily tuned to full effectiveness.

Fish traps can be used for freshwater and saltwater fish. They are very effective but take a good deal of effort to make and are difficult to carry if you decide to move on.

FISH TRAP IN STREAM

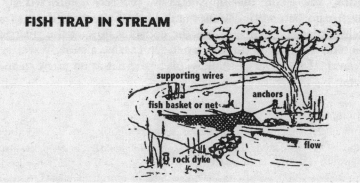

supporting wires

fish basket or net

anchors

flow

rock dyke

Gill net in a stream

The gill net is perhaps the best way to catch fish, but again it takes time to make it. Stones are used to anchor the bottom of the net and wood floats are set along the top. The net is set at an angle across the river from a suspension line between two suitable anchors.

GILL NET IN STREAM

Maze traps

These are the simplest traps you can construct. They are simply holding pens, which fish can enter easily but cannot leave because of the design of the entrance. When you make this type of trap, make sure that the stakes are securely hammered into the stream bed with a stone maul. Lash the tops of the stakes with cordage – your trap has the constant flow of the river to contend with. If you do have a net, set it across a straight section of river. If the river is shallow, place the net at an angle in the water.

FISH MAZE TRAP AND BASKET TRAP

The maze trap

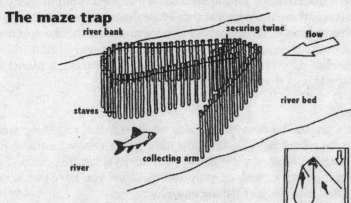

The trap is made up of wooden staves hammered into the river bed with a supporting line connecting the tops of each stave. The trap takes some time to build, but is very effective. The collecting arm should cover the main flow of the river so that the majority of fish swimming upstream are directed into the trap. Each stave should be at least 2 cm thick.

The basket trap

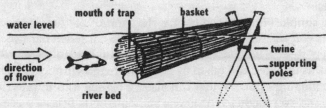

This fish trap is made up of wooden staves bound together to form a telescoping basket. In the faster-flowing parts of the river the fish swims into it but cannot turn round to get out, and finds itself beached at the end of the trap.

Basket traps
Basket traps are slightly more complicated to make than maze traps, but have the advantage that you can carry them easily to wherever there are the most fish. Place the basket so that the river current flows into the basket entrance and raise the downstream end out of the water. Secure the basket with rocks or slim willow branches. If you have time you can also construct a funnel of stakes to lead the fish into the basket.

Nets
Nets are the hardest fishing aids of all to make, requiring great lengths of cordage. Unless you have nylon cord to unravel for netting material or a gill net in your survival kit, this method of trapping is an unrealistic proposition. When you have one, a net is a first rate piece of fishing equipment.

Hook and line
If you have them, fish hooks and line can be used in an endless variety of ways. The easiest and most effective set-up is to set a fixed line across the river and suspend hooks from it at different depths. In this way you can fish several different levels of the river at the same time. Always make absolutely certain that your hooks are tied on securely – your life may depend upon them.

In the wild, on your own, you may not be lucky enough to have any hooks or line. But you can improvise them from natural materials.

The simplest improvised hook is the "gorge" or "toggle" hook. For this you will need a piece of bone or fire-hardened hardwood. Sharpen this at both ends and secure your line to its middle. When this is baited and taken by the fish it toggles inside the fish's throat, lodging tight. Thorns can also be turned into improvised hooks, and you might even carve a standing hook from a piece of bone.

Fishing line is far more difficult to improvise than a fish hook. The strongest line you are likely to be able to make is a very thin rawhide line. Although rawhide loses much of its strength when wet, it is still appreciably stronger than most of the plant fibres you will have available. Simply cut a piece of rawhide in a spiral until you have a long, thin fishing line. Soak the line before use and don't leave it submerged for more than a day or two.

Of the plant fibres you can use, nettle fibres are among the best. But, as with all plant cordage, you will need to gather a lot of nettles, and the process of turning them into cord is slow and laborious. Gather the longest nettles you can find and lay them out to dry in the sun. Once dry, they will have lost their sting and can be handled more easily. Take a mallet and split the stems, remove the pith until only the fibres remain. These can then be rolled on your thigh to produce strong cordage.

SECRET SET LINE

You may not want to risk using a set line in an evasion situation, but you can use a set line, known as a stake-out. This is a fishing device you can use secretly by setting a line in darkness between two reeds or similar with lines and hooks attached. Check the line at two-hour intervals until dawn, and then remove.

Meat

Meat is the most nourishing food for man, and certainly the most satisfying for the fugitive who is surviving for any length of time in the wild. Collecting and eating grubs may be an easier option than trapping larger animals, but you have to get through a lot of worms and caterpillars to beat a decent rabbit or duck. Here we describe how to set about catching whatever you find.

The first thing to know is that all animals are edible (but not necessary the whole of the beast). The second thing is that they're nearly all very difficult to catch and you'll have to use all your skills to be successful; and that means understanding the animal's way of life.

Daily habits

Animals are usually fairly regular in their habits, using the same paths and trails, drinking at the same places on the river bank and from pools, sleeping in the same sheltered places. They also have a timetable, and stick to it; if an animal went to a certain place to drink at dawn this morning, there's a very good chance that it will do the same again tomorrow. Spend time looking for signs of animals.

If there's a lot of animal activity going on, find a hiding-place and stay in it until you recognize the local wildlife patterns. It will make trapping or hunting them a great deal easier. All you've got going for you is your intelligence; they've lived there all their lives!

Unless you have an accurate weapon, such as a rifle, shotgun or crossbow, hunting will be a lot less likely to provide you with dinner than trapping. In a hostile environment, where there are enemy forces or natives, hunting is almost certain to be impossible anyway, but let's look at some of the basic skills you'll need to hunt game in the wild.

Always assume that any small animals in the area will be wary and quick to run away. If they spot you, hear you or smell you (remember that their sense of smell may be a thousand times better than yours), they will either go to ground or disappear off into the distance. Seeing them before they become aware of you greatly increases your chances of catching them. They often use the same pathways and drinking places, and make permanent homes. Look for their signs – tracks, paths in grass, faeces, dens, feeding-places – and use that intelligence to help you set up a plan to catch them.

To survive in the wilderness you have to become a predator – and that means you have to compete with other animal predators for the same prey. You can learn a lot about survival by watching the animals around you. Notice how the animal that makes the kill isn't always the one who enjoys the meal.

You can always let predators do your hunting for you. Watch until you can work out their pattern of activity, then wait for them to make a kill. If you rush them you'll often cause them to drop their prey.

Camouflage and approach

Remember, the fieldcraft that makes you a good foot-soldier can also make you a good hunter. Always obey the rules of camouflage and approach. Never silhouette yourself against the skyline, even in woodland. Always move upwind or across wind. Approach streams, rivers and waterholes very carefully, especially around dawn and dusk. Find cover and get into it, and wait for the animals. And stay still! Fidgeting may cost you a meal – and that may end up costing you your life. Larger game, even if it sees you, may not take flight straight away. Stop and keep still until it loses interest, and then approach in a wide zigzag. In hills and mountains, always try to get above the animal you're stalking.

Shooting

If you are shooting game, the best targets are the head, neck and the spine just behind the shoulder. Take your time, and make the first shot count – because you're not likely to get a second chance. If you hit and wound the animal and it runs off, follow the blood trail. A badly wounded creature won't have the strength to run far. Give it the chance to go to ground before following it up. Approach slowly and then make the kill. Don't waste ammunition if you can finish it off by clubbing it.

Trapping

Hunting, however, should take second place to making and setting traps. Traps are much more likely to provide you with a lasting supply of meat. Simple ones are very easy to make and set: the simplest of all is a snare – a slip noose firmly pegged into the ground or anchored to a rock or tree. Make them from wire if it's available, or use plastic fishing line, string or even line made up from natural fibres.

These snares are especially effective when you set them at the entrance to burrows and dens.

Set them in trees to catch squirrels, or make a "squirrel pole": an 8-12 feet (2.5 to 3.5 m) pole with perhaps half a dozen snares around it, leaned up against a tree used by squirrels. It may sound too easy, but squirrels are inquisitive creatures and will often investigate something new just for the fun of it. You're not likely to be able to kill anything larger than a rabbit or a small cat with a wire snare, though you may slow down larger animals so that you have a better chance of clubbing them to death.

Trapping, even more than hunting, depends on how well you can read the signs. There is no point in placing a trap just anywhere hoping that an animal will stumble into it by chance! Entrances to burrows and tunnels are the best place. Look for signs that they are occupied – fresh droppings, signs of feeding and movement in and out.

A POLE TO CATCH SQUIRRELS

Take a pole, fix some wire snares to it and lean it up against a tree where you've seen squirrels. It may seem too simple to be true, but these inquisitive creatures are quite likely to get caught up before too long.

Hanging snares

Hanging snares are a more secure way of holding on to the animal that you've caught. They use the creature's own weight to keep it from wriggling out of the noose. Apart from the wire noose itself, to make a hanging snare you need a sapling close to the run you've chosen, and a forked stick, or one bent over into a hoop. The forked stick is used as part of the trigger, holding the wire noose down in the animal's way and presenting the bait. You can even scare off large animals this way – cats and bears, for instance. Building a fire when you've frightened them off will often make them stay away long enough for them to forget you've robbed them of their meal. But unless you're well armed, don't be too ready to take on these large predators yourself.

Unless you're using wire for the snare, which may stand up on its own, you will have to make a stand to hold the noose open. Two twigs, one each side of the mouth of the burrow or the path, will do, with another one perhaps placed across the top to support the trap.

Human scent

Don't forget to cover your scent; both on the snare itself and on the surrounding ground: soaking the snare in a stream after you've made it and before setting it is one way. Or you can rub it with cold ashes, or disguise your own scent with something stronger – urine from the bladder of a dead animal, for example. Animals are usually attracted to urine from their own kind.

Improved noose
You can improve on the simple noose, and make it more difficult for the animal to escape from the trap, by intertwining two lengths of wire. Use the two strands that are left at the end to make up a double running loop. These two loops will naturally catch in the twists of the wire that makes the body of the line and noose, and will make it much more difficult for the animal to wriggle out of the noose.

Obvious targets
Don't go around chasing squirrels while ignoring more obvious targets such as cows, sheep and other domestic animals – including cats and dogs. They're all food, and often they're just standing around waiting to become somebody's meal – it may as well be yours. Bats and mice make good eating, but do not eat any of their innards, and immediately discard their heads, skin, feet and tails.

SKINNING SMALL ANIMALS

1. Lay the animal down on its back, spread all four legs wide, and cut from the anus up to the breastbone, taking care not to rupture the intestine.
2. Cut the skin through around all four paws at the first joint. Remove the guts, starting from the throat and working downwards. Do not eat these innards.
3. Now you can peel the skin off. You may find it necessary to remove the tail first.
4. Take the skin off in one piece. A firm grip and a quick pull are all that is needed.
5. The last thing to do is to remove the head. Keep the skin for making clothing.

Snails (Helix pomatia/Helix aspersa)
You can't afford to be squeamish in a survival situation. And if you are squeamish, put on a French accent and call them 'escargots'. Most snails are safe to eat, and the *Helix pomati* and *Helix aspersa* common in Europe certainly are. *Helix pomatia* is the

official 'edible snail', and used to be farmed by the Romans. The shell is creamy-white going on brown, usually with smudgy brown bands. Since it requires undisturbed loose ground to bury in for hibernation and egg-laying it is a creature of wasteland, pastureland and heath. (In England, but not the rest of the UK, the edible snail is a protected species, and off the menu.) The garden snail (*Helix aspersa*) is smaller than its cousin mollusc, and a darker brown in colour, with yellowish hoops. Both species of snail are vegetarian.

You'll find snails hiding under stones, rotting vegetation and cracks in walls. Alternatively, lay some large leaves on the ground in the evening, and you will find in the morning that the snails have come to you.

Since snails involuntarily ingest toxins when grazing, whether man-made (pesticides, herbicides) or naturally occurring (from poisonous plants, such as deadly nightshades), they need to be purged before consumption. Place 20-30 snails in a large metal bucket (or similar) with a little water and a handful of dandelion leaves. Cover the container with cloth, to keep the snails in. The herbage feeds and flavours the snails, but you will need to clean the snails out every day, and replace the water and fodder. Do this for at least five days. Clean the snails in running water.

To cook: Plunge the snails into boiling water for three minutes. Remove from shells, cut off the tortillon (the last bit out of the shell), and rinse in clean water. Simmer for 60-90 minutes in any vegetable soup you can manage.

Preserving food in the wild

You have to protect your kill from being stolen by other animals – not all of them friendly. You also need to protect your food from the hordes of bugs and flies that want to eat your food and, worse, lay their eggs in it. With care and the right techniques you should be able to keep your kill at least for long enough to let you eat all of it safely, and with practice you can even preserve your food indefinitely.

Preserving meat

First decide whether or not you intend to hunt large game. Preserving a large animal such as a deer will require considerably greater effort than will preserving a rabbit. The deciding factor is how long you expect to be stranded. If it's likely to be a long time, killing a large animal means less hunting and brings with it a large and useful skin. But it also involves hard work to preserve the meat. Until you become expert at preserving meat you will find it easier to rely on smaller game to stock your larder.

Because all wild meats can carry parasites harmful to man, they must be cooked thoroughly before consumption, regardless of how you preserve them. Efficient cooking destroys parasites and is therefore an essential part of field hygiene.

Drying

Drying, or "jerking', is the easiest way to preserve meat under survival conditions. First slice the meat into strips, approximately 2 inches (5 cm) wide and ¼ inch (0.5 cm) thick. Then string them on a thin stick or drape them over a bar on your drying rack. Make sure they are not touching each other.

Smoking meat

Smoke your meat over a wood fire using timber from a deciduous tree, ideally willow or birch. Do not use conifers like pine or fir trees because their smoke will impart a vile taste to the meat. You can hang meat high above a slow, smouldering fire, but a quicker method is to dig a hole about a metre (3 feet) deep and 50 cm wide. Get a fire going at the bottom and pile on green wood to create the smoke. Place the meat on an improvised grate over the hole. One night of heavy smoking will preserve meat for five to seven days; two nights and it will remain edible for two to four weeks. When properly smoked, the meat will look like a dark, curled stick. It is highly nutritious and, best of all, it tastes good.

The smoking can be stopped once the surface of the meat is dry. Allow the meat to hang in the sun or a dry place until it is brittle. It can then be stored, wrapped in dry grass and bark, until you need it. To use dried meat you can rehydrate it for boiling or steaming or, better still, just add it to a stew.

Pemmican

Once you have a store of dried meat, you can consider making pemmican, the survivors' home-made, high-energy, high-protein emergency ration. Pemmican is ideal for long hunting trips or if you intend to make a break from civilisation.

Take your brittle dried meat and pound it between two rocks until it is a powder. You now have the equivalent of a survival stock cube. Next, mix the powdered meat with sun-dried berries and plenty of rendered fat. Form the resulting sticky mass into palm-sized pellets and place these in the cleaned large intestine of an animal. Seal the ends by tying and with fat. You now have a survival sausage which can be eaten as it is, or sliced and added to stews, or fried on a hot stone.

Precautions against flies

Until the surface of the meat has dried you run the risk of flies laying their eggs in it. You can prevent this with two simple precautions. Either site your drying rack in a sunny and windy location or, the more effective method, lay a slow smouldering fire under the rack. This will speed up the drying process as well as keeping off insects. Make absolutely certain, however, that the fire is giving out only a low heat and not much smoke. Don't use green vegetation to produce the smoke, or you will taint the meat. If you need to increase the smoke, use some damp wood chips or bark from a non-poisonous tree.

Freezing

In Arctic conditions you may be able to store your meat by letting it freeze. But remember – even when frozen, the scent of the meat will be detected by other hungry predators. Make certain it is out of their reach.

Be sure that you will be able to cope with the meat once it is frozen. The most common mistake made by survivors is to freeze large pieces of meat. Instead, butcher it into meal size.

Preserving fish

Your fish can be preserved along with your meat. Treat fish in the same way as meat – dry it, or make it into pemmican. The only difference is that fish goes off far more quickly, so it must be dried as fast as possible. In all but the sunniest weather, this will mean you have to use a smudge fire or a smoke house.

Smoking

You can also deliberately flavour fish by smoking it. To do this you will need to hang the fish in a smoke house. Score the flesh before hanging, so that the smoke permeates the flesh better. Smoking fish in a smoke house is little different to operating a smudge fire. A slow trickle of wood smoke does the trick. Once you have started smoking the fish, check it on a regular basis. There are two stages in smoking fish: half smoking and full smoking. Half-smoked fish is still soft and flavoured of wood, ready for eating. Fully-smoked fish is dry and brittle. Treat it the same way as dried meat.

Fish pemmican is certainly an acquired taste when eaten raw. But it is an excellent addition to soups and stews, and can be fried to make delicious fish cakes.

Preserving fungi

If you are lucky you may be stranded during a glut of edible fungi. To preserve them for future use, you can dry them. First clean each individual fungus, cutting out any parts attacked by insects. Be particularly thorough with fungi that have gills or pores, as these are a favourite breeding-ground for grubs.

Preserving plants

In general, plant foods are best used fresh. But at the onset of winter, you must certainly consider stockpiling your supplies. The easiest parts of plants to preserve are the young green leaves used for teas. Don't pick the leaves and store them in containers – simply dry the stalks of the plant itself. With plants such as nettles, use the fibres in the dried stem for cordage. Store bundles of useful herbs in your shelter or smoke house. Dry and grind up roots to use as flour, or bury them in layers of dry sand. Cover this to keep it dry.

Preserving nuts, fruits and seeds

Nuts are best stored either as a flour or in open containers, still in their shells. Keep them dry and stir them regularly to prevent mildew. Dry fruits by laying them on warm stones in the sun with lids. Above all keep them dry.

The best way to store seeds long-term is by parching them.

Only make flour in small batches. Otherwise you risk losing your whole crop to weevils.

Storing food

Your food store must be safe from mammals, must be dry, and must have a constant temperature. A properly-constructed smoke house will meet many of these criteria, but don't use it to store all your food. "Never keep all your eggs in one basket" is the golden rule when storing your life-saving food.

The easiest larder to make is an underground cache. Try to find a dry sheltered piece of ground – for example, under an overhanging bush or log. Dig a hole about two feet deep and line the pit with bark slabs. Birch or cherry bark is ideal for this. Further line the pit with dried and, if possible, smoked grass. Place your food packages into the pit, followed by more grass. Then add dried aromatic herb (such as marjoram) to disguise any scent from the food. Finally, seal the pit with bark and the soil you originally removed.

Take care to note exactly where you have buried the food, or mark the location so that you can find it again even after a heavy snowfall.

Scavenged food

No animal will stop itself stealing your food out of a sense of fair play. In the same way, don't miss any opportunity to steal from a wild animal. You can turn even the rotting remains of a predator's meal into a life-saving stew if you are hungry enough, Skin and gut the remains in the normal way, and then thoroughly boil the rancid meat for as long as possible. To eat the stew you will need to hold your nose, but it will keep you alive.

This emergency stew *cannot be re-heated*. Discard what you don't eat. If you re-heat it, a dangerous botulism results.

Medicinal plants

On the run from enemy forces behind the lines, or stranded in the middle of nowhere with no resources apart from your personal skills, you have little access to modern medicine. You must learn how to use whatever is available.

The first lesson of survival medicine is not to get sick or injured to start with. This is not as silly as it sounds. Soldiers have the advantage of being young and fit, inoculated against some diseases and trained in hygiene, but over-confidence can undo all this. A Para once got his jaw broken after prodding a 600-lb black bear with a stick, and another squaddie on exercise in the UK was bitten by an adder that was sunning itself on a rock. He thought he was quick enough to catch it behind the head with his finger and thumb: when he woke up in hospital four days later, he knew he wasn't!

Treat all animals with respect, particularly large, nasty ones and small venomous beasts. Generally speaking, if you don't bother them, they won't bother you. All animal bites are danger-ous. They easily go septic, especially bites from carnivorous animals whose fangs cause deep, narrow wounds that soon close, leaving bacteria behind:

Sensible precautions

As a lone survivor you have to take good care of your feet. Keep your shoes on and improvise some footwear if you haven't got any. Your feet might be hardened against stones you tread on, but they won't protect you against snakes.

Don't paddle about in water with bare feet. Poisonous fish such as the lion fish lie motionless in the sand, with venomous spines waiting to be trodden on. If you have to go barefoot through the shallows, shuffle along rather than taking proper steps, and prod the ground in front of you with a stick to clear anything nasty out of the way. This is not a problem confined to the tropics: on a recreational outing in Yorkshire in the UK, some-one stood on a weaver fish and within an hour was unable to walk. Imagine that in a survival situation.

Never wade, swim, or even walk through fresh water in the

tropics. In much of Africa, South-East Asia and South America, the bilharzia worm is endemic. It burrows through your skin to lodge in your bladder, bowels, liver or intestines. If you have to drink water from such a source, boil it thoroughly, chlorinate it or leave it for 48 hours: any of these methods kills off the larvae.

It is wise to keep reasonably covered up to avoid insect stings, even in a hot climate. The vile-smelling leaves of the elder tree rubbed on exposed parts will keep the worst of the insects at bay. Peppermint and bog myrtle are also fairly effective, as is a decoction of pine bark or, in the tropics, camphorwood. None are as effective as chemical bug juice.

These common-sense precautions may seem obvious and even tiresome, but remember: it is the man who has the self-discipline and character to observe the do's and don'ts, even when at the end of his tether, who is most likely to survive.

How to use herbs
To get the maximum value from herbs you have to know the processes used to extract the goodness, how to apply them, and whether they may be used internally or externally. Different herbs and treatments require different methods.

Internal preparations
Infusion: An infusion is made by pouring boiling or near-boiling water on the relevant plant or parts of a plant. Leave for 3-5 minutes; longer for tougher plants.

Decoction: Boil the plant for as long as needed to get the goodness from the herb. The tougher its tissues, the longer you have to boil. Decoctions are usually necessary for bark, stalks, roots and seeds. A cup of tea is an infusion; a pot of non-instant coffee is a decoction.

Maceration: Chop or crush the plant and leave for several hours in water. Use within 12 hours.

Powder: Dry the plant and then crush it. Be careful; powders are very concentrated.

Preparations for external use
Poultice: Chop or crush the plant into a mash, then heat it.

Contrary to popular belief, it does not need to be very hot. Apply the poultice to the appropriate area and remove after five minutes, then re-heat and re-apply. Several short applications are better than one long application.

Compress: Soak a piece of cloth or a chunk of suitable moss in a strong decoction or infusion and hold it in place for about 10 minutes.

Dressing: Dressings are simply compresses made from weaker mixtures. Change the first few dressings on a wound or ulcer every two hours, then gradually increase the time between changes to a maximum of 12 hours.

Herbal remedies

Like most worthwhile skills, learning about herbs takes time and effort. Don't wait until you need them before you try to use them. The golden rule is: do not swallow anything unless you have made a positive identification. In the UK alone there are at least a score of plants that can kill you and many more that will make you very ill. The following are very safe, very effective and easily-identifiable herbs which have preventive and curative properties.

Garlic

The onion family includes leeks, chives, shallots, garlic, garlic mustard ("Jack by the hedge") and ramsons ("bear's garlic"). Hedge garlic and ramsons are very common in temperate climates and the sub-tropics. They are safe to use: if it smells like garlic, it's a member of the garlic family. Garlic was so revered as a healing plant by the Egyptians that they worshipped it as a god. As a lone survivor, you may come to appreciate their point of view.

Garlic contains an antibiotic (allicine) and vitamins A, B and B2. It is an intestinal disinfectant and helps protect you against food poisoning, amoebic dysentery, typhoid and other infectious diseases (which is why it was used by medieval grave robbers). It kills tapeworms and round worms if eaten in large quantities, relieves cramps, lowers blood pressure and fights fever. Garlic aids digestion and stimulates the appetite. It can also be used as a compress.

The most common garlic is garlic mustard, followed by ramsons. The latter is delicious: you will find it forming thick carpets in damp woods, ravines and riverbanks. The whole plant is edible and the seeds (which taste incredibly strong) can be kept for years.

Thyme *(Thymus serpyllum)*

Wild thyme is common throughout the temperate zone and sub-tropics. It contains thymol, a very strong antiseptic with few side-effects: it is retained in the gut and released into the blood-stream to counter infection throughout the body. Thyme helps kill worms and cures diarrhoea, although not quickly. For the evader it has another advantage: it reduces your body scent, which can give you a valuable edge against tracker dogs.

Delicious when added to stews (the best way to take your medicine), it can also be used to make a tea. Sip it for coughs and gargle with it to ease sore throats.

Comfrey

Comfrey is the best herb to help mend broken bones. The plant contains starch and sugar, particularly in the roots, and it is rich in mucilage (a gum-like substance) and tannin. The old country names for it are "boneset" and "knitbone", which describe one of its many uses. Its chemical action reduces swelling at the site of a fracture and fosters union of the bone, and the root can be used to help make a cast because the mucilage causes it to stiffen as it dries, providing the vital rigidity.

The plant grows 3-5 feet (1-2 m) tall in ditches, by roadsides, on waste ground, beside river banks and in woods. It flowers blue, purple or white between June and October. The yellow tuberous comfrey flowers from March to June and lacks the thick root of the common comfrey.

Anaesthetics

Many plants in Europe can reduce the agonising pain of bone-setting and other injuries. The snag is that they can also produce unconsciousness or death. Their chemical composition, and therefore their effects, vary according to the soil, weather and time of year, so never experiment with any of the following: hemlock, dropwort, thorn-apple, henbane, deadly night-shade, wolfsbane or yew. Some of their poisons are used as homeopathic remedies, but a little learning is a dangerous thing: unless you are thoroughly trained, leave these plants alone.

Feverfew is your best herbal anaesthetic. It is chemically similar to aspirin, but takes some time to have an effect. It is sometimes prescribed as a cure for migraine: you can buy it in tablets which cost less than the price of a prescription for similar controlled drugs, or you can eat it in its natural form – one leaf a day is the dosage. Unfortunately, it tastes disgusting: roll it into a "pill" and knock it back quickly. Incidentally, don't neglect the humble aspirin tablet in your kit – it is a very useful and effective drug.

Treatments
Because you can't foresee the terrain where you will be injured, make yourself familiar with plants from many different habitats. The following cures are from ten of the safest and commonest medicinal plants to be found in the temperate zone. Familiarize yourself with these before studying further.

Bleeding
A plant with haemostatic properties will help stop bleeding. You probably won't have such plants readily to hand when you first find yourself in survival conditions, so prepare and store these herbs in your survival medicine chest. The dried and powdered root of bistort (*Polygonum bistorta*) can be applied direct to external wounds.

Use an infusion of the green stem of horsetail (*Equisetum arvense)* to wash the wound. It will help stop the bleeding.

Antiseptic
To prevent wounds becoming infected they can be washed with an infusion made with these medicines:

1. Greater plantain (*Plantago major*) leaves and stem. In an emergency, chew the leaf of this plant to a pulp and use it directly on the wound.

2. Selfheal (*Prunella vulgaris*) flowering stems. This plant too can be chewed, for a quickly prepared pulp.
3. Dried burdock (*Arctium lappa*) root, made into an infusion. This is ideal to prepare for long journeys. The leaves can also be infused but are less potent.
4. Birch (*Betula pendula*) leaves when infused make an all-purpose disinfectant.

Digestive disorders

An excellent cure for diarrhoea is charcoal and a herbal tea. Remember to keep your fluid intake high when suffering from diarrhoea.

Five plants to aid digestive disorders:

1. Dandelion (*Taraxacum officinale*) leaves, washed and eaten raw, or cooked like spinach, are an excellent aid to digestion. Try to include some in your survival diet as a preventative.
2. Dog rose (*Rose canina*) petals and/or hip are a very good stomach-settler. Before eating any of the vitamin-C-rich hips, remove the hairy seeds inside them.
3. Water mint (*Mentha aquatica*) leaves and stems can be used as an infusion. This plant is also useful to flavour survival stews. Don't eat large quantities.
4. Horseradish (*Armoracia rusticana*) roots and leaves in your daily diet will add digestion and help prevent problems. The scrapings from the root make a strong flavouring for stews.
5. Selfheal flowering stems, infused, ease upsets. You can also prepare the leaves like spinach and include them in your diet.

For severe digestive disorders such as dysentery, use an infusion of powdered bistort root.

THE HERBAL COMPRESS

1. Open wounds are vulnerable to infection, especially as your body's resistance will be low after a prolonged period in the field. A compress of an antiseptic plant like greater plantain is made by

pulping the plant with a stone. Make sure you wash the stone beforehand.

2. Mop up the juice of the plant with the remaining flesh and gather it into a ball.

3. Apply the herbal pulp firmly into and around the wound. Do not attempt to stitch up wounds of a superficial nature as you may stitch in the infection, and pressure caused by the infection and the stitching may lead to restricted blood flow to the area and then perhaps to gangrene. Cuts left open that heal in this way do leave nasty scars, but in the absence of sterile conditions and antibiotics this is the safer course.

4. Keep the herbal pulp in place and maintain pressure on the wound with a wrapping of dock leaves held in place with strips of animal skin.

Insect bites and stings

Insects are always an irritation for a survivor. Besides the diseases, such as malaria, that they carry, their bites and stings can quickly become painful festering sores if scratched. Use infusions of horsetail, burdock, plantain or birch to soothe the inflammations. You will probably find that after a couple of days of eating wild herbs insects will pay less attention to you, particularly if you include a small amount of plantain in your daily diet.

Deal with stings from stinging nettles by rubbing them with a fresh burdock leaf or a dock leaf.

Bruises and headaches

You are certain to suffer some bruises and strains. To ease these, make compresses from bistort, horsetail or plantain.

Headaches are often encountered by survivors in the first few days of being stranded. Effective cures are soothing teas of mint or rose hips and/or petals.

Toothache

Minor cuts, bruises and bites are relatively easy to deal with under primitive conditions. But when it comes to survival dentistry there is very little you can do. Rose tea can ease pain, but the best answer is to care properly for your teeth. This means regular visits to the dentist, and especially before going on extended operations. When stranded, clean your teeth with ash or alder *(Alnus glutinosa)* bark.

Jellyfish

Jellyfish and other sea creatures can give you nasty wounds. Stingrays, weaver fish, lion fish and zebra fish venoms cause excruciating pain, swelling, vomiting and diarrhoea, and can slow your heartbeat. Box jellyfish and Portuguese men o' war cause the same symptoms, and paralysis of your breathing muscles and fits as well.

Treatment for all these nautical disasters is the same. Apply a tight tourniquet between the wound and your heart. Remove tentacles or spines, but not with your bare hands. Any form of dilute acid, e.g. vinegar or lemon juice, prevents further releases of venom. Fish venoms are destroyed by heat and the pain is eased greatly by the application of hot water. Also, the venom has a short-lived effect, so a casualty who is not breathing and has no pulse can be brought round by cardiac massage and mouth-to-mouth resuscitation.

Snake bite

An old farmer in Texas who reared rattlesnakes for their meat and skin was bitten by them four times. He nearly died the first time. Later, when living with Navajo Indians, he was bitten again. They applied a tourniquet between the bite and his heart, which is standard procedure. But then they cut an onion in half and pressed it against the bite; when it turned green, they threw it away and applied the other half. The procedure was continued with more onions until no green showed. Although he continued to feel ill, the worst of the sickness passed in two days instead of the normal five or six.

The moral is that with a knowledge of both modern and folk medicine, you can adapt to find the best possible course of action in circumstances where most people would give up and die. (For more information on snake bites see p317.)

Tips on preparing medicines

The secret of successful cures lies in how you choose and prepare your herbs. Try to collect only healthy plants, from areas of unpolluted ground. In wilderness areas, the best places to search for herbs are by water sources and where forest meets grassland. In escape and evasion situations, the edges of fields and along forestry rides are the places to search.

Having gathered your herbs, shake them clean of dust and insects. Most of the cures involve infusions, which basically means preparing the herb as a tea. Never boil your herb. Instead, allow it to brew in water just off the boil. This will retain all of the goodness in the plant.

Make paste for poultices by grinding up the herb between two rocks, with a little water. Apply this directly to the wound and wrap with cloth or large leaves.

You will have to judge the strength of your herbal cures by eye, as each plant has its own character, depending on the season or its location. If in doubt, always under-medicate.

Tools and Equipment

Survival knives

A civilian stranded after a disaster such as a shipwreck or a plane crash will not have chosen a survival knife. He will have to make do with whatever he's got with him – perhaps a piece of sharpened fuselage, or at best a Swiss Army Knife. But soldiers and adventurers operating in remote regions of the world will almost certainly have a knife with them at all times, and they will have made a choice. The wrong choice could be fatal, as a knife is literally a life-line in the wilderness, upon which you must be able to rely completely. It's too late to find out your knife is not strong enough when you are trying to cut yourself free from a capsized white water raft heading for a waterfall!

NOT A WEAPON

The survival knife is just that – for survival. The characteristics of a good survival knife are not those of a weapon.

Besides, the law in many countries is strict and you may be committing a crime if you own one without good reason – and in some places if you own one at all. They are not for kids. When you buy one you also buy into a professional, adult level of responsibility in its use and security.

Selecting the knife

When choosing your knife, find a reputable dealer with a large range of quality knives. Often the best shops stock custom knife maker ranges. Do not limit your choice of knife to those described as "Survival Knives": there are many hunting knives eminently suited to survival use. Try also to be practical. There are many beautiful knives for sale, well made and by top-class manufacturers; but they are not all practical for the specialized use you will be demanding.

You must always carry your knife with you; you never know when you'll need it. This means that your knife must be a convenient size to be carried without becoming a drag, and must also be capable of carrying out all those basic camp chores such as opening tins, hammering tent pegs, cutting string and so on. And if you become stranded or have to go to ground, it will have to do the job of a small axe as well, so it must be strong. Generally speaking, a fixed blade is the better option as it is stronger and more rugged, but most professionals carry two knives: a large fixed blade and a small folding blade.

The metal

There are really only two basic choices: carbon steel or stainless steel. Carbon steel will rust (generally speaking) unless cared for, whereas stainless steel should not. It is widely recognized that carbon steel takes a keener edge than stainless, although in some modern aircraft and cutlery, stainless steels are challenging this traditional concept. Stainless steel should hold its edge longer than carbon steel, but is in many cases harder to sharpen.

In most cases, stainless steel would be the best choice. Take the advice of a reputable dealer, as there are many varieties in use, in many cases alloyed with other metals such as vanadium, molybdenum and chromium to change their qualities. In general, avoid divers' knives (unless made by a reputable manufacturer), as the steel is usually very poor.

When you are finding out about the type of steel used, try also to find out about the temper. If a knife is under-tempered it will be strong but will not take an edge; if it is over-tempered, it could shatter in use. There is a tendency for manufacturers to over-temper blades!

Size, weight and balance
The wise traveller tries to reduce the weight of his pack, but when travelling far off the beaten track don't try to economize on the weight of your knife. You need a knife with a weighty blade, as this reduces the force you need to apply and allows more control and efficiency. But if you choose a blade that is too heavy, it will cause fatigue in your fingers, wrist and arm, and this can lead to dangerous accidents.

The length and weight of your knife are critical factors, bur no real formula exists to help you choose. In jungles, machetes and long, light knives are the norm, but for more general use these are really too long. As a rough guide, don't choose a knife that is more than two and a half times the length of your hand, and no less than one and a half times long.

Leverage principle
To illustrate the principle, imagine that you are striking a nail into a piece of wood with a one-metre steel bar. If you want to achieve the same result with a bar 50 centimetres long, you must either use a lot more force or a heavier bar. The shorter, heavier bar is more controllable as it exerts less leverage on the wrist, and can be used in more confined space. The same is true of knife lengths.

Once you have chosen the length and weight of your blade, try to decide where the point of balance lies. Ideally it should be just in front of the guard. This means that the knife is slightly blade-heavy, yet easily controlled by adjusting your grip. If the point of balance is too far forward it will cause muscle strain, which makes the knife slip from your grasp. The more common fault is that the knife is too handle-heavy. Excess weight in the grip is a burden, as it does not contribute to the blade's cutting ability.

Features and fittings

Grip: The most important fitting to your knife is the grip; probably the commonest fault in most survival knives is the way by which the grip is attached. The part of the blade that goes to make up the handle is called the "tang". In many knives, this narrows at the join of the guard and grip. This is an inherent weakness, at the point of greatest strain. The ideal attachment is what is called "full tang", where the blade remains the width of the grip throughout.

Guard: The guard is an important feature of any survival knife. Its purpose is to prevent your fingers slipping forward onto the sharp edge while using the knife. Remember: even the smallest cut can fester and prove fatal under survival conditions.

Point: The point of your knife is another important feature. It needs to be sharp, and strong enough to pry with. It is an advantage if it falls below the horizontal mid-line of your knife: this is a "true drop point", and prevents the point snagging the flesh of an animal's stomach wall during skinning and gutting.

Saws: Saws are a regular feature of survival knives. Do not expect them to saw through wood. They will, however, cut grooves in wood and cut ropes, making them a useful additional feature, although not essential.

Gristle saws are sometimes found in front of the guard. These again are a useful additional feature that will find many uses.

Hollow handles: Designed to accommodate useful survival tools such as fishing lines or firelighting aids, they are an excellent addition as long as they do not weaken the grip. Hollow handles do often mean, however, that the tang not only narrows but also shortens as well. While not all hollow handles are weak, take great care in your choice.

Sheaths: Sheaths are an important feature of any knife. As well as protecting the knife, they must be strong enough to protect you from injury if you fall on the encased blade. Good-quality leather sheaths are almost as good as the very strong scabbards being made from modern plastics, but beware of cheap leather. If you find a good knife that has a poor sheath you may be able to have a better sheath made for it.

The method of carrying the sheath is entirely up to you, and you may want to make some modifications. You may also consider taping additional survival gear to the outside of your scabbard, as long as you don't end up looking like a Christmas tree.

Personalising your knife

Having carefully selected your knife, work it in, personalise it, practise using it and, above all, look after it. Your life may one day depend on it. Your choice of survival knife speaks of your knowledge of survival; the state it is in and the way in which you use it speak of your experience. To a survivor, a knife is the most versatile life-saving aid. To a survival expert it is a craftsman's tool, treated with the same care and attention as a master carpenter's chisels. It is not toyed with: it remains in its sheath until it is needed, and is then used with great dexterity and ease for a multitude of tasks before being returned to its resting place.

The grip: The best place to begin your personalisation. It is an essential feature of your knife, and must allow for exact and secure control of the blade in many differing uses and environments.

1. If a grip is too large you will not be able to hold onto it for heavy cutting.
2. If a grip is too small you will have to clench it tightly for heavy cutting; this is very tiring and dangerous. Blisters and severe hand cramps can result.
3. If a grip is too long it may pull out from your hand.
4. If a grip is too short you will not be able to hold onto the knife correctly, which may be dangerous.

As a general rule, it is better to have a grip that is slightly too big, as it is less tiring to use than too-small grip – and when your hand tires you will have accidents. A large grip is easier to hold when wearing gloves. Your grip should be easy to hold in a variety of different ways, with no sharp edges or protuberances that will impede its use. It should be the correct shape in cross section, which is a blunt oval shape.

GRIP CROSS-SECTIONS

Altering the grip may seem a drastic thing to do, but once the knife fits your hand, there will be a visit improvement in its effectiveness as it will take less effort to use.

Improving the shape

1. If your grip is too round you may be able to build it up using gaffa tape or nylon webbing and a strong resin. Very often round grips are all-metal: these are best covered, as metal is a "non-friendly" material, hot in the desert, dangerously freezing in the Arctic and always hard. Remember that whatever you use as a grip covering must be resilient to a variety of temperatures and environmental conditions.

2. If your grip is too square you may (if the grip material is soft or man-made) be able to file or sand it to the correct shape. This is preferable to covering because the performance of the grip will not be impaired by changing climates. If your grip is of bone it may feel as though it is more comfortable when gripped as for hammering. In this case there is usually little that can be done other than replacing the grip entirely.

The blade: Having set up the grip, give your knife a "road test": there should be an immediate and definite improvement in its performance. But the blade is where the major transformation will occur. You will have to alter the angle of the edge to improve its cutting ability, which in most cases means a long session of filing. Avoid using a high-speed grinding wheel, unless you are very expert in its use, and back-street knife sharpeners, as the risk of the blade overheating and losing its temper is high.

To help you, some of the better established knife manufacturers will supply a knife with a "professional edge", but only on request. Once the edge has been altered you should never have to re-grind the edge, because you will now "parallel sharpen".

Sharpening

To sharpen your knife you will need a stone. The best type of stone is still a natural stone such as a Washita or Soft Arkansas stone, although there is much to be said for the strength of a diamond whetstone for field use.

At home base you should have a large stone. This makes sharpening an easy task, using six long strokes on the left of the blade, six on the right, and six alternately. In the field you will need a small pocket stone, or failing this a suitable local stone or large pebble. Hold the knife steady and move the stone: the opposite to home sharpening. Whenever you sharpen your blade, maintain an even pressure across the full width of the edge. If you place too much pressure on the edge itself you will not be sharpening parallel to the edge angle you originally laboured to achieve, but will be gradually blunting the knife.

PARALLEL SHARPENING

Once you have a professional edge, make sure you do not destroy it while honing. A common failing is to tilt the edge too sharply; this gradually blunts the knife. These cross-sections of the blade show the right and wrong methods, and the results of each.

Honing

Having sharpened your knife, a really razor-like edge can be achieved by lightly honing with a ceramic rod. Use this before all major cutting to help maintain the edge.

Common uses for your knife

Slashing: Grip the knife as far back as possible. Use long, sweeping motions with a straight arm.

Chopping: Grip the knife further forward, with your cutting action more from the elbow than the shoulder.

Stake pointing: Hold the grip even further forward and, using mainly wrist action, cut away from you.

Hammering: Use the flat of the blade, keeping the edge aimed away from your body.

Draw knife: Fit a makeshift split stick-handle to the point end of your knife to create a second handle.

Sawing: Sawing is not designed to cut through wood but is mainly for grooving wood and cutting ropes. Cut on the draw stroke.

Rasping: If your knife has a saw back, you can set it into a log and work bone on it.

Whittling: Control is the name of the game. If you can lever with the thumb of your free hand, on the back of the blade, do so. Otherwise take your time with many small, shallow cuts.

Splitting: This is an important operation. Strike the blade through the work piece with a wooden baton (not stone or metal).

Professional use

In the hands of a professional a survival knife takes on jobs that seem impossible. This is because he has learned to use the correct cutting techniques and angles. Experience and practice will be your best guide here, although the most basic principles are:

1. Safety first.
2. Cut with the grain in your favour.
3. Always follow through.
4. Use smooth, steady cuts, the fewer the better.

Making other tools

A professional's knife is a tool to make other tools. Wherever possible he avoids any use of the knife which may result in its damage or loss. If a root needs to be dug up, make a digging stick; if a spear point is needed, whittle one.

Safety first
1. When you carry your knife, carry a first aid kit.
2. Plan every cut before you make it.
3. Keep all limbs away from the arc of your cut.
4. Always cut away from the body.
5. Be aware of what is going on around you.
6. Replace the knife in its scabbard immediately after use.
7. Never lend your knife; you may never see it again.

IMPORTANT: *The privilege of owning a survival knife is one that all survival students must uphold and defend. Be professional in your approach and your use of your knife, and be seen to be professional.*

Bows

One surprising omission from most survival training and survival literature (including Special Forces) is a weapon that has been used by millions of men and women, and all young boys, from the Stone Age to the present: the bow and arrow. This may be because the skills of bow-maker, arrowsmith, fletcher and archer are not perfected overnight, and you don't learn them best in a survival situation.

The bow and arrow have been ignored in survival training because some knowledge of tree types is necessary, and professional bow-makers insist that wood must be seasoned for three years to make a bow. Neither of these notions will hold water. A soldier should be knowledgeable about nature, especially if he is trained in survival techniques. But, yes, a longbow must be seasoned for three years – if you want one that will last for years and can drive an arrow-head through the breastplate of a knight at 400 metres. But that's rather unlikely on the modern battle-field. Most survivors or evaders, if offered a weapon that would get their dinner and kill an enemy at a range of up to 150 metres, would say, "That'll do nicely, thank you." That weapon can be made in as little as four hours, and not more than a couple of days depending on materials available, and the power required.

Bows and the law

Game hunting with bows is illegal almost everywhere, so don't do it. Target shooting can teach you the basics of archery, but it cannot prepare you for survival archery. The nearest you can get is to try the sport of field archery, in which you shoot different-shaped targets at unknown ranges deployed in woods and fields. This enables you to practise instinctive shooting without getting jailed for poaching.

Shooting tips

A strong upper body is both necessary for, and developed by, archery. You need this strength to draw the bow and to hold your aim. In a survival situation your strength may be reduced, perhaps greatly, by hunger, fatigue, illness or injury. If so, do not try ambitious shots. Use a shorter "draw length" – the distance the arrow is drawn – and engage your target from as close a range as possible. A quick, instinctive shot is less likely to be wrong because of fatigue. In fact, this is often the best way to shoot in any case. Field archery is mostly snap shots, perhaps at moving targets, and target archery bears as much resemblance to it as shooting on the range does to field-firing or combat shooting. Some archers are always more accurate with an instinctive shot than an aimed shot. Use the style that suits you best.

What to wear

Note the dress of the bowman. Do not wear headgear with a peak – a fatigue cap for example – even when shooting into the sun, as it will foul your draw.

Gloves are one of the most under-emphasized survival items. After a few days of using fires, building or collecting and using sharp or toxic materials, your hands will get rather painful. For the archer, gloves prevent your holding arm being painfully bruised by the string. Pressure on the fingers on your drawing hand can be very painful without gloves, and is distracting in the aim. But you can make a "shooting tab" and a bracer from hide.

If the skirt of your jacket is hanging, or if the sleeves are bulky, remove the jacket, or it will foul the string when you release it, causing loss of speed, range and accuracy.

Making a bow

The first step on the road to equipping yourself with a bow and some arrows is to find the materials from which you'll make them – which means knowing how to recognize the right wood where it's growing. You may already be familiar with the species of tree and shrub mentioned already, of course. If not, the best ways to find out about them are to ask someone who's country-wise to show them to you, or to go to a botanical garden. If the idea of visiting a botanical garden seems weird, bear in mind that paragraph 87 of the old Air Ministry publication on jungle survival recommends unit visits for aircrew. Servicemen in survival-oriented units should ask their CO to arrange a day visit, which most parks and gardens anywhere in the world will be happy to set up. A day's visit will give you all the knowledge you need about trees to find the material for a bow. On top of that, you'll learn to recognize a huge variety of edible, medicinal and otherwise useful plants. If you think it's a waste of a day's training, just think about it – it beats the hell out of square-bashing, or humping a loaded Bergen over 50 kilometres.

Let's assume you've now armed yourself with a fair knowledge of the local flora. So what do you look for?

Hard, well-seasoned, springy woods are best for making a bow. Don't even think about making one from softwoods such as pine, fir, new elder shoots, larch, spruce, and so on. You'll only be wasting valuable time and energy. Look for hardwoods like wych elm, elm, oak, ash, rowan, birch, greenheart, wild rose, hornbeam, dagame (lemonwood), osage orange, juniper and ironwood. Some of these will make a good bow, and some will make a passable one. None will make a bow equal to the king of bow woods, the yew.

POISONOUS YEW

Yew grows in most of Asia, the Americas and throughout Europe. It's very common in southern England, and you'll see it in churchyards, estates, parks and gardens. Be careful with it. The leaves, berry arils (an extra covering over the fruit) and sap contain a deadly nerve poison, taxine. Celtic warriors dipped their arrows in the yew sap, just to make sure! So don't use the leftovers from

your bow-making as skewers or spoons or whatever. You won't
come to any harm from handling yew, though, as long as you
wash the sap off your hands.

A QUICK ONE
You can make an excellent bow very quickly – seasoning the
wood in a day, over a fire – from rowan. (This is sometimes called
mountain ash in England). Ideally, you should take the wood
from a slim sapling growing in dense wood. This is because trees
growing close together have to "shoot for the sun", and so grow
slim and straight with few branches low on the trunk: just what
you need for a bow. You don't harm the environment by taking a
few of these saplings, since you help the other trees to spread.
And if you cover or dirty the stump, you won't leave any sign of
your presence to be spotted from the air.

Rowan bows are "sweet" to use, giving no jar or kick. But they
do creak ominously when you're shooting them in. It takes fine
judgment and a steely nerve to find out how far you can draw
them – but then a good bow properly drawn is seven-eighths
broken!

THE CORRECT SIZE OF A BOW
When deciding what length to make your bow, consider the
following:

1. The longer the bow is, the better it will resist a given pull.
2. If you change your mind and shorten an existing bow it will
   shoot further for the same draw but will be harder to pull
   and is more likely to break.
3. Experiment to find your ideal draw length and try to make
   your bow to suit, but any bow drawing between 60 and 90
   cms (2 to 3 feet) will be sufficient for most "survival
   archery". A bow should not bend in the middle – the central
   foot or so should be rigid. To determine the position of the
   handgrip, find the centre of the bow, then mark 75 mm (3
   inches) below and 25 mm (1 inch) above. This section will
   be the handle. The arrow is shot from the bow centre while
   you grip beneath it. The upper part of the bow should be

cut slightly more than the lower in order to compensate for the handle. Trim your bow to its finished size, then cut the nocks at either end.

TOOLS

Once you've selected your bow stave, you'll need some tools to carve the actual bow from it. Professional bowmakers first use a hammer and steel wedges to split logs into workable dimensions. Then a small hand-axe trims the stave to the rough shape and size of the bow. A spokeshave brings it down to the exact size, with final minute shavings removed with shards of glass. In the middle of nowhere and on the run you're not too likely to have any of these. But an issue-type machete or a heavy survival knife will do the job, given some skill and elbow grease.

It's always worth having at least Stanley knife blades in your survival kit. You can use them on their own as scalpels for fine work, and you can use one to cut its own wooden handle. You can use the Stanley to make your bow from scratch, but it's invaluable for making arrows. If you haven't got any of these, then it's back to basic Stone-Age survival technology.

SEASON THE WOOD

Now to making the bow. Look for a branch or trunk of the right wood that's as straight as possible. It should be at least 6 feet 6 inches (2 metres) long, although you can go as short as 4 feet (1.25 m). If you can get a piece of seasoned – that is, properly dried-out – wood, terrific. Look for uprooted trees, cuttings and trimmings, at rail and roadsides, and near farms and houses. In conventional bow-making the entire log is seasoned, sometimes for years, and then thinned down to a bow. Survivors have to reverse the process, and cut out the rough bow and then dry it. This is a lot faster, though it may cause some warping. Trim the stave to the approximate size of the bow, leaving a good quarter-inch surplus in both thickness and breadth.

DRYING OUT

At this point, decide how quickly you need your bow. Some

woods you can use straight off, but all of them improve enor-
mously with drying out. In a very hot climate a day or two makes
a huge difference, and the bow keeps improving as you use it. In
cold or temperate climates you will have to dry it over or near the
fire. Yew and rowan make the best quick-dried bows. While you
have the bow near the fire, you may as well make sure that the
stave is straight when viewed from the back or belly.

If you heat – or, preferably, steam – the staff where it's bent,
you can put it permanently into shape by applying pressure in the
right direction. This doesn't set up any stresses in the wood.

You can also re-curve or reflex the bow by the same method.
But if the stave you've chosen is naturally reflexed, or re-curved
at one end or the other, don't straighten it. If it ain't broke, don't
fix it!

MAKING THE STRING

The English longbowmen of the Middle Ages used bow strings
able to take a weight of 140 lbs (60 kg), and these were made
from the stalks of the common stinging nettle. Unfortunately this
takes a long time to master, so the average survivor must improvise. Silk is ideal for a bow string because it stretches very little,
but it is not available in every survival situation. Nylon paracord
is a more feasible material. Although it does stretch a little, this
can be taken up when bracing the bow. Paracord has the bonus of
being near rot-proof and very strong.

BRACING A BOW

Putting the string on a bow is called bracing, and it is very important to get this right. Place your hand "thumbs up" on the back of
the bow: the string should touch your thumb when correctly
braced. You need not be too slavish to this rule with a survival
bow, but the nearer the better. Use a timber hitch to tie the bottom
end of the string permanently in place and a simple loop to attach
it at the top. When you need the bow, brace it and slip on the top
loop. Always unstring the bow when not in use or it will lose
strength, and never leave it standing on end.

Arrows

The arrow is at once both beautifully simple and extremely sophisticated. It is a missile, developed by human ingenuity over thousands of years. Many of the lessons learnt in the manufacture of millions of these missiles, with hundreds of variations, were forgotten after the Middle Ages, only to be painstakingly re-learnt by twentieth-century missile scientists. For survival purposes, you will not have to make an arrow anywhere near as good as those used at Agincourt, which had heavy armour-piercing warheads and had to withstand 120 lb of thrust from the string.

The first thing to learn about arrows is that the missile (the arrow) must match its launcher (the bow). At this stage, an explanation of what's known as the Archer's Paradox is helpful.

Due to the impact of the string, the inertia in the arrow, and the fact that the arrow is set at an angle to the string (which is in line with the centreline of the bow) and the edge of the bow, the arrow actually bends over the bow when you release it. You will not see this with the naked eye, but it does happen. When it leaves the bow, the arrow springs the other way and, after a few more bucks, straightens out and flies off to your target. If the arrow is too weak for the bow, therefore, it will wobble in flight and lose power. It may also break, usually about six inches from the nock (the notch into which the bowstring fits), usually with jagged edges, and usually getting stopped by the inside of your wrist, which is damned painful. If the arrow is too strong, it will go off a little to your left (if you are right-handed).

For survival purposes, you don't have to match bow and arrow exactly. Instead, learn how each of your arrows flies. It is better in every way to err on the side of the strong arrow.

WOODS TO USE

So now we have the theory, let's make some arrows before we starve to death! Good woods are birch, ash, hornbeam, alder, willow, bamboo, ramin (gonystylus), pine, fir, oak, elm, beech, elder, dog rose, bramble and some reeds. As a survivor you will do best by not confining yourself to the rules, but to use your common sense.

The simplest, quickest and most versatile wood is bamboo,

which is *not* confined to the jungle but common worldwide. Bamboo breaks always have many dead canes amongst the green: these can be used instantly – dry the green ones near the fire, or leave them for a few days after cutting. Don't forget that you can eat the young shoots, raw or cooked, after you remove the poisonous hairs along the edges of the leaves! Next (for ease, not quality) come strong reeds, followed by willow. Surprisingly, thick bramble and wild rose can provide good arrows. The thorns are easily removed with your front teeth, leaving a nice round shaft.

THE SHAFT
The arrow should be as straight as you can make it, as bends and kinks cause inaccuracy and wind resistance. Use steam, or bend it over a warm stone, to straighten it, as you did making your bow. Some woods you can straighten cold, either by bending and holding for a minute, or by tying the bow with thread or string and leaving it for an hour or so.

It is easier than you think to cut an arrow from a billet of wood, especially the softwoods such as pine, using your knife or, better still, your Stanley blade from your survival tin, suitably mounted.

If you have the time, it is then back to Stone-Age technology for a sanding block, to give perfect roundness. Make this from two pieces of sandstone, about 2 ½ by ½ by 1 inch. Chip out a semi-circular groove along the length of each one. When you put one on top of the other, they should make a circular groove that's the same diameter as you want your arrows to be. Draw the arrow through these blocks until it's smooth. A far better device, if you can make one, is a small steel plate   inch thick with a "V" cut in it. This cuts better, and allows you to vary the diameter of the arrow.

THE FLIGHTS
By far the easiest way to fit the flights is to use plastic – not quite as good as feathers, but requiring much less skill, time and effort. Sadly, there is no shortage of plastic litter anywhere. Near houses, where farmers, climbers and forestry workers are, along any roadside, beach -in fact, just about anywhere – you will find a profusion of plastic drink bottles, oil cartons, milk cartons, etc.

Cut them into strips with your Stanley blade or knife. If necessary, put them momentarily in boiling water or near heat for a few seconds to soften them, then smooth them flat. Fix them by cutting one slot through the arrow for a pair of flights and a groove at right angles for the third flight.

If you use feathers, those of geese or large gliding birds are best – for example the eagle, buzzard, hawk, flamingo, pelican, crow, seagull or turkey. Good places to find them are farmers' or gamekeepers' gibbets: rows of dead crows hanging upside down on fences to scare other crows away. Use the large flight feathers from the wing. Do not mix feathers from right and left wings, if you can help it – it causes wobbling and loss of power, as they set up opposing wind currents.

POSITIONING THE FLIGHTS

The flights should be positioned at 120-degree intervals. Plastic flights will need a little moulding to give them a slight curve, and if you are using bird feathers do not mix the feathers from either wing: this will make the arrow wobble and reduce its velocity.

ARROWHEADS AND NOCKS

You can make your arrowheads out of steel, slate, stone, bone, flint, horn, glass, or just sharpened wood. You can even use staples from a fence post. For the nock, it's simplest just to groove the wood. Put a whipping above the nock to prevent it splitting, if necessary.

Shooting the bow

Although you can shoot without them, it is far better to have a pair of gloves, or a shooting tab and a bracer, to stop the inside of your bow arm being bruised by the string. You can easily make a bracer out of rabbit skin or hide, and a shooting tab too. If you have a jacket with close-fitting sleeves, you can do without the bracer. But a glove or shooting tab is virtually indispensable, as the pressure of the string on the fingers is painful and can be very distracting in the aim.

BRACE THE BOW

First you've got to "brace" or put the string on the bow. The correct height from the back of the bow to the string was covered in "Making a bow". Don't be a slave to this dimension for a survival bow, especially when you first use it. Use a timber hitch for the bottom end, permanently in place, and a simple fixed loop for the top. When you need to use the bow, just brace it by slipping on the top loop.

Shooting

Archery can be broken down into five component skills: standing, nocking, drawing, aiming and loosing. The principles outlined below hold good in target and field shooting, although it is not always possible to stand correctly in field shooting.

Here are the ideals in the five disciplines.

STANDING

Put your feet in the "stand at ease" position, at right angles to the target. Leave only about eight inches between your heels. Keep your knees straight, body upright and turned towards the target, so that if a line were drawn through your shoulders it would run to the target

NOCKING

Hold the bow with your left hand (right hand for left-handed people). Without touching the flights, engage the nock in the whipping on the string (if fitted). The nock should be in the exact centre of the string, with the arrow resting on the mid-point of the bow, on the left-hand edge of the bow (right-hand side for left-handed people). You can make a mark in the middle of the bow to ensure quick, accurate nocking.

DRAWING

Place the fingers with index finger above, and next two fingers below, the arrow. You will probably prefer the three-finger draw, but the two-finger draw did not harm mediaeval Englishmen! If the terrain permits, your weight should be evenly distributed on both feet. Bring your bow across your body at waist level, and slightly incline the head. This helps the chest muscles to assist the draw. Both arms should be bent at this point, and your body relaxed.

Begin to straighten your arms and bring the bow up as you continue the draw smoothly and continuously to the full draw position.

For target archery, exactly the same draw length is taken for every shot. In survival archery this is not always possible (due to illness or fatigue), or desirable. And you are not very likely to have produced such perfectly matched arrows; it is far better to know how each arrow flies.

AIMING

Make a straight mark, or marks for different ranges, on the outside of the bow. If your arrow lengths and draw lengths are uniform, line up the arrowhead on the point of aim. Remember that the target and the point of aim may not be the same, due to windage (air resistance or wind force on the projectile) or range. The trick is to get the line of sight between your eye, sight marks or arrowhead, and the aiming point to coincide with the trajectory of the arrow. In field archery it is usually far better to make a quick draw, aim and shoot.

Remember the Archer's Paradox? This can affect your aim at very close range (up to 10 yards/9 metres), and if the arrow is too rigid it will tend to go to the right, at any range. Compensate for these problems by aiming off.

LOOSING

Letting go of the string, or loosing, is one of the most important aspects of archery. It is a lot easier to achieve a correct loose than it is to describe it accurately – a fact agreed upon by all writers on the subject!

The loose should be both sharp and smooth, with the bow arm kept rigidly in place. This is important, as the sudden release of the load on the muscles of the bow arm tends to make you push the bow to your inside before the arrow has cleared the bow, or to pull hard the other way in anticipation. Something similar happens when a rifleman or machine-gunner tenses in expectation of the recoil after squeezing the trigger, and pulls or pushes his weapon off the aim.

STAY IN THE AIM

It is best to "follow through", that is, stay in the aim, eyes on the aiming mark, until the fall of the shot, just as you do with a fire-arm – unless, of course, your target can do you some damage, or is likely to escape!

In all the above aspects of archery, strange as it may seem, your posture and movements should be smooth, graceful and pleasing to the eye of the beholder. This has been accepted by all writers and instructors of archery through the centuries. It is not just for aesthetic appeal: for various reasons, if it is not done gracefully and smoothly, missed targets and pulled muscles are the result!

The quarry

This may be fish, fowl, four-legged and furry – or your enemy. It is important to have the right bow and the right arrow for your particular prey. A heavy bow, shooting steel broadheads, will kill anything including an elephant – if it hits it. The bows and arrows in English fifteenth-century warfare would kill a man at 300 metres – even through chain mail and steel plate. But this is ridiculous overkill for fish and birds: a heavy bow is difficult to aim, tiring and unnecessary. Ordinary arrows are all right.

On larger game, you achieve the kill by penetrating a vital organ, or by causing a haemorrhage. Tests indicate that flint has better flesh-penetrating properties than steel. American archer Bob Swinhart boasted of shooting buffalo and rhino with a 90 lb bow and steel broadheads, leopards with a 70 lb bow, and a five-ton bull elephant from 15 yards using a 100-lb bow and *five* arrows. But he did have a back-up rifleman beside him, and it would have been some sort of world record to have missed an elephant at 15 yards!

Barbed arrows are only for holding fish; on birds and game they are cruel and unnecessary. For an evader they can be positively fatal – to you. If you shoot game with an *un*barbed arrow it either kills it, or falls out in a very short time. If you do not retrieve it, there is not much chance of it being found by anyone. But a barbed arrow will stay in, and if you don't find your prey, it will probably fester. A dead animal surrounded by scavengers will surely be spotted, and *you* have left your calling card stuck in it!

IMPORTANT SAFETY NOTE
Bows can kill! Treat them like a firearm. Never point your bow and arrow at something you do not intend to shoot. When practising, check your backdrop: if you can't see that it is safe to shoot, don't. Never shoot at anything on the skyline.

Spears
On your foraging excursions, you have spotted signs of large mammals. If you can catch one you will provide yourself with a large amount of meat that can be preserved and stored, as well as useful skin and bone. But how do you catch the animal? Of the many hunting techniques at your disposal, the age-old method of spear hunting is a practical answer. Spears are easy to make, easy to learn how to use, and allow you to hunt while on the move. In fact, spears are so effective that early man, hunting in bands, was able to catch animals as big as mammoths. In areas where there are large carnivores that pose a serious threat to your survival (obviously best avoided), a spear is about the most effective deterrent you can carry with you, as these predators will almost certainly have encountered horns and antlers and have therefore learned to respect long, sharp points. There are even Native American tales of grizzly bears backing away from spears, but don't count on it!

Simple spears
The quickest and simplest spear you can make is the "self spear". In its crudest form, this is simply a straight piece of hard, natured wood with a sharpened point. You can vastly improve it by fire-hardening the point and fashioning it into a leaf-shaped blade. But the self spear is a primitive and brutal weapon and a skilled survivor should make every effort to kill as cleanly as possible, reducing the suffering of his prey to the minimum.

An effective spear must have a sharp cutting-edge that is wide enough to cause maximum bleeding, but not so wide that it prevents the spear penetrating to the vital organs. So the most important part of a spear is the point. As a survivor, you can never be certain of precisely what raw materials you will have to hand, so the broader your knowledge of spear design the better.

Basically, spears fall into one or both of two categories: thrusting spears and throwing spears. As the name suggests, thrusting spears are used at very close range, so the spear point can be broad, as the impact force is guaranteed to be great. Throwing spears, on the other hand, are used at a distance: they need to be light so that they can fly fast, and the point needs to allow penetration, as the impact force of a throwing spear can vary greatly. Throwing spear points are also often barbed. The design you choose should be tailored to meet your circumstances, and with a specific prey in mind. Obviously you will be limited in raw materials. If you have difficulty finding a suitable spear shaft, consider using a lighter material – reed bamboo or elder – with a short, hardwood foreshaft. The length of the spear is also important. Where dangerous animals are concerned, you will obviously need a long spear, but if you are in an area of scrub bush you may find a long spear too unwieldy. Try to achieve the right balance of factors. Lastly, make sure you are happy with its feel and heft.

Hunting with spears
To hunt with spears you need to be as close to your prey as possible. You can do this only by careful stalking and attention to camouflage and descenting.

Hunting with thrusting spears
These are used from "lying-up positions" beside frequently-used animal runs. As the animal passes by, you thrust the spear into it. The best hiding-place is in a tree above the run, as large game rarely looks up. An added bonus in such a hiding-place is that you can drop on your prey, imparting the full force of your body-weight to your spear. The disadvantage of this hunting method is that it is static: you may spend many fruitless hours waiting to pounce with no luck.

Hunting with throwing spears

Success comes more from stalking than from throwing, and a good stalker should be able to get within touching distance of most prey. If necessary, though, a throwing spear can be used over some distance.

Throwing a spear is not like throwing a javelin. Having stalked to within a few metres of your prey, you cannot risk a "run-up" or a large movement of your throwing arm, "pulling back" before the throw. You should launch the spear before your prey detects any movement at all. Try at all times to remain hidden: if your first shot misses, you may be allowed a second chance.

Having stalked close to your quarry, very slowly draw your throwing arm back like a coiled spring. Do not draw it back beyond your shoulder: to do so means that you will have to turn your body. Instead use the resistance of your shoulder as the buffer from which all your throwing force is generated. If you feel it will help, raise your free hand as an aiming aid. When you are ready, cast the spear like a dart in one explosive movement. Follow the movement through and be still. Do not chase after the wounded animal but remain hidden, until the prey is lying down, then swiftly put the injured animal to sleep.

This is the theory, but even for experts things do not always go so smoothly. Whatever happens, remain calm.

THE DESERT

The very word "desert" conjures up images of shimmering sand dunes and oases of refreshing sweet, blue water surrounded by vivid green palm trees – but in deserts like the Sahara reality is very different. Only 17% of the Sahara's 3.5 million square miles consists of sand dunes. The rest is a mixture of broken plateaux, weird rock formations, endless gravel, dust plains and arid mountains. The Sahara, from the Arab word meaning "empty place", is truly vast. Solitude and loneliness, coupled with fear, become a real test of your character and will to survive in this intimidating place. The world's other great deserts are scarcely less daunting: the Arabian (500,000 square miles); the Gobi in Mongolia (400,000 square miles); the Kalahari in southern Africa (300,000 square miles); Patagonian desert (Argentina, Chile, 260,000); Great Basin Desert (USA, 190,000); Great Victoria Desert (Australia, 134,653).

Basic rules

If you're not acclimatized to the desert be extremely cautious during the critical first three or four days of working in summer heat. Sweating washes salts and other minerals out of the body, so make it your business to increase your water and salt intake to compensate. Avoid salt tablets – they can cause damage to your stomach lining by lying undissolved against the stomach wall. Simple table salt taken with water is adequate. A guide to how much salt you need is taste. If the salt seems to have little or no flavour, increase your intake until it tastes normal.

Diarrhoea is doubly serious. While you suffer, fluids and essential salts tend to pass unused through the body. Cooling fluids fail to reach the skin surface in the form of sweat, your body thermostat fails and you'll have heat illness as well.

Serious sunburn also damages the sweat ducts and so stops the skin surface cooling.

Choose lightweight, loose and comfortable clothes. The looseness provides insulation and prevents excessive evaporation of sweat. Dress like the Bedouin of North Africa, light and *light-coloured* – which reflects heat. Make sure your head is covered, and if necessary wrap material over your mouth to keep out sand. Members of 22 SAS wear the traditional Arab head-dress, the shemagh, a fringed-cotton wrap-around scarf which can be used to protect the head, eyes, nose, mouth and neck from sun and sand. Sandals are common favourites for footwear, but beware of thorns, snakes and scorpions. If you expect the going to be rocky or difficult, military-pattern or lightweight desert boots are best. You will appreciate the ankle-support that boots give you. Every time you don footwear check for scorpions of other dangerous fauna.

Remember, survival in the desert is a matter of knowledge of the terrain, and minimising risks. As with all other extreme environments, you should not expose yourself to danger without proper training. The heat and the sun are your enemies; water and shelter are your friends. Without water you will be dead within a day; and if you can't find shelter, wear loose clothing. Try to avoid exposing yourself to the sun; you don't see desert nomads working on their tans!

Surviving the desert – a checklist

Survival in a desert as in any area depends upon your knowledge of the terrain and the basic climatic elements, your ability to cope with them, and your will to live. Every year the desert continues to kill the unwary, the unprepared and the foolish. BEFORE THE OFF, CHECK THE TERRAIN YOU ARE HEADED FOR.

Types of terrain
Each type of terrain seemingly blends into another. There are five different types: mountainous, rocky plateau, sand dune, salt marsh and highly dissected rocky terrain called "gebel".

Sand dunes: These are usually extensive areas covered with sand and gravel. Some dunes may be over 300 metres high and 10 to 15 miles long; others will be completely flat. They can be devoid of plant life or covered in scrub up to two metres in height. Any form of travel through sand dune deserts should be avoided.

Salt lakes: If a large volume of water enters a basin, a lake may develop. However, the water has a very high salt content and is undrinkable.

Salt marshes: This type of terrain has a highly corrosive effect on boots, clothing and skin.

Rocky plateau deserts: These are characterized by many solid or broken rocks at or near the surface, and there may be sand dunes around the plateau. Rock outcrops may offer cover and shade. The rocks often form natural cisterns which collect water after rains.

Mountain deserts: High-altitude deserts have thin air and little or no vegetation. Sunburn is a real danger, and movement at altitude requires extra physical exertion.

TEMPERATURE CONVERSION
Most of the world's military use the Celsius scale, but some readers may be more familiar with Fahrenheit. Here are some approximate conversions.

50° C	120° F
30° C	90° F
20° C	70° F
10° C	50° F
0° C	32° F
-10° C	15° F
-24° C	-5° F
-30° C	-20° F

Climatic elements
Temperature variation: The temperature may vary from as much as 55° C during the day down to 10° C at night: warm clothes are essential. Obviously, work or travel at night requires less water than day, but in most deserts, moving by night is so hazardous as to not be a viable option.

It's counter-intuitive but prepared for dangerously low temperatures in the desert – the legendary SAS 'Bravo Two Zero' mission of the Gulf War was severely hampered by freezing weather, which caused the patrol to become split up.

Rainfall: It does rain in the desert on high ground, and when it does, rainwater runs off very quickly in the form of flash floods. The floods excavate deep gullies and ravines known as "wadis".

Vegetation may appear after rain, but the water evaporates, leaving the lands as barren as before.

Burning sand: The temperature of the desert sand and rock averages 15 to 20 degrees more than that of the air, so if the air temperature is 45° C then the sand would be around 60° C. You will be unable to walk around without adequate foot protection.

Never attempt to cross a desert area in a single vehicle; always travel in convoy. The best way of surviving is not to endanger yourself in the first place.

First aid

An individual first aid kit for the desert depends on personal choice and allergies. Seek your doctor's advice if you have any doubt about personal medications. You may also need a prescription for some of the items suggested. Your kit may contain some or all of the following:

Butterfly sutures

Surgical blade

Plasters – assorted sizes and waterproof

Potassium permanganate as general disinfectant

Mild painkillers for toothache, headaches, e.g. codeine phosphate

Intestinal sedative, e.g. Immodium

Antibiotic cream and tablets

Anti-histamine for bites, stings, irritant rashes, e.g. Piriton

Water sterilising tablets, e.g. Puritabs

Anti-malaria tablets, e.g. Paludrine, Daraprim, Mepachrin

Water

Remember, it is the water in your body that keeps you alive, not the water in your water bottle. Don't ration your water intake to little sips: that will not prevent dehydration. If you drink only enough to satisfy your thirst you can still suffer from dehydration. Your water intake must remain sufficient to make you urinate three times daily. Healthy urine is a pale straw colour.

In summer in the Sahara, you will need to drink up to 6 litres (10 pints) of fluid daily – and may well need 8 litres. Keep your clothing on, as the insulating effect of a layer of clothes will reduce evaporation of sweat and reflect direct sunlight.

Dehydration
The maximum water loss your body can tolerate is probably as high as 20%. However 12% is a more practical maximum. You won't be capable of making rational decisions after losing a fifth of your body fluids.

The body absorbs heat from direct sunlight and from the atmosphere. You will also absorb heat reflected from the ground or from direct contact with the ground. Any increase in body temperature of 3 or 4° C (6 to 8° F) above normal (98.6° F or 37° C) for any extended period can cause coma and death. Your body attempts to dispose of this excess heat by sweating, which can lead to loss of body fluids and dehydration.

Drink early in the morning while temperatures are low.

If you lie up during the heat of the day, remember that ground temperatures may be as much as 15° C hotter than the air temperature. Break through the crust of the desert into soft sand and you will find the temperature is as much as 30° cooler at 45 cm deep. So try to rest in deep shade or about 45 cm above or below ground level. Bushmen of the Kalahari Desert urinate into holes in the ground and lie in them in the heat of the day to reduce sweating.

Don't smoke or breathe through an open mouth. This exposes the mucous membrane to the dry atmosphere, increasing your rate of dehydration. Reduce conversation for the same reason.

AVOIDING DEHYDRATION
Keep activity to a minimum during the day to minimize water loss. Take sips of water often rather than normal drinking or gulping.

Finding water
If you are near a water supply stay there and set up ground-to-air distress signals. If you have to keep moving, look for signs that indicate the direction of a water supply.

Water sources are often indicated by animal trails and

droppings or birds in flight. But don't rely entirely on wild animals as a guide to water in the desert. Some are so adapted that they do not need a regular water intake as we do. Dorcas gazelles, jerboas and gerbils, for example, extract all the moisture they need from their foodstuffs. Foxes, jackals and hyenas, however, do not stray too far from water. Listen for the sounds of birds and baboons at early morning or evening. Quail fly towards water in the evening and away from it in the morning. Doves use the water both morning and evening, but it may be a long way off. Some turtle doves will fly 50-75 kilometres to water. Camels will eventually lead to water – but remember that a camel can walk vast distances between water stops. In camels, the water is stored in the stomach, and Arabs in dire straits have been known to kill the animal and use this store of water.

Don't make the mistake of thinking that tyre tracks will lead to water – you could mistakenly follow your own tracks or those of someone else who is equally lost. In some parts of the Sahara the "main" road is as much as 15 kilometres wide.

Study the rock in your surroundings: sandstone will absorb water after a rainstorm, basalt-type rocks will pool it on the surface. Dry stream beds or wadis sometimes have water below the surface: finding it is the problem. Look for greenery on the outside of a bend in a water course, and dig at its lowest point. You may have to dig deeper than your own height. Kalahari bushmen cut a hollow stem from a bush, pack and wind dry grass around the bottom to act as a filter, then insert this into moist sand in an old riverbed and suck. Eventually water comes into the mouth. You may find it infinitely easier to pack wet sand into a sock or cloth and wring hard. If you do find water, think before you camp in the wadi itself. If it rains, wadis fill up with remarkable speed and become raging torrents.

Only drink your own urine in the direst emergency; it contains a lot of salt.

The desert still
The first attempts to extract moisture from air pockets within the desert sand were carried out simultaneously and independently

at opposite ends of the world. Today, we accept the desert survival still as being a normal aid to survival in any desert.

To make a still, dig a hole roughly one metre square and 70 cm deep. Put a container at the bottom of the hole. Then put the end of a drinking tube at the bottom of the container. Cover the hole with a polythene sheet about 2 m square, threading the drinking tube under the edge of the sheeting. Then seal it all round the edge of the hole with sand or stones. Let the sheet "belly in" – you can help by placing a stone in the centre of the sheet. This creates an inverted cone over the container at the bottom of the pit. The polythene must not touch the sides of the pit, or the container itself – if it does the condensed fluid will be wasted.

Theoretically, the sun's rays heat the ground inside the hole and cause the moisture trapped inside to evaporate. The moisture then saturates the confined air space and condenses on the cooler surface of the plastic sheet. This runs down into the container, where you can drink it through the drinking tube without having to destroy the still. A still like this can produce up to a litre of water a day in some parts of the desert. In other areas very little is produced at all, unless you add greenery or urine in the evaporation space under the plastic sheet.

Purifying water

Treat all water in the desert, no matter where from, as suspect. Filter dirty water through several layers of cloth or a Millbank bag to remove solids. Even radio-active fallout can be removed in this manner. Purifying the water involves killing the germs. To do this use purifying agents such as Puritabs, Halzone, Chloromine T, iodine, permanganate of potash, or simply boil it for between three and five minutes. Add charcoal while the water is boiling to remove disagreeable flavours. Agitate it to restore its taste, or add a small pinch of salt. There are many chemical purifiers, and the choice is a matter of personal taste. Generally, the water needs to stand for up to 30 minutes to allow the chemical time to act properly.

The penalty you will pay for not purifying your water properly or neglecting to prepare food carefully, or for lack of hygiene generally, is a severely upset stomach. This in turn can lead to dehydration and heat illness through loss of body fluids. Treat an upset stomach with a proprietary preparation, or if you don't have one, use crushed charcoal or burnt crushed bone. Neither taste very pleasant but both are effective. The tartaric acid in a very strong brew of tea will also help. Continue to drink plenty of fluids during treatment.

PROPRIETARY CHEMICAL PURIFIERS

Chloromine T: 1 cm/ inch of matchstick loaded for 22 litre/5-gallon can.

Tincture of iodine: 3 drops per litre of water.

Household bleach (5.2% sodium hypochlorite): 2 drops per litre for clear water, 4 drops for cloudy water. Water will taste of chlorine.

Puritab: 1 small tablet for 1-litre bottle. 1 large tablet for 5-gallon can.

Potassium permanganate: enough to colour the water pink.

Plants that provide water

Date palms: Cut branch at base and water should seep from cut. Also a good food source.

Cactus: Some cacti will provide water if their innards are pulped and squeezed; however, you do need to know your cacti types, as some members of the family are poisonous.

Prickly pears: Both fruit and lobes contain water.

Baobab: Water collects in trunk; will almost certainly need to be purified. The fruit ('monkey bread') is edible, as are the leaves.

Bloodwood desert oak (Australia): Roots lie near the surface; cut and suck.

Saxaul: Cut, pulp and press bark

Carrying water

If you have any control over your circumstances, think about how you will carry your water supply. Always take 25% more than you think you need, in several containers of unbreakable material. Glass and thin plastic containers are non-starters. Conventional military water bottles in tough plastic or aluminum are reliable, as are some of the civilian versions. Avoid carrying single one- or two-gallon containers. Desert terrains are unforgiving – a slip can result in all your water supply being lost. A condom from your survival kit (carried inside a sock for additional support) makes an excellent portable container.

Building a desert shelter

This shelter reduces the midday heat by as much as 15 to 20 degrees. However, it does take more time and effort to build than other shelters so build it during the cool night to prevent dehydration during the day.

1. Find a low spot or depression between the dunes or dig a trench 45 to 60 cm deep and wide enough to lie down in.
2. Pile the sand from the trench around three sides to form a mound.
3. On the open end of the trench, dig out more so that you can get in and out easily.
4. Cover the trench with material such as a parachute or poncho.
5. Secure the cover in place using sand or rocks as weights.

You can reduce the temperature of the shelter further by adding an extra layer 30 to 45 cm above the first, creating an air space between the two layers.

Remember: radios and other sensitive items of equipment are likely to fail when exposed to direct sunlight in the desert. They need to be covered – as does ammunition, which is affected by high temperatures.

Desert survival kit

This could be combined with the first aid kit in a single pouch in the pack or on the belt. It is not to be treated as a kit to be opened only in an emergency. Use and familiarize yourself with the contents of your kits. Don't wait until you get into trouble before practising your survival techniques.

Wire saw with loop handles
Second compass (button or lapel type)
Waxed non-safety matches that will strike on rough surfaces
Single large candle or three birthday-cake candles
Flint and steel
Cotton wool packing for use as fire-starting aid.
Table salt in small container
Signal flares
Pen torch
Tube of Dextrose tablets
Heliograph
Ground-to-air recognition tables and Morse code sheet
Marker panel in fluorescent material
Whistle
Condom for water-carrying
Water purification tablets
Magnifying glass

Desert hazards

Many of the creatures that live in the desert are potentially dangerous, from bats and snakes to scorpions and centipedes – and even dogs and spiders. Heat exhaustion, malaria and storms all offer their own hazards as well.

Bites

When on your own in the desert, avoid suspect animals at all times. Rabies virus is carried in the saliva of an infected animal and enters your body through breaks in the skin. Even a lick from a friendly but infected animal can infect you through a cut or abrasion. Potential carriers include dogs, cats, bats, and some types of rodents. If you are bitten by any animal get a tetanus booster as soon as possible.

Scorpion stings

There are two common types of potentially lethal scorpion in the Sahara: *Androctonus australis* and *Androctonus buthidae* (also known as fat-tailed scorpion because of its massive tail), which is often cited as the world's most dangerous. Drop for drop, their venom is as toxic as that of a cobra and can kill a man in four hours. If the scorpion stings in self-defence it will usually inject the maximum dose of poison.

The sting of a buthid scorpion produces intense pain at the site of the sting, often without discoloration apart from a small area of gooseflesh. A feeling of tightness then develops in the throat, so that the victim tries to clear imaginary phlegm. The tongue feels thick, and speech becomes difficult. The casualty becomes restless, with involuntary twitching of the muscles.

Sneezing bouts and a runny nose follow. There is an uncontrolled flow of saliva, which may become frothy. The heart rate will increase, followed by convulsions. The extremities turn blue before the casualty dies. The whole sequence of events may take as little as 45 minutes or as long as 12 hours.

Snakes

Snakes are permanent residents in most parts of the desert. They hibernate, however, and so you'll see fewer snakes in winter. Most are venomous, so regard any snake bite as suspect and treat it as promptly as possible. Simple precautions against snake bite include shaking out boots and sleeping bags before you use them, and using a torch after dark. Don't go barefoot: certain types of snake actually bury themselves in the sand, leaving only their nostrils and eyes showing. They ambush their prey – including you – in this fashion and are extremely difficult to spot.

If you get bitten by a snake, study the pattern of teeth punctures. If there are two well-defined punctures, the bite will be that of one of the viper group. Non-poisonous snakes with solid fangs, and mildly venomous back-fanged snakes, make a horseshoe-shaped row of teeth marks. It takes only 5 mg of venom from the saw-scaled viper to kill a man. As with scorpion stings, defensive bites tend to contain the maximum amount of venom.

However, not every snake bite is fatal. You're more likely to survive a bite to the shin than one deep in the muscular tissues of the thigh or calf.

The ideal treatment for a snake bite is to immobilize the casualty and administer sedatives. Ice is put on the bite site, a tourniquet is applied and loosened at frequent intervals, and the casualty is evacuated to hospital for treatment with antivenin (an anti-venom product), adrenalin and plasma. The snake is killed for hospital identification.

In reality, you will probably be able only to attempt to restrict the amount and rate of venom entering the bloodstream by applying a tourniquet between the bite and the heart. The tourniquet must not cut off the blood supply entirely – this can cause tissue damage and possibly gangrene and kidney failure. Release the pressure each half-hour until you get help. The patient must also be rested as much as possible, and kept calm. Panic can become a major problem – it increases the heart rate and so speeds the circulation of the venom in the blood. Physical exertion must also be avoided.

This list is far from exhaustive, but you will want to familiarize yourself with the following species of snake at least:

Egyptian cobra: Typically about 2 metres long, the Egyptian cobra can be black, brown or yellow. Some examples are light brown with darker cross-bands. It likes cultivated land, rocky hillsides, old ruins and even rural villages. The venom is a very powerful neurotoxin: it attacks your nervous system, making it hard to breathe.

Sand viper: Well camouflaged and only about 60 cm long, the sand viper is found throughout North Africa. Its venom is haemotoxic: it attacks your circulatory system, causing tissue damage and internal bleeding.

Boomslang: Deadly poisonous and found throughout sub-Saharan Africa.

Horned desert viper: Found in Africa, Iran, Iraq and the Arabian Peninsula. Buff-coloured with scale over each eye. Dangerously poisonous.

Puff adder: Found in a range of yellow, orange and brown hues, but with distinctive black/brown chevrons. Dangerously poisonous. Found in Africa, Saudi Arabia and parts of the Middle East.

Death adder: Deadly. Found in Australia, Moluccas, and New Guinea. Between 1 foot 6 inches and 3 foot in length, with colour ranging from brown to yellow.

Taipan: Deadly. Found in Northern Australia and southern New Guinea.

Mojave rattlesnake: Found in Mexico and US. Sandy in colour, with diamond-shaped marks on the tail. Grows up to 4 feet in length. Deadly.

Other dangerous bites and stings
Camel spider: The camel spider, or "wind scorpion" as it is known to the Arabs, grows to 15-20 cm in length and has some very anti-social eating habits. When not eating its fellows, the camel spider will eat beetles, scorpions and even small lizards at great speed by injecting a venom that dissolves the internal organs of the prey, and then sucking out the resulting juices.

   Mexican bearded lizard: Grows up to 3 feet in length. Black or black and bladed yellow. Found in Mexico and Central America. Dangerously poisonous.

Bites and stings: emergency first aid
Opinions differ on whether to "cut and suck" or not. This treatment may worsen the situation, as any wound inside the mouth will allow the venom to enter into the system. When you're on your own, there may be some value in cutting and bleeding as an alternative to simply sitting and hoping that the snake was not venomous. You can easily shed a pint of blood without any ill-effects, and this may be all you need to do to save your life. Simply cut yourself deep enough to bleed freely with a clean knife at both

entry points. Then wash the cut in a solution of potassium permanganate. Do not urinate into the cut.

Overheating

Two conditions can arise from overheating; heat exhaustion and heat stroke. Heat exhaustion usually affects people performing strenuous physical exercise in hot, humid climates, and is caused by loss of salt and water from the body. It will be aggravated by stomach upset, diarrhoea or vomiting. Remove the casualty to a cooler environment and replace lost fluids and minerals. Seek medical aid.

Heat stroke is caused by a very high environmental temperature or a feverish illness (such as malaria) and leads to a greatly increased body temperature. It develops when the body can no longer control its temperature by sweating and can occur quite suddenly. Reduce the casualty's temperature as quickly as possible and get medical help.

Malaria

This very debilitating illness is caused by the bite of the female *Anopheles* mosquito, which breeds in stagnant water. Take a course of anti-malaria tablets before you enter into an area where the disease is endemic, continue the treatment throughout your stay in the country and for the medically-advised period on your return. See your doctor for advice on the type of anti-malarial treatment recommended for the area. In an emergency, quinine is an effective if unpleasant treatment.

Dust storms

Generally, these are either limited to a height of about 6 feet or rise hundreds of feet high. In either case, if visibility is restricted, seal all equipment likely to be affected and be prepared to sit it out. This is preferable to getting lost or even injured in the poor visibility. During severe dust storms, the air temperature can soar up to 58° C (135° F), while simultaneously the moisture content will drop to only a few per cent. A long-lasting dust storm can cause serious dehydration; you can lose up to a quart of moisture in sweat in one hour in these conditions.

A side-effect of a prolonged severe dust storm is the rise in atmospheric electricity due to sand friction. This can cause severe headaches and nausea, but can be neutralized by "earthing" yourself to the ground.

Magnetic compasses will be affected in these conditions. The wisest course will be to stay where you are. Always carry a spare compass.

Emergency survival

When you find yourself stranded in a desert, you'll have to make up your mind whether to stay where you are, or try to move on. It's a decision governed by circumstances. If you've been travelling by aircraft, the pilot will have filed a flight plan. Similarly, employees of oil and water prospecting companies and suchlike organisations file a route plan with an estimated time of arrival. In the event of your non-arrival, a search-and-rescue plan will be put into action. Clearly, the best course here will be to remain with the aircraft or vehicle until help arrives.

The problems arise if you're stranded while engaged on military activities or on expeditions to more remote regions, where the chances of rescue are slim at best. In one region of the Sahara, some 43 people died in a single year. These are recorded deaths: the actual figure may be higher. In temperate or tropical zones the environment is relatively kind, and the survivor is rarely far from materials water, foodstuffs and people to assist in an emergency. The desert militates against this, and the decision to stay or move is much more difficult to make. You must consider your assets, equipment, physical state, mental state, navigational skills and equipment, water, food, location and the size of your party. Then you must weigh these against the distances involved, the terrain, your chances of rescue, weather, temperatures, etc.

VITAL SKILLS
To improve your chances of survival in the desert, learn and practise these basic skills before going abroad. The average soldier will be familiar with most of the following but may find one or two techniques that aren't in the Army manual.

- Map reading
- Compasses, bearings, back bearings and variations
- Direction-finding using sun and stars
- Direction-finding using shadow-stick methods
- Water location, extraction and purification
- Heat and its effects and how to avoid them
- First aid
- Signals – ground to ground and ground to air

How far can you go?

By walking slowly and resting for 10 minutes every hour, a man in good physical condition can cover between 20 and 30 km (12 and 18 miles) per day if he has sufficient food and water. If you plan on walking during the day, you may get 16 km (10 miles) to one gallon of water. At night, you could possibly double that distance, since you will dehydrate less. If a lack of water is a problem then moving at night is more sensible, but only if the terrain allows safe travel. The disadvantages are that you may bypass water supplies and habitation.

Choose the easiest route. Go round obstacles, not over or through them. Zigzag to prevent over-exertion when climbing. Visibility for a man six feet tall is limited to between five and six miles when standing on a flat plain.

The seashore

No, not a desert, but sand anyway, and there are plenty of barren islands where you may be forced to search for fresh water. You can be sure of finding fresh water where rivers discharge into the sea. (The term "fresh" means non-salt, rather than drinkable). All water will be heavily polluted, so take all precautions to make sure the water you drink is sterile. You can also get "fresh" water by digging several beach wells. Dig the holes a safe distance above the high-water mark, and deep enough to permit water to collect in the bottom. Skim off and use only the top layer of water – this will be less salty than the denser sea water below it. Obviously, the sea shore also has plenty of things living or growing on it that you can eat, starting with seaweed.

'Mayday' Signals

Set signal fires in threes, arranged in a large triangle with sides approximately 20 metres long. In daylight the glare from the ground and from the air reduces the visibility of wood fires as wood in the desert is so dry that it is smokeless. Add oil, rubbery plastic or green plants, if available, to generate smoke.

You can also use mirrors for signalling over long distances in the desert. Fluorescent signal panels are another useful addition to your kit.

Set ground signals too. These last a long time and need little or no maintenance. Lay out a large SOS in stone, preferably of contrasting colour to the ground, but at least large enough to cast a well-defined shadow. There is an international system of ground-to-air signals which is worth carrying in your survival kit.

GROUND AIR EMERGENCY CODE

If friendly forces are going to be looking for you, all means of communication are important, so do not assume the radio will work. This signalling system will work wherever you have air superiority; hilltop village sites are usually clear enough to set this up.

NOTE: leave a space of about three metres between each element where possible

1 Require doctor, serious injury
2 Require medical supplies
3 Unable to proceed
4 Require food and water
5 Require firearms and ammunition
6 Require map and compass
7 Require signal lamp with battery and radio
8 Indicate direction to proceed
9 Am proceeding in this direction
10 Will attempt take-off
11 Aircraft seriously damaged
12 Probably safe to land here
13 Require fuel and oil
14 All well
15 No
16 Yes
17 Not understood
18 Require engineer

You should carry a copy of the Morse alphabet in your survival kit and try to memorize the Mayday signal along with the newer Pan signal. This is a lower-priority signal recognized by all international maritime and aircraft crews. Learn the international distress signal, and the reply. The distress signal is six flashes of light, six blasts of a whistle or six waves of a signal flag followed by a break of one minute before repeating the sequence. The response is three long blasts, waves or flashes.

The heliograph

The Mk 3 signal mirror issued to US forces is a handy heliograph which you can hang around your neck when not in use. Make sure the reflective side is against your chest when not in use.

1. Reflect sunlight from the mirror on to a nearby surface like a rock or your hand.
2. Slowly bring the mirror up to eye-level and look through the sighting hole. You will see a bright spot of light which is the aim indicator.
3. Hold the mirror near to your eye and move it so that the aim indicator is on the target.

CAUTION:

Don't flash the mirror rapidly. In a combat zone, a pilot might mistake the distant twinkling for ground fire and treat you to a rocket attack! Don't hold the light on someone's cockpit either, or you could dazzle the pilot. Mirror signals can be seen for many miles, even in hazy weather, so keep sweeping the horizon even if nothing is in sight. In a combat zone where you could attract the enemy's attention you must obviously wait and positively identify an aircraft before signalling.

Signalling with an air signal panel

Air panels are light, easy to carry and should be carried by at least two members of a patrol. The US issue VS-17 signalling panel is a simple plastic sheet that is violet on one side and orange on the other. Use the orange side to initially attract the pilot's attention. Flashing the panel will make it easier to spot. You can then use the panel to pass information as shown. You can use any reasonable substitute for the panel, e.g. life raft sails, bright-coloured rain jackets, etc.

Navigation

With a map and compass you should be able to establish your position. Without these, you will have to improvise. Here is a reminder of some simple orientation methods previously described.

To find north, first establish south by pointing the hour hand of your watch towards the sun. Then find the mid-point between the hour hand and the 12 o'clock position. The line from the centre of your watch to here points south. Remember that if you are in a desert in the southern hemisphere the procedure is slightly different. Point the 12 o'clock position towards the sun and bisect the angle between the 12 o'clock position and the hour hand. This points north. A digital watch can be used for the same task, despite opinion to the contrary. Either mark with a grease pencil or imagine the conventional watch face and hands that show the time overlaid on the digital face. Then continue as above.

Remember that the sun rises in the east and sets in the west to within a few degrees. Remember also that in the northern hemisphere the sun is to the south of us and in the southern hemisphere the sun passes to the north of us.

The east-west line

Place a one-metre stick vertically into the ground and mark the top of its shadow with a stick or stone. After 15 minutes, place another stick or stone to mark the tip of the new shadow position. Then the straight line that joins these two points indicates roughly east-west.

The north-south line

Put a stick in the ground in the morning and mark the tip of its shadow on the ground. Using a piece of string anchored to the base stick, draw an arc. The arc must be the same length as the shadow line you've just drawn. In the afternoon, when the tip of the shadow touches the drawn arc once more, draw a further line from the arc to the base stick. Bisect the angle formed between the two lines and the resulting line will indicate north-south.

Night navigation

If you move at night, you will need to be able to recognize certain star constellations that either point the way north or point to the North Star (sometimes known as the Pole Star).

The constellations to learn are the Plough, Orion and Cassiopeia. They appear at different times during the night throughout the year and revolve, so they may well appear upside-down when compared with conventional star charts. You must learn your constellations before you set out on any journey that involves the risk of being stranded. And practise all your survival skills before you need to use them.

Survival tips

Staying put

Aircraft wrecks: In some desert areas there are many aircraft wrecks left over from the war. These usually have "wreck" painted across the wings. Make sure your aircraft cannot be mistaken for a wreck by having at least one signal operative at any one time. If you can, put out a large SOS in wreckage or stone on a stretch of the beach.

Aircraft kit: All commercial aircraft must carry a dinghy if they are travelling over water. In addition you will have the survival kit in the dinghy, a first aid kit and what you can salvage from the aircraft itself.

Air panel: Make sure you carry a fluorescent air panel in your survival kit. These can be used not just to draw the initial attention of a rescue aircraft but also to pass messages to the aircraft.

Signal fires: Signal fires should be set in the shape of a triangle with the fires 20 metres apart. These are useless in the intense sunlight of the day unless you use plant material or oil to produce smoke. Smothering a fire with leaves tends to produce white smoke, and oil produces black smoke. Make sure you produce a colour that contrasts with the background.

Limit movement: Any essential work should be done at night. During the day, get under cover, put something between you and the hot ground and stay there. Stay in the shade: If you stay in the shade quietly, fully clothed, not talking, keeping your mouth closed and breathing through your nose, your water requirement will drop dramatically and consequently you will last a lot longer.

Conserving sweat: In this situation you are not going to have unlimited amounts of water, so if you cannot control the amount of water you take in, you have to control the amount your body loses. This means complete body coverage. Roll your sleeves down and cover your head and neck. This will protect your body from the hot sand-laden winds and the direct rays of the sun. Your clothes will absorb your sweat and keep it against your skin so you gain the full cooling effect.

"Voluntary dehydration" is a risk: when you are thirsty you will generally drink only 65% of your daily requirement. To avoid this voluntary dehydration at temperatures below 35° C/100° F drink one pint of water every hour. At temperatures above 35° C/ 100° F drink two pints every hour.

Food discipline: If water is scarce, do not eat. Water is required for digestion of food, and you need that water for cooling.

Health hazards: The sudden and extreme temperature shifts from day to night can cause chills, chest infections and even pneumonia.

Insects: Lice, mites, wasps and flies which are drawn to man as a source of water and food are extremely unpleasant and may carry disease. Old buildings, ruins and caves are favourite habitats for spiders, lice, scorpions, centipedes and other wildlife that can make life unbearable. Take extra care when sheltering in these areas. Always wear gloves, and do not sit down or lie down without visually inspecting the area first.

Moving out

You must prepare for every eventuality: that includes having to walk out. Do it with a 5-gallon water jerry-can mounted on an aluminium rucksack frame with shelter kit and sleeping bag fixed on top.

Estimating distance: If you do decide to send off a party to find help, remember that in the desert things always seem closer than they are by a factor of three. So a rough guide is that anything that looks one mile away is in reality three miles away.

Night marching: Although you will conserve water by moving at night, visibility on moonless nights is extremely poor and travelling is very hazardous. Dangers include getting lost, falling into ravines and missing water sources. Conversely, moonlit nights are usually crystal-clear, with none of the problems associated with daylight moves; winds die down and haze and glare disappear, you will be able to see lights at great distance and noise will carry further.

Sandstorms: Sandstorms or sand-laden winds occur regularly in most desert areas: for example, the "Siestan" or desert wind of Afghanistan and Iran can blow up constantly for up to 120 days. Wind speeds in the storm could reach 70 to 80 miles per hour by early afternoon. Major dust storms can be expected at least once a week. When confronted with this you should take cover and mark its direction of travel. These storms will affect radio transmissions.

THE JUNGLE

Tropical jungles are characterised by high temperatures, frequent and heavy rainfall (more than 6 feet per annum), and high humidity. "Typical" jungles occur in South and Central America, South-East Asia, West and Central Africa. Primary jungles contain trees that can grow up to 60 metres, forming a thick canopy preventing light from reaching the jungle floor. In secondary jungle, which results from the clearance of primary jungle for cultivation, light reaches the ground, leading to a dense growth of grasses, ferns, vines and shrubs which makes travel difficult.

Whether primary or secondary, the jungle environment tends to produce a combat scenario where engagements are close-up. Hacking through the jungle is noisy, leaves an obvious trail, is exhausting, and is likely to produces masses of cut-off plants, all of which can scratch your skin and produce a wound through which bacteria can enter. The SAS, who call the jungle 'the ulu', aims to make 100 yards an hour in the jungle.

Basic rules

An environment with thick, often sharp, vegetation, together with a host of biting insects, leeches, scorpions, snakes, centipedes and chigoe fleas or jiggers, requires clothing that will repel these "enemies". In the jungle, remaining healthy and free from disease is paramount. Wear thick trousers and specialist lightweight boots, the US-issue jungle boot being a favourite. The feet and legs must be protected at all times. Use insect repellent to keep biting insects at bay.

Special Forces soldiers are instructed to have two sets of clothing with them: a 'wet set' for wearing in the humid jungle during the day (keep wrapped in plastic), and a dry set to wear at night.

Shelter

Flooding, snakes, and millipedes are all good reasons for a platform shelter with a base off the ground. Find four trees, or position four wrist-thick poles into the ground at the corners of a rectangle big enough to take your body. Lash poles cross-across at both shorter ends, then lash poles along the long sides so the ends also rest on the shorter poles. You now have, when looked at from above, a square frame. Lay cross bars all along the length of the bed, and cover with leaves. Finally, lash a light pole horizontally to the top of the uprights to create a sloping roof. For waterproof roof "tiles" and walls use overlapping or woven leaves of atap (the nipa palm), banana, elephant grass or similar. Bamboo makes an excellent building material, but beware it can split and painfully injure than unwary handler.

If you cannot make a shelter, a hammock will serve you well, especially if it is a specialist one with an integrated mosquito net. Outside a combat zone, build a smoky fire to keep insects at bay at night.

Rags tied in petrol can be attached to the uprights of your shelter as a deterrent against bugs and beasts. *But if you do use petrol as a repellent, do not position a fire nearby.*

Water

Although water is often plentiful in the jungle, this is not always the case, and you will be needing an intake of around seven litres of water a day (because of high perspiration-rate) to remain healthy.

Finding water

The best source of water in the jungle is a fast-flowing stream: look for bees, finches and pigeons, all of which will head for water during the course of the day. Water from a clear fast-flowing stream with a stony bottom is likely to be safe, but boil or purify if in doubt.

Hollows and some plants will collect water, and a rain trap can easily be made with large leaves to funnel water into a receptacle. If there is no rain, you can make a version of the desert still (see xxx), or vegetation stills. For a vegetation still, tie a translucent plastic bag around a leafy branch in a sunny location. The branch should be bowed (by tying) so the water from transpiration will collect at one end.

Plants that provide a drink

Green bamboo: Bend over a piece of bamboo, and tie it down. Cut off the leafy end; the stem will drip water into a receptacle overnight.

Plantain or banana tree: Cut the tree down to leave a two-foot-high stump. Dig a bowl shape in the top of the stump. Water will rise into the bowl from the roots. Or insert a "tap", a hollow tube (bamboo will do), into the trunk at a slightly down-pointing angle, and water will drip into a waiting receptacle.

Coconuts: Green, unripe coconuts provide "milk"; avoid drinking from fallen ripe coconuts.

Bromelids: These are members of the pineapple family with a rosette of leaves that produces a natural water tank. Beware: the water is likely to contain animal droppings and quite a lot of "protein" – over 200 organisms are found in the water. Common throughout the tropics of the Americas.

Traveller's tree: Contains about 2-4 pints of water in the leafy stalks which attach to the trunk. Found in Madagascar.

Plants that provide food

The standard Special Forces test to determine whether an unrecognised plant is toxic or an allergen is to run a small amount on the skin; if there is no reaction, try a small piece on the lips; if there is still no reaction after two hours, lick it; if there is still no reaction, eat a little. If again nothing happens, eat a little more. In general it is inadvisable to eat any plant that is brightly coloured, as shrill coloration is often a warning that the plant is poisonous.

Bamboo: Found in many parts of the world; young shoots can be eaten raw, but *remove the black hairs which are irritants*.

Bael fruit: Found in Burma, India and throughout South-East Asia.

Bignay: Shiny evergreen, common throughout South-East Asia and northern Australia. The red or black fruit can be eaten raw.

Breadfruit: Tree with dark green leaves and large, green, round fruits, which can be cooked in a multitude of ways: baked, boiled, roasted, fried. Found in the South Pacific, Polynesia and the West Indies.

Coconut: Common throughout the tropics, particularly near the coast. Aside from the white 'meat' inside the shell, the palm 'cabbage' at the top of the tree can be cooked.

Mango: Grown throughout the tropics, with the large fleshy fruit familiar from supermarket shelves.

Manioc: Also known as cassava or tapioca, and produces large tubers that are a staple in many parts of the world. However, the tubers are poisonous raw and must be cooked.

Rattan palm: Common in rainforests. Roast or eat the palm heart raw.

Water lily: Widely found on waterways and lakes throughout temperate as well as subtropical regions. Roast seeds and roots.

Taro: Plant which grows to 3 feet high with distinctive heart-shaped leaves. Poisonous raw, so boil roots, young leaves and stalks.

Wild yam: Ground creeper common throughout the tropics, whose tuber is a staple starchy foodstuff. Again, can be poisonous raw, so cook.

Wild rice: Tall grass found in areas producing the familiar grain. Needs to be threshed and winnowed to be made easily palatable.

Few Special Forces troopers are vegetarians, and there is plenty of fauna in the jungle. Wild deer, pigs, and birds can be hunted. (see p267 for trapping). Snakes and lizards can also be eaten. Rivers are full of fish, but boil the fish well on catching, as they can be full of parasites. Keep your eyes open in rivers: some fish are dangerous (stingrays, piranhas) and rivers are the abode of poisonous snakes and dangerous animals, such as crocodiles and hippos.

Making a fire

Since everything in the jungle is wet, fire-starting can be a trial. You need to take standing dead wood and shave off the outside. Dead bamboo makes good tinder. So does a termites' nest.

Insects, snakes and parasites

As well as stout boots and trousers (Special Forces never wear shorts in the jungle), you will need an insect repellent. If you do not have one, smearing mud on your face and hands will offer some protection. If you take off your footwear, always check for scorpions, snakes and insects before donning in the morning. Shake them out. Likewise, shake out any clothes and check pockets before putting on clothes.

Leeches are widespread in the humid jungle environment, and are not just found in water. Usually they take their fill of your blood, then drop off. If you need to remove them, *do not pull them off*. Their jaws will remain locked in your flesh and turn septic. The tried and tested method is to apply a cigarette to their rear end; if you don't smoke (and if you are intending to join Special Forces you should not be a smoker), dab them with a flame, salt or alcohol.

For snake bites see p317. Spider bites should be treated in the same manner. Snakes are best avoided; if you have to kill the snake strike it on the head.

Jungle hygiene

Cuts and scratches must be cleansed and covered as soon as possible. Defecate in a river (as the locals are likely to do), or scrape away an area of earth and bury. For once, shaving can be dropped due to the dangers of infection in cuts. In the jungle, water for washing – let alone drinking – may need to be purified before use. Among the waterborne diseases prevalent in the tropics is leptospirosis, spread via the urine of infected aaimals, notably rats.

Poisonous snakes and spiders

It's a jungle out there, and home to some of the most venomous snakes and spiders in the world, including:

Bushmaster: Deadly poisonous. Grows to around 8 feet, and is pinky-brown with dark triangular markings. Found in the lowland tropical forests of Central and South America.

Coral snake: Distinctly banded red, yellow, and white. Found in the southern US and South America. Deadly poisonous.

Bush viper: Widely distributed throughout Africa. Lives in trees but hunts on the ground.

Green mamba: Deadly poisonous. Found throughout Africa.

Russell's viper: Found throughout much of South-East Asia. Grows to 4 feet, and is brown with reddish spots ringed in black.

Krait: Grows up to 5 feet, banded black and white, or black and yellow. Deadly poisonous. Found in Indonesia and India.

Funnelweb: Spider, found in Australia. Deadly poisonous.

Travel in the jungle

The density of the jungle makes navigation difficult. Special Forces troops are taught "cross-graining", where you follow a compass and pace the distance travelled, working out your position by dead reckoning. Any paths used by locals are liable to be places where ambushes are mounted. Patrol movements are likely to be single-file, and to avoid the difficulties and dangers of hacking paths with machetes progress is likely to be slow. If you wish to return to a position, mark your trail by cuts in trees or piles of stones. In a survival situation head for water, and follow the downwards course of a stream or river – eventually you will encounter human habitation. Rafts can be made from the abundance of local materials. Cut notches in the wood for ropes (vines are fine) so they do not slip. When hacking through the ulu is the only option, chop down at an angle with a machete rather than horizontally. Keep the blade sharp.

Weapon-handling

Standard patrol rules in the jungle include each man being equipped with one magazine full of tracer bullets, which can be used to identify enemy positions. Magazines in ammo pouches are usually placed upside-down, with the bullets pointed away from the body; this keeps dirt and water out of them. Grenades are not carried on the chest.

On patrol in the jungle, Special Forces troopers do not shoot from the hip: they keep the butt against the shoulder, the trigger-finger on the trigger guard. At the first sign of trouble, the

Special Forces soldier can raise the gun and fire, leaning into the weapon as he does so. Since weapons must work each time, every time, in the jungle it is standard that weapons are cleaned and oiled at night.

THE ARCTIC

Survival in Arctic and sub-Arctic conditions is survival against constant attack. Day and night, without respite, the cold lays siege to your body. There is no let-up; staying alive requires attention to detail for 24 hours a day. Clothes, shelter and food are your major weapons against the cold – plus a strong will to survive. Without the will, the battle is already lost. Air temperatures of -40° C and wind velocities of 30 knots are common in Arctic and sub-Arctic terrains. In these conditions, without clothes, you would be dead in about 15 minutes.

Basic Survival

Clothing
The most effective clothing provides a system of layers that trap warm air to form an effective insulation. If you are caught out in Arctic conditions because of vehicle failure, air crash, etc. improvise layered clothing and insulation.

Outer-shell garments should be windproof. Arctic conditions are usually dry, and waterproof outers (unless they are of "breathing" material such as Gore-Tex) should be avoided, as they cause condensation to build up inside, soaking your inner garments. Many fabrics lose their insulating efficiency when they are wet. Goose and duck down, very popular in dry-cold outer garments, clump disastrously when wet, losing the "lofted" air spaces that give them their insulating qualities. Cotton garments and kapok quilt fittings also become heavy and cold. Wool, on the other hand, functions well when wet, as do a range of modern synthetic materials such as polyester, which can be woven into single-layered clothing, used as quilting fillers, or processed into thick piles and fleeces which have the added advantage that they "wick" moisture away from inside layers.

Keep clothing dry

In cold temperatures, your inner layers of clothing can become wet from sweat, and your outer layer, if not water-repellent, can become wet from snow and frost melted by body heat. Wear water-repellent outer clothing, if available. It will shed most of the water collected from melting snow and frost. Before entering a heated shelter, brush off the snow and frost.

Despite the precautions you take, there will be times when you cannot avoid getting wet. At such times, drying your clothing may become a major problem. On the march hang your damp mittens and socks on your pack; sometimes the wind and sun will dry this clothing. Or you can put damp socks or mittens, unfolded, near your body so that your body heat can dry them. In bivouac, hang damp clothing inside the tent near the top, using drying lines or improvised racks. You may even be able to dry each item by holding it before an open fire. Dry leather items slowly. If no other means are available for drying your boots, put them between the sleeping bag shell and liner. Your body heat will help to dry the leather.

The effort expended in keeping warm should be regulated carefully to avoid overheating and sweating. Chopping a tree down to make a shelter could be a fatal expenditure of energy, burning up vital resources and soaking clothing with perspiration.

Ten key clothing tips

1. *Underclothing:* This should be a polypropylene shirt and pants: the material allows ventilation, the zip is shielded from the skin, the cuffs can be extended over your wrists, and a broad tail on the shirt prevents a gap when you bend over.

2. *Thermal clothing:* This is your second layer and is ideally a "duvet" jacket with hood and salopettes. This type of clothing should not be worn when on the move unless it is extremely cold.

3. *Combat shell clothing:* The third layer is usually a windproofed camouflaged smock and trousers, loose and baggy and so trapping a layer of "dead" air that is warmed by your body. The trouser legs open on the outside from ankle to knee to permit them to be removed without taking your boots off.

4. *Waterproof clothing:* This fourth layer should ideally be made of Gore-Tex, which is waterproof but allows body-heat condensation to escape. It should not be the top layer when the temperature is at or below freezing point, because escaping condensation will form an ice shell that will lower your body temperature.

5. *Over-whites:* The fifth and top layer is a set of lightweight oversmock and trousers. When the weather is not too bad, this can be the top layer, omitting the camouflage smock and waterproofs.

6. *Cap comforter:* Elite units prefer a dark-coloured wool watch cap, but on issue are cold-weather caps with protective flaps. Balaclavas and ski masks are also used, but remember that when your ears are covered your hearing – the first line of defence against the enemy – will be impaired.

7. *Eye protection:* Wear polarized sunglasses on bright days. As extra protection in wind and snow you will need goggles.

8. *Mitts:* Must be worn to prevent frostbite and especially when you have to touch anything metal. Mitts have a special trigger finger so that you can fire your weapon. Link one mitt to the other by a cord through the sleeves of your smock so that you can take them off without losing them.

9. *Socks:* Feet must be kept dry. Wet socks should be changed as soon as possible and dried.

10. *Boots:* These should be well insulated and preferably be sealed with Gore-Tex gaiters. Wash the boots inside and out once a month.

Dangers

Frostbite

The prime dangers of cold-weather conditions are frostbite and hypothermia, as the cold strikes at both the outer and inner body. Your extremities – hands, feet, ears and nose – are particularly susceptible to frostbite, but any exposed skin is at risk, and the risk is multiplied by wind speed.

The wind-chill factor transforms modestly-cold temperatures into deadly, tissue-destroying assaults on the body. An 18-mph wind in a 9.5° C temperature results in a -23.3° C wind-chill temperature. At wind-chill temperatures below -6° C exposed flesh freezes in 60 seconds or less. An ambient temperature (measured by thermometer) of -28.8° C is converted by a 35-mph wind into a deadly -59.4° C wind-chill temperature. At this level, flesh freezes in 30 seconds.

Removing a mitten long enough to undo clothing and urinate can result in frostbitten fingers. Deep frostbite, which can result in lost fingers, toes or even limbs, kills by incapacitating the victim. But gangrene can also easily set in, and that will indeed see you off unless you get medical help. The first sign of frostbite may be a waxy whiteness on the skin. Keep a close eye on your companions for these patches. If you are on your own periodically feel your face and ears for the typical numbness.

It is easier to prevent frostbite or to stop it in its early stages than to thaw out and take care of badly-frozen flesh.

1. Wear enough clothing for protection against cold and wind.
2. Clothing and equipment must not restrict the circulation.
3. Do not touch cold metal or oils at extreme low temperatures.
4. Avoid unnecessary exposure to strong winds.
5. Exercise the face, fingers and toes to keep them warm and detect any signs of numbness.
6. Watch your buddy for any signs of frostbite; he should do the same for you.
7. Thaw any frozen spots immediately.

If you encounter frostbite:

- Rub snow onto the area until the whiteness or numbness disappears.
- Alternatively, gently compress the affected area with a warm hand, or put affected hands inside clothing near the body, or if feet affected put inside companion's clothing near body.
- Do NOT vigorously rub the frostbitten area directly; you are likely to break the skin, leading to an open wound and infection.
- Do NOT burst blisters; dust well with antiseptic powder instead.
- Do NOT put affected areas into warm water; use body warmth.
- Seek medical help asap.

Hypothermia

Hypothermia occurs when the temperature of the inner body core, which houses the vital organs, falls below 35° C. The normal inner body temperature is 36.8° C. As hypothermia sets in, movements slow up, thought processes are dulled, and you begin to lose co-ordination. You're dying on your feet, though you probably won't know it. Your speech becomes slurred. When your body temperature falls to 25° C and below, death is almost inevitable.

One of the best ways of dealing with hypothermia is to put the victim naked inside a sleeping bag with another person, also naked. A second person can also administer the warm sweet drinks (such as honey, dextrose, sugar or cocoa) and food necessary for recovery. *Do not force an unconscious person to drink.*

If you manage to get back to civilisation, the hypothermia victim's torso can be immersed in a warm bath – that is, a bath just right for a baby. Dip in your elbow: if the water temperature is comfortable for your elbow it will be comfortable for the patient (about 38-40° C). *Be careful*: start with the trunk area first, otherwise there's a risk of cardiac arrest and shock when the whole body is immersed. The patient will be needing to lie near flat on his back with his legs out of water. A victim will also need some time to recover, because the attack will have profoundly affected the circulatory system.

Overheating

When you get too hot, you sweat and your clothing absorbs the moisture. This affects your warmth in two ways: dampness decreases the insulating quality of clothing, and as sweat evaporates, your body cools.

Adjust your clothing so that you do not sweat. You can do this by partially opening your parka or jacket, by removing an inner layer of clothing, by removing heavy mittens or by throwing back your parka hood or changing to a lighter head covering. The head and hands act as efficient dissipators when overheated.

Trench foot

Trench foot and immersion foot result from many hours or days of exposure to wet or damp conditions at a temperature just above freezing. The feet become cold and swollen and have a waxy appearance. Walking becomes difficult and the feet feel heavy and numb. The nerves and muscles suffer the most damage, but gangrene can also occur in extreme cases and it may become necessary to have the foot or leg amputated. Trench foot was a common ailment of soldiers in the First World War, hence its name.

The best preventative is to keep the feet dry. Carry extra socks with you in a waterproof packet. Wet socks can be dried against the body. Wash your feet daily and put on dry socks.

The treatment is to clean the feet with soap and warm (not hot) water, dry them and keep them raised. Put on dry socks. *Do not massage or rub feet.*

Dehydration

In cold weather bundled up in many layers of clothing, you may be unaware that you are losing body moisture. Your heavy clothing absorbs the moisture, which evaporates in the air. You must drink water to replace this loss of fluid. Your need for water is as great when it's cold as when it's hot.

One way to tell if you are becoming dehydrated is to check the colour of your urine in the snow. If it makes the snow dark yellow, you are becoming dehydrated and need to replace body fluids; if the snow turns light yellow or remains normal, you're OK. Dehydration is also likely to cause headaches.

There's a condition called "cold diuresis", which is an increased output of urine caused by exposure to cold. It decreases body fluids, which must be replaced.

Sunburn

Exposed skin can become sunburned even when the air temperature is below freezing: the sun's rays reflect at all angles from snow, ice and water. Extra-sensitive areas of skin are the lips, nostrils and eyelids. You should apply sunburn cream or lip salve whenever you are out in the sun. You can get sunburn more easily at high altitudes during the same time of exposure to the sun.

Snow blindness

This is caused by the reflection of ultra-violet rays from the sun shining brightly on a snow-covered area. The symptoms of snow blindness are a gritty feeling in the eyes, pain in and over the eyes that increases with eyeball movement, eyes watering and becoming red, and a headache, which intensifies with continued exposure to light. Prolonged exposure to these rays can result in permanent eye damage. To treat snow blindness, bandage the eyes until the symptoms disappear.

It is vital to protect your eyes in bright sun and snow. Wear your sunglasses. If you don't have any, improvise. Cut slits in a piece of cardboard, thin wood, tree bark or other available material. Putting soot under your eyes will reduce glare.

Constipation

If you put off relieving yourself because of the cold, eat dehydrated foods, drink too little liquid and have irregular eating habits, you may become constipated. Although not disabling, constipation can cause discomfort. Increase your fluid intake to at least two quarts per day and eat fruits, if available, and other foods that will loosen your bowels. Eating burnt wood and charcoal may help!

Hygiene

Although washing yourself daily may be impractical and uncomfortable in a cold climate, you must do it. Washing helps to prevent skin rashes that can develop into more serious problems.

In some situations, you may be able to take a snow bath. Take a handful of snow and wash your body where sweat and moisture accumulate, such as under the arms and between the legs, front and rear, and then wipe yourself dry.

If you cannot bathe, periodically wipe yourself dry in these areas. If possible, wash your feet daily and put on clean, dry socks. Change your underwear at least twice a week. If you are unable to wash your underwear, take it off, shake it and let it air out for an hour or two. If you are with natives or using a shelter that has been used before, check your body and clothing each night for lice. If your clothing has become infested, use insecticide powder if you have some.

You have to strike a balance between hygiene and warmth. Shaving daily, for instance, may well be discouraged, because it removes oils that protect the face from frostbite.

Keep clothing clean

This is always important from the standpoint of sanitation and comfort in winter, but it is also important for warmth. Clothes matted with dirt and grease lose much of their insulation quality. If the air pockets in clothing are crushed or filled up, heat can escape from the body more readily.

A heavy down-lined sleeping bag is one of the most valuable pieces of survival gear in cold weather: make sure the down remains dry. If wet, it loses a lot of its insulation-value. Beat and brush your clothes: this will help get rid of the lice, but not their eggs, which will persist in the folds.

Shelter

The Arctic terrain of, for example, northern Norway restricts freedom of movement and is well suited to defence by small units. On the other hand, transport of logistic support and reinforcements is very difficult. Even if you do receive reinforcements you will still be heavily outnumbered by enemy forces, and so there is a good chance that, either alone or with your unit, you will find yourself in a struggle for survival as you try to evade the enemy. If you are in the treeline, you may find that the snow is not deep enough to build snow shelters, but you can make brushwood shelters. There are five basic designs which you can adapt to suit your purpose or the conditions:

1. Single lean-to shelter
2. Double lean-to shelter
3. Wigwam-style shelter
4. Tree pit shelter
5. Fallen-tree shelter

Basic building rules

The lean-to designs are the simplest, but the wigwam is the best, warmest and most comfortable. The tree pit and fallen tree are best used in tactical situations. If you have these basic designs in your mind, you can adapt them to most circumstances.

Build the main wall with its back to the prevailing wind, and weave it thickly with whatever wood or branches are available. A small wall can be built downwind to provide reflection for the heat from a fire. You can use snow to reinforce the woven wall, but it should not go too high up or it will melt into the "bivi" from the roof.

If possible, dig down to ground level for the fire. If this is impossible, build a good solid firebase of mixed layers of logs, snow and brushwood. You can burn an open fire in all types of brushwood shelter except the tree pit: in this case the walls are inclined to melt back and the "bivi" collapse.

The single lean-to shelter: The only problem with these shelters is that you must have a knife, saw or axe. The Eskimos have shown that with a knife you survive; without one you need a miracle.

When building this lean-to make sure it is tactically located so that you can build a fire large enough to spread the warmth equally throughout the shelter. The shelter is improved by using a reflector of green logs with the fire. With the reflector correctly placed, the warm air from the fire should circulate as shown below. It is vital the sleeping shelf is insulated from the ground, as without it you will rapidly lose body heat to the ground.

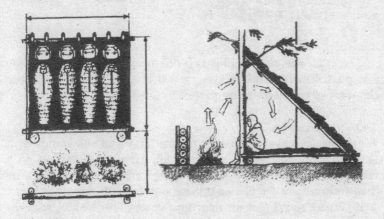

The double lean-to shelter: A larger group will be able to produce the more ambitious double lean-to, which is a lot warmer than the single lean-to. It consists of two singles with the high, open sides facing each other across the fire. The fire reflector is not required. As with the single lean-to, side walls can be added.

Teepee or wigwam shelters: This is a tent construction which can be easily built using a parachute (parateepee). It is possible to cook, eat, sleep and make signals from inside. You need a number of good poles about 3 to 4 metres (10 to 13 feet) long, or you can improvise as shown.

The tree-pit shelter: This is a good option in an evasion environment when the only people looking for you are the enemy. The only drawback is that a fire tends to melt the walls and cause a collapse.

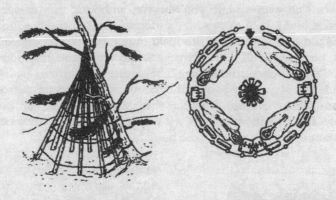

The fallen-tree shelter: This is a mixture of the teepee and the tree-pit solutions, and its design will contain greater or lesser elements of each according to the circumstances.

Tents and tentsheets

Tents can sleep five or ten men and are large and bulky; they tend to be used in base areas, and generally have to be carried on a vehicle or on a "pulk" – a man-towable sledge. The tents used by British forces are the Canadian single-pole or British ridge tent.

If you are working in small groups you will not be able to carry a tent, so you will each carry a tentsheet. In its simplest form this is a diamond of canvas with buttons and buttonholes on each edge. They can be joined together to form a tent of almost any size, but normally it would be for eight to ten men: the tent group. Tentsheets give you a portable, windproof, lightproof, robust and flexible system that meets all the needs of survival and tactics. It takes time to construct a shelter using tentsheets, and you will need to be able to do it quickly when the temperature is 20° C below freezing, so practise now. And learn to live in it.

The two-man tent group: The tentsheet is the basic unit from which you can make a simple two-man tent, using two sheets. Kit layout is all important. These tents are extremely cramped and you must decide where everything is stored, so that you can move out at speed and your oppo can pack your kit when you are not there.

The four-man tent group: The way in which the tentsheet is folded and joined to produce different-size tents is not obvious and must be thoroughly practised in dry training before you get out on the ground. Each man in the section must have an exact "job description" so that the tent is erected as a drill.

The five-man tent group: This is the usual half-section or fire-team layout complete with stove. Ideally you should not use ski poles in the construction of the tent as you may need them in a hurry.

The seven-man tent group: Everyone's feet face the door and the cook sleeps next to the stove. If you are operating a sentry stag, make sure the stag list is written so that the sentry wakes up the person who sleeps next to him, which means sentries do not have to trample over people looking for the next man on the stag list.

Storage and care of skis and weapons: Weapons should be stored outside because, if they become warm, snow will melt on them and then freeze again when they're next taken outside. They are stored in numerical order so that their owners can find them easily. However, from a security point of view, keep one weapon inside the tent for instant use, and free from snow.

In cold temperatures lubricants tend to thicken, meaning that weapons may be more sluggish, or even fail to work at all. Weapons therefore need to be stripped, and leaned; only the camming surfaces are lubricated, and then only sparingly.

Skis are stored horizontally in a pit, again in numerical order, with brushwood or poles underneath so that they do not freeze to the snow. The pit will absorb any new snow during the night, leaving the skis exposed so you will be able to find them.

Striking your tent or tentsheet

This is not difficult, but you must get it down to a fine art: you'll get cold if you find yourself standing around. Work out how long it takes you; this is your "pull pole" time. It should be around 15 minutes when properly practised. This will help you make plans to go straight from the tent to work that keeps you warm. Brush off ice and snow before packing away, or you will be carrying unnecessary weight and it will take you longer to put the shelter up again.

THE TENT GROUP
COMMANDER'S DUTIES

As commander, it is your responsibility to plan and organize the following:

1. Correct pitching of the tent or tentsheets
2. Allocation of sleeping space
3. Storage of weapons and equipment
4. Sentry roster and alert states
5. Routine for drying clothes
6. Fire precautions
7. Blackout drills
8. Track and camouflage discipline
9. De-icing of tent
10. Foot inspections
11. Overall welfare of your men

The tent group commander will direct this very simple drill for pitching a tent.

- *Select the best site:* Look for shelter from wind and the enemy, and make sure the snow is deep enough to dig your shelter in.
- *Stow your kit:* This should be neatly stowed to one side, normally to the left of the intended doorway.
- *Level the site:* Level to near ground level. The tent group commander will designate the area to dig.
- *Find insulation:* At the same time, designated men find brushwood and undergrowth to use as insulation.
- *Install cooking kit:* The designated cook unpacks the cooking kit, lights the stove and gets the rations ready for cooking. The lamp is lit.
- *Lay the tent:* The tent is laid out with the door positioned away from the enemy (and, ideally, away from the prevailing wind) so that they will not be able to see any light.
- *Raise the tent:* Peg the edges down and raise the tent on its own poles, if you have them; otherwise use brushwood poles. Do not use your skis or sticks except in an emergency. The cook takes the lamp, cooker, rations, etc into the tent.

- *Settle in*: Weatherproof the edges of the tent with snow (thrown over brushwood, which prevents icing and allows easy dismantling). The cook begins to heat the water (use clean, fresh snow, stored in plastic bags). Pass in sleeping mats and bags and lay them out. Make sure the floor is flat or everyone will slide during the night and lose sleep, and the snow will harden into uncomfortable lumps. Dig a hole by the door.
- *Food and warmth*: By now it will be pretty warm from the stove and the lamp. Two men will finish off the outside ski pit, weapons rack, fuel pit and latrine, but everyone else is thinking about food and admin, such as weapon and equipment maintenance. When you have eaten, night routine will begin.

It's -20° C, but you have got your drills right and so you kept warm while the shelter was erected. Now you're inside you're comfortable in your shirtsleeves! It only took 15 minutes – and that's as good as a fully trained Arctic soldier.

Once the tent is up, your immediate priority is camouflage. Issue white netting gives good cover, but you must use poles to distort its outline and avoid shadows formed by the shape of the tent. Snow walls around the tent provide cover as well as protection from the elements. The fighting position can be camouflaged with a few branches to minimize the shadow of the trench from the air.

Tent group routine

The group will evolve its own routine depending on tactical conditions, but the commander and cook always sleep by the door. Cooking is also done by the door (in case of fire and to allow moisture to escape) or in the cold hole. Other points for comfortable tent life are:

1. *Control your kit:* You will be cramped, so keep your kit packed unless you need it. Don't lose your gloves or hat.
2. *Keep clothes dry:* Dry damp clothing by hanging it in the ceiling of the tent. When the heat is off, take it into your sleeping bag; this includes your boots.
3. *Check your feet:* You and your buddy should help each other

to do this. Powder them and put on dry socks. If your feet are cold, rub them or, even better, warm them in your buddy's armpits! If they are seriously cold, don't rub them; just use the armpit method.

The tent group commander must make sure that the following are carried, and that they work.

1. Pulk
2. Tent (5- or 10-man)
3. Snowshoes (if not being worn)
4. Snow shovels (2)
5. Stove and spares (2)
6. Pressure cooker
7. Lantern with case plus spares, including mantlets (1 or 2)
8. Machete (gollock) and case
9. Saucepan
10. Fuel funnel
11. Fuel containers: 2-gal, 1-gal or half-gal
12. Ski/pulk repair kit

Note: The amount of fuel carried will depend on the time to be spent in the field.

Making a fire
The skill to make a fire means the difference between death and survival. You should have waterproof matches in your kit.

1. Dig down to the frozen earth for your firebase. If this is not possible, build a base of logs over the snow. You need a layer of brushwood, a layer of snow, then another layer of each, finally topped off with good thick layers of logs.
2. Build your fire on this base.
3. Use tinder to start the fire. If tinder is a problem, you can always find dry spruce twigs in the lowest branches, peel off birch bark, or use fir root. All contain high concentrations of tar and burn with a long-lasting flame. Fir root is especially good.

4. If you need to use fuel to help the fire along, dip your twigs in it and soak them. Don't waste fuel by pouring it on.
5. Use dead tree logs as the main fuel. It burns best. "Live" birch will burn if split. Eskimos use Arctic bell-heather (*Cassiope tetragona*) when there is no wood, or dung, or dry grass.

Snow shelters

You've been separated from your kit, but you've got your first- and second-line survival kit with you. It's a long way to base camp and there's only just over an hour of light left. A light snow is beginning to fall, and the wind's come up, but it's not too bad yet. You haven't got a tent. You're facing the prospect of a night in the open in worsening conditions. This is an emergency survival situation. Stay calm. Think. You've got a number of options, and you've practised them all. And best of all, you've got your rations!

The simplest way of building a shelter is to use snow. You can make a snow grave, a snow hole or an igloo; all three are better than a tent. *Make sure the entrance is lower than the sleeping bench; this will trap the warm air in the living space near the ceiling.* Even a burning candle will keep the temperature at about 0° C. Always smooth off the ceiling to prevent dripping. This, though, will make the shelter airtight, which can lead to lack of oxygen, especially if you are using a cooker, so punch a ventilation hole using a ski stick.

Keep a shovel in the shelter to dig yourself out if it blizzards or if the cave collapses; if the temperature is above freezing the snow conditions will not be quite right and the roof may start to fall in. For this reason, don't practise building snow shelters unless it's below freezing point.

Snow trenches

You need about one metre of snow – the deeper the better – into which you dig a simple trench. Make the bottom wider than the top, especially if there are two of you. If it's not quite deep enough build up a bit at the sides. Now smooth off the sleeping bench, insulating it with brushwood, if you don't have your sleeping mat with you. Then dig a cold hole next to the door: this acts as a sump for the cold air. Then dig an entrance and move your kit inside, and put the roof on. This can be tricky, especially if your trench is too wide. The simplest way, if the snow is compact, is to cut blocks and place them over the top, then add more snow. If you find you need support for the snow blocks use brushwood or tent sheets. You can use skis, but only as a last resort: if you do, put them in upside-down, as this helps to stop them freezing in. Then add more snow.

Snow hole or snow cave

If there are two or more of you, you need a large bank or drift of snow about three metres wide and two metres deep. An avalanche probe will come in handy to gauge depth. Put on waterproofs if you have them as you will get wet. There are two methods of digging: the tunnel method, and the block-and-cave method. The latter can be used when the snow is compact enough to be cut in blocks. Dig along the full length of the intended cave, using as many men as will fit, while one digs the entrance off to the side. Once you have dug the sleeping benches, build up the open side of the cave with the excavated snow blocks until it is sealed in. Only the entrance remains open.

Using the tunnel method, only one man can work until the building of the sleeping benches is started; it therefore takes much longer than the block-and-cave method.

You will find a snowhole rather oppressive at first, but it is the most comfortable and warm form of shelter in the Arctic and much preferred by Arctic troops.

Snow house (igloo)

The igloo – the traditional home of the Eskimo – needs experience and practice to build, and snow must be of the right quality to cut into blocks. Loose snow is useless; and the more granular it is, the smaller the igloo must be.

Work from the inside, cutting out the centre and using your carefully-cut blocks to form the base of the wall. Work progressively upwards in a spiral, shaping the blocks as you go, and leaning them just slightly further inwards with each spiral. Finally a key block is inserted – carefully – either by widening the centre hole or trimming the key block until it drops gently into place. The wall should be chest- to shoulder-high.

The entrance to your snow house should be small; a large doorway is simply an easy way for heat to escape. Ideally, it should be an S-shaped tunnel away from the prevailing wind. In deep snow, this can be underground. Construct sleeping benches inside and fill in any holes in the walls with loose snow.

Snow wall
In dire emergency a simple semi-circular snow wall will keep the worst of the weather at bay and provide shelter from the wind, allowing you to cook and sleep for a limited period.

Living in snow shelters
Follow these rules for safety and comfort:

1. Strip off to avoid sweating; the sweat may freeze later. But wear waterproofs when digging or you will get soaked.
2. Make sure your shelter is adequately ventilated at all times.
3. Mark the entrance to your shelter so you can always find it. This will also help rescuers if the cave collapses.
4. Brush loose snow from yourselves before entering. This prevents damp developing on your clothing in the warm interior of the shelter.
5. Take all your equipment in, *especially* a shovel.
6. Remove wet clothing and try to dry it overnight.
7. Take your boots into your sleeping bag and keep them near your stomach area. This will help to dry them.
8. Don't boil water for too long: its vapour will cause condensation and dampness.
9. Keep a candle burning to give light and warmth – but keep an eye on it.

Food and drink

Arctic rations
However tired you are, you must eat all your rations. In the Arctic you burn enormous amounts of energy, and your rations are geared to replace this loss fully. It's all freeze-dried for convenience and lightness, and you melt snow to add to it. Meat/rice rations must be simmered for about 20 minutes to make sure they have completely absorbed the moisture – otherwise, when eaten, they may cause stomach pains and will certainly contribute towards dehydration. The diet in the ration pack is balanced and is very nutritious, with plenty of "brews" in the form of tea, coffee and beef stock. Again, you must drink well, and one of the cook's main jobs will be to see that plenty of hot water is available to top up Thermos flasks.

You have four types of pack to choose from. Breakfast is always porridge and hot chocolate. The main meal is usually eaten in the evening, and you carry the snack pack in your windproof for eating throughout the rest of the day. You may get a little fed up with the chocolate, but eat it: it contributes as much as anything else to your diet and well-being. One little tip is to carry some curry powder with you to add to any food you're getting bored with.

Duties of the cook

Follow these drills and responsibilities and you will ease congestion in your tent or tent sheet when you first pitch it. A familiar routine will also keep you spirits up! The cook should:

1. Be the first man in – with his cooker and lamp – and may raise the pole.
2. Arrange the sleeping mats and bags as they are passed in to him.
3. Arrange the collection of rations, and clean snow.
4. Cook the rations and with the help of other members of the tent group, arrange:
   - The filling of stoves and lamps. Initially all stoves should be used: snow takes a long time to melt.

- The collection of more clean snow and ice for melting.
- The collection of rubbish.
- A constant supply of hot water. Empty flask are used for storage.
5. Organize a hot drink, if flasks are empty.
6. Use his imagination to make the ration as satisfying as possible; for example curry powder, onions and bacon all add flavour.
7. Have the next meal prepared, as far as possible; this saves time and effort later.

Remember: the health and morale of your group hinges on your expertise and hard work as the cook.

Lamps and cookers

There are various types, but they work on the same principle. All burn de-leaded petrol (naphtha), which is the only fuel that should be used, except in emergency. Leaded fuel causes poisoning and "tent eye". Even with naphtha you need some ventilation.

Your cookers are vital equipment. Check them constantly – nuts, bolts, and gaskets tend to come loose – and carry spare parts in your pulk.

Light and fill cookers and lamps in the open – particularly in training. On operations, you may have to risk lighting them inside your shelter. Make sure the filler cap is properly screwed on, and use the filler funnel to avoid waste. Remember, the naphtha must live in its pit outside your tent. Most lamps and cookers need pre-heating to generate a gas-pressure build-up before you can light them. Use "meta" (methylated spirit impregnated blocks) to do this – never use naphtha.

THE ARCTIC PARAFFIN LAMP
1. Fill the tank and screw down the cap firmly.
2. Check that the mantle is undamaged.
3. Lift the glass by slackening the ventilator nut and place four lighted meta blocks around the bottom.

4. Pump up the pressure vigorously while the metal blocks burn.
5. Switch the fuel on and if you have sufficient pressure the fuel will vaporize and the mantle will glow. If not you will end up with a small fire in the glass. If this happens, switch off the fuel and start again.

Arctic tent group stores

The list below gives the usual cooking and lighting equipment for an eight-man tent group. The kit is set up and used by the cook but is distributed throughout the group to spread the weight. Ideally it will be carried on a pulk, as the tent group can survive without it.

Paraffin fuel containers
Funnel
Paraffin lamp
Lamp carrying case
Saucepans for melting snow and ice for cooking
Pressure cooker
Peak fuel cooker
Issue fuel cooker
Snow melting tins
Meta fuel blocks (for lamps)

Water

Thirst is a major problem in the Arctic. In order to conserve fuel for other purposes, the survivor often deprives himself of drinking water from melting ice and snow, and the time and energy required to chop and collect ice for water also limits the supply. You may become dangerously dehydrated in the Arctic as easily as in the desert.

Remember:
1. You need about 50% more fuel to produce the same quantity of water from snow than from melting ice.

2. It is safe, within limits, to eat snow, as long as you allow it to thaw sufficiently to be moulded into a stick or ball.
3. Do not eat snow in its natural state: it will cause dehydration and chill your body.
4. Do not eat crushed ice, as it may cause injury to your lips and tongue.
5. Any surface that absorbs the sun's heat can be used to melt ice or snow, e.g. a flat rock, a dark tarpaulin or a signal panel.
6. The milky water of glacial streams can be drunk once the sediment has been allowed to settle out.

Rules of health

Keep fit: You burn enormous amounts of energy just doing simple jobs. The fitter you are, the less energy you burn, and you can work without becoming exhausted. This reduces the danger of freezing.

Drink plenty of water: Dehydration causes tiredness. Drink even if you are not thirsty.

Eat your rations: Even if you're not hungry, keep eating. Regular hot food will keep you at your peak.

Maintain a positive attitude: Keep alert and, above all cheerful. You can make it!

Elements for survival

The secret of successful travel in the Arctic is adequate clothing, sufficient food, rest and a steady pace. You must have your kit; unless properly equipped, the best course of action is to "hole up" and hope that the friendlies find you before the enemy does.

Emergency food

There is little to eat in the Arctic in winter, but in an emergency there are some possibilities. Look out for bird and animal tracks: these may lead you to their sources of food, which will probably be safe to eat. But beware: if you find berries or something you don't recognize, they may be poisonous. Try a small quantity on your tongue first of all, and if there are no ill effects eat a little; wait up to eight hours and then eat a bit more. If after another eight hours you are all right, you can be reasonably sure that the food is safe. Be especially wary of fungi: don't touch them in training unless one of you is a real expert.

Kelp and many types of seaweed are edible. Look out too for:

Rock tripe: Common name for lichen that grows on stone and boulders. Top of plant is usually black. An irritant when raw, a survivor's staple when cooked.

Reindeer moss: All of the plant is edible, but soak before boiling.

Crowberry: The small black berries of this low-growing shrub are an important source of Vitamin C for the Eskimo.

Arctic willow: Both shoot and roots are edible. Peel first.

Iceland moss: Comes in brown or grey-green forms. All parts of the plant are edible, though best soaked and boiled.

Bearberry: Grows in mats with pinky-white flowers. The red berries, usefully, can be eaten raw. The leaves make a tea.

Animals

Arctic animals range from reindeer, moose and bear (brown and polar) to hares, rabbits, squirrels and lemmings (look under rocks for these). You will also come across wolves and foxes. Look at the snow in the mornings and you will realize from the number of tracks just how much wildlife there is. The closer to the treeline or shoreline you are, the more abundant wildlife becomes, even in winter. Hunting animals is a skill, but you will soon master it if your life depends on it. Points to remember are:

- Always hunt up-wind (with the wind in your face).
- Move slowly.
- Try to stalk from above.
- Crawl if you are on exposed ground; move while the animal is feeding, and freeze when it lifts its head up.
- Don't take too long a shot, and if using issue ammo (which has solid heads), shoot through the heart, although small ground game may have to be shot through the head.

- A sharp whistle will cause most animals to stop; time enough to give you the chance of a shot.

Seals and walruses are found along the coastline or, on a good day, lying next to their breathing holes out on the ice. Both have large amounts of blubber, which is useful for cooking, heating and lighting, and is also edible, along with the flesh. You need to take great care when stalking a seal, and ideally you should shoot it through the head: this will make sure it cannot reach its breathing hole, and if it's in the water it will float.

> REMEMBER that polar bears are predators. Ensure that you are not hunted yourself. They may be attracted by your smell, as well as the smell of any "kills" you make.

Birds

The most common Arctic bird is the ptarmigan or snow grouse, which is relatively tame and can be killed with a stick or stone in a trap. There are owls and ravens too, but both are wily and you will need a baited trap. Near the coast, you will find gulls; these can be killed with a gorge hook. To trap birds you need some sort of cage system to be triggered as the bird takes the bait or by you from a hidden position.

Trapping and fishing
Snares
If you do not have any customized snares you can use string or light wire. The secret of success is to make sure that the slide moves smoothly; you can improvise with bone or a button, or a spring-loaded system. Once it is set, run a flame round the snare to reduce human smell. Set the snare on a natural game trail, preferably in a narrow place or gap. Use bait if you can.

Fishing
There is an abundance of fish in the Arctic, not only in the sea but also under the ice of frozen lakes, generally towards the inflow or

outflow. You will have to cut holes in the ice for your lines. Make hooks from safety pins, tin openers, bones, etc.

Bait can be inedible parts such as the entrails of animals or fish. The best fishing method is to put out night lines, which you check each morning, but where the bait needs to be moved about you must make "jigs" using discarded food tins, silver paper or other shiny material. Cod will take your clasp knife! For weights, use stones; for floats, a piece of wood. Animal tendons make very strong traces which are almost invisible and ideal for attaching hooks to lines.

Fish can be caught in winter, through a hole in the ice. Once you have cut it you can stop it freezing over by covering it with brush and heaping snow over the top. Fish tend to gather in deep pools, so if you are lake fishing cut your hole over the deepest part. You will need several holes which you can fish simultaneously using the "automatic fisherman". The fish pulls the flag upright. You need a one-metre pole and enough line to reach well beyond the ice. Attach a spoon-shaped spinner from a ration pack can to the line and place a hook slightly below it.

Fish hooks can be improvised from:

Wood skewer: Buried in the bait this hook sticks in the side of the fish's mouth

Thorn: An awkward piece of thorn can be effective when buried in bait. Look for a thorn bush with large rearward-pointing barb.

Bone: A sharp piece of bone can be fixed to a suitable piece of wood.

Nails: Ordinary nails can be bent into shape or set into wood.

Preparing fish
See diagram.

Bleeding
As soon as you catch a fish cut out the gills and large blood vessels next to the back-bone

Scaling
Remove the scales by scraping with a knife

Gutting
Gut the fish by cutting it open and scraping out the guts.

Skinning
Some fish such as catfish, have no scales and can be skinned

Traps
Fall log trap for big game: Large and medium-sized game is usually caught in deadfalls. However, this method is only worthwhile if there are sufficient quantities of larger game available.

   Spring and spear trap: The spear trap is another method of catching larger mammals, but requires very careful construction to be effective.

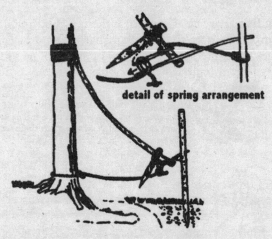

detail of spring arrangement

Trip deadfall: A rock deadfall stretched across an animal trail is effective as long as you are able to canalize the animal into the trap.

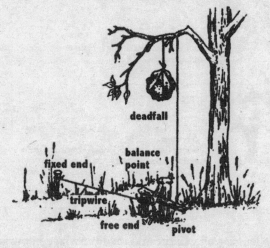

Harpoons and spears

You can make these from a piece of stout timber, their tips hardened in a fire, or with a knife or suitably-shaped stone or bone bound on to one end. They are best used to finish off an animal that has already been caught in a trap.

If you are near shallow water (waist deep) where fish are large and plentiful, you may be able to spear them. Try to find a straight sapling with a solid core that you can sharpen to a point. If not, tie a bayonet or pointed piece of metal or sharp bone to the end. Next, find a rock or bank which overlooks a fish run and wait for the fish to swim past.

The Arctic is harsh, but you can still live off the land as long as you have one or two basic items with you. Go for what seems to be plentiful; don't waste time or energy; and above all be patient and determined.

24-hour Arctic ration packs

Spare Arctic ration packs are carried by each man as part of his survival kit. These rations will buy you the time to find help or find or catch food. The packs contain:

Sugar packets
Powdered milk
Beef stock drink
Instant tea
Instant coffee
Instant dried apple and apricot flakes
Vegetable soup
Dehydrated beef curry
Rice
Dried peas
Tissues
Matches
Salt
Chocolate drink
Rolled oats mix
Sugar
Biscuits (fruit)
Nuts and raisins
Biscuits (brown)
Toilet paper
Milk chocolate
Beef spread
Chocolate and biscuit bar

Dextrose tablets
Chocolate covered caramels

Travel

Deep snow means deep trouble if you're on the move. On foot or in an ordinary vehicle, you've got very little chance unless you've taken precautions beforehand. As well as the difficulty of moving through the snow itself, there are other less obvious things to worry about. To start with, deep snow will change the appearance of the countryside, turning navigation by map into a nightmare. Secondly, the snow will hide all sorts of obstacles and dangers. Falling into a ditch filled with three metres of soft snow may sound like it could be fun, but the reality is deadly. You would find it very difficult to climb out before you were overcome by exhaustion and died of exposure. That is, unless you drowned in the snow first.

Consider and conserve

So what can you do to make your way through Arctic, sub-Arctic or Alpine conditions?

First, you must stay calm and conserve as much energy and body water as possible. If you're carrying a heavy load of equipment, weapons and ammunition you'll be unable to travel far if there's more than half a metre of untrodden snow on the ground – even if the country is flat.

You have to spread the weight of your body and your load. The two most usual ways of doing that both have their drawbacks – skis are hard to control unless you know how and anyway, are almost impossible to make from the sort of material you'll be able to gather. Snowshoes, the other real way to get about, are very tiring unless you're used to them, but they can be improvised using natural materials. If you're properly equipped, of course, you'll have both available: skis to use when you're travelling any distance, and snowshoes for use in camp, where there are lots of people about – or in heavy brush or undergrowth, where two metres of ski on each foot would make you a little clumsy!

THE JELPER SLEDGE AND GPMG PULK

The Jelper Sledge is the equivalent of the stretcher. It is the Arctic method of casualty evacuation, although it is also used for carrying light loads. The central sheet has an idiot's guide on how to make up the Jelper Sledge from ordinary skis and ski poles and the kit. It is designed to use one man's ski kit in its construction, for obvious reasons.

A specialist pulk is available for the CPMG in the sustained-fire role and enables the weapon and the huge quantities of ammunition it requires to be pulled into position and deployed at speed. You can fire off the pulk.

Skiing

A fit, experienced skier can keep up a solid 10 kilometres an hour for days on end, even when carrying a full load of equipment. That's an awful lot more than you could manage on foot, and it requires a lot less effort, so there is much to be said for learning how to do it.

There are two main types of ski: Alpine skis are the shorter of the two types, and have fastenings for both the toe and heel of the boot; cross-country or Nordic skis are longer and narrower, with a hinged fastening at the toe only, so that the heel can be raised. This allows you to do a push/step movement that covers the ground remarkably quickly.

Military cross-country skis

Standard military issue skis are 208 cm (6 feet 10inches) long (big by Alpine standards). They have a hole in the tip to allow you to tow them in an improvised sledge, and are grooved at the heel to accept mohair "climbers". To the non-skier it may come as a surprise to learn that you can actually walk uphill wearing skis. Originally, people stuck strips of sealskin onto the soles of their skis, with the pile of the short, stiff hairs pointing backwards. The British Army uses mohair instead, but the effect is the same.

The length of a pair of skis isn't terribly important, but the length of the poles is. They're much longer than the poles used in downhill skiing, coming to just below the shoulder. In the British forces they come in three lengths: 51 inches (130 cm), 54 inches (137 cm) and 58 inches (147 cm). Don't damage the points of your poles. They are intentionally sharp to allow you to get a purchase on hard ice.

FIELD SIGNALS FOR SKI TROOPS

1 – Patrol adopt arrowhead formation.

6 – Obstacle ahead

2 – Patrol adopt single file formation

7 – Gun group move to the right

3 – Patrol adopt file formation

8 – Gun group move to the left

4 – Patrol adopt staggered file formation

9 – Gun group go forward

5 – Patrol adopt extended file formation

10 – Halt

Improvising snowshoes

The traditional snowshoe looks a bit like a big tennis racket, but more modern versions are a rounded oblong shape, around 50 cm long and 25 to 30 cm wide, made up of a lightweight frame interlaced with straps of some sort. These straps can be made from any suitable material, and so can the frames, which means that at a pinch you can make a pair of snowshoes for yourself. Use stripped straight branches for the frame and webbing, animal hide cut into strips or even bark for the cross straps.

You don't need clever bindings on an improvised snowshoe: a single piece of rope, doubled and knotted twice around the foot and ankle, will do fine. Do not bind the ankle to the snowshoe – allow it to lift in the same way as your heel lifts while walking normally.

Walking at night

In an operational or hostile situation, travel during darkness, unless the weather has closed in sufficiently during the day to hide you in low cloud or fog. Even then take care: bad weather can lift very quickly, leaving you exposed and unprotected. And beware travelling in "white-out" conditions: the lack of contrasting colours makes it impossible to judge the nature of the terrain. And do not travel during blizzards – they are deadly. Moving at night can be tricky, as any light from stars and the moon is made even brighter when reflected off the snow.

Plan your moves

Make a plan to work from one feature to another, for shelter and concealment, rather than to trek straight out into open country.

Sound travels easily in cold climates, so you should keep very quiet and stop to listen every so often.

Always cross a snow bridge at right angles to the obstacle it crosses. Find the strongest part of the bridge by poking ahead with a pole or ice axe. Distribute your weight by crawling or by wearing snowshoes or skis.

Cross streams when the water level is lowest. Normal freezing and thawing action may cause a stream level to vary as much as 2 to 2.5 metres per day. This may occur at any time, depending on the distance from a glacier, the temperature, and the terrain. You should also consider this variation in water level when selecting a campsite near a stream.

Choosing your course

Consider rivers, frozen or unfrozen, as avenues of travel. Frozen rivers are frequently clear of loose snow, making travel easier than on the land. Avoid snow-covered streams: the snow, which acts as an insulator, may have prevented ice forming over the water.

Your course should be determined by your location and the terrain. In mountainous or wooded areas, it is advisable to follow rivers downstream towards populated areas (Siberia, where rivers flow northward to the high Arctic, is an exception). When travelling cross-country, try to follow the contour of the land; however, note that valley floors are frequently colder than slopes and ridges, especially at night. Head for a coast, major river or known point of habitation.

Going the right way

Navigation is tricky in the Arctic. You're near the magnetic pole, so compass readings may be erratic; take more than one, and average them out. Use the shadow tip method or use the sun and stars to show you in which direction north and other points of the compass lie. Nature itself can give you a few clues:

1. A solitary evergreen tree will always have more growth on its south side.
2. Bark on poplar, alder and birch trees will always be lighter in colour on the south-facing side.
3. Trees and bushes will be bent in the direction that the wind normally blows, so if you know the direction of the prevailing wind you can work out north and south.
4. The snow on the south side of the ridges tends to be more granular than on the north.

5. Snowdrifts usually are on the downwind side of protruding objects like rocks, trees or high banks. By determining the cardinal points of the compass and from the direction of the drifts, the angle at which you cross them will serve as a check point in maintaining a course. In the Southern Hemisphere of course, the opposite polarity applies.
6. Birds generally fly out to sea in the morning and return in the afternoon.
7. Moss is generally thickest on the north side of trees and rocks.
8. Lichens are more numerous on the south side of rocks and trees.

Pay attention to staying on the right track. You'll get some help in this during the clear weather by looking back at your tracks in the snow. But, of course, that's a sure sign to enemy forces that you're around. You have to be very cunning in the snow to cover up your tracks: stick to the treeline wherever possible, or use existing tracks and patches of broken snow. If you're travelling as a team keep in each other's tracks. Be careful how you plant your poles: always put them in the same holes as the guy ahead of you – then the enemy won't know how many there are of you. Alternatively, make lots of holes to confuse them.

CROSSING THIN ICE
If you have to cross thin ice remember these rules:

- One man at a time.
- Take your hands out of the loops of your ski poles.
- Put your equipment over one shoulder.
- Think about distributing your weight by lying flat and crawling.
- Bear in mind these thicknesses of ice and their corresponding capabilities: 5 cm supports 1 man; 10 cm supports two men side by side; 20 cm supports a half-ton vehicle.

If you fall through the ice, get your kit off and up onto the ice; use your poles to help you out. Don't get too

close to a team mate who has fallen through: you'll
only end up in there with him. Throw him a line so
that you can help him out from a safe distance.
Hypothermia will set in very quickly after immersion,
so carry out emergency re-warming straight away.

Distance

It's very difficult to judge distances in the Arctic as there are so
few visual clues, and the clear air makes estimating distances
difficult; they are more frequently underestimated than overesti-
mated. The simplest way of estimation is to pace out a given
distance yourself, but this must be practised to be anywhere near
accurate. Another method is for rope or some signal wire of a
given length (say 50 metres) to be strung between two men. The
first man moves off, and when the slack is taken up the first man
stops and the second man joins him, and then repeats the exercise. Simple mathematics can be used to estimate the distance
achieved after a number of repetitions.

Weather patterns

There is no fixed weather pattern in Arctic and sub-Arctic
regions, but the west coast of Scandinavia is affected by the meeting of the warm air masses off the Gulf Stream (which keeps
most of Norway's ports ice-free) and the cold polar winds from
the polar ice cap and the land mass of the USSR. This leads to
great instability along the coast, with considerable variations in
temperature, high snowfall, rain and fog. Mountain flying is
impeded by poor visibility, white-out and icing of rotor blades.
High winds lead to drifting, and snow builds up on downwind
(lee) slopes, with a strong possibility of avalanches.

When planning an operation, try to build up a picture of the
weather you are likely to meet. As well as checking with weather
stations, get the feel of local conditions. Observe the clouds:
watch for a build-up in the mornings – particularly of layers of
cloud on the mountain-tops. Snow clouds are generally light in
colour, with a slight yellow tinge. A watery moon or sun can also

indicate poor weather to come. If the mountains look hard and clear, this too is a bad sign. A south or south-westerly wind, or wind moving anti-clockwise towards the south, also portends bad weather. There are many other smaller indications, but these are the main ones and should influence your plans.

Avalanches are likely to occur after heavy snowfalls, often backed by a wind, or after a period of rising temperatures. Sometimes they happen for no apparent reason. "Slab" avalanches consist of wet snow that has been heavily compacted by wind; soft snow avalanches involve loose powder snow travelling at up to 400 kilometres per hour and creating enormous pressure waves in front of them. Avalanches occur on slopes greater than 15 degrees and up to about 70 degrees. A powder avalanche may occur with as little as a third of a metre of snow at about 20-25 degrees, and wet avalanches on slopes as low as 15 degrees.

Arrive and perform

Special operations often take place far from any means of support. You may have to travel long distances in the harshest of conditions to reach your objective, and you must be fit enough to do the job when you get there. Arriving as a casualty puts the whole team at risk, and not arriving at all means that the operation will fail. To be a successful Arctic warrior is more than survival: you have to be able to travel, fight and win.

Transport

Mobility is the key to successful Arctic operations. A thorough understanding of the capabilities of your vehicles, and the techniques needed to overcome the problems you may encounter, is vital to effective movement.

A variety of over-snow tracked vehicles is available to help you move around the difficult terrain of the Arctic. Two such vehicles are the BV 202 and BV 206. The latter vehicle is relatively new, whereas the BV 202 has been in service for over twenty years. The infantry, engineers and artillery generally have one of these vehicles per section, but fewer in logistic units. The 206 can carry everything that is needed by a section, including all the men, but the 202 can only carry the section kit, although it will pull sledges and troops.

Skijoring

The technique of pulling troops is called "skijoring", and requires a lot of skill to master. In skijoring, two 50-metre ropes are attached to the back of the vehicle at each corner. The troops attach themselves to the outside of the rope by twisting their ski sticks into it; the weight on the rope ensures that the ski sticks stay in place, and troops just hold on and are towed along. A "guard" sits in the rear of the vehicle to make sure that the vehicle stops if any men fall, using a buzzer to communicate with the driver. Once the technique is mastered, troops can be moved very quickly with little exhaustion. But the reverse is true if the terrain and going are poor and can result in chaos; you must decide carefully when to skijor, or whether it would be quicker to ski. Broken birch country and forests are very difficult to skijor, but open snow fields above the treeline are ideal and you can cover up to 15 kilometres per hour. Moving at speed through cold air can cause wind chill and frostbite, and orders of dress must be given. You should normally wear the Arctic hat, with flaps down, a face mask and toe covers. Halts may have to be taken as frequently as every 20 minutes to allow blood circulation to be restored to reduce the risk of frostbite.

Vehicle mobility

The most likely problems you will come across are navigating, traversing a slope, ravines, ice crossings, rivers and icy roads as well as heavily-laden vehicles becoming bogged down on steep inclines. Route planning and preparation require a great deal of time, and large numbers of troops may have to be used for route construction and maintenance work.

To overcome some of the problems faced by vehicles you will have to learn a number of tricks. To traverse a steep hillside, dig a road to avoid shedding tracks or overturning. If you become bogged down, anchor your skijoring ropes to a tree and the other ends to the vehicle tracks; then simply drive out as the ropes wrap themselves around the tracks. Use this technique to maintain grip when heavily-laden vehicles slip on icy mountainous roads. Winching is another option, and many vehicles are now fitted with efficient winches that can be used with "A" frames to solve most problems. (Another tip: if your Land Rover loses a back wheel, stick a stout log under the mud-guard into the suspension unit until you reach safety; the end of the log simply slides on the ice-packed road.)

Crossing rivers

If your route involves crossing a lake or ice-covered river, an ice recce must be done. This involves drilling holes in the ice with an auger and measuring the thickness. Do this over the entire length of the crossing at 10-15 metre intervals and at smaller intervals if you think the ice may be rotten or unsupported. Sometimes you will find layers of water between the ice – beware: the load-bearing capabilities are considerably weakened.

Make sure that crossing-points avoid the inflow and outflow points on rivers and lakes, or bends in rivers which accelerate the flow, and areas where banks are difficult to prepare. Lakes behind hydro-dams are particularly dangerous as the water level falls in winter leaving an enormous gap between the ice and water – sometimes up to 20 metres. You won't recover a man or vehicle if they go through the ice in these conditions.

Even after making a sensible choice for a crossing-place, you will still encounter problems. The underside of the ice may melt and scour as the weather conditions change, and cracks will occur: cracks which are parallel to the direction of travel are the most dangerous; those at right-angles less so. Cracks can be repaired by filling them with hay and straw and then pumping water onto the surface which freezes layer by layer. This is the principle for reinforcing any crossing that is deteriorating, but timber planks, steel mesh, trackway, hessian, brushwood and other materials can all be frozen onto the surface as reinforcement. The idea is to spread the load as widely as possible. This requires a great deal of effort and if the temperature is in the region of -10° C it is more economical to pump on layers of water to build up the depth of the ice.

Ice bridges

Find a slow-flowing straight section of river away from any previous crossing sites and put out protection parties to cover the work party. Prepare and reinforce the banks and mark out a suitable block from the upstream bank. Once cut, using ice saws, the bridge can be floated into position using ice pitons and mooring lines. The bridge may weigh several tons and simple pulleys can be used to manoeuvre it. Once in position, the bridge can be cemented in place by pumping water on to reinforcing material at the edges.

Approaches to bridges will also deteriorate as the ice tends to be thinner at the banks. The bank and bridge should be reinforced with timber and frozen snow to form a base for an "approach" bridge on to the ice. This relieves the load on the ice near the bank and maintains safe entry onto the main bridge. If there is open water between suitable ice banks you can cut a large section of ice and float it into position to bridge the gap. The ice should be good quality and of considerable depth – about 40-50 centimetres initially – and with temperatures below -10° C it can be reinforced like a standard ice bridge if it is needed for any length of time.

The most robust type of bridge is one that fits into notches cut into both banks. The notches should be cut with standard power saws and must be at least 20 feet deep, so that the bridge can freeze into place or be reinforced if it does not fit exactly. Lines attached through holes in the ice and toggled underneath are used to control the bridge as it is put into position. If the ice breaks, this technique can be used to make repairs, as the ice will quickly re-freeze at low temperatures. Angle-iron pitons can be used instead of toggle ropes, but these are not always readily available.

"Skewed" bridge

The previous type of bridge is probably the most stable, but it is time-consuming to make. A "skewed" bridge can be used as an alternative. The principles of its construction are the same, but the anchorage is less secure. The bridge has rounded ends that rest on both banks, which are again anchored by either toggled ropes or pitons. In the same way an ice ferry (an ice floe) can be constructed to move light loads; the load bearing/flotation capacity can be worked out using a simple calculation. The ferry is hauled, using a hand or vehicle winch, across the gap collecting and delivering its load.

Remember, ice is dangerous. To use it requires a great deal of study and understanding, which is built up by many years of experience. Ice recce is extremely time-consuming, because the ice engineer cannot afford to make mistakes; but ice is one of nature's phenomena that can be used to great advantage to speed up mobility in the Arctic.

Vision

Low light, flat light or white-out blizzard conditions may also occur when drivers will be unable to distinguish the type of terrain, any obstacles or direction, even on a marked route. The main problem is that the driver has nothing to focus on, and no depth of vision. This is very dangerous as he may drive over a cliff. The only solution is for two skiers to go ahead of the vehicle and act as reference points so that he can judge the rise and fall of the land; they will also navigate for him. If the conditions are really bad the skiers should be changed every 20 minutes to stop them freezing.

Helicopters

Helicopters are an invaluable asset, speeding movement over the inhospitable terrain, often where no roads or track communications exist. They can undertake a wide range of roles and jobs – the ferrying of men and supplies, forward and flank reconnaissance, fire direction, liaison, casevac and, if necessary, armed action. The main types used in the Arctic are the Puma, Sea King, Lynx and Gazelle; the USA uses the CH-53.

Helicopter operations are not easy at the best of times, and in the Arctic can be highly dangerous. Pilots, ground crew and the troops that are to be carried all need considerable raining. The biggest enemy of course, is the weather, affecting every aspect from flying to maintenance. For example, the helicopter will need "pre-heating" before flying, which means blowing warm air into the engine and body from hot-air generators. Visibility is crucial when flying, and "white-out" conditions where no depth or land-mark can be seen by the pilot will curtail an operation. Another danger is icing-up, caused by being caught in freezing rain or sleet.

All landing sites should, where possible, be flattened by an oversnow vehicle to create a hard landing-pad. This avoids snow being churned around by the blades, which is hazardous to the aircraft, and to everyone on the ground: the pilot can lose his bearings and high-speed whirling air can cause frostbite within minutes. To overcome the visibility problem, mark the landing site with a black, snow-filled plastic bag or with coloured smoke that stains the snow. If no markers are available, a marshaller will have to lie down to provide a marker. To avoid frostbite everyone on the ground must wear full protective clothing and masks, particularly the ground crew.

Maintenance
Maintenance is very difficult in cold temperatures, particularly at below -15° C, where skin sticks to metal. Heat is essential, and is provided by a portable air generator inside a tent or, in the case of larger helicopters, a large cover such as a parachute. Fluid leaks are frequent as seals can contract and crack with the cold, so ground crew must be particularly alert.

Emplaning and deplaning
Drills for embarking and disembarking must be practised. Take great care to avoid damaging the helicopter with the large quantities of heavy, cumbersome equipment, such as skis and sticks,

that must be manhandled in difficult circumstances. In the Arctic, the technique is that the helicopter will land almost on top of you; your section will lie beside or on its equipment, acting as a marker, and the pilot will put down beside you. The section then emplanes through one door, equipment going in last. You strap in and raise your right arm to indicate to the loadmaster that you are secure; the helicopter then takes off.

When deplaning, Bergens and men are offloaded through both doors, but the pulk and skis always go through the starboard (right) door. Troops should adopt fire positions until the aircraft is clear, and they then go to cover, where reorganisation and ski fitting takes place.

Snow scooters

Most forces who operate in the Arctic make use of snow scooters as a means of easing travel in the snow-covered terrain. In the military context, snow scooters have their plus and minus sides. They can carry out a variety of roles:

1. Liaison and communications (dispatches)
2. Casevac
3. Line-laying
4. Ammunition resupply
5. Route recce and deep patrols
6. Weapons deployment – off-route, e.g. anti-tank weapons

However, they do have a number of major disadvantages.

First, they are difficult to drive without considerable training and experience. Secondly, their engines are temperamental, although the modern machines are much more reliable and robust; they need constant maintenance, which may be difficult if deployed forward of their own troops. Thirdly, they need a reasonable amount of snow in which to operate successfully, so route planning is just as important as when moving vehicle-borne or ski troops to a target. They suffer high wear on open roads and off snow they are difficult to manoeuvre. A wheel can be attached to or in place of the front ski for road use.

Snow scooters are not particularly fast, but have powerful engines and a wide range of low gears to cope with snow, particularly heavy wet snow, which tends to clog the driving belts. The heavier machines, the "workhorses", have twin tracks that give them greater grip and thrust through all types of snow and allow them to pull large loads.

Driving a snow scooter demands skill, which you often have to learn the hard way! The trick is to counterbalance the machine in the traverse – it will always try to slide down the slope, turning over on you if it can. Leaning into the slope while driving across it is physically and mentally demanding and takes confidence to master, particularly when pulling a fully-laden sledge, but it is exhilarating and fun, and once mastered will allow you to use snow scooters as a significant contribution to Arctic operations.

Avalanches

Avalanches are difficult to predict, so avoid any slopes that look suspicious, especially when the temperature is rising or after blizzards. Avoid skiing in a traverse across the face, but if you have to, go as high as you can, and only one person at a time. Try to move from firm ground to firm ground if possible, to reduce the risk for example from a boulder to a clump of trees. Appoint someone as sentry to observe the crossing at the bottom of the slope and to one side if possible, although this may not be tactically permissible.

Avalanche awareness

Avalanches come in four different types:

1. Soft slab: snow fallen on lee slopes which fails to bond with older snow.
2. Hard slab: a deceptively hard surface formed by high winds and cold air temperature.
3. Airborne: new snow falling on an already hard crust.

4. Wet snow: usual in spring thaw, often after a rapid temperature rise.

Some avalanches can reach 200 miles per hour and carry with them thousands of tons of snow, ice and rock debris, burying a victim up to 10 metres below the surface. Here are some basic precautions to keep you away from danger areas.

- Stay high.
- Don't ski across rotten snow, new falls or very steep slopes.
- Don't travel alone, but do keep a safe distance between group members.
- Stay out of gullies – you never know what will come down from above.
- Keep a close watch on the temperature, both of the air and of the snow; check them often, especially in the spring. Sudden changes bring about avalanches.
- Dig pits from time to time to check on the condition of the snow lower down.
- Watch for recent avalanche signs; they often come in groups.
- Keep a very, very careful listening watch.
- Don't assume, because one group's got across, that it is safe. They could have triggered an avalanche.
- Avoid convex parts of a slope: this is where fracturing of the slab commonly occurs.
- Keep below the treeline – it's generally safer.
- Keep away from slopes of angles of between 30 and 45 degrees, which are often the most dangerous.
- The deeper the snow, the greater the danger.
- Avoid new snow: it takes a minimum of 2-3 days to settle.
- Travel in the early morning before full sun-up.
- Do not adopt a "lightning never strikes twice" attitude, or assume that if there's been an avalanche the danger is past. Avalanches occur in the same place all the time.
- On ridges, snow accumulates on the lee side in overhanging piles, called cornices. These often extend far out from the ridge and may break loose if stepped on, so do not stray unless you are sure of your ground.

Crossing a danger area

Do everything you can to stay away from areas that look or feel like they might be about to avalanche. There may come a time, however, when you just have to go through one! Before you cross, loosen your bindings, hold your ski sticks in your hands only (no straps around your wrists) and be prepared to unclip your Bergen in a hurry. Do not rope up with your colleagues, but unravel your 30-metre avalanche (lavine) cord if available or your 5-metre cord. If you are buried, the cord may float on the surface and indicate your position.

Here are some rules that will increase your chances of making it safely – and some hints as to what to do if you get caught:

- If you have to cross an avalanche area, travel across the slope one at a time.
- Follow in the same tracks as the man in front of you.
- Loosen your ski bindings and take your hands out of the loops on your poles.
- Slip any rucksack straps off your uphill shoulder so that you can ditch it easily.
- Fasten you smock hood over your nose and mouth to reduce the chances of drowning if you go down in powder snow.
- Walk downhill; don't ski!
- Go straight down, not in a traverse.
- Keep high and stick to concave slopes.

Caught in an avalanche

If you feel or hear an avalanche coming, you must move fast but carefully – a fall now will almost certainly mean your death. Don't panic. If you stay calm you have a good chance of coming out of it unscathed. Here is the Rule of 10:

1. Ditch your kit.
2. Find out where you are in relation to the avalanche. You may not be in its path. If it's going to miss you, don't move.

3. Look out for your team mates. Remember their positions. You may have to dig them out.
4. Ski away in a steep traverse. Don't go straight down the fall line. The avalanche may be travelling at anything up to 200 miles per hour.
5. If you are in the path of an avalanche and cannot ski out of the way, try to find an anchor point (a boulder or tree) or sit down with your back to the slope, Bergen behind you, having kicked off your skis and sticks. *Immediately the snow hits you, begin swimming, and try to stay on the surface. The swimming action should help to clear an air space, which you must achieve as the avalanche comes to rest, and the snow re-sets.* Remain as calm as you can; there is little point in wasting energy if you are trapped under the surface, where no-one will hear you.
6. If you get caught at the side of an avalanche, dig outwards – it's easier.
7. Make an airspace around your nose and mouth, but keep your mouth shut. In a powder avalanche, try to get a cloth over your nose to act as a filter.
8. *Determine which way is up and down – perhaps by dribbling.*
9. Start digging your way out before the avalanche has time to settle and freeze into position.
10. If you're covered in powder snow, try a swimming motion. Backstroke is the most effective.

Rescue

If attempting a rescue, you must start a systematic search immediately, in two phases. Post a sentry to watch for new avalanches, and send for help immediately. Organise a helicopter landing-site close by, to which the rescue services can fly: this will often be the only way in.

Your buried person is likely to be somewhere in a vertical line from the point of disappearance to the bottom of the slope. The first phase of the search is a "coarse" one: starting at the bottom, with a man every half-metre, using avalanche search poles or ski sticks to probe the snow every 30 cm. Maintain a tight pattern on the search line, and probe delicately so that you do not injure the lost person. If you touch something soft, dig. Mark the area as you search it.

Specially-trained search dogs are available in most countries where avalanche risk is high, and they are invaluable. Ideally they should search the slope prior to any other human interference, but this will not always be possible as time is important; however, clear the slope of human searchers as soon as dogs become available.

Modern technology has also provided personal radio transponders and seekers. They are generally only available to troops who are at high risk, such as reconnaissance units, who work in small groups high in the mountains. The beacon works by sending a radio "bleep" every second. Everyone's transponder is switched to "send" at the start of the patrol. If anyone gets lost, all beacons are switched off except one or two that are switched to "receive". Searchers then systematically quarter the site of the avalanche looking for the strongest signal, which strengthens as they get close to their target. At the location of the strongest signal, dig.

An injured man should be treated as for shock: make sure his airways are free, keep him warm and give him a warm drink. An unconscious man will need artificial resuscitation, and look out for other injuries that may not be obvious.

Arctic combat

Combat in the Arctic is probably the most challenging of all military skills. It is the soldier, either as an individual or as a team, against the cruellest climate in the world; a climate with no sympathy for men or machines. It requires constant practice, and minute attention to planning and detail, because if things go wrong there may be no way out. Arctic warfare demands the highest of conventional military ability, plus a whole range of extra skills.

Care of equipment

We will start by looking at the basics. You will have to learn to look after your equipment and pay special attention to the range of spares that you must carry. Because of the intense cold, equipment tends to be more brittle and may break more easily, and the harsh terrain also takes its toll. Among the most essential items that should be carried by each section are spare ski binding straps, poles and mittens together with emergency ski tips.

Weapons

Your weapons also require special attention. Some of the main problems that you may encounter when shooting are:

• Working parts break more easily at low temperatures.
• Ice may form on working parts after firing.
• Ammunition lethality is reduced, and it may become fouled by ice or snow.
• Your hands are less effective when wearing bulky mittens.
• Weapons need a firm base to fire.
• Fog that forms during firing may interfere with the optical sights.

The above problems can be overcome, with maintenance becoming second nature. The muzzles of all weapons require a cover to prevent snow from entering the barrel and firing mechanism. Use light oil (normally a mixture of oil and naptha/petrol) to lubricate, but if this is not available, just dry-clean your weapons. To overcome sweating and thus freezing, leave your weapons outside your tent sheet. Make a weapon rack and cover it if possible, but always remember to brush off any snow when picking up weapons. If the temperature is above freezing, the weapons can be put in the tent.

During pauses in firing you may find that the ammunition freezes in the barrel. To overcome this, work the bolt/cocking handle every few minutes until there is no possibility of freezing. This is painstaking work and could take up to an hour, but is well

worth it. Ice fog which forms around automatic weapons during
high rates of fire may force you to fire at a reduced rate. Alternative
firing positions should be considered if possible. Also take care of
your ammunition, keep it in its liner, remove any oil and avoid
getting snow on it.

Always ensure that your mittens are dry. If your mittens are
wet when throwing a grenade, it may freeze to them – think of the
effect of that if you had pulled the pin! Another useful trick to
prevent the grenade sinking in the snow is to tie it to crossed
sticks or a board. It will then explode near the surface and have a
much better effect. Remember that all your weapons will sink in
soft snow, and it will be difficult to attain muzzle clearance. You
must put "feet" on your machine-gun bipods, light mortars, etc,
and there are special techniques for rifle shooting using ski sticks
to prevent your elbows from sinking into the snow. You can use
snowshoes on the bipods, but most light machine guns are
specially equipped in Arctic trained units. Light mortars require
a steel plate placed on the compacted snow, which the unit LAD
(Light Aid Detachment) will make.

Radios

Radios and batteries should be looked after, particularly batteries.
These lose their power in half the time in Arctic conditions sometimes even quicker. So if a battery is not in use make sure that it
is on charge or in a warm place – which may have to be inside
your smock if you're on the move.

IMPORTANT ARCTIC WARFARE KIT
Kit to be kept in your pocket
First field dressing; earplugs; lip salve; plastic spoon;
snow goggles; plastic whistle on lanyard; survival/Silva
compass; hat ECW; headover; toe covers; snowbrush;
wristlets; contact gloves; survival bag (if bivi bag not
issued); survival ration pack; Arctic mittens (if not
worn); safety pins; ski scraper/waxes; M&AW safety
guide; notebook & pencil; map and torch (remember
to keep this warm).

Kit to be kept in your patrol pack

Windproof trousers; Thermos flask; tent sheet, reversible waterproof or Gore-Tex suit, jacket and trousers ("Chinese Fighting Suit"); shovel; 24-hour ration pack; snow shoes; No. 6 cooker (one between two); fuel and matches; steel mug.

Belt order

Right/left pouch; rifle magazines; rifle-cleaning kit (REK); bayonet; snowbrush (if not in smock); water bottle pouch; emergency rations; string; candle; waterproof matches; steel mug; No. 6 cooker and fuel (if not all in patrol pack).

Other items on belt

Avalanche cord (10 metres); survival knife (Collock); rope and karabiner; bivi bag.

Individual camouflage

Camouflage starts with the individual, and good use of a mixture of DPM (Disruptive Pattern Material) and white overalls is important. For example, if you are working in a forest a DPM suit is probably most suitable, whereas near the treeline or snowline a white jacket or white trousers may be worn. Above the snowline use the full white suit. Weapons and webbing must be camouflaged using white tape, and special helmet and Bergen covers in white are available. Adjust your camouflage to suit your background, and use cover such as hollows, broken ground, trees and birch scrub as normal.

Movement is often the great giveaway, as it is very difficult to camouflage ski and vehicle tracks. Where possible use the shape of the terrain, moving in hollows and shadows. Tracks should run under tyres if possible, and sharp edges that might cast shadows in bright sunlight should be broken up by the last man or vehicle dragging a small pine tree along the track. In a camp where digging is necessary, remove snow from under the trees and throw it onto the tracks. This may deceive air recce but not ground patrols, although it all adds up to making it as difficult as possible for the enemy to spot you.

The disruption of sharp edges also applies to field defences, the entrances to tents and the tents themselves. Field defences should have rounded edges, smoothed to blend in with the shape of the ground. Fill in the bottom of trenches with snow to prevent black earth showing, and remember that tracks within the position will need filling and smoothing daily. Pitch tents under trees or, if this is not possible, dig them in and camouflage with white nets or parachutes. Use track plans and discipline, particularly in camps, and try to set a series of deception tracks away from your position. Construct "dummy" positions using spare tents to draw enemy fire and deceive the enemy about your strength.

Mountains

Mountains often contain vast tracts of open, unbroken snow fields, but the lower slopes are generally covered in pine and dense birch scrub. No amount of snow can fill all hollows or conceal all rock and scree, so natural cover does not exist. You will have to use deception extensively and reduce noise to a minimum, as sound travels over long distances in still air. There is also the problem of human-induced fogs of vehicle exhausts and cooking fires, as warm, damp air condenses in the cold conditions.

Arctic camp

We will now look at how the above techniques can be applied to set up an Arctic camp. Whatever the size of the camp, whether a patrol camp or a major formation base, the principles for setting it up are the same. Select the site carefully, considering concealment defence, routines and administration.

Initially you will set off with your recce party, which runs one or two hours ahead of the main body. The recce party will contain 2ICs and guides from all your sub-units. What will you be looking for? A map study may have produced some likely areas to look at: you need an easily defendable area with good concealment, good snow cover for digging in and with the possibility of good administration. The position should avoid low-lying ground, which is likely to be on a marsh and may get very cold. Try to find a piece of forested high ground, or ground that is broken up with good fields of fire, limited access points or access routes which can be dominated by outposts. As far as administration is concerned you will probably have to consider fresh water, covered vehicle access from main routes, and helicopter landing sites.

Having made your selection, mark out the camp and brief your commanders and guides on areas, defensive work, sentry posts, arcs of fire, stand-to positions, track plans, areas for cutting brush-wood, latrines and a host of other measures.

The deception plan

Then consider your deception plan, which may require the assistance of your main body. You will require a false trail beyond the camp area, and possibly a "dummy" camp using spare tents. Vehicles may have to be used to produce long fake trails, creating confusing and large-scale defensive track plans.

The "jump-off"

For small units without vehicles the entry track to the camp will be a "jump-off" from the ski trail. A professional enemy may be able to detect the change in the track, and it is possible to tell from a ski trail how many men actually passed along it, and in which direction, by examining the number and angle of the ski-pole plants in the snow and their compactness. The idea of a "jump-off" is that the patrol halts, but the lead skier or skiers lay a false trail beyond the "jump-off". While they do this the remainder of the patrol leaves the main track, often through a thicket or where the snow is broken. The skiers laying the false trail then return to the "jump-off", camouflage it (it may be disguised as a fallen man, and many similar dummy "jump-offs" will have been laid previously) and then re-join the rest of the patrol. The job may of course be done by the main body, depending on the number of men you have and your standard SOPs (Standard Operating Procedures).

Camp discipline

When the main body arrives at the camp, the sub-unit commanders are briefed, and work begins with the minimum of noise and disturbance to the snow. A track plan is established and should be used by everyone. Vehicles are tucked under trees and camouflaged; slit trenches are dug; tents and shelters are put up; weapon racks are built and food and drink are prepared. At last light, patrols depart to lay mines and trip flares and to establish listening posts beyond the perimeter on likely enemy approaches. Each tent group has a man on sentry duty, connected to the tent group commander by a vine or string to ensure a silent call-out. Sentries are changed every hour, and in extremely cold weather as often as every 20 minutes. The camp then settles into night routine, which includes minimum movement (except for sentry changes and patrols leaving the camp), no lights and minimum sound – radios are on mute, but vehicles may have to be run occasionally to keep them warm and their batteries charged.

Navigation

The ability to navigate accurately in the Arctic is vital. It saves time and energy, and poor navigation could lead to death. The principles of navigation are the same as those in a temperate climate, but there are more problems: snow changes the shape and nature of the terrain, and it is much more difficult to relate the map to the ground. Add to this white-out conditions, when it is impossible to judge relief and distance, and freezing conditions, when it is difficult to handle both map and compass, and you can see the problems. It is also difficult to pace distance accurately, particularly on skis, so you must rely on obvious features – easier said than found!

The following techniques will help you. First, select your route carefully from a map. This is vital to avoid obstacles such as steep ravines and slopes, forests and open water. Study the contours in detail as you draw in your route, trying to ensure gentle gradients.

En route, try to navigate parallel to a major feature or aim at a marker. For example, a river bed on a flank will act as a guide; or navigate towards a fixed feature such as a hut, tree or rocks. You can use a star for short periods (20 minutes), but remember that stars move. If you are navigating towards a fixed feature, e.g. a hut on a road, aim to the right or left of the hut by a few miles. Then when you reach the road you know you are on one side or the other of your objective.

Distance is probably the most difficult element to judge, particularly in white-out or at night, and on skis. Use the mileometer in your vehicle, or for more accurate measurement use two men tied together with a piece of rope of a known length (e.g. 50 or 100 metres). One man acts as anchor while the other skis forward to the rope's limit; then they swap roles and the anchor man skis past the skier. The distance is calculated by counting the number of rope lengths. This method is time-consuming but can be vital in poor conditions.

Being lost can be very worrying, but don't let it affect your reasoning. Using a map and compass, select a linear feature and march on a compass bearing towards it – you should eventually hit it. Without a map and compass things are more difficult, and you will have to use your memory, your watch (if you have one) and try to relate your route to a linear feature. Make use of the sun (if it is up) or the North Star at night (this does not move). Draw a diagram on paper or in the snow, noting the position you want to get to, any roads or linear features, and the position of the sun at various times of the day, remembering that it rises in the east and sets in the west. Try to put in a north pointer. Then march in the direction you require, keeping your direction relative to that of the sun (at that time of the day) or to the North Star at night. It is not very accurate, but that is not the point: you are aiming to hit a large feature and then refine your route from there, so trust your plan. If the conditions are not good, you may have to consider going into a survival situation with shelter, warmth and food.

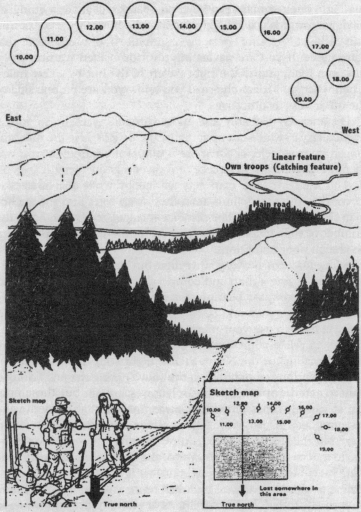

If you are caught out without a map and compass, you can navigate using the position of the sun and your watch. At 12.00 noon you will have a rough indication of north as shown above. You can then prepare a rough sketch map to hit a large feature eg a road by relating the map to the position of the sun.

If you lose your compass don't panic. Look out for the natural signs above and remember that the shadow cast by a straight object perpendicular to the ground at midday will indicate north and south.

Then there are the stars: In the Northern Hemisphere, true north can be deduced from the constellation of the Great Bear (Ursa Major) which points to the North Star; in the Southern Hemisphere the southern cross indicates the direction of south.

Special operations

In spite of the hostility of the terrain and climate in the Arctic, there is still a requirement for the specialist skills provided by the Special Forces. Troops who are specially equipped and trained in deep penetration behind enemy lines are often employed, but very careful logistic planning and subsequent mission supervision is required for success. Like other troops, Special Forces will need acclimatization, and they should also have the experience to operate independently. Most northern armies maintain such forces: some are assigned to land operations and others to operations at sea.

Soldiering in the Arctic requires determination, skill, and a great deal of hard work. Troops will be delivered to the target by boat, submarine, parachute or helicopter, followed by a long, hard ski march. Some armies use snow scooters, but these are only suitable if the terrain is reasonably flat. Most movement will be at night, and if a large unit is required to reach the target, infiltration tactics will be required. An individual's skiing ability and fitness must be exceptional, and accurate navigation and survival skills are required.

Most Special Forces will be involved in strategic tasks. These encompass simple observation and reporting, target reconnaissance and attack, sabotage, ambush on lines of communication and beach reconnaissance, which is vital for successful amphibious landings.

Raids and ambushes

A typical raid by a Scandinavian Special Forces unit is pre-planned, with many small units infiltrating from temporary lying-up positions to the main RV in order to mount the operation. A classic ambush is to attack a convoy on a route, using "stand-off attack" tactics to reduce casualties to their own men, and making follow-up more difficult. The unit will covertly dig in about 150 metres from the route, and camouflage their position from both ground and air. The positions are well equipped as troops are likely to occupy them for considerable periods of time. Any tracks into the area should also be camouflaged and any likely follow-up routes booby-trapped and mined.

Remote control

A wide range of remotely-fired devices should be positioned in the main killing area to deal with armour, soft-skinned vehicles and personnel. The ambush may be initiated by blowing two culverts with improvised changes at each end of the convoy. Anti-tank weapons of the LAW type are strapped between two posts or a tree and a post, and are aimed at a marker on the far side of the killing area. The firing mechanism is simply operated by a piece of string, attached to a piece of wood to give sufficient leverage to the trigger when the string is pulled and the rocket fired.

Various types of mine are also sown for both defensive and offensive use. The defensive mines will largely be anti-personnel, and there are two main offensive directional mines: first, the well-known Claymore-type mine (No. 13) which fires a large number of ball-bearings into a fixed killing area – ideal for soft-skinned vehicles and troops; and secondly, the anti-vehicle mine, which will damage and immobilize most vehicles. If the killing area is properly mined and booby-trapped there would be little requirement for supporting fire from the main position.

Once the ambush is over, a rapid withdrawal is undertaken through the usual RVs.

Attacking a railway

To achieve the best effect when attacking a railway both a train and a line should be destroyed together. In order to cause even more disruption and delay the recovery of the train and repair to the line, the area around the ambush site should be booby-trapped.

The most suitable places to launch an attack are embankments or cuttings, or where the train is likely to be travelling at high speeds. The area should be ideally be covered by forest or brushwood, but the line should be visible from 100-150 metres. A further obstacle between the line and the firing position would also provide additional cover.

The mines are dug in under the rails into the trackbed, which may require the use of hammers and chisels if the ground is solid rock. The mines are then linked together with a detonating cord, and a fuse is run back to the remote firing-point, the base of a tree ideally, where it terminates in a firing-cap pull switch. This in turn is attached to a pull cord. Great care must be taken to bury the mine and fuse and to camouflage any disturbances to the ground. Sometimes snow will have to be collected from an area well away from the line and used to fill any holes produced in laying the device.

Remember to position sentries, linked by radio, well out to the flanks (at least 400 metres away). The line may be patrolled or an unexpected train may use the line, and you must have early warning so you can return to cover. Initiation is by pull, which is followed by immediate withdrawal along a pre-planned route using the usual anti-tracking and anti-follow-up tactics.

As can be seen, Special Forces have their place in the Arctic, and can have an effect that far outweighs the effort and resources committed to the tasks. It is vital, however, that any such operation is properly prepared and mounted, otherwise it will end in disaster – and never more so than in the Arctic.

PART V

MISSIONS

LANDINGS AND RAIDS ON ENEMY TERRITORY

Special Forces teams take the battle to the enemy on his own ground. Working behind the lines, their missions can vary from intelligence-gathering to sabotage, and organising guerrilla resistance movements against the enemy. It is a war without rules. The Special Forces soldier can expect no mercy from the enemy.

Many operational techniques are made up on the spur of the moment, to take advantage of a tactical opportunity. But that doesn't mean there's no formal training. The US military forces all have special detachments, and they all take as their guide FM 31-20, the US Army Special Forces Operational Techniques field manual. Because they are "Special Forces", their job is impossible to describe without listing all the possibilities. It is safer to say that as a member of Special Forces team you have to be prepared to tackle just about anything that comes up. One of the most important tasks is intelligence-gathering – e.g. locating hidden "Scud" missile sites in western Iraq. Another is the instruction of locally recruited guerrillas in military and other techniques – anything from personal hygiene to farming methods. The aim is to prove to the local population that you have their best interests at heart, a tactic pioneered by the SAS in the jungles of Borneo.

Winning the battle for the "hearts and minds" of the people is really much more important than taking an objective by armed force. But you can't win either of them until you get to the battlefield itself. Inserting agents into hostile territory has been a frontline intelligence task for thousands of years. There are two main methods: false identities and disguise, and covert operations.

False identities

The biggest advantage of the first approach is that once you have got through the identity checks at the frontier you will be able to live openly in enemy territory. You will be living a double life, with slim chances of survival if the enemy identify you – but no-one said Special Forces work would be easy. Disguising your identity in peacetime is essential if you are to succeed in such a task: this is why the US Special Forces do not allow their personnel to be filmed after they complete basic training.

Covert operations

Covert operations involve entering the enemy's territory without his knowledge. It can mean trekking across a border in remote frontier regions, or parachuting from an aircraft at very high altitude to freefall most of the way.

Infiltrating Special Forces teams

Airborne landings
When preparing a team for infiltration by parachute, remember the following:

1. Aircraft load capacity may limit the equipment and personnel you can take.
2. The presence of a reception committee on the drop zone makes "sterilising" the area and hiding your parachutes less of a problem.
3. You must ensure you take the equipment needed for your initial tasks.
4. The detachment commander places himself in the best position within the stick for controlling the team.
5. Team recognition signals, and signals for contacting the reception committee, must be decided in advance.
6. The primary assembly point should be 100 to 200 metres

from the drop zone, and you should have a secondary point 5 to 10 km from the DZ for use in an emergency.

Insertion from an airborne operation is popular because no area is inaccessible by air; it's quick and, when organized properly, minimizes the risk both to the carrier and to the passenger and his reception committee. There are three normal variants:

1. Low and normal altitude parachuting.
2. High Altitude Low Opening (HALO) parachuting.
3. Air Landing operations.

The objective is to insert agents without the enemy's knowledge, so you must take his capabilities into account. How good is the enemy radar? Are adequate drop or landing zones available? Are there personnel on the ground who could act as a reception committee and help transport people and supplies to safe locations and "sterilize" the drop zone after use?

You must consider many of the same factors when planning an infiltration from the sea. First of all, what sort of coastal areas are available, and how vigilant are the enemy defences? Do you have the right sort of marine craft to hand? Do you have the facilities to make sure that sea water can't affect vital pieces of equipment? Submarines are widely used to land Special Forces. Modern submarines are difficult to detect and Special Forces personnel can exit underwater and stay that way until they reach the beach.

Infiltration overland is very similar to a long-range patrol in enemy-held territory and can be the most secure way of all of getting the Special Forces gear into place, especially if time is not crucial. Distance is not necessarily a problem to well-equipped Special Forces personnel trained to use their skills, wits and resources.

Local assistance

Where you can get help and assistance from "friendlies" already
in place, to provide food, shelter and intelligence, overland infiltration is often the most effective of all. Because drop zones and
landing zones are unlikely to be next door to the area of operations, both air and seaborne insertions will probably end up as
overland journeys as well. So there is a lot to be said for relying on
your own two feet rather than on technology; man can escape
detection a lot more easily than a machine. One factor is common
to all three methods of insertion that we've looked at so far – the
availability of people on the ground to act as porters and guides
and provide security for the infiltrators. But it may not always be
that way. In some cases the members of your team will have to go
in "blind", relying exclusively on your own skills and resources –
not to mention a degree of luck!

Planning Airborne operations

Airborne operations are the arteries and veins of Special Forces
operations in enemy-occupied territory. In most cases, it's just
not possible to get men and supplies in and out of operational
areas by any other means, and so a great deal of effort goes into
making them as safe, secure and simple as possible.

The DZ or LZ

The first stage of any airborne operation is the identification and
selection of Drop Zones (DZs) or Landing Zones (LZs).

Drop zones and landing zones must please both the aircrew
who are to fly the mission and the reception committee who
will be there to meet the consignment and passengers. From
the aircrew's point of view the zone should be easy to identify
from above and the countryside around it relatively free of
obstacles.

All-round access

Flat or rolling countryside is best, but if the Special Forces operation being supported is located in mountainous country, this may not be possible. In that case, it's best to choose sites on broad ridges or plateaux. Small enclosed valleys or hollows, completely surrounded by hills, should be avoided whenever possible.

To give the aircrew as much flexibility as possible in the route they will take to the zone, it should be accessible from all directions. If an approach can only be made from one direction, then the area should be free of obstacles for five kilometres on each side to give the aircraft space to perform a "flat" turn.

Level turning radius

Drop zones with a single clear line of approach are acceptable if there is a level turning radius of 5 km each side (1.5 km for light aircraft). Remember that these are minimum distances, and if you reduce them the aircraft may be endangered or fly higher than desirable when making the drop, leaving your supplies drifting on the wind away from the DZ.

1. The general area surrounding the drop zone must be relatively free from obstacles that might endanger the aircraft. Flat or rolling terrain is the best, but plateaux in hilly country can be suitable.
2. Small valleys surrounded by hills should not be used for drop zones.
3. For night operations you must avoid using drop zones with ground rising to 300 metres within 16 km of the site level.

Even particularly tall trees can be a potential danger to an aircraft doing a low-level drop. Where the operation is to take place at 130 metres or less, the safety requirements are that there should be no obstacle higher than 30 metres within 8 kilometres, if possible. Where the aircrew have no choice but to put up with such obstacles in the immediate area of the DZ, their location must be well known.

Dispersion

The DZ should be equally accessible from all directions, so the best shape is round or square, even though the various packages that make up the consignment will land in a line parallel to the course of the aircraft. Dispersion – the distance between the points where each component will hit the ground – is mostly controlled by the speed of the aircraft over the ground, and the time it takes to get the whole consignment out through the hatch.

The rule of thumb for low-level operations is that half the speed of the aircraft in knots (nautical miles per hour: 100 knots – 115 mph), multiplied by the time it takes to get the whole consignment out of the aircraft, will give the dispersion in metres on the ground.

Drop zone axis

If you have to use an oblong DZ, it must have its long axis in absolutely the right direction, to allow the pilot of the aircraft the best possible chance of completing his mission safely and delivering the consignment into the right hands. It must make some allowance for sidewinds, because this will dictate how far to the side of the aircraft's track the drops will land. It's not sufficient to expect the pilot to compensate completely for sidewinds by "aiming off".

TAKE-OFF & APPROACH CLEARANCES
FOR FIXED-WING AIRCRAFT
Minimum landing-zone sizes
Light aircraft: 305 m x 15 m
Medium aircraft: 920 m x 30 m
Add a 15-metre cleared strip each side as a safety margin.
This is the critical distance, because it determines how long the zone needs to be. If possible add at least 1,000 metres to each end as a safety factor. Sometimes it may be impossible to find a potential DZ as wide as it is long that meets all the other requirements.

Dispersion pattern

The first man or package out of the aircraft will obviously tend to land some distance behind the last man out. You can calculate the dispersion as follows: half the speed of the aircraft in knots multiplied by the exit time in seconds, equals the dispersion distance in metres. The dispersion distance is the absolute minimum length of the drop zone.

The surface

The surface of the DZ should be level and free from obstructions such as rocks, fences, trees and power lines. Where personnel are to be dropped at high altitude (15,000 metres and higher), try to locate DZs in soft snow or grassland. Parachutes fall faster in the thin, high air, and so the passenger will hit the ground harder.

Dangerous drop zones

Swamps and marshy ground, including paddy fields, are suitable both for personnel and bundles of goods in the wet season, and for bundles when they are dry or frozen.

It is possible to drop into water providing special precautions are taken. The water should be one and a half metres deep; it should be cleared of obstructions both on and below the surface; it must be 10° C or warmer; it must be free of swift currents and shallow areas; and there must be a foolproof recovery system that ensures that personnel don't stay long in the water.

One particular problem that dropping into water minimizes is that of cleaning up the DZ after use, so that no tell-tale signs of the operation are left. Be particularly careful when dropping onto agricultural land. If the fields in question are cultivated, it will be next to impossible to eradicate all traces of the drop.

Landmarks and way-points

The further an aircraft has to fly on a compass course, without way-points (visual checks on position) the more likely it is to be off the correct course. The main causes are tiny inaccuracies in the compass and other instruments and external factors such as wind. Special Forces re-supply missions rely on being pinpoint-accurate first time: the pilot hasn't time to fly around the countryside looking for the drop zone. The usual procedure is to select an easily identified landmark somewhere between 8 and 24 km away from the DZ itself. The pilot then takes his bearings from this point and flies on a compass heading for a pre-determined time to bring the aircraft over the zone.

Features that stand out from the ground may well not make good landmarks from the air especially at night. These are the sort of things you should be looking for:

1. Coastline in distinctive stretches, especially with breaking surf or white sand beaches, river mouths over 50 metres wide, or sharp promontories or inlets.
2. Rivers more than 30 metres wide. Heavily wooded banks will reduce their visibility.
3. Canals: their straight course and consistent width make them easy to spot, except where the surrounding countryside follows a uniform pattern.
4. Lakes at least a square kilometre in area with a distinctive shape or feature.
5. Woods and forests a square kilometre and more in size with clear-cut boundaries or some special identifying feature.
6. Major road and highway intersections.
7. Railways especially when there is snow on the ground.

Para dropping behind enemy lines

Resupplying Special Forces teams that are operating behind enemy lines is a difficult business. Because radio communications can be detected, the supply drops often have to be at pre-planned times. Since the Special Forces teams cannot guarantee their arrival at a specific drop zone either, the US Army units have a system for area supply drops. The aircraft arrives at point A and flies to point B. Below the flight path there are several possible drop zones, but the aircraft does not need to know which one the ground troops want to use. The aircrew simply fly along the route and drop their supplies when they see DZ markings. The distance between points A and B should not exceed 25 km, and whatever DZ is chosen should not be more than 1 km away from the line of flight.

How to request a para drop

Whenever you use a radio, keep the three principles of use in mind: Security, Accuracy and Discipline (SAD).

Security
Remember the eternal triangle of sender, receiver – and enemy monitor. Keep your transmissions as short as possible, always encode your own and enemy grid references, and be careful not to use names or appointment titles on the radio. If in doubt, encode it into battle code (BATCO). Watch your speech mannerisms: these can also give you away and are a vital source of long-term intelligence.

Accuracy
You must encode and decode accurately. BATCO leaves no room for mistakes. Corrections take up valuable seconds that could lead to a message being intercepted and a traumatic experience: for example in a 40-second fire mission a battalion of Soviet BM-21 multi-barrelled rocket-launchers can deliver 14 tonnes of HE (high explosive) or chemical agent onto your position.

Discipline
You must obey radio net discipline, provide constant radio watch and answer calls correctly and quickly. Use correct voice proce-dure, apply the rules of BATCO and this will help prevent enemy electronic warfare units from breaking in on your net.

Radio voice
You must also be aware of your radio voice. It should differ from

normal speech in the following respects: Rhythm, Speed, Volume and Pitch (RSVP).

Rhythm: Divide the message up into logical portions, and deliver it at an even rhythm with pauses. Remember, the recipient has to write it down.

Speed: BATCO delivered too quickly will lead to mistakes; delivery must be slightly slower than normal speech.

Volume: Speak slightly louder than normal, but don't shout – this just distorts the message.

Pitch: Try to pitch your voice slightly higher than normal: this enhances clarity.

Marking drop zones

Even if his navigation is excellent and his instruments spot-on, the pilot should still be helped in the final stages of the approach by signals from the ground. At night these can be made by electric flashlights (torches), flares, small fires or vehicle headlights.

In daylight, the best DZ marking method is the square panels that are supplied as sets to Special Forces units. If they're not available, use bed sheets or strips of coloured cloth, but make sure they stand out against the background. The squares or strips are used to make up distinctive shapes or letters, which are changed every day according to the unit's Standard Operating Instructions.

Using Reference Points

Help the aircraft find your drop zone by providing reference points with three-digit bearings and distances measured from the centre of the Drop Zone. Dangerous obstacles like radio masts or high hills should also be reported in the same way. Smoke grenades or simple smudge pots of burning oil aid identification considerably. Radio homing devices become more and more popular as the technology that supports them improves, but remember that they need to emit a radio signal to operate. Any signal that you can pick up, the enemy can pick up too.

Ground Release Points

The ground party has a much better chance of computing the Wind Drift Factor (the distance that bundles and personnel will be carried by the wind) than the pilot does, so they allow for it when marking the Ground Release Point.

The wind doesn't start to act on the load immediately it leaves the aircraft. The rule of thumb is that the load will travel in the same direction as the aircraft for around a hundred metres before starting to slip off to the side. Drift is calculated by a simple formula: aircraft height in feet, times wind velocity in knots, times a constant – three for bundles, four for personnel. Release Point Markers can then be offset according to the likely wind drift. Obstacles along the flight path might prevent the pilot from seeing the markers, and to reduce this possibility there must be a clearance on the ground of 15 metres for every metre of the aircraft's height above the ground. An obstacle 30 metres high mustn't be closer than 450 metres from the ground markings.

Markers should be sited in such a way as to be visible only from the direction from which the aircraft is approaching. This may mean screening them on three sides, placing them in pits with the appropriate side sloping or, in the case of panels, mounting them at an angle of 45 degrees.

Unmarked drop zones

In particularly sensitive operations it may be necessary to make deliveries of personnel and equipment to unmarked drop zones. This usually means a daylight or full-moon drop into a zone that has a particularly well-marked geographical feature to identify it. Because of the need for security, the ground party will have no way of directly communicating with the aircrew. The pilot will have to calculate wind drift himself, using the latest available weather reports as a guide and make allowances accordingly. Electronic homing devices should be used whenever possible to help the aircrew recognize the DZ, but very careful arrangements are necessary to keep transmissions to a bare minimum.

High Altitude Low Opening

Precision skydiving (an increasingly popular sport) grew out of a Special Forces infiltration technique known as HALO – High Altitude Low Opening – parachute infiltration. Dropping from around 1,000 metres, the parachutists fall free, controlling their direction with hand and arm movements that act in the same way as the control surfaces of an aircraft.

If the wind speed is over 20 knots the jump should be aborted. By laying out a pre-learned arrow patterns on the ground you tell the pilot and parachutists the direction and strength of the wind, which enables them to judge the timing of the jump.

DZ markings indicate the landing point itself in this technique, because the parachutist is able to make corrections for windage. In the last few hundred metres of the descent, however, he will be subject to the same forces that act during a normal descent, and so it is necessary to show wind speed and direction by arranging the target marker in the shape of an arrow pointing into the wind. Up to five knots of wind are indicated (standardly) by an arrow head, adding one additional marker to form a tail, for every further five knots of wind speed.

The use of sophisticated electronics renders it unnecessary for the target area to be visible from the aircraft, so the HALO jump can be made from above cloud or at night. Equipment can be freefall-jumped too, using altimeter-triggered or timed parachute release and the same aiming techniques used in high-altitude precision bombing.

Helicopter landing

For maximum effective use of the helicopter you should position the landing zone to allow take-off and landing into the wind. At night the helicopter will usually have to land to transfer personnel or cargo, but during daylight hours it can fly a couple of metres off the ground and the team can leap out of the back.

Altitude and temperature

Remember that at high altitudes and high temperatures the

density of the air is sharply reduced. This means the helicopter cannot carry as much cargo, and will need a longer distance to take off and land.

Approach path
Helicopters need at least one approach path 75 metres wide. For a night landing a helicopter requires a minimum space 90 metres in diameter.

Surface and slope
The surface chosen for the landing zone must be relatively level and free from obstructions such as logs, rocks, ditches or fences. The maximum ground slope permitted is 15 degrees. In dry conditions it is a good idea to dampen the area to reduce the tell-tale dust cloud which also hampers the pilot's visibility.

Noise
The noise of a large helicopter such as the Chinook coming in to land will reveal your position to any enemy forces nearby. For this reason, helicopter landings must be conducted away from the enemy unless you have a powerful security detail in position.

Water landings
Helicopters like the Chinook can land in a water course provided the bottom is firm and the water no more than 46 cm deep.

The reception committee

The reception committee is split into five parts, but a single person may, of course, take on more than one role. The five functions are:

1. *Command Party* – to control and co-ordinate the operation and provide medical support.
2. *Marking Party* – which sets out and collects markers and assists in recovering equipment and personnel and sterilising the site.

3. *Security Party* – which ensures the unfriendly elements don't interfere with the operation.
4. *Recovery Party* – ideally two men for each bundle or parachute. They should be spread out along the drop axis at the same interval as the drops are expected. Any back-up should be stationed at the far end of the drop track, because the drop is more likely to overshoot than undershoot. The recovery party is also responsible for the clean-up "sanitisation" of the drop site, and that includes briefing all members of the reception committee on proper procedures. A surveillance team should keep watch over the DZ for 48 hours after the operation to warn of enemy activity.
5) *Transportation Party*, responsible for getting personnel and

Sterilization procedures
The reception committee will clean up the drop zone after the operation. Here's a basic check list:

1. Collect cigarette ends and food wrappers; mislaid equipment; human waste.
2. Collect rigging straps and parachute line.
3. Count all items of equipment out and in.
4. Bury any waste or unwanted equipment, preferably in a number of different places, at the base of large bushes.
5. Erase drag marks, footprints and impact marks. Use a leafy branch and disguise the freshly-cut end on the tree with mud.
6. Avoid trampling vegetation, especially in cultivated areas.
7. Maintain security on the way in and out of the DZ.

Security

Because security and concealment are so important to Special Forces operations, you must pay a lot of attention to these considerations when selecting reception zones. Three factors are important: freedom from enemy interference on the ground; accessibility by means of concealed or secure routes for the reception committee; and proximity to areas suitable for hiding supplies and equipment.

Avoiding the enemy

It goes almost without saying that the aircraft's route into and out of the DZ must avoid enemy troop installations. There must be a very high level of patrol activity around the DZ for some time before the operation is due to take place. When the aircraft is actually scheduled to land, rather than merely drop a consignment from the air, vehicles mounted with automatic weapons should be available, to keep pace with the aircraft on both sides during landing and take-off (bear in mind that the vehicles will have to be moving and up to speed at the point where the aircraft will touch down). If incoming fire is received the crews of these vehicles must be in a position to suppress it immediately.

LOLEX

Vital cargo can be dropped without landing with a technique known as Low Level Parachute Extraction Resupply System (LOLEX). The aircraft flies a couple of metres above the ground and a parachute fitted to the cargo pulls it out of the rear door.

Waterborne landings

Landing from the sea
Special Forces operations often start and finish on a beach. Even though airborne insertion is faster and more flexible, when safety and secrecy are the first considerations the unit commander will often opt to go in by ship or submarine, landing his men from inflatable boats or getting them to swim.

Submarines are self-contained, safe from prying eyes. They mean that amphibious special operations can be mounted at extremely long range – from the other side of the world if necessary. The long journey time can be an advantage in itself because it allows the operation to be studied, pulled apart and put back together again until it is close to foolproof.

The first consideration is the type of boat available to carry the team to the landing site. When security comes first, this will usually be a submarine, but that choice will put a severe limitation on the amount of equipment that can be carried, which may mean that a resupply mission will be needed. However, for infiltrating small-groups of people into existing operations, or for mounting hit-and-run raids, the submarine is ideal. Space is very limited in submarines, but there is room in flooding compartments for kit such as inflatable boats and that is where they are carried.

Submarines are self-contained, safe from prying eyes. They mean that amphibious special operations can be mounted at extremely long range – from the other side of the world if necessary. The long journey time can be an advantage in itself because it allows the operation to be studied, pulled apart and put back together again until it is close to foolproof.

The mission can be split down into four stages:

1. Movement to the disembarkation point. This part of the operation is normally under the control and charge of regular navy personnel.
2. Transfer from ocean-going vessel to the landing craft and movement to the landing site.
3. Disposal of the landing craft. This may mean destroying it, hiding it or navy personnel ferrying it back to the mother ship.
4. Sanitisation of the landing site and movement to the operational area.

Keep fit

Physical exercise plays a big part in the shipboard life too, to ensure that the team is in top condition for the operation. This is a particular problem when the mother ship is a submarine making a completely submerged passage. The modern generation of submarines routinely crosses oceans without ever surfacing, and there's not a lot of space on board for callisthenics or aerobic exercises!

Transferring at sea

From a surface ship, the transfer procedure is quite simple. The landing craft are inflated and sent over the side. A scrambling net is let down, and the operational team install themselves in the inflatables, stow their equipment and set off on their long journey to the beach. And it will be a long journey. To maintain security, the mother ship will never come above the horizon as seen from the shore – maybe a distance of more than 20 miles.

Outboard engines are notoriously noisy. There are electric versions which are almost silent, but they have a very limited range. To get around this problem the landing craft may be towed in close to shore by a purpose-built tug – low to the water and fitted with a heavily-silenced inboard engine. The landing craft then make their way the last two or three miles to the beach under their own steam – or rather, by the muscle power of the Special Forces team who are paddling them.

Transferring from a submarine to the landing craft is either a lot easier, or a lot more difficult, depending on which one of the three methods is chosen. If the submarine can come to the surface, the inflatables can be dropped over the side, the landing party boards, and away they go. In one interesting variation to this method the boats are placed on the deck of the submarine and the crew get aboard then the submarine submerges gently beneath them. Alternatively, the submarine commander comes up to just below the surface, exposing only the very tip of the conning tower and presenting a very small picture, even to enemy radar. The landing party exits and either swims to the landing point, on a compass bearing, or inflates the boats in the water and paddles in. The most secure technique of all requires the landing party to exit the submarine underwater, usually with the boat completely stationary and sitting on the bottom. Team members wearing SCUBA (Self Contained Breathing Apparatus) then emerge from a hatch connected to an air-lock, and swim under water to the landing place.

SIX THINGS TO REMEMBER
WHEN LEAVING A SURFACED SUB

1. Crew members and troops should be fully briefed on the debarkation plan.
2. Inspect all your kit before the debarkation.
3. Wait for the crew to man their debarkation stations first before going to yours.
4. Swimmers debark in pairs from the conning tower of the submarine, which will surface with its decks awash.
5. Form up in the control room with all your kit. If there is space, the first pair can be in the conning tower ready for the submarine to surface.
6. If possible, rehearse the whole debarkation procedure before you do it in a tactical situation.

Special Forces personnel who undertake missions like this have to be highly trained and very, very fit. If it's necessary to use this "locking out" technique with technicians or mission specialists of any kind, then the lead pair will exit with inflatable boats and set them up on the surface. The rest of the team can then make "free ascents" using the submarine's ordinary escape hatch, join up with the divers, and make their way to the beach in the normal way.

Underwater infiltration

As radar and anti-aircraft weapons become increasingly effective, underwater infiltration has become an increasingly important method of infiltrating Special Forces troops. The key to any successful infiltration may be summed up as Short, Simple and Secure. Underwater operations using SCUBA equipment provide an extremely secure method of infiltrating short distances by water.

Shallow depth

Try to make your approach at the shallowest possible depth so that your air supplies last longer, and you and your equipment do not suffer the problems associated with sustained diving at great depths. There is another reason: swimmer detection systems find it harder to detect people at shallow depths.

Security
Part of the team should land ahead of the main body to check that the beach is clear. Surfacing and removing their masks outside the surf zone, the security team goes ashore and signals "Clear" to the rest of the troops when it has examined the beach area.

Combat loads
Combat loads must be light and small and should include only equipment, weapons and ammunition needed for the mission. You must have a proper equipment unloading plan and preferably have it rehearsed before landing.

PRECAUTIONS AT SEA
1. Is the area used frequently by passing enemy patrol boats?
2. Fishing boats can cause embarrassing confrontations and must be avoided.
3. Rocks and any other hazards that are likely to make navigation difficult have to be noted and passed on.
4. Sometimes underwater obstacles will be in the way, so a route through to the shoreline has to be checked.
5. A close check on weather conditions is important, and prior to the raiding force landing a meteorological report should be sent back.
6. You need a secure landing point that will enable the raiding force to disembark safely and without making any noise.
7. The reconnaissance team will have been given a time and a date for bringing in the raiding troops and by this time all their work must be complete. They should know the lie of the land like the back of their hands, and in particular which routes afford the best cover. Having checked the state of

the sea and sent their met report back, they will then stand by at the landing area to receive the raiding troops.

Swimmer delivery vehicle

The furthest reasonable distance the swimming team should have to cover is 1,500 metres. If the submarine cannot approach this close to the target area then swimmer delivery vehicles should be used to reduce fatigue.

On the way in

In anything but a flat calm it will be impossible to see the shore for most of the journey in, except when you get up onto the crest of a wave. Even then you probably won't have time to get a fix on your objective. You have to navigate by compass, and that will be satisfactory as long as you know where you are.

Unfortunately, the seas and oceans never stand still. Except for a very short period at high and low tides (called "slack water"), they are constantly in motion – and not just straight in to the beach and out again either. On top of that there are coastal currents to contend with, and though they may run in the same direction all the time they certainly don't always run at the same speed.

These factors are much worse in some parts of the world than in others. The Mediterranean, for example, has no tides to speak of, while the Bay of Fundy and the Bristol Channel have up to 15 metres between low and high water. And around the Channel Islands there are four tides a day instead of two! It's impossible to compensate for all this, and the commander of the mother ship will have calculated the transfer point to take account of all the known factors. Even so, the landing party will have to work hard to keep on course and will be grateful for all the help they can get.

Choosing a landing place

The ideal site for a seaborne landing has very similar features of a good airborne drop zone: it's easy to identify from a distance; is free of obstacles; has good and secure access and evacuation routes for both the transportation group and the reception committee; and is largely free from enemy activity. The main differences lie in the sea and under it.

Any reasonably competent observer can evaluate an inland drop zone just by looking around carefully. To do the same for a seaborne landing requires a certain amount of training in the science of hydrography. Tides and currents are more difficult to deal with than underwater obstacles – at least these don't move around all the time!

Navigation at sea or even on inland waterways is much more difficult than on land, chiefly because it's difficult to know exactly where you are at all times. Modern small radar equipment can solve this problem, but leaves you exposed if the enemy detects the radar emissions. A better solution is offered by satellite navigation (satnav) hardware, which will tell you where you are to within 100 metres anywhere on the earth's surface. Because it's completely passive (it transmits nothing itself but only receives) you don't risk giving away your position when you use it.

Find the beach

If there's no reception committee on the beach, the landing party will navigate for themselves, using the compass, sun or star sights and shoreline observation, and will be rather lucky to hit the beach at precisely the right place except under the easiest possible conditions. If there is a beach party it can help with visible light, well shielded and only allowed to shine out to sea; infra-red beacons, which the boat party can pick up using special goggles; underwater sound; and radio.

The surf zone doesn't stretch very far out from the shore. When the landing party are close to its outer limit they stop and maintain position. Scout swimmers get into the water, approach the beach and check it out. When they are sure there's no enemy activity they signal the rest of the party to come in.

There are no exceptions to this procedure. Even though there may be a reception committee waiting with established perimeter security and reconnaissance patrols, the landing party still performs its own reconnaissance.

The raid goes ashore

The transit to the area may take some time, and distance will depend entirely on fuel consumption. The troops must also be prepared for a wet and bumpy ride, and wear adequate clothing.

At a certain distance from the objective the boats slow their engines to cut down on noise. At this point their greatest allies will be wind and the crash of the sea, which will disguise any noise they make. From there they move slowly up to a rendezvous point, within a visible distance of their landing site. It is important to note that good radar can pick up and identify small boats, and you should remember this when planning the route.

Once at this RV point the troops wait for a pre-arranged signal from the reconnaissance team ashore to notify them that all is clear to move in. It may be that something has occurred ashore and therefore no signal will be given, in which case the boats will return. Having received the signal, the boats move in with engines cut and the troops paddling. This depends on the weather conditions, but it is essential that from here on as little sound as possible is made. One man in each boat has a gun trained on the shore as a precaution. Once in, everyone disembarks as quickly and quietly as possible, and moves to a given area to await the next stage. Meanwhile, the boats wait in the most concealed area, along with a guard force, their bows pointing back out to sea.

The raiding force commander and his team leaders are then given a final brief by the recce team commander. This gives everyone an opportunity to confirm any last minute details and to make any changes. Once everyone is satisfied, the team leaders carry out a briefing for their teams and then at a given time, they move off. It may be necessary at this stage for teams to split and approach the target from different angles. In this case each team is led by one member of the recce force, who takes them up to a starting line. Quite often the recce team acts as a fire support group giving whatever help they can when required.

River raiding

Infiltration is by no means the only type of amphibious operation. There are lots of important military targets underwater, in the water or close alongside, and all of these are vulnerable to attack from combat divers either operating submerged or approaching secretly, landing and approaching the target from an unexpected – and therefore poorly-guarded – direction.

Breathing apparatus
Underwater operations like this generally require the diver to stay submerged for some considerable time, and that means breathing apparatus. There are two types of SCUBA: open-circuit, where the bottles are filled with compressed air and the outbreath is vented into the water; and the closed-circuit system, where the diver breathes the same air over and over again, each breath being "topped up" with pure oxygen carried in the tanks, and exhaled carbon dioxide absorbed by a special chemical.

Closed-circuit SCUBA is particularly difficult and dangerous to use, and even preparing the equipment is risky in itself – pure oxygen is highly explosive in the right circumstances. The advantage is that it doesn't leave a stream of tell-tale bubbles to give away the diver's position.

Even with the danger of being spotted, open-circuit SCUBA can sometimes be used, but the surface of the water must be broken and turbulent to minimize the risk. The advantage is in its ease of use and much greater safety.

As well as laying demolition charges, the combat diver may be called upon to reconnoitre minefields and other underwater obstacles, check out harbours, docks and dams, establish and recover underwater caches of equipment, and find essential equipment that has had to be abandoned in an emergency.

Because it's bulky and difficult to conceal, equipment for underwater missions will have to be air-dropped to established undercover Special Forces teams as they need it.

Small boat operations
In many countries, rivers and inland waterways take the place of roads as the prime communications routes, and Special Forces, with their comprehensive training, are very well equipped to make good use of them. River craft and small inflatables are better suited to transportation than for use as fighting vehicles,

however, though you must always be prepared for ambushes, for example, which will force you to fight from the boat. This possibility will influence the team leader's decision when it comes to choosing between boats or travelling overland. The one great advantage to travelling by boat is the speed. It's quite in order to estimate average speeds of 35 to 30 miles per hour (55160 km/hour) in areas where the waterways are widely used and kept free of debris and other obstructions

Inflatable boats

Inflatables, which ride on top of the water, are much more manoeuvrable than displacement craft, which may draw anything up to two-thirds of a metre. They are also very light in weight, and so can be carried for short distances if necessary. Purpose-built inflatable assault boats do have their disadvantages however. There's no disguising them: their outboard engines make an awful lot of noise, and they are very easily damaged by water-logged trees and other debris floating on or close to the surface.

When he decides whether or not to use boats in a particular operation, the team leader has to think of the operation as a whole, and choose the ways and means most likely to get the job done successfully and in the shortest possible time. The rule of thumb must be: use boats when they offer a quicker way of getting from place to place; abandon them and set off across country when that looks like the better solution. The same applies to using divers: hit the enemy where he's weakest, from the direction he'll least expect.

This training in small boats and underwater operations is just one more example of the flexibility of the Special Forces soldier, ready to go anywhere and do anything at a moment's notice.

Raids and ambushes

Special Forces units operate deep in the heart of enemy-occupied territory, undertaking both active and passive missions. A typical passive operation involves moving into position in the utmost secrecy, setting up a concealed and secure observation post, and then passing information about enemy troop strengths and move-ments back to HQ. It may be months before the observers can be extracted or even re-supplied, so their training has to make them self-sufficient, allowing them to operate in the most hostile envi-ronments, where one false move, day or night, could give the whole thing away.

Active operations such as raids and ambushes call for a differ-ent sort of courage. Daring instead of patience, decisiveness instead of caution. This section on Special Forces Operational Techniques looks at the way active clandestine operations are planned and executed, and takes FM 31-20, the US Army's field manual for Special Forces, as its source.

A Special Forces raid is a surprise attack on enemy force or installation. It breaks down into four parts:

1. Clandestine insertion
2. Brief, violent combat
3. Rapid disengagement
4. Swift, deceptive withdrawal

Raids may be mounted to destroy enemy equipment and installa-tions such as command posts, communications centres and supply dumps; to capture enemy supplies and personnel; or simply to kill and wound as many of the enemy as possible. They may be used to rescue friendly forces or partisans too, and can also serve to distract attention away from their operations.

Organising the raid

The purpose of the mission, the type of target and the enemy situation will all have a bearing on the size of the raiding party. But whatever its size it will always have two basic elements – an assault group and a security group.

The assault group conducts the operations itself. Here are the troops who go in and demolish installations, rescue the prisoners, steal the plans and code books or whatever the objective may be. As well as out-and-out fighting men, the group may include demolition experts, electronics technicians, and whatever specialist may be needed – a pilot, for example, if the object of the operation were to steal a specific enemy aircraft.

The security group is there to protect them, to secure the area and stop enemy reinforcements from becoming involved in the action, to stop any would-be escapers, and to cover the withdrawal of the assault group.

Special Forces units have a well-deserved reputation for aggressiveness. Not one man amongst them will want to be idling away his time, and so they are always on the look-out for potential targets. Before operation planning can begin, each one is assessed for importance, accessibility and recoverability, taking into account distance and terrain and the strength of raiding party required.

FIVE POINTS
FOR A SUCCESSFUL AMBUSH

1. Set the ambush in a site you can move into and out of unobserved.
2. Use a night ambush if the mission can be accomplished by a short intensive burst of fire.
3. Use a daytime ambush if a follow-up is required.
4. Choose a site where the terrain forces the enemy to bunch up.
5. Bear in mind that you may need a secondary ambush if enemy reinforcements can reach the scene quickly.

Local repercussions

Another important factor is the likely effect of the raid on friendly natives and others. There are countless examples of tens of local people being executed for every one occupying soldier killed. Planning for this possibility always forms part of the back-up organisation to the raid, and psychological operations experts (psy-ops) will also be ready to exploit any successes to the full.

Keep it simple, stupid

Pretty much the motto of Special Forces: KISS. Although it should be accurate down to the last detail, the plan must be essentially simple. If success depends on a large number of factors coming together at the right time, any one of them going wrong will probably blow the entire operation. If you doubt this, read about the debacle that was Operation Eagle Claw, the US attempt to rescue hostages from the nation's embassy in Tehran. (see pp515–519)

Time – of day and of year – is a crucial factor in the plan. When the operation is straightforward and the physical layout of the target is well known, it's probably better to operate during the hours of darkness. Where intelligence is less complete, go for dawn or dusk.

Launching a raid

1. Whatever the mission and whatever the size of the raiding party, the principles of a guerrilla-style raid are the same. The actual assault team must be protected by security elements who will prevent enemy interference with the operation.
2. As the explosive specialist lays charges underneath a railway, for example, on-the- spot security is provided by a small team of Special Forces soldiers. This team will take out any sentries on the objective, breach or demolish obstacles and provide close protection for the main mission.
3. After the target has been destroyed, the security groups provide cover on the flanks for the assault team to retreat. If the enemy follow the raiders, one security group should try to draw them away from the main assault force.

Withdrawal

Dusk is the best time for withdrawal: it gives you the advantage of the last minutes of daylight to exit the immediate area of the operation, and darkness to slow the enemy down during any follow-up.

But in any event, choose the time very carefully, to give yourself the greatest possible advantage.

Withdrawal after a large raid can be conducted with the party split up into small groups. This denies the enemy a large target for an air or ground strike, but an alert and aggressive enemy may be able to mop up the force one unit at a time.

In some circumstances it is safer for the entire party to stay together and operate as a fighting column, but it will all depend on the situation of enemy forces, the terrain and the distances to be covered. An overt withdrawal, with no attempt at secrecy, will require a great deal of external support. There's very little chance that the extraction force, if there is one, will escape enemy attention.

Intelligence

It may seem obvious, but it's impossible to over-stress the value of accurate intelligence. There are three main sources.

1. Local agents
2. Reconnaissance
3. Satellite and high-level flights

Local knowledge is of the utmost importance. Whenever possible, friendly locals should be recruited to act as guides, and may even be employed in the raiding party itself if security considerations permit.

In the movement towards the objective, take every precaution so as not to alert hostile troops to your presence. Avoid contact, but make sure that the enemy suffers one hundred percent casualties if the worst does happen.

Test your weapons

Where conditions allow, conduct a weapons and equipment test before the assault phase, replacing any pieces of kit that may be faulty. Personal belongings should be "sanitized" at the same time, even down to removing clothing labels if necessary.

Size of raiding party

Well-defended objectives sometimes demand large raiding parties – perhaps in battalion strength or greater. Surprise is just as important as in a smaller raid, but will be much more difficult to achieve. A large raiding party will usually split into small groups and move towards the objective over a number of different routes. That way, even if some components are detected the enemy may still be in the dark as to the real target. Control and co-ordination of a large raiding party is more difficult, too, especially with regard to timing. Only a high degree of training and excellent standards of equipment operation can make it easier.

Raiding a shore installation

The first priority when mounting a raid on the enemy coast is to carry out a thorough recce of the target area; it is unusual for you to have enough information available without sending in a reconnaissance team. They will be looking for the following:

1. The exact location, size and structure of the target.
2. Any fortifications, minefields, searchlights and wandering guard patrols, checking their routines.
3. The nature of the surrounding terrain
4. The best route from the sea to the target
5. A place where the boats can come in and be hidden while the attack goes in.
6. A position to place any covering fire or mortar teams.

Blowing up bridges

For complicated structures, two sets of cutting charges are required to cause collapse of the bridge. These should be placed equidistant from the centre of support. Cutting charges must be placed on beams and crossbraces as well as on the floor plating.

Stone arch bridges are best demolished by placing a charge to blow out the keystones.

Small stone arch spans are easily demolished by a row of

cutting charges across the centre, which destroys the integrity of the arch.

Remember that only one person should prepare, place and fire explosive charges. Never divide responsibility: that is how expensive mistakes can occur. To destroy a bridge abutment use 18 kg TNT charges in holes 1.5 metres deep at 1.5 metre intervals across the width of the bridge, and 1.5 metres behind the river face of the abutment.

Timber-cutting charges

If you can drill into the wood and place the explosives inside, you can use a much smaller charge for exterior explosives. Calculate the charge using the formula, D2 divided by 40. (D = least dimension in inches). This gives the number of pounds of TNT needed.

Railways and waterways

Railways themselves are always relatively open targets. Just removing the rails will bring the system to a halt. The attacking force tries to derail as many wagons and carriages as possible and leave the wreckage blocking the track. This maximizes the damage to stock, passengers and material and slows down the work of repairing and reopening the permanent way.

If the attack party is large enough, they assault the train with automatic weapons and grenades. Part of the raiding party's security element will remove sections of the track in both directions, some way away from the scene of the ambush. Explosive charges should be used to destroy the level rail-bed itself. This will prevent any possibility of reinforcements arriving unexpectedly.

Traffic on inland waterways – barges and smaller craft – can be disrupted in much the same way as railway trains, and the same technique is used against columns of vehicles on roads.

Ambush

An ambush is a raid on a moving target. The only real difference is that the timetable of the operation becomes much sketchier and unreliable. Even excellent intelligence sources can't really predict the enemy's operational delays, and so the raiding party will often be in position for some time before the target comes along, considerably increasing the chances of detection.

Ambushes are conducted to destroy or capture enemy personnel and supplies or block their movement. A systematic approach can channel the enemy's communications and re-supply operations, and force him to concentrate his movements onto main roads and railway lines, where they are more vulnerable to attack, especially from air strikes.

As the SAS discovered to its satisfaction in 1965 when undertaking a mission deep inside Kalimintan during the Borneo Crisis, river craft are often best attacked from the rear (i.e. when the craft has floated past), since this avoids a "broadside" from any troops on board and may well set the fuel tanks on fire.

EVASION, CAPTURE AND ESCAPE

"Captured Special Forces troops must be handed over to the nearest Gestapo unit . . . these men are dangerous."

order by Adolf Hitler

There are any number of situations where you as a soldier will need the skill to evade. For example:

1. An escape from a surrounded position in small numbers or as an individual.
2. As a result of the disruption of boundaries, between units after a tactical nuclear exchange.

3. As a result of becoming lost on patrol and straying into the enemy positions.

4. When your defensive position is overrun and not cleared.

5. Make no mistake: Special Forces soldiers who have engaged in sabotage action behind enemy lines are not generally well-treated by an enemy, especially if wearing disguise. The infamous 'Hitler order' above was only a sign of things to come. Thus you may well wish to use evasion skills when having broken out of a POW camp or holding area.

Equipment

Could you survive and fight if you were captured and lost all your equipment except the clothes you stand up in? What if you were searched by an enemy soldier and had everything in your pockets taken away from you? He might not be thorough enough, though, and you have had the foresight to conceal enough equipment in your clothing to enable you to escape. If you are captured, the man searching you is going to be so interested in retrieving stuff such as notebooks, maps and knives that he will not even think about looking in the other places where small items of equipment can be concealed.

Hiding places

He will find the tobacco tin containing your survival kit, and it is probably best not to hide any equipment in your jacket or smock as this will probably be taken off you straight away. Your shirt, jersey or trousers are, however, ideal hiding places for escape and evasion equipment.

SAS belt order

Sabre squadron troopers always carry E & E equipment as part of their belt order. This is not the definitive layout: individuals are allowed to carry what they like once they are on squadron.

1. Belt, pouches and water bottles
2. SLR magazines
3. Rifle-cleaning kit
4. Purse net
5. Fishing kit
6. Snares
7. Mess tin lid and rations
8. Torch and filters
9. Button-compass
10. Wire saw
11. Fire-starting kit
12. Lock picks (note: these are illegal in the UK)
13. Clasp knife
14. Prismatic compass
15. Mini flares
16. Millbank bag for filtering water
17. Field dressing
18. Survival ration
19. Heliograph
20. Silk escape map

Useful things to conceal in clothing are:

1. Wire saw
2. Compass
3. Sharpened hacksaw blade
4. Fishing kit
5. Sewing kit
6. Condoms
7. Scalpel blades
8. Map
9. Firelighting oil

You can usually feed the wire saw into the waistband of your combat trousers: remove the rings from the saw, and replace them with bootlace or nylon cord. Likewise, you can feed fishing line into the seams of your clothing or under the collar of your shirt. Some soldiers remove all the buttons on their trousers or pockets and re-sew them using fishing line.

Fishing hooks are, however, a different problem. If you sew them into clothing unprotected, they may pierce the cloth and injure you; wrap them in duct tape first. The same applies to needles and scalpel blades.

Boots are often cited as good hiding-places for escape and evasion equipment, but beware: walking is probably the only way you will be able to travel, and if your boots are uncomfortable or unable to protect your feet you will be in trouble. If you have very thick shock-absorbent insoles in your boots you can hide things beneath them, but check regularly to make sure the insole is not being worn away. Obviously only very thin items can be concealed this way, and nothing over about 8 cm long, as it may puncture the insole and your foot when the sole of the boot flexes.

Condoms also need to be concealed with care: if they are unprotected the plastic wrapper will eventually wear and damage the contents, so when you come to use one in a survival situation it has a hole in it! Strap them in PVC tape (ideally, a minimum of five should be carried).

If you can conceal a flint and steel firelighter in your clothing so much the better, but make sure you know how to use it before sewing it in, otherwise the space is wasted.

Small compasses are fairly easy to conceal, and the small RAF button compass can even be swallowed and retrieved at a later date! However, these compasses only really give an indication of magnetic North, and are not accurate enough for bearings.

Rough maps of your operational area are not as difficult to construct as you may think. Pilots and Special Forces are often issued with elaborate maps, printed on cloth or silk and disguised as handkerchiefs or sewn into the lining of clothing.

The most useful item of E & E kit is something you can usually guarantee not to be without: your brain. No-one can take away your skill or experience so prepare now.

One painless and profitable way of preparing for the eventualities of escape, evasion or being taken POW is to read the memoirs of those soldiers who have done these things. A useful library of escape classics comprises:

Airey Neave, *They Have Their Exits*. Neave was the first Brit to make a "home run" from Colditz POW camp in the Second World War.

John McCain (with Mark Salter), *Faith of My Fathers*. The Republican politician's account of his years as a US Navy pilot held POW by the North Vietnamese.

Chris Ryan, *The One That Got Away*. Evasion in the Iraqi desert by a 22 SAS NCO.

A.J. Evans, *The Escape Club*. First World War escape classic.

M.C.C. Harrison and H.A. Cartwright, *Within Four Walls* – Another Great War POW escape classic.

CONDOMS

Every Special Forces soldier's friend, for all sorts of improbable reasons. Can be used as:

1. *Water carriers:* Each one will take about one and a half pints. Remember to put the whole thing in a sock for support.
2. *Surgical gloves:* Bullet wounds are usually already highly contaminated, but if you are clearing out a wound put condoms on your fingers to reduce the chances of further infection.
3. *Signalling devices:* Useful for ground-to-air signalling: simply blow them up and place them on the ground in the desired pattern.
4. *Waterproof containers:* You can use them to protect kit or maps and for hiding things internally, and for keeping water out of weapons and radio equipment.

REMEMBER

1. Every piece of kit you smuggle through the first search will help you to escape.
2. If they keep searching, eventually they will find everything.
3. Make sure the piece of kit can be retrieved once you have escaped – e.g. that it is not so well sewn in that you can't get at it.

4. Make sure you know how to use the kit you've hidden.
5. Your escape map should be a very simple affair, with only large towns, major roads, railways and rivers marked on it. Any other detail would be useless and confusing. Combined with your simple compass, it just makes sure you walk in the right direction. It is best drawn on rice paper or airmail paper, folded and wrapped in Clingfilm or Saran Wrap and sewn behind a unit or rank patch or hidden under the insole of your boot.

Evading Dogs

Every breath you take, every move you make, a dog can detect it. Perhaps as much as a mile away under the right conditions. And an attack dog, trained to silence, can be on you literally before you know it. Travelling at 15 metres a second and weighing anything up to 45 kilograms, it is as lethal as any bullet. What can a man working behind enemy lines do to protect himself against these killers? In this section we're going to examine some of the dog evasion techniques taught to British Special Forces units.

Dogs of war are trained to do specific jobs. Guard and attack dogs are trained to detect, engage and, in some cases, to savage intruders or evaders either under the command of a handler or running free. Search dogs are adept at picking up and finding the source of airborne scents and are allowed to run free, going over an area of ground yard by yard. Tracker dogs, on the other hand, run on a long leash with a handler. Ground scents are the trackers' speciality. Search and tracker dogs lead their handlers to their target, but do not usually assault the fugitive, leaving that to the attack dogs, to the handlers or their combat back-up.

Eyes and ears

Like most mammals except man dogs have very poor eyesight. They don't see colours at all, only shades of grey, and then not very clearly. They can see you moving, of course, and this is very likely to attract their attention. Because their eyes are low down to the ground they're quick to see movement above the skyline. If a dog's eyesight is only half as good as man's, its range of

hearing is twice as good. How far away they can hear you is affected by weather conditions, especially wind and rain. If the wind is blowing away from you and towards the dog, he's a lot more likely to hear you. Rain creates a background noise, and makes individual sounds much more difficult to pick out. So take advantage of rain to get on the move.

It's not just that a dog can hear you a long way off: he can also hear sounds that man can't. High-pitched squeaks and whistles that you don't know exist are part of a dog's everyday life. So tape loose pieces of equipment to stop them rubbing and catching. Think about the way you use radios and other items of hardware. A clink of cooking utensils, a match being struck, even the sound of the flame when you're cooking your meal, can give away your position to a well-trained dog.

In fact, if you were cooking a meal the chances are that he would smell you first – from anything up to a couple of miles away under the right conditions! Because while a dog's hearing is a lot keener than ours, his sense of smell is many thousands of times better.

The strongest human body odour comes from the sweat glands, especially under the arms. Moving quickly, particularly when carrying a heavy load and wearing too many clothes, makes you sweat heavily. So does being tense, nervous or frightened. Eating various types of strongly flavoured food makes it worse, and so does not washing regularly. And it's not just the natural smells of our bodies that provide a target for the tracker dog's nose. Clothing, especially when it's wet; soap and deodorants; leather; tobacco; polish and preservatives; petrol; oil; and many, many more smells that are a natural part of our everyday lives – all can give a dog a clue to your presence.

A dog picks up scent in two different ways: from the air, and from contact with the ground, trees, plants and buildings. Airborne scents do not last very long; they are blown away by the wind quite quickly.

Traces of movement

A ground scent, on the other hand, may be obvious to the dog for anything up to 48 hours. Ground scents are caused not just by you leaving your own smell on things you touch, but also by the movement itself. If you're walking on grass or pushing through vegetation you will crush leaves and stems with every movement. Even on bare ground you will release air and tiny quantities of moisture that have been trapped in the soil, which smell quite different from the fresh air above the ground. From the scent "footprints" that you leave behind a dog can even tell in which direction you're moving. And because you push off each step with your toes, the front of the footprint is more obvious than the heel, and it only takes a few steps for a dog to work out which way you're travelling.

Just as each person's footprints look slightly different to the eye, so to a dog is the mixture of scents in the smell footprint slightly different. The dog recognizes this difference, and so may be able to track one person even where there are a number of people travelling together or where there are animals present.

Methods of evasion are detailed in the special sections, but remember the general point: although a dog can out-hear, out-smell and out-run you, you can out-think him. To do that you must assess the skills of the dog opposing you, and use your wits and tactics to confuse all or most of its senses. Outwit the dog or handler and you may escape where others may not.

Combatting attack dogs

Guard dogs and attack dogs either operate with a handler or are left to run free in a confined area. A dog that is running free in a compound may not even recognize his handler, but will attack absolutely anyone who comes into his territory. But whether the dog is on a leash or running free, its training is designed to do just one thing – catch anybody who shouldn't be there. You do have one slight advantage when dealing with a guard dog: he's fixed in one place, more or less.

1. Always approach from downwind.
2. Take it slowly and easily to minimize exertion, and thereby cut down the amount of smelly sweat you secrete.

3. Keep as low as possible and use natural features of the ground. Windborne scent doesn't quite travel in straight lines, but any natural obstacle will help.
4. Approach along paths used by other people.
5. When you get within 200 metres of the objective, don't stop for anything – dogs have been known to pick up scents even against the wind at this sort of distance.
6. If you're dealing with a dog guarding a building, try to get above the ground floor if you can: dogs have difficulty detecting people way above their heads.
7. If you find yourself close to a dog and handler unexpectedly, keep still. Guards have been known to pass within 10 metres of an intruder who's keeping perfectly still without detecting him.

Sacrificial defence

If you can't evade the dog you have to immobilize him. And you can't do that effectively until the dog is within attack range. You have to let the dog bite you. Wrap protection around the forearm of the hand you don't use by choice. Arrange it in three layers. A soft one on the inside as padding; a hard one next to stop the dog's teeth penetrating; and lastly, another soft layer to give the dog something to get his teeth into.

• Protect your forearm with three layers of padding
• Allow the dog to grab your protected arm. If you're still standing you can club the animal.
• If the dog leaps on you, roll over with him and keep his body tight to yours. Work your way around onto the top and back of the dog to immobilize it.

Don't discourage the dog from attacking you, but make sure he takes the offered target; he will be more difficult to deal with the second time. When he's sunk his teeth into the padding, he's within reach, and you can deal with him.

Protect your forearm with three layers of padding

Allow the dog to grab your protected arm. If you're still standing you can club the animal.

If the dog leaps on you, roll over with him and keep his body tight to yours. Work your way around onto the top and back of the dog to immobilize it.

Evading tracker dogs

So what can you do to fool the dog? Let's split the mission up into four phases: lying up, pre-contact, distant contact, and close contact.

Lying up

If you have to spend any length of time in a lying up place always obey these simple rules, even if you have no proof that a search dog is operating.

1. Keep as close to the ground as possible.
2. Put most of your clothing over you so that the ground absorbs your scent rather than letting it out into the open air.
3. Breathe down into the ground or at least into the vegetation.
4. Keep as still as possible.
5. Bury rubbish under where you are lying.
6. No smoking, no fires wherever possible.
7. If you're discovered by anyone move away as fast as you can.

Pre-contact

Use all the normal physical camouflage tricks to blend into the environment, plus a few that are designed to throw the dog off the scent.

1. Travel over ground already used by other people or by animals. This makes the dog work much harder to keep on your track.
2. If you're travelling as part of a group, split up from time to time. Double back on yourself. Leave a false trail wherever possible.
3. Use streams and running water to confuse the dog, but don't try to walk for too long in the stream itself – it will slow you down too much. Instead, cross the stream diagonally, doubling back perhaps two or three times so that the dog can't tell which of your exit tracks is the real one and which ones are dummies.
4. When you're preparing food, pay close attention to the direction of the wind. You must bury all wrapping and containers, but remember too to handle them as little as possible. The smell of the food is one thing: your smell on the wrappers tells the dog that it was your food. When you bury the remains, don't touch the ground with your hands. Use a metal tool of some sort. Whenever you can, sink the rubbish in deep water. The same goes for urine and faeces.

Distant contact
If you're sighted from a distance, speed becomes important.

1. Try to tire the dog and handler team; it will be easier to destroy their confidence in each other if they make mistakes through tiredness.
2. If you're part of a group then split up straight away, and arrange a rendezvous for later.
3. Make for hard ground. A road or a rocky surface makes and holds much less scent than a soft one.
4. If you are in wood country or scrub, double back and change your direction as often as you can.
5. The tracker dog will be on a long lead. If you can get him tangled up you can increase the distance between you and him and maybe break off the contact entirely.

Close contact
If the dog catches up with you you're in deep trouble. Not so much from the dog – he's done his job in finding you. Now you're in trouble from the handler and whatever combat back up he may have available.

1. Forget the dog for the moment. You'll know from the look of him whether he's an attack dog or a tracker. If he's a tracker, he probably won't come near you.
2. Move as fast as you can. Get out of sight of the handler.
3. Get rid of loose pieces of clothing, food (especially food – the dog may be distracted by it when he comes looking for you) and any other pieces of kit that aren't vital to your mission or your survival.
4. If the dog sticks with you, you must kill or immobilize it.

Evasion and capture

To be taken prisoner is the worst thing that can happen to a soldier. Death is quick; a wound will see you evacuated to a field hospital for treatment; but capture exposes you to a nightmare of torture, indoctrination and exposure. An army is a part of a nation, an arm of government, and every government goes to great lengths to protect its soldiers from every danger, including that of mistreatment as a prisoner of war.

Techniques in which Special Forces are trained are not widely published, but reliable sources applying to all soldiers do exist. The United States Army issues Field Manuals – FM 2L-76 and FM 21-78 – that deal only with evasion, escape and survival. This section is taken from those manuals. It deals with evading enemy forces and how to behave if you're captured. The manuals put a new word into the English language – the evader. A man, probably on his own, being hunted by enemy troops in unknown country. The chances against him are enormous, but if he keeps his head and remembers his training, he just might escape – against all the odds. Evaders are split into two types: short-term and long-term.

Short-term evasion

You're a short-term evader if you or your unit are temporarily cut off from the main body of your forces. This can happen quite frequently – while you're on patrol, for instance – and is actually the way of life of long-range patrol units (known as LURPS in the US military). When you know you're going to be separated from the main force, navigation and fieldcraft are your best friends. Knowing where you are and which direction you're heading in is going to help save your life, and your own skill in moving cross-country or through town will finish the job.

Long-term evasion

Very few people have to evade the enemy for long periods of time or cross long stretches of enemy-held territory. The only people likely to have to undertake this most difficult and arduous task are aircrew who have been shot down, and escaped prisoners of war, though patrols are sometimes sent so far out that the same principle applies to them.

Try to relax. Fear and tension will only force you into making mistakes. Time is on your side. It doesn't matter how soon you get back to your own people, as long as you do get back. This may mean lying up for weeks or even months and applying all your survival skills. Under military law, a soldier must make every effort to return to his unit. If captured, it is his duty to try to escape – though few ever do so successfully. Getting "home" will be a lot easier before you're captured. You must use all the tricks of camouflage and concealment to stay hidden from the enemy. Rely on your own resources. Don't trust civilians unless you absolutely have to. Their whole way of life will be strange to you. A gesture that in your home town might mean "welcome" could mean the very reverse in enemy territory.

It's not a good idea – ever – to try to disguise yourself as a native. Even if your colour and clothes don't give you away, and you happen to speak the language, the smallest gesture will be enough to show an experienced observer that you're not what you're pretending to be. If you have been lucky enough to make contact with a friendly local group, be guided by them – but remember that no conventions of war apply to them. Any civilian found helping you will probably die for it. Take every opportunity to distance yourself from your helpers. If you have to travel with a member of a local resistance group, for instance, don't sit together. Arrange a system of simple signals so that you don't have to speak. Be ready to go it alone at any moment, and don't carry anything that could point a finger of suspicion at anyone who might have helped you. No names and addresses written down; no marked maps. Remember that you're a representative of your country – perhaps the first one the natives have actually met. Even under the hardships that an evader must endure, it's up to you to make a good impression. Remember, you're fighting a war that requires their co-operation.

Communicating

If you do get the chance to talk to natives and feel secure enough to ask them for help, communicating is going to be a big problem. The chances are you won't speak each other's language, so you'll be reduced to making signs and gestures. To make this easier, the

US, for example, issues each soldier with what is known as a "Blood Chit". A Blood Chit is an American Flag, printed onto cloth, with a message in English, and all the other languages you are likely to come across in the area in which fighting is taking place. The last, and most important feature of the Blood Chit is a unique number that identifies the person it was issued to. The message asks for help and assistance. It promises that this will be rewarded. Don't give up the Blood Chit itself. Anyone who helps you will get their reward just by quoting the number. Give them the number but don't give them the chit itself.

Evasion: the basics

It's easier to evade than to escape from a POW camp. By travelling just five miles you increase the enemy's area of search to some 75 to 80 square miles. The longer you evade, the more obsolete any information you might have becomes. Thus, if you get caught and are tortured into talking you won't be giving them anything useful; indeed, your captors know this and may well press you less. Try to remain hidden for at least 48 hours.

During survival training you will have been taught how to build a variety of shelters: Build them, for your comfort and for camouflage. Don't hide in caves or choose isolated cover. Pick an unlikely spot that stands a good chance of being over-looked. If possible, try to hide out fairly close to a water source, and go for high rather than low ground.

Once in position, avoid making tracks. Use the same route in and out. Don't leave the shelter unless you have to. Keep still and quiet, and stay alert. If you are a smoker, throw away your cigarettes so that you are not tempted. Bury all refuse, and when you eventually move out, don't leave any traces of your stay.

After two or three days you might consider moving on. Before doing so, bear in mind the "Five Ps": Prior Planning Prevents Poor Performance. Decide where you are going and, if possible, plan on the route. Take only what you need. By now you will have an idea of what is essential. Conceal everything else. As always, use your common sense. Move only at night and avoid people, built up areas and roads.

During your trek across enemy terrain you could be presented with an opportunity to hit at the enemy. You will definitely be in a unique position to observe him at first-hand. Remember anything that might be of use to Intelligence. This is assuming you can pass on that information within a reasonable span of time.

You may be aware of an escape net operating in the country you are in. If you manage to contact such an organisation you will, initially, probably be treated with distrust. This is understandable, as such people survive by being extremely cautious. Once contact is made, be prepared to be left alone while they observe your reactions. You will probably then be blindfolded before being taken away for questioning. If the escape organisation is satisfied by your replies, you can then expect them to help you. Of course, the enemy could impersonate such a group, so never give away classified information, and take care not to implicate anybody else.

In exceptional circumstances you could be in for a long journey before reaching the safety of a neutral country. You could be shot down in the middle of summer – and find yourself still on the run at the onset of winter. Your trek to freedom could take months, even years. One German paratrooper, captured by the Russians during the Second World War, took three years to reach his homeland during his escape from Siberia!

If the prospects of a long uncomfortable journey, fraught with danger, seems too grim, try to remember why you should continue:

* An evader is a *free* man!
* Special Forces soldiers are rarely treated kindly by the enemy (to put it mildly).
* You can re-join your unit, and carry on serving your country the best way you can.
* You will see your family and friends again.
* Your evasion is a victory over the enemy.

And if that is not reason enough, bear in mind that according to regulations: "Any person . . . shall be guilty of an offence against the appropriate section if . . . he . . . fails to take . . . any reasonable steps to re-join HM Service which are available to him."

In other words it is your duty to survive, to escape to fight again!

9 POINTS FOR SUCCESSFUL EVASION

1. Large groups are easily detected. If there are a lot of you, split into four-man teams, which are a lot harder to detect.
2. As long as you are wearing your uniform you can attack enemy military targets, but not civilians.
3. Do not disguise yourself as a local unless you can do so convincingly. Amateur disguises and ignorance of local language and customs will quickly betray you.
4. If you landed by parachute, you should assume that the enemy spotted your descent, and get out of the immediate area as fast as you can.
5. Observe the basic rules of camouflage, concealment and movement at all times.
6. Take your time when travelling: hurrying makes you less alert and tires you out.
7. Avoid populated areas and busy routes wherever possible. If approached by strangers pretend to be deaf, dumb or just half-witted; it often works.
8. If you are being helped by the local population, do not make any marks on your map: if you are captured with it, the enemy could work out who was assisting you.
9. Observe enemy troop movements, military positions, weapons and equipment if you have the chance – but do not write anything down, or you risk being treated like a spy.

Re-joining your unit

If you're out on patrol there will be an established method of re-joining your own forces – direction of approach, safe periods, recognition signals, password and all the other ways of making sure that you don't come under fire from your unit. You won't have the benefit of these safeguards, so you must follow basic rules when re-joining:

1. Get in a position close to the front line.
2. Watch and wait for a friendly patrol.
3. Let them come to you.
4. Don't give away your position – or that of the patrol – to enemy forces.
5. Show a white cloth.
6. Shout out an unmistakeable greeting.
7. Don't fool around. The patrol will believe you're the enemy trying to trick them until you prove otherwise.

If you get caught without map, compass or other navigating equipment, use your memory. Orient yourself by listening to the fighting. Use your time behind the enemy lines to gather intelligence. Take a prisoner if you think you have a reasonable chance of making it back to your own lines with him. You must think positively all the time. Fear is your worst enemy.

If you lose your Blood Chit, report it straight away. It's a very valuable document. If it falls into the hands of the enemy's Intelligence Section they could very easily use it to discover which members of the local population are likely to be friendly to you, and this will probably get them shot. It will certainly make sure that no-one trusts the chit – or you.

It may be possible for your own people to rescue you, most likely from the air. To stand a chance of this being successful you must know the standard ground-to-air distress signals. Don't call down a rescue attempt unless you are absolutely sure that the area is safe. Remember that a helicopter is most vulnerable to attack when it's taking off and landing. Make sure that any signals can be removed or covered up very quickly in case an enemy air patrol should appear.

Save the wounded

If there are casualties, make sure they get off first. If you do have seriously wounded men in your party, you must always consider whether their best chances of staying alive are to surrender (United States law allows that). Obviously, local conditions will be important – a man with a light wound surrendering to troops who are known to kill all prisoners, despite the Geneva Convention, is not helping himself!

Intelligence of all sorts – and evidence of the blood-thirstiness of enemy troops is only one sort – is really vital. Use every means you can to learn about enemy troop movements and placement, and the attitude of local non-combatants. Try to keep abreast of the progress of the war as a whole, too. You may be hiding for nothing! Remember that some Japanese infantrymen were still living concealed in the jungle of the South Pacific islands 25 years after the end of the Second World War because they didn't know it was all over.

If the worst does happen and you face capture, your first decision will be whether to try to fight your way out. If you're alone and unarmed this is not likely to be an available option, but if you're with your unit and your armament is up to strength, you may stand a very good chance of winning a fire-fight even against a larger enemy force, because surprise will definitely act in your favour – the last thing the enemy force will expect is an armed and trained group of soldiers behind its own lines.

THE "GO-PACK"

Irrespective of whether you fly in a single-seat jet or a multi-seat aircraft, you will always carry emergency survival equipment. The Personal Survival Pack (PSP) carried underneath your seat holds the bulkier, heavier kit. However, the PSP may well get lost if you are forced to bang out (eject) in combat. In the event of coming down behind enemy lines you may have little or no time to retrieve it.

For this reason, all aircrew should carry a "Go-Pack". The official RAF version contains: a 7 foot x 3 foot polythene sleeping bag, fire-lighting kit, 4 grips, a compass, 4 rubber bands, an instruction sheet, 6 plastic ties, one 5 foot x 150 lb nylon cord and three 6 inch x 10 inch polythene bags. However, most aircrew prefer to make up their own Go-Pack – the contents of which are often carried in a container such as an Emergency Flying Ration tin. For those who can afford a little extra room, a container measuring approximately 18 cm x 10 cm x 4 cm can accommodate: a 7 foot x 3 foot sleeping bag, a candle, a Melinex sheet (space blanket), fishing kit, fire-lighting kit, fire blocks, a compass, needles, a scalpel, water purification tablets, cotton wool, nylon cord, brass wire, wire saw, water carriers (i.e. *unlubricated* condoms), instruction sheet and a couple of Tampax (ideal for fire-lighting).

Urban Evasion

Urban evasion, like its rural equivalent, varies according to the climate and wealth of the country you are operating in. For example, a country with strong family or local loyalties, or with a restrictive political regime, will be harder to move about in than one in which there is a large "floating" population, a high level of personal wealth and public transport and facilities. The important considerations will be the sense of national threat and suspicion that has been generated by war.

A large Western city can be a very anonymous place. Even to members of ethnic minorities it offers a level of concealment. Citizens will keep to themselves and as long as your manner and appearance do not attract attention you can move fairly freely. Always include a shaving kit in your E & E gear – unshaven men will always attract attention. Trains, entertainment centres, etc. can offer protection from the weather by day and sometimes by night: evasion is not helped by standing around.

Movement by day

Generally, moves by day are not a good idea, but are sometimes unavoidable. If you have to move by day:

1. Be confident: look as if you know where you are going, do not loiter and do not appear furtive.
2. Obtain some unobtrusive clothing and try to assume a definite identity; e.g. steal a donkey jacket and carry a spade.
3. Keep clean, and shave if possible.
4 .If you can get hold of a bike you are doing well, but assess the risk before you steal it. Use public transport if you are completely confident that you know how the system works.
5. Keep away from stations and bus terminals.
6. Rivers are an excellent escape route, but the larger ones will be watched.
7. Watch out for children and dogs. Children are not bound by grown-up conventions of social behaviour, and when they see something peculiar they will point it out loudly.

Checkpoints

If you have to pass through an area covered by a checkpoint, imitate the silhouette of the enemy sentries as far as possible, especially headgear, which is a common recognition feature. Learn at least one phrase in the local language along the lines of "Don't shoot, you idiot – it's me!" – and make sure it is fluent.

Movement by night

Virtually all evasive moves should be made at night. Do not be over-confident: don't forget that the enemy has night-vision devices. You will always have to compromise between choosing the easiest route and not going where the enemy expect. Remember:

1. Learn the route.
2. Unless you have foolproof documentation and the right clothes, never move on roads.
3. Never cross bridges: use improvised rafts or swim.

Weapons

You will have a good chance of bluffing your way out of a stop-and-search check if you have the right documents and kit and know the language. In this case, do not blow your chances by carrying a weapon. If you have no chance of bluffing then consider carrying a weapon; silenced firearms are ideal, but otherwise choose something that is concealable or not in itself harmful, e.g. a screwdriver or chisel. Silenced firearms are ideal, but realistically a meat skewer is more the sort of thing you can hide in your kit.

Capture

If you are caught in civilian clothes you will not be able to claim protection as a POW; you will probably be treated as a spy and eventually killed.

Slumming it

One way of surviving is by becoming a vagrant. This is not as easy as it may sound. In many cities there is a well-developed underworld of vagrants and drop-outs, and your arrival among them will not go unnoticed. The vagrants may include informers or drug addicts, who are an easy target for pressure by the police or enemy security forces. But if you can degenerate to a low enough level you will become an unlikely suspect. You may have problems with your health and in protecting yourself against bad weather if you adopt this technique.

Scavenging for food is easy in a wealthy environment as long as you are prepared to examine the contents of café and restaurant dustbins. This type of odd behaviour will also add to your cover as a vagrant. Dustbins are an excellent source of food and useful kit. Use the lid to sort through the stuff or lay it out on some paper so that you do not make a mess. If you take things away you must fill the bin with newspaper and try to leave the top layer undisturbed: people notice how full their dustbins are.

The vagrant approach to urban evasion depends on the society in which you are on the run. A European vagrant could be the object of great interest in some African or Far Eastern cities, and this would not assist your attempts at concealment. You may wish to give off the appearance of madness; people are less likely to approach you.

Deep cover

Food can be a problem, depending on how you intend to work. If you go into deep cover and remain concealed in a "safe house", you will depend on your hosts. There may be problems where food is rationed or controlled. Within the house you will, as in an OP, need a look-out position and, most importantly, a place to hide. Many modern houses are built to well-known specifications; a search team will perhaps have plans, or at least have a good knowledge of the type of house. Older houses, on the other hand, may have common roof space that allows you to move from house to house in a run of terraced buildings. Flats that have been converted from larger buildings offer good hiding places, but may be less sound-proof.

The ideal hiding place should be small so that its presence does not detract from the space or comfort of the house. However, it should not be so small that prolonged occupation becomes uncomfortable. Water and a bucket for waste matter are the basic priorities, and good ventilation is essential. A bench or seat is welcome. The walls of the hide should be thick enough not to sound hollow. Various types of sound insulation can be added to the inside to give the impression of a solid structure. Lay in a store of simple foods that will not deteriorate over time and which have basic wrappings.

When you have prepared the inside you should practise a "crash-move" – getting into the hide from "a standing start" from somewhere else in the house or flat. When you are under cover, the householder will have to remove any trace of your presence in the building. This can include extra food, and plates, books and magazines, clothing of the wrong size or sex and even the extra toothbrush or towel in the bathroom. This type of concealment assumes that your evasion is assisted by relatively well-paid people with a circle of reliable contacts. Such people do not normally have a traditional fear of authority, but neither do they have the skills of deception and concealment.

The grey man

The mid-way approach to evasion is to adopt the "grey man" technique. Here you aim to have as anonymous an appearance as possible. Clothing should be neutral, and your behaviour will have to be that of a "solid citizen" – such people do not sit around in public parks or search through dustbins: they are on their way to or from work.

But this can be very tiring, and you will need a good command of the local language. The advantage is that, unlike the vagrant, you are less vulnerable to assault by other vagrants or bored members of the enemy police force. Your travel through the country is less likely to be questioned, but – and this is critical – you will need the right paperwork, work permits, identity cards, even documents for travel in restricted areas such as the border, and you must also have money.

It may be that you can make the transition from deep cover to a grey man role. During your time in cover you will be able to learn some language and local knowledge before venturing out.

Seasonal advantages
Though evasion and escape can be easier in the country in spring, summer and early autumn, the city can have attractions in the winter. The major disadvantage is that contact with enemy citizens or even occupying powers is inevitable, and this can compromise you.

Jungle Evasion

Evasion in an environment such as tropical jungle, savannah grassland or deep temperate forest can be a case of survival rather than evasion. Enemy hunters may find searching for you or your group as difficult as locating the proverbial needle in the haystack. But your movements may be predicted by shrewd hunters and they can place ambushes or stop lines on features. You will probably have a compass and basic survival kit and even if you escape from a POW camp or convoy you need a sense of direction, particularly if moving by night. Hunters will try to put stops between you and friendly forces or an open border or sea coast. They will also look at the easy routes, for instance tracks or river lines. Roads and railways are often covered by transport police or civil security forces.

Security versus speed

You will be faced with a trade-off between security and speed. Movement by day is faster, and in deep jungle movement by night is almost impossible. But grassland should be covered at night, since helicopters or fixed-wing aircraft can cover large areas very easily by day.

Jungle varies between primary and secondary, and though the high canopy of trees in primary may obscure the horizon and make navigation difficult, it is excellent cover from the air, and the going on the ground is easy. However, it does not adequately conceal you from enemy troops.

Secondary jungle gives excellent cover, but is very hard going on foot and can house dangerous plants and animals. But among these threats to life and health there will be edible plants and scope to make animal traps – you have to wait for the trap to be sprung, and it may be found by local people who will report its presence to the enemy.

Finding water

Water can be collected from plants or as rainfall, but avoid streams unless you have sterilising tablets in a survival kit. There are a vast number of killing or incapacitating organisms in many rivers.

Savannah and bush have water holes and do give you a better chance to kill game, but remember that you will have to cook it. Cooking takes time, requires a fire and the trade-off of the nutrition of the meat against time and vulnerability is a decision that you or your team will have to make on the ground. Dried or smoked meat is one way of making the most of game that you may have killed.

Talking to the locals

You may be obliged to enter a village, perhaps because you need urgent help or simply through bad navigation. Most villages have dogs, and dogs bark. This will warn the locals that there is a stranger about. Avoid crossing rivers downstream of the village:

there may be sewers as well as the "launderette". Remember that infection can enter your body through your skin as well as your mouth. You will be an object of great interest to the locals, but not necessarily an object of hostility. Your colour, clothing and equipment will be observed.

If you are going to approach a village a thorough recce is essential. Before going in, decide whether you stand a reasonable chance of winning if you do have to fight. If you come to the conclusion they would easily kill you, do not risk provoking them; stash your rifle where it can be retrieved later. When you approach the village, do so openly so that they have plenty of warning and will not be forced into a snap decision, such as killing you. Take off your helmet, and bin anything that makes you look like a spaceman. They are less likely to kill you if you look vaguely like them. Items such as survival knives and water bottles or footwear will be examined; be prepared to demonstrate them in the spirit of mutual interest – the locals are professional hunters who kill to live, and should be extended respect and courtesy.

Village leaders
It is a fair bet that the older men are the village leaders. Treat them with respect and you will ensure that the village will respect you – if you are brash, threatening, or offhand with them you will probably find enemy troops on your tail within hours of your exit from the village.

Local hospitality
It is worth remembering that not all villages in remote rural locations or deep jungle see their government as friendly. You may have more in common with them than they with the soldiers, and a lost, perhaps wounded and frightened man will merit traditional hospitality extended to any stranger. But do not overstay your welcome – the villagers' resources may be limited, your presence will become known through tribal gossip and sweeps by enemy soldiers may pick you up.

The longer you stay, the more vulnerable you make the villagers to enemy reprisals. One night – or a brief stop -can always be explained away to the enemy; they can say you were armed and threatened them. If you stay longer it will be obvious that they co-operated with you.

Respect for women

An important rule when visiting a village is to extend a dignified respect to the women – whatever their age. It is very unlikely that they have the same values as your culture. If you are in a group, keep an eye on anyone who is likely to breach the social etiquettes.

Disguise your route

If you discuss your proposed route with the villagers, do not tell them which one you decide on, and do not leave in the direction you intend to travel. Go west if you plan to go north, and change route after you are away from sight. The villagers may wish to guide you on your way; accept with gratitude and when they have gone cover your tracks. Even if they have been friendly, they may be naive people who will subsequently betray you.

Capture

If you are captured, you are required to tell the enemy only four things: your name, rank, serial number and date of birth. Say nothing else. Don't refer to your unit by name, don't talk about your superior officers, don't identify the leaders of your group. The smallest piece of information may be useful to the enemy.

Searching and handling by captors

This is how you can expect to be treated by an enemy who plays by the rules.

- You will be made to stand; they will work from top to bottom and check your clothing. Expect your groin and armpits to be checked.
- You will be made to lean standing against a wall, with your weight off-balance to prevent reaction or flight. Again, expect top-to-bottom search, including armpit and groin.

- Even a "fair" enemy is likely to be verbally abusive and physically rough. Being "frisked" by an enemy is an inherently demeaning experience. Keep cool, and don't rise to provocations.
- Two-man search: one enemy soldier fixes you with an arm lock while the other applies pressure points and searches.
- You may be tied and bound. Do not resist: it's a waste of energy you'll need for later. That said, make sure all muscles are imperceptibly expanded so the constraint is not too tight. This is for your comfort; but also a "loose fitting" may enable you free yourself later.

The laws of war

The news of your capture is supposed, under the Geneva Convention, to be passed to a body called the Protection Power, often the Red Cross or Red Crescent, so that they can pass it on to your own government. That's the only reason for giving away even such simple information as your name, rank, number and date of birth. If you're captured by a terrorist group, however, they probably won't do this – even some governments don't, which is why so many US prisoners of the Vietcong and Pathet Lao are still recorded as MIA (Missing in Action) following the war in South-East Asia.

The Geneva Convention

The Geneva Convention is an international agreement first formulated in 1864 to establish a code of practice for the treatment of wartime sick, wounded and prisoners of war. These are the major elements of the Geneva Convention as it affects prisoners of war:

1. *Interrogation:* A POW is required to provide only his name, rank, service number and date of birth. The use of physical or mental coercion to obtain information from POWs is prohibited.
2. *Movement:* POWs must be moved under humane conditions.

3. *Environment:* The internment environment must not be unhealthy or dangerous.

4. *Food:* Food must be of sufficient quality and quantity to maintain good health.

5. *Clothing:* Suitable clothing must be provided.

6. *Health, Hygiene and Well-being:* The detaining power must ensure that adequate hygienic facilities are provided. The POW is entitled to treatment by medical personnel from their own country where available. The seriously wounded or sick are entitled to special treatment and may be transferred to a neutral nation.

7. *Protected Personnel:* Captured medical personnel and chaplains are treated as protected personnel and are to be free to circulate among the POWs tending to their spiritual welfare and health.

8. *Religion, Recreation, Education and Exercise:* Each POW has the right to practise his religion, and to engage in physical exercise, education and recreation.

9. *Work:* All enlisted personnel below NCO rank are subject to work details, but these shall not be dangerous or unhealthy. NCOs may be called up to work in a supervisory capacity; officers may work voluntarily. The Geneva Convention prohibits the use of POWs for mine clearance and lays down working conditions, pay, fitness for work and the treatment of POWs working for private individuals.

10. *Outside Contacts:* POWs have the right to write to their families on capture. The convention outlines postal privileges and rights pertaining to the receipt of packages.

11. *Complaints:* POWs have the right to complain to the military authorities of the detaining powers, and to representatives of the neutral protecting powers recognized by both sides.

12. *Representatives:* The senior POW will be the prisoners' representative. In a camp where there are no officers or NCOs the representative will be chosen by secret ballot.

13. *Legal Proceedings:* POWs prosecuted and convicted for offences committed before capture retain the protection afforded by the convention. They may not be tried for any

action which becomes illegal after the act is committed. The captors may not use force to gain a confession.

14. *Punishment:* Cruel and unusual punishments, torture, collective punishments or unfair punishments by a biased court are prohibited.

15. *Escape:* Attempted escapes, or non-violent offences committed only to aid escape and not involving theft for personal gain, the wearing of civilian clothes or the use of false papers, are subject only to laid-down disciplinary action.

Interrogation

To the army on the move, taking prisoners is more than a waste of time: it's a waste of precious manpower to guard them and rations to feed them. It's often only some respect for the laws of warfare and the fear that they would be treated the same way themselves that keep them from shooting everybody.

To the intelligence specialist, though, the prisoner is not a waste of time. He's precious. He may be pure gold. The information about troop strengths and positions that he has in his head – perhaps not even realising that he has it – could be the difference between a battle lost and a battle won. The US Army knows this, and spends a lot of time training its men how to combat enemy interrogation techniques. Field Manual FM 21-76 is the source for this section on how to get through a hostile interrogation while giving away as little information as possible.

Your conduct

You don't have to tell them what branch of the service you're from, though they may be able to guess that themselves from your uniform and equipment. Some personnel traditionally get a hard time, notably members of Special Forces units and fliers.

Try not to get noticed and singled out for interrogation. Don't exhibit bravado or humility. Just fade into the background. There's no point in not being respectful and polite – in fact, to behave in any other way is extremely stupid. It will only earn you harsher treatment and probably get you beaten up and deprived of food. At the same time, don't give the interrogator the idea that you might be willing to co-operate. All you'll succeed in doing is prolonging the interrogation.

There's a world of difference between acting ignorant and acting dumb. The interrogator may say something like, "We know there's a build-up of troops at such-and-such a location. Does it contain armour?" If your answer was, "I don't know, sir, I've never been in that location," it sounds a lot more convincing than "Piss off". But beware of seeming to be trying to be helpful.

Watch out for apparently innocent enemy personnel such as doctors, nurses, orderlies and cleaners. Never talk in front of them: they could well be intelligence agents, operating under-cover – perhaps not even revealing themselves to other enemy agents on the spot.

The enemy interrogator will be very keen to turn you into a collaborator, too. The two main methods are threats – of physical torture or death, to you or to another member of your squad or promises – and bribes – of better treatment, medical attention for someone badly wounded, or almost anything else that seems attractive. After all, they can promise you anything – you're not going to get it anyway.

Tip: SAS troopers are taught to act tired if captured. The interrogator is more likely to press an alert man than one seemingly incapable of understanding through fatigue.

The interrogator's skill
The interrogator prepares himself before interrogating his prisoner:

1. *Intelligence:* The interrogator studies any information he may have acquired from initial searches, overheard conversations and background material gleaned by intelligence workers operating in the captive's own country.
2. *Weak or strong?* He also builds up a picture of the POW's make-up: is he weak or strong? Can he take punishment? What gets to him? Is he cold or emotional? How has he adjusted to POW life?
3. *Softening-up:* You'll be softened up, either by rough

treatment, starvation, thirst, sensory deprivation and sleep-lessness, or by solitary confinement. The interrogator will set up the place where he'll ask his questions so that it's intimidating and unfriendly.

4. *Disgrace:* He will try to destroy your confidence by disgracing you in the eyes of your fellow prisoners or your family or comrades at home, or will simply try to make you feel ashamed of yourself.

5. *Lesser of two evils:* The captor will give you a choice between two evils, one of which is less damaging than the other. He knows that you will choose the least damaging, and that is the one he can use for his own purposes.

6. *The file:* Your interrogator may start by asking you a harmless question about yourself. If you give a false answer he checks his intelligence file on you and gives you the right one. You begin to think this guy knows everything. "What's the use of holding out?" Don't give in. He is telling you the little he does know; if he knew everything he wouldn't have to question you further.

7. *Hidden eyes and ears:* You may have looked and found nothing, but the enemy has probably bugged the camp, so watch what you say, everywhere.

8. *The silent treatment:* You may be put into solitary confinement, or held in a room with an interrogator who says nothing. Don't be afraid of silence: come to terms with it.

9. *Repetition and monotony:* Your interrogator may ask you the same question in the same tone over and over again. Let him: if you get riled, he'll win; if you maintain control, the psychological victory will be yours.

10. *What's the use?* "Why hold out?" "Why suffer?" "You are at our mercy." "We'll get the information out of you anyhow." "Make it easier on yourself." These are all statements that you must learn to resist.

Be on guard

As well as trying to convince you that other prisoners have been co-operating, your interrogator will try to get information from you about them which in turn will allow him to put subtle pressures on anyone you talk about ("the Double Game"). Don't give out any information about any of your comrades. Don't admit to being in the same unit with them. Watch out for false questionnaires "for the Red Cross", for instance. The aid organisations need to know nothing more than your name, rank, number and date of birth. Any information you provide on a form like this is only for the enemy intelligence officer's use. Never make any statement of any kind. Not in writing, nor spoken, where it might be recorded.

Don't try to impress the interrogator by boasting about things that you and your unit have done, whether they're true or not. He's not going to let you go because you make yourself out to be some sort of superman! At the same time, don't try to deceive him by volunteering false information, no matter how subtly you think you do it. He knows the wide intelligence picture and will ask you the same questions over and over again, perhaps with days in between. He'll record everything you say, and look for differences in your answers. Don't look into the interrogator's eyes. You may give away information without meaning to. Pick out a spot between his eyes or in the centre of his forehead and concentrate on that.

Once he has you talking, it won't take a skilled interrogator long to get the truth out of you. Don't put yourself into a position where you find that you're having a conversation with him. Let him do all the talking, and limit your answers to "No" and "I don't know anything about that".

Never drop your guard. You can be taken off for further interrogation at any time, at any hour of the day or night.

Try to win a victory every time you're interrogated, no matter how small. Having worked out how, pass it on to your fellows, so that they are morally stronger. The longer the interrogation goes on, the safer you are. More prisoners will be arriving and needing your interrogator's time, and your information will become more and more out of date. What will prolong the nightmare is your partial co-operation. One snippet of useful information will convince your interrogator that he may be onto a good thing, and he'll carry on until he gets the lot, no matter what it takes.

Forcing co-operation

These are some techniques that POWs have been subjected to in recent times.

Torture

Technique: extreme dislocation of body parts, e.g. arms, legs, back, etc by twisting or pulling; beating, slapping, gouging, kicking; inserting foreign objects such as bamboo slivers under the finger-nails; electric shocks.

Effect: crippling; partial or total temporary or permanent loss of use of limbs and senses; loss of normal mental functioning; extreme pain; lowering or breaking of ability to resist captor's demands. TORTURE IS THE MAJOR MEANS OF FORCING COMPLIANCE.

Threats

Technique: Threats of solitary confinement, non-repatriation, death or beatings to oneself or other POWs; threats regarding future treatment; threats against family.

Effect: Unreasonable anxiety; loss of hope and confidence; despair.

"Now and then" treatment

Technique: Occasional favours such as release of food packages and better living conditions; promise of big rewards for helping captors.

Effect: Tempts the POW to go along with captors; presents the captors in a favourable light; makes resistance to questioning seem a bad idea.

Isolation or solitary confinement

Technique: Total or partial isolation by rank, race, degree of compliance, etc. or total solitary confinement.

Effect: Keeps POW away from anyone who can give any kind of support, moral, physical or psychological.

Hints that captors are in full control of everything in camp
Technique: Use of information from other sources to make POW believe the captors know more than they really do.

Effect: Makes POWs suspicious of each other and makes resistance seem futile.

Show of power over life and death
Technique: Use of executions or torture; introduction and withdrawal of better conditions and medical care; complete control over physical aspects of camp.

Effect: Breeds extreme caution and the belief that the captor is boss.

Deliberately-caused physical deterioration
Technique: Extremely long interrogation sessions; long periods in leg irons and stocks; bad food.

Effect: Drastic lowering of resistance to interrogation.

Enforcement of minor rules and commands
Technique: Overly strict demands for compliance with instructions and expected courtesies; forcing POWs to write or verbally repeat nonsensical words or phrases.

Effect: Causes automatic obedience to commands.

Lowering of self-respect of POW
Technique: Lack of privacy; ridicule and insults; prevention of washing; keeping living conditions filthy, insanitary, full of vermin, etc.

Effect: Humbles POW and makes giving in an attractive prospect.

Control over physical senses
Technique: Placing in isolation with no stimuli, or giving extreme stimuli such as no light or sound or too much light or sound; dripping water on forehead.

Effect: Makes POW think that captors have total physical control; causes extreme discomfort and distress.

Surviving as a prisoner

A prisoner-of-war camp can be anything from a huge barbed-wire compound holding tens of thousands of men to a crude shelter in a jungle clearing and one or two men in a bamboo cage. Once your interrogation is over you're of very little use to the enemy, unless he can exploit you for political purposes. You're just a drain on his resources. The men he has to use to guard you, the food and medicines he has to send to keep you alive – all of these could be better used on the battlefield. So it's going to be tough. The US Government has spent a great deal of time and money to find out what gives its soldiers the best possible chance of getting through a period spent as a POW.

Strength through unity

No matter how few of you there are, you must have an organisation. One man must be in command. Chances are that your captors will try to force someone of their choice on you.

If they try to set up an organisation amongst the prisoners, then the best thing to do is to appear to go along. But you'll know who the real Senior Ranking Officer is. He, not the enemy's puppet, will appoint his Adjutant, his Quartermaster, his Welfare, Education and Entertainments Officers, and set up the rest of the POW infrastructure.

Eat the food

You will get less, worse and stranger food than you have ever had – a poor version of the stuff the enemy eats. If you are a finicky eater, get over it. Many men have died in a short period of captivity because they could not adapt to the food – they have starved themselves to death.

Add to your diet with roots, weeds, bark, a hidden garden, animals or reptiles. Ants and grasshoppers are good sources of protein. Cat, dog and monkey meats are staples of many diets.

Steal from your captors. If your Senior Ranking Officer approves, trade with the enemy, and share with those POWs who need it at least as much as you do. If it's edible, eat it.

The enemy knows that lack of enough food or the right kinds

of food decreases mental and physical powers, making you less able to resist and easier to manipulate. Therefore he will withhold food to make you do what he wants.

Drink the water

You must drink, even though your water smells bad, is dirty and is alive with bugs. Strain or purify it with chemicals or by boiling if you can. Make a still to obtain water or suck the juices from fruits. Tomatoes are an excellent source of fluid. Catch rain or snow. If you think, you'll drink; if you panic, you'll dehydrate.

Exercise for survival

Try to take some sort of exercise every day. Keep up your muscle tone, but don't overdo it – you won't be getting the proteins and carbohydrates in your diet that will allow you to do strenuous exercise.

Keep your mind active too. Try to be learning something new all the time. If you're in a large camp, with lots of other people, the chances are that you'll be able to learn pretty much anything you can think of. You'll have skills that others will want to learn too.

Play can be just as important as work. Not just physical games and sports, though these are very important, but entertainment of all kinds. Painting and drawing and writing need very little in the way of materials, and they don't just keep you busy – they allow you to express yourself, your inner thoughts, in an important way. Remember, it may be hard work trying to stay fit and healthy, but it's nothing compared to the problem you'll have if you lose your health and fitness and then have to get it back again. Your captors will like it a lot better if you just sit around doing nothing all day and every day, weakening your own morale and destroying your will to stay awake and alive. Don't do it! Your life is in your own hands.

Join in

The men appointed to the jobs of Sports, Education and Entertainments Officers will want to set up as many activities and events as they can. Get involved in them. It doesn't matter if you're not too good at whatever it is – what matters most is that you get busy and active and stay that way.

The folks back home

Keeping in touch with your family and friends is very important for both sides. You need to know you're not forgotten, and they need to know that you're as safe and well as possible.

Letters and photographs are the only way you'll be able to keep in contact, and the enemy will know this and use it to weaken you. Be ready to share your letters, photographs and parcels, if you get them, with the people around you. The SRO will put someone in charge of mail, and keep an accurate list of letters sent and received.

Outgoing letters are often a source of intelligence for the enemy. Try to restrict yourself to a brief note like "I'm alive and well", and if you're in any doubt about the value to the enemy of something you want to say in a letter home, ask the SRO's advice – that's another one of the many things he's there for.

Make sure that you circulate any scraps of news that you get in your letters. The best way is for a group of people to produce a camp newspaper. It needn't be more than a handwritten sheet that gets passed on from person to person around the camp. If that's not possible, then you'll have to do it by word of mouth.

Get one over

Let no chance go by to "get one over" on the enemy, and make sure that everyone knows about every little victory. Give all the guards and camp personnel nicknames – the crueller the better! Don't use them to their faces, of course, but in private use every chance you have to make fun of them. Leave them in no doubt of what you think of them.

Camp communication

There are many ways to communicate with other prisoners. The POW isolation barrier and enemy-imposed ban on communication must be broken. If you can see, hear or touch other POWs, or if articles are brought into and taken out of your place of confinement, you can communicate.

Sign language

The standard deaf-mute language may be learned, but it is diffi-cult. There is a simple variation that is quicker to learn, using hand signals. Either hand can be used. Numbers are rotated to indicate that they are numbers and not letters. The code uses the standard US Navy hand signal numbers: zero is shown by rotating the letter O. Let your hand drop slightly after each series of letters or words. To indicate "I understand", the receiver may nod slightly in a pre-arranged manner. Different body movement such as blinking the eyes, flexing the hands or arms, shrugging the shoulders, etc., – all natural and meaning-less to the enemy – can be worked out in advance to indicate different responses.

Tap codes

The Morse code can be learned quickly. But it has a serious drawback: it consists of dots and dashes that sometimes cannot be distinguished. There is a better system that consists of a square marked off in 25 sub-squares: 5 across and 5 up and down, with the letters of the alphabet in the sub-squares (the letter K is not used because it sounds like C). The squares running from left to right are rows; the squares from top to bottom are columns.

Taps are used to identify the letters. The first series of taps gives the row; after a short pause the second series of taps gives the column. The letter is in the block where the row and column meet. To find the letter O, for example, three taps would desig-nate the third row (L-M-N-O-P); a slight pause followed by four taps would designate the fourth column (D-I-O-T-Y); the row and column meet at the letter O.

A longer pause indicates the end of a word. Two taps indicate that the word has been received. A series of rapid taps indicates that the word was not received or not understood. When a receiver has enough letters to know what the word is, he gives two taps and the sender goes on to the next word. Each time the code is broken by your captors you can rearrange the letters.

The methods of getting a message across with this code are almost unlimited. The code can be tapped, whistled, winked, coughed, sneezed or hummed; you can nudge the guy next to you; you can use finger movements, eye movements, twitches, broom strokes, push-ups; or you can bang objects together.

Word of mouth
This can sometimes be dangerous. To disguise the content from the enemy, language variations can be used – subculture language (street language of minority groups), for example, or pidgin English, ordinary slang, etc.

Talking through the wall
Roll up a blanket in the shape of a ring doughnut and put it against the wall. Put your face in the centre of the doughnut and talk slowly. The receiver puts his ear against the wall on the other side or presses the open end of a cup against the wall with his ear against the other end.

Different noises
Various sounds such as grunting, coughing, sneezing, blowing your nose, whistling or humming can be used as pre-arranged signals to pass messages such as "All is well", "Enemy around", "Stop", "Go", etc.

Writing messages
You will not usually have writing materials available, but you can improvise: use charred wood, fruit juices, ashes mixed with any fluid, etc. Use any pointed object as a writing implement. Leaves, wood, cloth, toilet paper and any material can be used as a writing surface.

Mail deliveries
As well as personal deliveries, messages can be left in any hiding-place – latrines, trees, rocks, crevices, holes, etc; the best places are those that the enemy would expect you to visit normally. The hiding-places should be changed frequently, and couriers should deposit and collect their dispatches at different times.

Escape

The first hours

The best chances to escape will come straight after your capture. You'll still be close to your own forces, and so you'll know which direction to head in, and you may even be familiar with the country. You'll be fitter and healthier than after any time in captivity, and if you can keep your wits about you, you may be able to take advantage of the confusion that is usually to be found just behind the fighting front, with reinforcements and re-supply trying to go forward and medevac and empty re-supply units trying to move back.

You'll be in the hands of combat troops, not people trained in holding prisoners, and their inexperience may give you opportunities. But at the same time they'll be psyched up for battle, so will probably shoot rather than ask questions. They might just shoot you for the fun of it.

For all these reasons every army has a plan for dealing with prisoners of war, for getting them out of the combat zone as quickly as possible, so that they can be interrogated while the information they have about troop strengths and movements is still worth something. The chances are that if you're captured on your own, or as part of a small group, you will be held somewhere like the regimental command post, and then transferred to the rear echelon headquarters run by intelligence security units, military police or internal security troops. This will not be far from the fighting front.

In transit

When enough prisoners have accumulated, you'll be moved back, being kept to open country and avoiding towns and villages. The enemy is likely to be short of motor transport – or, at least, will give a very low priority to the transportation of prisoners, so you may well find yourself evacuated on foot. He'll be short of personnel, too, so the POW column may have too few guards, who may even be unfit for active duty – walking wounded perhaps, themselves on their way to rear-echelon hospitals. That means that there will be more chances to escape. If the guards are placed at the head and tail of the column, as is often the case, pass the word through the ranks of prisoners to spread out and make the line of marching men as long as possible.

Keep the pace as slow as you can. At a bend in the road, you may suddenly find that the head and the tail are out of each other's sight, which means that men in the centre of the column can slip away to either side of the road and get quickly into some kind of cover. The larger the number of men who make the break, the greater are the chances of their absence being noticed straight away. One or two men missing probably won't be noticed until the next head count is made, and that may not be until the end of the day.

Take advantage of any diversion, too. Artillery bombardment and attack from the air or extreme weather conditions, for instance, are likely to cause a lot of confusion, and may permit men to slip away while the guards' attention is distracted.

If you're being transported by truck out of the combat zone, you will probably be moved by night. If the guards are not alert and you are not locked inside the vehicle, you may get a chance to jump for it when the truck slows down – climbing a hill, for instance, or negotiating a section of damaged road. Try to sabotage the vehicles – put sugar or sand in the petrol, for example – so that they are forced to stop. Once again, an air raid may give you the necessary cover.

Permanent POW camps are usually placed as far away as possible from the battlefield and from borders with neutral or enemy territory, so the last move will probably be made by train. Large groups of prisoners in transit are usually locked into freight cars, the guards relying on the physical security of the locked wagons to stop escape attempts. The conditions inside these cars, especially during a long journey in the middle of summer or winter, can become lethal, and the fact that you'll probably be packed in very tightly doesn't help. Even so, because you'll have long periods without observation this may provide your best chance. Try to break though the floor, the walls (especially at a window or a ventilator) or the roof. If you're travelling in passenger coaches, then you have two other advantages, even though you may have guards to worry about: it's much easier and quicker to break out through a window than the solid sides of a freight wagon, and you'll probably be able to communicate in some way with prisoners in other compartments or even in other carriages.

Don't relax for a moment, but always stay alert to any possibility, because you never know if you'll ever get another chance. If you're not in a position to escape yourself, help others to do so even if it means that you'll be punished for it later.

In the camp

Escaping from an established prisoner-of-war camp is a much more difficult task than making a break from a train or from a column of marching men. The camp itself will have been built specifically to keep you in: barbed wire, electronic surveillance, floodlights, watch towers, dogs and thermal imaging for tunnel searches are just some of the weapons at the enemy's disposal. And even if you do succeed in getting out of the camp itself, you're still faced with a difficult and dangerous journey through enemy territory, where just your physical appearance may be enough to give you away.

The escape committee

Part of the prisoners' secret organisation in the camp will be devoted to the business of escaping. There will be very few ways of making an escape from a camp, and each time an attempt is made it will cut down those possibilities even further. The escape committee will co-ordinate escape attempts, to try to ensure that each one has the best possible chance of success and also set up the infrastructure that each will need – tools, diversions, false documents, intelligence and so on. You should collect and hoard everything, even useless articles: these will mask the useful ones if you are searched by camp guards. Most escape attempts will need this sort of organisation – but that doesn't mean that you shouldn't go for it on your own if a chance presents itself unexpectedly, perhaps from a labour party working outside the camp.

Documents and disguises

Before you get too far in your escape planning, you have to think how you'll cross the enemy territory that lies between you and neutral or friendly forces. There are two methods: either you try to blend in with the local population, or you try to stay hidden. If you try to fit in, you'll need clothing, documents, money and at least some knowledge of the language, all of which will either have to be produced inside the camp or stolen once you get outside.

In order to forge documents, you have to know what they look like to start with, and you must have the right sort of raw material available – paper, inks and dyes, pens and so on, not to mention the skill to do it. And as magnetic encoding like that used on credit cards gets more common, the chances decrease of producing forged documents that will pass any sort of examination.

The other option is to travel in secret, using your survival training to keep out of enemy hands. In many ways this is more practical. and at least you know where you are when you depend only on your own skills.

POW rescue

As technology takes over from human observation and scrutiny, escape has become more and more difficult. But what technology has taken away with one hand it has given back with the other. Spy satellites and high-altitude observation flights give intelligence officers a clear view of every part of the Earth's surface. That means you have a way of signalling to your own people, no matter where on Earth you may be. There's no need to rush it. You can trace out the letters of a message in the soil of a compound – or even stand around in groups that shape the letter in human bodies – in such a way that the enemy won't even be aware that you're doing it. Make certain that each arm of each letter is at least two metres long or it might not be seen from above. But remember, it's as likely to be seen by enemy satellites as your own.

You can also signal to aircraft, of course. To attract the

attention of friendly aircraft you need to make a large sign which will stand out: again, letters should have arms of not less than two metres. Alternatively you can send the emergency "SOS" signal in Morse code. Look around for any useful material: stones, fertilizer sacks, anything that can be arranged into a shape to catch the pilot's attention. Or when on parade in POW camp, form your parade up so that it spells out the letters "SOS" as shown above.

Once your position has been identified either by these methods or by a successful escaper being de-briefed, a coded letter getting through, or an enemy national selling the information, it may be possible for a rescue mission to be put together. Even if you're four or five hundred miles from the nearest friendly border or sea coast, your own authorities may be able to get a rescue force through.

The odds on a successful rescue will be a lot greater if there's a channel of communication from the would-be rescuers to you, and that probably means coded radio messages. There have been many cases of prisoners building radio receivers in camps, and here technology lends a hand once again, modern radio receivers being small enough to be easily hidden in all sorts of places.

Any information should include a validation code, such as mention of a pre-arranged subject like trees or weather, or even the days of the week. Leave this code off only when under duress. Every piece of information that you can exchange with the people planning the rescue attempt will increase its chances of success. One of the most vital will be to set up the signalling system you'll use to call the rescue force in at the last moment. The chances are that it will be helicopter-borne, and the pilots and mission commanders will need to be shown exactly where to land to be most effective, and advised of wind direction, where to expect resistance, and perhaps even where the prisoners they've come to rescue are to be found.

HIJACK AND HOSTAGE RESCUE

Personal survival
You switch on the 6 o'clock news and once again you see an
airliner parked at the end of a runway. It shimmers in the heat
reflected from the concrete and you can see armoured cars and
troops lurking by the control tower. The terrorists' demands seem
wearily familiar, and there's no comment yet from the White
House. But hijacks don't just happen to other people. One day it
might be you.

You can survive some hijacks, like some ambushes, by careful
planning and thinking ahead. Don't just follow the crowd: think
through your schedule, the different routes to your destination
and the airlines you might fly with.

Are you a target?

The very first priority is to establish if you, or anyone you might
be with, is a potential target. Remember that you are more likely
to be singled out because of what you represent than who you
actually are: terrorists often attack people just because of their
nationality. If they simply want Western hostages, you might fit
the bill very nicely just because you happen to be in the wrong
place at the wrong time.

Choose your carrier

The second area of prior planning is the booking, route, carrier
and seat. Make two bookings on different airlines, but only pick
up one. Collect these tickets at the airport, so that your movements are known to a limited number of people. Choose an airline
like Finnair which has no political associations. Some of the US
carriers are obvious targets, as are Middle East airlines. Go for

the neutrals – even countries with former colonial empires can be targets.

If you are flying to a potential trouble spot some airlines are noted for their high level of security – El Al insists on searches of baggage as well as electronic and body checks of passengers. It is also one of the many airlines that now operate with "sky marshals". El Al may be a target, but it is a "hard" target.

Avoid stop-overs

Try to make sure that you have a direct route with no stop-overs – this is particularly important with the Middle East. Some airports have very sloppy security, and while you may have had a thorough scarch when you boarded at your departure, other passengers at other stops may board less thoroughly checked. If there is a stop-over, a walk around the terminal will get you away from the vulnerable aircraft – some terrorists have boarded aircraft disguised as cleaners during stop-overs, so a stroll reduces your chances of being caught in the hijack.

Pick your seat

Your seat could be a lifesaver. Aisle seats put you within reach of the hijacker. Window seats are safer, and exit seats may give you the chance to escape if the aircraft is on the runway of an airport. "Neutral" seating in tourist class is less likely to attract attention than first class. If the terrorists wish to show their determination they may shoot hostages, and these are likely to have been chosen from passengers who are obviously important.

Be a grey person

Your dress and manner will also make you a target. In some countries blue jeans are seen as Western clothing, and so are suspect. Ex-army clothing is to be avoided, combat jackets being the most obvious. Baggage also draws attention either by its opulence or by being service-issue, for example kitbags or rucksacks.

Labels should only have a business address, and the baggage

should not sport hotel labels from around the world (incidentally, these precautions also reduce the chance of theft at airports). Jewellery, striking T-shirts and obvious ethnic clothing can also be a liability and reduce your ability to be the "grey man", a neutral unnoticed among the passengers.

Finally, your passport and wallet can contain a goldmine of information. Try to avoid collecting visa stamps from countries that have a terrorist problem – many countries will stamp entry and exit visas on a separate piece of paper if you ask. Your job description can be a major liability – government or service personnel are seen as "targets" by many hijackers and natural targets for hostage executions. Photographs of relatives and children are always worth including in your wallet or passport. You will be seen as a family man or woman with dependents and thus a less suitable person for execution. At the other extreme, the bathing-costume picture of a wife or girlfriend may cast you as a corrupt and decadent Westerner in the eyes of some hijackers.

Action

If the worst happens and you are on the aircraft that has been hijacked, follow the old army adage: "Keep your eyes open, your mouth shut and never volunteer for anything". The last part can be modified if it allows you to escape. As the hijack is taking place the armed men and women will be very nervous, and rapid or unexpected movements from the passengers may produce violent reactions. They may assault you, note you as a future execution victim, or kill you as a suspected sky marshal.

HOW TO AVOID AND SURVIVE A HIJACK
1. Travel with an airline that has no or few political enemies.
2. Do not wear army or ex-army clothing.
3. Do not carry your luggage in service-issue kit bags or rucksacks.
4. If the plane is hijacked keep quiet and do not draw attention to yourself.

5. Observe the terrorists' activities very carefully: if you do escape you'll be able to help the security forces.

By quiet observation you will be able to build up a picture of the numbers of hijackers and their mode of operation. In a large aircraft they may collect everyone together, or position themselves at different points around it to cover the passengers.

Tiredness and tension

As time passes everyone will be affected by fatigue and the need to perform bodily functions. This will increase tension, and the presence of children will be a further aggravation. The hijackers will probably release women, children and elderly people if the aircraft has landed at a location where negotiations are taking place. These released passengers will be able to give details of the hijackers to the security forces, assuming that the aircraft is in a reasonable pro-Western country.

If you have a seat by the door there may be an opportunity to escape. However, if you are travelling with a group this may make them potential execution victims. Note how the hijacker is armed – if he has a handgun you have a better chance of surviving, and there may even be a chance to overwhelm him. The most dangerous situation is a group with automatic weapons and explosives. The explosives may be positioned around the aircraft, with the threat that they will be detonated if there is an attempt at rescue; automatic weapons are notoriously inaccurate in untrained hands, and could cause casualties if a firefight with a sky marshal developed. *If there is a firefight, stay as low as possible*. Window seats give better cover, though they are less easy to escape from. The sky marshal will probably have a low-velocity weapon with ammunition that will not damage the fuselage, but the hijacker may be using a 9-mm high-velocity weapon – and if this punctures the aircraft fuselage there may be decompression.

Rash rescue attempts

However, the aim of the hijacker is to get the plane to a place where the bargaining can begin. There have been examples where hastily-mounted "rescue" operations have caused more casualties than were expected when the rescuers stormed the aircraft. If a rescue operation takes place the most likely course of action will be for the assault team to order the passengers to keep down. In this way they can identify the hijackers, who are likely to be on their feet in the aisle.

Your best course is to keep down and wait for the shooting to stop: the assault team will be looking for any violent or un-expected movement. They will have preceded the assault with stun grenades, and both passengers and hijackers will be suffering from temporary shock. The team will then aim to have the passengers off the aircraft as fast as possible, so you should follow their instructions.

Keep cool

If, however, the aircraft arrives at a neutral or "friendly" country where the hijackers can negotiate, the advisable course is to assess the situation. There may be friends of the hostages at the airport who will take over the negotiations with a friendly power and be more rational than the men and women who hijacked the aircraft. In this situation, a leader for the passengers may emerge; he could be the pilot or a mature and experienced passenger. Such a person will be able to make representations about the health and welfare of the passengers. By this stage the aircraft and passengers will have become bargaining counters and their safety will be more important.

Now it may be a time for patient waiting. If you find you are moved from the aircraft to hotels or holding areas, try to take some hand luggage or toiletries – there may be nothing when you arrive. Staying clean and presentable will also sustain your morale. The in-flight comforts will stop almost at once if a hijacking happens, since the stewardesses and stewards will be seen as conduits for information as they move around the aircraft. It is advisable therefore to keep hand luggage that contains simple toiletries and any medication you may need ready to hand.

For many people hijacks, like other man-made or natural disasters, are experiences that happen to other people and are reported on the news. But they could happen to almost anyone, even if they see themselves as "Mr Average": they may be on the flight with an important traveller, or they may just be unlucky.

Sweating it out

Some hijacks are over in hours. But others can last for days, as the aircraft is directed from international airport to international airport. While in flight, the air-conditioning will work and the physical conditions will not be too bad. On the ground, however, the aircraft will be reliant on its Auxiliary Power Unit (APU), and so it can become hot and not very comfortable. The passengers' discomfort will be one of the bargaining counters that the hijackers will use as they talk to the control tower. Lavatories will become blocked, and food will be reduced to light snacks from the galley. Though the staff at the control tower may be able to send food as the negotiations continue, this cannot be relied on. These points will help you to get through a trying and frightening time.

1. Avoid provoking the hijackers by unnecessary demands or by eye contact that may be seen as critical.
2. If you have hand luggage that can be reached without creating problems, you may be able to use your sponge bag to keep clean and refreshed.
3. Eat any snacks or sweets you have packed, but avoid snacks that will make you very thirsty.
4. Try to contact your neighbours and take an interest in them. It will take your mind off your own situation, and may even enable you to place some leverage on the hijackers – for instance, if your neighbour is sick or elderly he may be evacuated from the aircraft as a humane gesture.
5. Contact with your neighbours will also allow you to work out any plan of action that may present itself – thus the

single hijacker may lay himself open to attack by the passengers if he turns his back on them as he moves along the aisles. If the situation deteriorates and an attack on a hijacker is the only option, remember that a tightly rolled-up newspaper makes a surprisingly effective weapon – jab the rolled end into the hijacker's face.

6. Avoid a rash attack on a hijacker. You may be happy to be a hero, but if you fail, the attack puts everyone at risk. Random shots may penetrate the fuselage or kill or injure passengers.
7. The hijackers may also see the whole aircraft as a threat and attempt to destroy it in revenge.
8. Attempts to disarm hijackers should be left to the skilled, experienced and brave, not the amateur and enthusiastic.

Ever since the series of "skyjacks" in the late 1960s, anti-terrorist units have been refining a series of methods for storming a plane on the ground. It is not an easy task. The terrorists have every advantage in their favour: they usually have a clear field of view and can slaughter the passengers in a matter of moments. If you are going to make a rescue attempt it must be planned to the last detail and executed with split-second timing.

Ending a hijack

In some instances hijackers have released men and women who are sick or very young or old. These people will be vital, since they will give information on the hijackers' numbers and their weapons and equipment. They will also provide more information on their level of training and motivation, though some of this will have been gleaned from the conversations with the control tower.

Wear them down

You will need to know how close you can approach without alerting the hijackers. Disguise as ground crew is good cover, though ladders and weapons and equipment can be difficult to conceal. Night is the obvious time when the hijackers will be fatigued and there is reasonable cover.

If the APU (Auxiliary Power Unit) cuts out through lack of fuel, the internal lights, air-conditioning and other power will cease, putting the aircraft in darkness. If the ground crew from the previous stop-over can advise on fuel states and it seems that there might be a breakdown, then an attack can be planned or the hijackers warned that the aircraft will be without power. Timing must be perfect: it was a failure to co-ordinate an APU breakdown that caused heavy casualties at Malta airport when Egyptian Special Forces attacked an airliner that had been hijacked.

Talking them out

The negotiating team can induce fatigue in the hijackers if they can keep them talking, although this must be balanced against the risk to the passengers, as well as their continuing discomfort. Sometimes the negotiators will be able to talk the hijackers out of the aircraft with no need to assault it, and no loss of life.

Losing patience

However, once hijackers lose patience with the negotiating team and start killing hostages to show they mean business, then the assault team must be ready to move in fast. Since hijackers are not likely to have weapons with rifle-calibre ammunition, your team could wear body armour, which will provide sufficient protection: the new lighter-weight Kevlar armour can be worn without reducing efficiency. The use of body armour is also important for the morale of the assault team.

Weapons for the assault team

The weapons for the job can include a linear cutting-tape charge, stun grenades and automatics. Linear cutting-tape is a flexible metal or plastic tube with a notch running along one face: when correctly positioned, it acts as a charge to cut through an aircraft fuselage to gain entry. It can be fixed magnetically or with adhesives, according to the target.

Weapons for the firefight

The handguns favoured by anti-hijack teams vary, though the preferred slugs tend to be hollow-point ammunition that flattens when it hits a target and has a devastating effect on soft tissue, but will not ricochet or cause damage to internal controls and fittings in the aircraft.

New ammunition

Some new plastic ammunition will slow down after a short range, but is lethal over the short distances in which the action will take place. Automatics with large-capacity magazines like the Browning High Power will give enough ammunition for the short but violent action that will follow the entry into the aircraft. However, you should carry spare magazines where they can be quickly loaded if there is a sustained firefight.

NINE QUESTIONS THE ASSAULT TEAM MUST FACE

1. How many hijackers are there?
2. Where is each one stationed in the aircraft?
3. What are they armed with?
4. Have they prepared any explosives to destroy the aircraft?
5. How fit and motivated are the hijackers?
6. How many passengers are aboard, and what is the seating plan?
7. Can the hijackers be tricked into gathering together in the cabin for a discussion with the control tower?
8. How many entry routes does the aircraft have?
9. Can the assault team practise on a similar aircraft first?

Entering the aircraft

If the hijackers are divided, with some on the flight deck and others amongst the passengers, then you will need to attack in two teams, and stage the assault so that one team fights towards the front and one towards the back of the aircraft. This way you should avoid firing into your own men. Entry must be preceded by stun grenades, which will temporarily disable the enemy but not severely injure the passengers.

Stun grenade effects

When a stun grenade explodes in a confined space like an airliner, anyone standing nearby will be completely deafened, and if you are very close your eardrums will be shattered. The flash leaves you temporarily blinded, and if you were looking towards it when it went off the image will be burned onto your retina for at least ten minutes, making it very hard for you to shoot straight.

Speed means success

However the rehearsals went, you must be ready for anything when you get inside the aircraft. The hijackers may not be where you expect them, and it's tempting to fight your way forward cautiously. But your attack will only succeed through speed. The volley of stun grenades and the suddenness of your assault throws the hijackers off balance and you must not give them time to recover. Shout at the passengers to lie down. This will keep them out of the line of fire and should make the hijackers better targets. As you move through the smoke-filled aircraft hunting a handful of terrorists amongst hundreds of passengers, it is horribly easy to shoot the wrong target.

Standing targets

This is the moment all your training is for, when life or death hangs on your split-second reactions. If Intelligence managed to provide you with photos of the terrorists, at least you have some means of identifying your target; if not, then you must sweep through going for anyone standing or armed.

Hostage survival

Keep low
As soon as the action starts, slide to the floor under your seat and stay there. Do not move into the aisles: any assaulting troops will flatten you in their rush to dominate the aircraft. Obey all orders from the assault team without question or protest. They'll treat everyone as potential threats, so you'll be handled very roughly until positively cleared. Tear gas will probably be used, so bury your head in the seat cushions. Do not rub your eyes – especially if you wear contact lenses.

Non-provocative stance

Do not pick up weapons as you flee the aircraft – you may be shot as a suspected terrorist when you get outside. As you exit, fall to the ground as though injured with your arms outstretched, and stay there until instructed to move by security forces.

The passengers can be removed from the aircraft as soon as the hijackers are cleared from a major exit. Station members of your team by the exits to make sure no hijackers try to sneak out the same way and to co-ordinate the security forces outside the aircraft. There have been cases when escaping passengers were shot by mistake as they fled from the fighting.

Assault team moves out

After the hijackers have been dealt with and the aircraft declared "clear" the assault team moves out. It is sensible to keep a low profile, because you do not want your arrival during a future crisis to be observed by the press and blasted over the TV and radio. This is why all Special Forces preserve the anonymity of their men. It may save their lives one day – and it may save yours.

Hostage rescue: equipment and training

Rescuing hostages is a dangerous business. Dangerous for the hostages, dangerous for the rescuers. The aim of the SAS is to make it terminally dangerous for the hostage-takers – whilst allowing the innocent to get out alive.

Although all SAS troopers are trained in hostage-rescue, the regiment has a specialist anti-terrorist team under the wing of the Counter-Revolutionary Warfare unit. Variously codenamed the "Pagoda Team" and the "Special Patrol Team", the anti-terrorist team is comprised of two "watches": Red and Blue. Together they give "24-hour cover", and all members are required on pain of "platform four" (being Returned to Unit) to carry an alert bleeper. Team members also have their movements restricted to a tight radius of Hereford to ensure quick recall in the event of an emergency. Training is mostly undertaken at the SAS camp at Pontrilas, south-west of Hereford, where facilities for hostage-rescue "games" include trains, a bus and even an aircraft fuselage. Needless to say, members of the anti-terrorist team are highly familiar with the "Killing House", the building dedicated to learning the skills of room combat. One particular skill honed is "the snatch", where a "hostage" is extracted by an anti-terrorist assault team. VIPs sometimes find themselves in the "hostage hot seat" – those having done so include the Queen and Prince Charles – but "hostages" no longer endure live rounds whizzing around them. An accident in 1985, when Sergeant Raymond Abbots of G squadron was killed, brought in a new training practice in which the anti-terrorist team fires at "virtual" life-size terrorists imaged on to bullet-absorbent walls in the Killing House.

In any hostage-rescue situation, the anti-terrorist team has a veritable arsenal of special weapons and equipment. Essentially, kit falls into three types: protective clothing for the SAS; devices to ensure quick "breaking-and-entering"; plus weaponry to eliminate the terrorists.

SAS anti-terrorist troopers wear clothing that keeps out bullets, fire, smoke and gas. Almost total protection, in other words. As standard issue comes the black assault suit made from flameproof

Arvex SNX 574 material, with the knee and elbow joints reinforced by retardant Pantotex felt, enabling the wearer to crawl
over hot and jagged surfaces. Extra protection comes from flameproof gloves and underwear. To keep out the bullets, troopers
wear, over the assault suits, Kevlar assault vests and "hard
armour" consisting of contoured ceramic composite plates. This
body armour is designed to defeat all 5.56 mm and 7.62 mm
rounds. A CT-12 respirator, meanwhile, not only looks Darth
Vader-menacing, it filters out (through carbon and wool sieves)
gas and smoke, while communication is enabled by mini-ear-
phones and a microphone. Other standard-issue assault clothing
includes a ballistic helmet and an assault belt rig, made of leather,
to carry personal weaponry.

If an SAS rescue is ordered, entry into the building, aircraft,
train or bus commandeered by the enemy is by any means possible – as long as it's fast. The quicker the SAS can get to the terrorists, the greater the chance of saving the hostages. The best
entrance of all is the surprise one that lands the SAS right on top
of the terrorists, thus dramatically reducing the latter's ability to
act.

To force doors, the SAS employs everything from mini
hydraulic battering-rams to a hefty kick of the boot. Remington
870 pump-action shotguns loaded with Hatton rounds are sometimes used to blow off door locks, and if the door won't open then
another American import is used – on the windows. This is the
"hooligan bar", a metre-long metal bar which smashes out most
of the window, with a pronged end that then removes debris.
Explosives are usually avoided, because of the danger of blast
damages to hostages – who are exactly the people the SAS are
trying to save. Even so, frame charges have found their place in
SAS operation (one was used to blow in the French windows of
the Iranian Embassy). Much the most effective means for a hole-
in-the-wall entry is the so-called "Harvey Wallbanger". This is a
wall-breaching cannon that uses compressed air to fire a water-
filled plastic projectile. The projectile breaches the wall, but as
soon as it has done so its energy is dissipated and it falls harm-
lessly to the ground.

Whatever mode of entry is employed, the anti-terrorist soldiers go into the building or transport in pairs. One trooper moves, while the other gives cover. Backs are protected and a wide arc of fire is maintained. On closing with the terrorists and the hostages, a shouted warning is given by the SAS to the hostages to lie down. Anyone who remains standing, anyone who is armed or threatening, will be shot on sight. In the event of a firefight with the terrorists, the SAS then uses its superior firepower.

The true superiority of SAS firepower lies in the calibre of the men selected for the SAS and the training they receive. Even so, the calibre of SAS weaponry is unlikely to be matched by that of the terrorists. The main weapon of the SAS anti-terrorist soldier is the Heckler & Koch MP5 sub-machine gun, although the Heckler & Koch Personal Defence Weapon began to be deployed on operations in 2002. The PDW is capable of firing 950 rounds a minute and, with armour-piercing bullets, can cut through more than 20 layers of Kevlar.

HECKLER & KOCH MP5

SMGs are by no means the only weapons of the anti-terrorist trooper. Strapped to the leg of the assault team member is a Browning 9 mm Hi-Power pistol. This is a semi-automatic pistol which holds 13 rounds in its magazine. Members of the SAS anti-terrorist unit can fire all 13 rounds in under 3 seconds – an annihilating rate of fire. Also to the regiment's liking is the Hi-Power's reliability and simplicity: it works even when covered in brick dust and can be stripped and reassembled in seconds. The only real contender for the title of "SAS Pistol of Choice" is the Swiss SIG-Sauer P226 which, according to tests done by the

Canadian "Mounties", has a malfunction rate as low as 0.007.

One more piece of the SAS hostage-rescue armoury deserves special mention. This is the stun grenade, which was developed by Royal Ordnance Enfield at the specific request of the SAS.

The stun grenade when detonated produces 160 decibels of noise and 300,000 candles-worth of light – and anyone close by is immobilized for nearly four seconds but not irreparably damaged. The magic ingredients are magnesium powder and fulminate of mercury. The official name of the stun grenade is the G60. SAS troopers know it by the appropriate nickname of "flash-bang".

APPENDIX:
SPECIAL FORCES UNITS
OF THE WORLD

ARGENTINA

Agrupación de Buzos Tácticos, APBT, "The Tactical Divers Group"

Main special operations force of the Argentine Navy. Based at Base Naval Mar del Plata (BNMP), the Buzos Tácticos was the first Special Forces division created in South America; the unit was established in 1952 with instructors who were former X-MAS Italian divers.

Operations

There is some evidence that undercover Buzo Táctico personnel accompanied the Argentinian scrap metal merchants who took over South Georgia on 19 March 1982. Later in the Falklands conflict a Buzo Táctico detachment, landed by the submarine *Sante Fé*, recced and secured the Yorke Bay beaches.

Division Especial De Seguridad Halcón

Also known as 'Falcon Group'. Consists of 75 operatives, and specializes in counter-terrorism and counter-insurgency. Formed in 1986. Similar to French GIGN. Took part in the battle of La Tablada in 1989, when guerrillas from the MTP (All for the Fatherland Movement) attacked the army barracks in Buenos Aires.

AUSTRALIA

Special Air Service Regiment (SASR)
Established in 1954 as 1st Special Air Service Company, the unit was expanded to three sabre squadrons in 1964, when it simultaneously gained regimental status as the Special Air Service Regiment. Officially abbreviated to "SASR", but usually known, like the British unit that inspired it, as the SAS. The SASR motto, like that of the GB SAS is 'Who Dares Wins'. Under the direct command of the Australian Special Operations Command, the SASR is based at Campbell Barracks in Swanbourne, Perth, Western Australia. Current strength: four squadrons of about 75 operators, each divided into three troops (Water Troop, Land Troop, Free-Fall). A signal squadron (152) is attached.

Major campaigns and missions

1965: Indonesian Confrontation as part of Operation Claret.
   1966-71: Vietnam. SASR squadrons rotated through Vietnam on year-long deployments, usually in Phuoc Tuy province east of Saigon. Specialised in long-range patrols, earning the nickname 'phantoms of the jungle' ('Ma Rung') from the Vietcong.
   1980: Zimbabwe (peace-keeping).
   1994: Somalia (VIP protection and rapid-response).
   1998: Kuwait; Operation Desert Thunder.

1991-2003: East Timor.

2001: MV *Tampa*; counter-terrorist squadron ordered to Christmas Island to board ship carrying illegal immigrants.

2003-07: Iraq.

2006: East Timor; Operation Astute.

2001-12: Afghanistan; including Operation Slipper; Operation Anaconda; in recognition of the operational actions of the Special Air Service Regiment (SASR) and 2nd Commando Regiment in summer 2010, the Special Operations Command was granted a battle honour, titled Eastern Shah Wali Kot.

BELGIUM

Special Forces Group
Traces its origin to the 1942 Belgian Independent Parachute Company, commanded by Captain E. Blondeel; this later became the Belgian SAS Squadron. The lineage of the Special Forces Group back to the Belgian SAS is somewhat tortuous (if not tenuous), though some of the significant way-stops, in chronological order, are the SOE (Special Detection Unit), the ESR-GVP (Specialized Reconnaissance Teams), disbanded in 1994; the new LRRP, which had a relationship with its predecessor; and was in turn disbanded in 2000 to become the 1st Company Special Forces. This was re-organized in 2003 as the Special Forces Group. Insignia is that of the British SAS, the flaming sword; mottoes are "Who Dares Wins", "Far Ahead" and "Never Surrender". In its various incarnations has been deployed in the Congo in 1964 (where it rescued European hostages), Zaire in 1978-79, Rwanda in 1990 and 1994, and Somalia in 1993.

CANADA

Joint Task Force 2 (JTF2) (*Deuxième Force opérationnelle inter-armées*, FOI 2)
Principally, though not exclusively, a counter-terrorist unit, which was established in 1993 in the wake of the closure of the Royal Canadian Mounted Police's Special Emergency Response Team. Members are mainly drawn from Princess Patricia's Canadian Light Infantry and the Canadian Airborne Regiment. The unit's strength is 600 personnel; the motto is *Facta Non Verba* (Deeds Not Words). JTF2 has been deployed in Bosnia, Haiti, Iraq, Rwanda, Libya and Afghanistan. The unit was awarded a Presidential Unit Citation by the US government for service in Afghanistan as part of Task Force K-Bar. Recognised as Canada's premier Special Forces unit. The other units JTF2 serves alongside in the Canadian Special Operations Forces Command are the Canadian Joint Incident Response Unit, 427 Special Operations Aviation Squadron and the Canadian Special Operations Regiment.

FRANCE

GIGN (Groupement d'Intervention de la Gendarmerie Nationale)
Formed in 1973 and essentially a counter-terrorist unit, drawn from the Gendarmerie Nationale, whose hostage-rescue operations have included the release of 30 French school children at Djibouti (1976), regaining the Grand Mosque in Saudi Arabia (1979), the liberation of 229 passengers and crew from Air France 8969 in Marseille (1994), and operations involving the arrest of war criminals in Bosnia.

GERMANY

GSG-9 (Grenzscutzgruppe-9)
Formed in the wake of the Black September attack on Israeli athletes at the Munich Olympic Games of 1972, GSG-9 is a counter-terrorist unit drawn from the para-military police force. 75% of applicants are rejected. Celebrated for its rescue of hostages, held by the Red Army Faction, from a Lufthansa 707 in Mogadishu, October 1977; code-named "Operation Fire Magic", it was the GSG-9's first real test.

At 1 p.m. on 13 October 1977, Lufthansa flight LH181 had lifted off from Majorca's Palma airport, with 86 passengers and 5 crew, and headed towards its destination, Frankfurt. It never made it. Shortly after take-off four terrorists, two men and two women, had broken into the flight deck and, with pistols smuggled aboard in their hand luggage, threatened the pilot, Captain Jürgen Schumann and his co-pilot Jürgen Vietor. The terrorists – Zohair Youssif Akache (aka "Captain Martyr Mahmoud"), Suhaila Sayeh, Wabil Harb and Hind Alameh – were a joint cell of the Popular Front for the Liberation of Palestine and the Red Army Faction called the "Martyr Halimeh Commando Unit". They demanded the release of eleven members of the Red Army Faction, together with a $15 million ransom. A haphazard flight across the skies of Europe, the Middle East and the Horn of Africa ensued, as the skyjackers sought a safe haven for their commandeered plane. Meanwhile, the West German Chancellor, Helmut Schmidt, approached Britain for help – specifically as to whether 22 SAS would aid GSG-9 in a hostage-rescue. Major Alastair Morrison, then second-in-command of 22 SAS, and Sergeant Barry Davies, one of the Regiment's counter-terrorism experts, were duly dispatched to Dubai, where the GSG-9 team was assembling and where the hijacked plane was about to land. Morrison and Davies took a box of "flash-bangs", the

SAS-invented magnesium-based concussion grenades, with them. In Dubai, they found GSG-9 commander Ulrich Wegner and two of his men under virtual arrest.

No sooner was this problem sorted out than the hijacked aircraft flew on to the Republic of Yemen. There the terrorist's leader, Mahmoud, killed the captain of the airliner, Schumann, for communicating with the security forces. The wild goose flight set off again, the Lufthansa Boeing now proceeding to Somalia on 17 October, with co-pilot Vietor in the control seat. Shortly after landing, the terrorists threatened to blow up the aircraft unless all their demands were met. They then threw Schumann's body down onto the runway of Mogadishu airport. Short of erecting a sign saying "We Mean Business" the terrorists could not have been more obvious in their implacability. There was now no real possibility of a peaceful outcome, short of conceding every one of the terrorists' demands. As a ruse to gain some time for the GSG-9 team to organize themselves, negotiators told the terrorists that eleven Red Army Faction members were being released. Even as this misinformation was being fed to the terrorists, the main body of the GSG-9 team was flying in from Turkey, and Wegner, Morrison and Davies were thrashing out the plan to storm the airliner. The operation was codenamed "Fire Magic" – *Feuerzauber*. At 1 a.m. on 18 October, GSG-9 assembled for the assault, and the team's snipers moved into position. Morrison and Davies prepared their "fireworks". Thirty minutes later the twenty-two-man assault team began creeping forward half-crouched, off the edge of the runway directly behind LH181. This was the aircraft's blind spot. To divert the attention of the hijackers' leader, "Captain" Mahmoud, the control tower engaged in intense conversation about the fictitious release of the Red Army Faction members; while Mahmoud was on the radio the assault ladders were erected against the Boeing's metal body. Morrison and Davies climbed cautiously on to the wings on either side of the aircraft, and the three GSG-9 teams climbed to the emergency doors. At 2.07 a.m. – twenty-three minutes before Mahmoud's final deadline – an oil drum was rolled onto the runway in front of the aircraft and set alight. While two of the terrorists rushed forward into the cockpit to see the diversionary pyrotechnics, there was a massive blinding flash, courtesy of the SAS men who threw their "flash-bangs" over the emergency exit and cockpit.

In almost the same second, GSG-9 troopers entered the aircraft via the rear starboard door, and shot a bewildered female terrorist. The terrorist leader, Mahmoud, was quicker on the uptake and rolled two grenades from the cabin towards the first class passenger lounge, where they exploded with a dull thud, though miraculously caused little damage. Inside the aircraft, recalled Barry Davies, 'gunfire rattled up and down the aircraft for what seemed a lifetime'.

In the mayhem, no one saw the terrorist Soraya dive into a rear toilet, from where she began shooting. She was wounded and incapacitated by a return of fire. With the rear of the aircraft secure, the fighting centred on the cockpit. It was soon over. Mahmoud was 'stitched' by an MP5 burst, and Wegner shot the last terrorist in the head with a pistol.

As the joint GSG-9–SAS team had calculated, the passengers, strapped to their seats, were below the line of fire. Save for the fragments of white metal from Mahmoud's grenades which caused minor injuries to stewardess Gabriele Dillmann, two passengers and one GSG-9 operative there no "friendly" casualties. Hurriedly, the passengers and crew were disembarked and escorted to the passenger lounge. Major Morrison, Davies, recalled, was particularly courteous to one of the eleven German beauty queens who happened to be amongst the passenger complement. Of the hijackers, Mahmoud died of his wounds, leaving Suhaila Sayeh as the sole terrorist survivor.

Watching the operation from the control tower was the German Minister of State, Herr Wischnewski. Immediately the assault was confirmed as successful by Wegner radioing the code "*Frühlingszeit! Frühlingszeit!*" ("Springtime! Springtime!"), Wischnewski in turn radioed the West German capital, Bonn: "Tell the world Germany has done it, the job's done." It was.

Other missions include the 1993 arrest of RAF terrorists Birgit Hogefeld and Wolfgang Grams.

Current strength 250 operatives.

ISRAEL

Sayeret Maktal
See pp64–70.

NEW ZEALAND

SAS (NZSAS)
Established in June 1955 as an unconventional warfare unit, and almost entirely modelled on the British SAS, down to the beige beret and the motto "Who Dares Wins". The unit has seen action in, among other theatres: Malaya, Borneo, Indonesia, Vietnam and Afghanistan (for which it received a US Presidential Citation). Based in Auckland, the NZSAS was granted regimental status in 2013, and currently comprises HQ, A, B, D, E and Support Squadrons.

POLAND

JW GROM (*Jednostka Wojskowa GROM im. Cichociemnych Spadochroniarzy Armii Krajowej*)
Formed in 1990, principally as a counter-terrorist unit, although its missions in practice have been broader in scope; in Afghanistan, for instance, it has been tasked with reconnaissance, and in Iraq it was detailed to seize infrastructure objectives. Of

the former Communist countries, Poland's GROM is the preferred working partner of most Western Special Forces.

RUSSIA

CIS

Special Forces are by no means exclusive to the Western powers. The Soviet Union had a number of elite units in the army, navy and marine branches of the military. These have resurfaced in the new CIS, the confederation of countries containing many of the former component republics of the USSR.

Spetsnaz, the Soviets' special-purpose troops, came under the direction of the GRU (Main Intelligence Directorate) and consisted of 16 Spetsnaz brigades, four Spetsnaz naval brigades, 4l independent Spetsnatz companies and the Spetsnaz regiments – the latter being available for senior commanders to use as the situation demanded. In peacetime, Spetsnaz numbered some 30,000 men in the event of war or crisis; those ranks could be expanded to 150,000. The conscript collecting centres took in newcomers twice a year – in the winter period or the summer period. Your birthday dictated which one you attended, as you were liable for service immediately after your eighteenth birthday. Women were not subject to compulsory military service, but were selected through the Communist social and youth organisations, KOMSOMOL and DOSAAF, if they were interested in joining the Armed Forces. At the centre, the conscript was interviewed, and his allegiance to the Communist cause was evaluated along with his wider suitability for Special Forces. Selection was of a similar nature and calibre to that for the SAS and Delta. Among other tests, Spetsnaz candidates were faced with a 5 km ski course (to be completed in 26-29 minutes), alongside the familiar endurance runs.

Successful candidates were divided out among the various Spetznaz units, with the crème de la crème going to the KGB and the GRU-controlled Alpha unit, a counter-terrorist force founded in 1974; many recruits ended up in the naval Spetsnaz which, with 1,300 men (and an unknown number of women) was the largest amphibious Special Force in the world. The brigade was the basic Spetsnaz unit, comprising 400-1,300 men, divided into *otrady* of about 200 men. Patrols were usually a four-man unit.

The Spetsnaz were well blooded in Afghanistan, where they exploited the carrying capacity of the MIL MI.26 "Halo" helicopter, probably the heaviest, most powerful helicopter in the world. The first Spetsnaz units in action were from Alpha and the so-called "anti-VIP companies" (euphemisms for assassination units), and proved themselves to be as murderous as their job title suggested. Alpha is generally credited with being the unit that attacked the Presidential palace in Kabul, Afghanistan, on December 28 1980 and murdered President Hafizullah Amin and his family. Spetsnaz were known to kill their own wounded rather than let them fall in the hands of the enemy. Follow-up units from Army Spetsnaz took the war to the Mujahideen in the mountains.

Following the collapse of the USSR and the birth of the CIS, Spetsnaz continued much as they always had done, though in the years of 'churn' they tended to be passed around from one military force to another. Eventually, the FSB (*Federal'naia sluzhba bezopasnosti*, "Federal Security Service") took over Alpha, but only after it had been under the control of three other agencies, including the police.

Alpha, whose strength is estimated at 300 operatives, continues to be the Russian unit closest in type and spirit to the SAS and Delta; like those units it has found itself used as a "fire-brigade", performing missions well outside its original remit: it was heavily committed in both the First and Second Chechen Wars of the 1990s.

Alpha group missions

1979: Operation Storm 333, the storming of the Tajbeg Palace, Afghanistan, and the killing of President Amin.

  1994-1996: First Chechen War.

  1999: Second Chechen War.

2002: Moscow theatre hostage crisis.
2004: Beslan hostage crisis.

UNITED KINGDOM

22 SAS
Formed in 1941 as "L" Detachment (see p48); has two associated territorial units, 21 SAS and 23 SAS.

Much of the purpose and point of the post-War SAS was given by Brigadier J.M. Calvert in a 1945 document "Future of SAS Troops":

We all have the future of the SAS at heart, not merely because we wish to see its particular survival as a unit, but because we have believed in the principles of its method of operations. Many of the above-named officers have had command of forces which have had a similar role to that of the SAS, as well as being in the SAS at one time. The object of this investigation is to decide whether the principles of operating in the SAS manner are correct. If they are correct, what types of units should undertake operations of this nature, and how best to train and maintain such units in peace, ready for war? I will not start now by writing about the principles of SAS, which have been an intrinsic part of your life for the past few years, but I will mention what I think are some of the most important points which need bringing out. The best way to do this is to consider the usual criticisms of the SAS type of force.

1. "The Private Army": From what I have seen in different parts of the world, forces of this nature tend to be so-called "Private Armies", because there have been no normal formations in existence to fulfil this function – a role which has been found by all commanders to be a most vital adjunct to their plans. It has only been due to the drive and initiative of certain individuals backed up by senior commanders that these forces have been formed and have carried out their role.

2. "The taking-up of Commanders' valuable time": This has often been necessary because it has very often only been the Comds of armies who have realized the importance of operations of this nature, and to what an extent they can help their plans. The difficulty has been that more junior staff officers have not understood the object or principles of such forces. They have either given us every help as they have thought us something rather wonderful, or they have thought we were "a bloody nuisance". I feel that the best way to overcome this is, that once the principle of the importance of Special Raiding Forces operating behind the vital points of the enemy's lines is agreed to, it should become an integral part of the training of the army at the Staff College, military colleges, and during manoeuvres, etc. Students should be asked not only what orders or directors or requests they have to give to the artillery, engineers, air, etc., but also what directives they would give to their raiding forces. There should be a recognized staff officer on the staffs of senior formations whose job it is to deal with these forces, i.e. the equivalent of a CRE or CRA. This should also be included in the text books FRS, etc.

3. "These forces, like airborne forces, are only required when we pass to the offensive, which – judging by all previous wars – is when the regular army has been nearly wiped out in rearguard actions whilst the citizen army forms, i.e. about 3 years after the beginning of the war." The answer here, I feel, is that it is just when we are weak everywhere that forces of this nature are the most useful, and can play a most vital part in keeping the enemy all over the world occupied. Also, there is little difference between the roles of SAS and "Auxiliary Forces" who duck when the enemy's offensive rolls over them and then operate against the enemy's L or C from previously constructed bases. An SAS formation, by its organization and training, is ideally suited to operate in this defensive role.

4. "Overlapping with SOE and other clandestine organizations": My experience is that SOE and SAS are complementary to each other. SAS cannot successfully operate without good intelligence, guides, etc. SOE can only do a certain amount before requiring, when their operations become overt, highly trained, armed bodies in uniform to operate and set an example to the local resistance.

SOE are the "white hunters" and produce the ground organization on which SAS operates. All senior officers of SOE with whom I have discussed this point agree to this principle.

5. *"SAS is not adaptable to all countries."* This has already been proved wrong. SAS is probably more adaptable to changes of theatres than any regular formation.

Also, as I have said in 4 above, SAS work on the ground organization of SOE. It is for SOE to be a world-wide organization with an organization in every likely country. Then when necessary, SAS can operate on this organization using their guides and intelligence knowledge, etc.

6. *"Volunteer units skim the regular units of their best officers and men."* Volunteer units such as SAS attract officers and men who have initiative, resourcefulness, independence of spirit, and confidence in themselves. In a regular unit there are far less opportunities of making use of these assets and, in fact, in many formations they are a liability, as this individualistic attitude upsets the smooth working of a team. This is especially true in European warfare where the individual must subordinate his natural initiative so that he fits into a part of the machine. Volunteer units such as the Commandos and Chindits (only a small proportion of the Chindits were volunteers although the spirit was there) have shown the rest of the army how to fight at a time when it was in low morale due to constant defeat. A few "gladiators" raise the standard of all. Analogies are racing (car, aeroplane, horse, etc.), and test teams.

7. *"Expense per man is greater than any other formation and is not worthwhile."* Men in units of this nature probably fight three or four times more often than regular units. They are always eager for a fight and therefore usually get it. If expense per man days actually in contact with the enemy was taken into account, there would be no doubt which was the more expensive type of formation. I have found, as you will have done, the "old familiar faces" on every front where we have seen trouble. I consider the expense is definitely worth it without even taking into account the extra results. One SAS raid in North Africa destroyed more aeroplanes in one day than the balloon barrage did during six years of war.

8. *"Any normal battalion could do the same job."* My experience

shows that they definitely cannot. In Norway in 1940, a platoon of marines under a sergeant ran away when left on its own, although they had orders to stay, when a few German lorries appeared. Mainly owing to the bad leadership of this parade-ground sergeant, they were all jittery and useless because they were "out of touch". A force consisting of two Gurkha Coys and a few British troops, of which I was one, was left behind in 1942 in Burma to attack the enemy in the rear if they appeared. The Commander, a good Gurkha officer with a good record, when confronted with a perfect opportunity (Japs landing in boats onto a wide sandy beach completely unaware of our presence), avoided action in order to get back to his Brigade because he was "out of touch" and could not receive orders. By avoiding action, the unit went into a waterless area and more perished this way and later by drowning than if he had attacked. My experience with regular battalions under my command in Burma was that there were only three or four officers in any battalion who could be relied on to take positive action if they were on their own, and had no detailed orders. This "I'll 'ave to ask me Dad" attitude of the British Army is its worst feature in my opinion. I found the RAF and dominion officers far better in this respect. I have not had experience with the cavalry. They should also be better. Perhaps cavalry could take on the SAS role successfully? I admit that with training both in Burma and North Africa there were definite improvements amongst the infantry, but in my opinion, no normal battalion I have seen could carry out an SAS role without 80% reorganization. I have written frankly and have laid myself open to obvious criticism, but I consider this such a vital point I do not mind how strongly I express myself. I have repeated this for five years and I have nowhere seen anything to change my views, least of all in Europe. I have mentioned some points above. You may not agree with my ideas but I write them down as these criticisms are the most normal ones I know. Other points in which the DTI wants to obtain information are:

1. *Obtaining of recruits.* Has anybody got the original brochure setting out the terms and standards required?
2. *Obtaining of stores and equipment.* Here again, I imagine SOE

has been the main source of special stores. My own HQ is producing a paper on this when in England.

3. *Signal communication.* This is of course one of the most important parts of such an organization and it has, as in other formations, limited the scope of our operation.

4. *Foreign recruits and attached civilians.*

5. *Liaison with RAF and Navy.*

6. *Command.* How is an organization of this sort best commanded and under whom should they be?

7. *Suggestions re. survival in peacetime including auxiliary formation, command, technical development, etc.* You may expect a communication from Lt Col Wigham. Please give your views quite candidly. They certainly need not agree with those I have written down. I am sending Lt Col Wigham a copy of this letter so that it may give you something to refer to if necessary. I hope, from the army point of view, and for all that you have worked for and believed in during the last few years, that you will do everything you can to help Lt Col Wigham to obtain all the information that he requires. We can no longer say that people do not understand if we do not take this chance to get our views put before an impartial tribunal whose task it is to review them in the light of general policy, and then make recommendations to the CIGS. Send along any reports or documents you have got. Lt Col Wigham is thirsting for information.

[Mike Calvert] Brigadier, Commander,
SAS Troops Sloe House, Halstead, Essex. 12 Oct 1945

Principal campaigns and missions

November 1941-January 1943: Raids on German and Italian airfield and installations in Western Desert.

February 1943-December 1943: 1 SAS renamed Special Raiding Squadron, and put under command of Lt-Col Paddy Mayne, transferred to Italy, along with 2 SAS (formed 1943).

June 1944: SAS units parachuted in France ahead of main invasion.

SAS Order of Battle for D-Day:

HQ SAS Brigade

1st SAS Regiment 2nd SAS Regiment

3rd (French) SAS Regiment 4th (French) SAS Regiment

5th (Belgian) SAS Regiment

1944-45: 1,2,3, 4, 5 SAS serve in, variously, France, Belgium, Holland, Italy and Germany.

October 1945: SAS Regiments disbanded; 3 and 4 SAS go to French Army; 5 SAS go to Belgian Army.

1949: 21 SAS Regiment (TA) (Artists), a Territorial unit raised in London.

1950: Major Jim Calvert raises the Malayan Scouts to fight Communists in Malaya.

1951: The Malayan Scouts and M Squadron 21 SAS combine to form 22 SAS.

1952-7: Malaya Campaign.

1958-9: 22 SAS serve in Oman.

1963-5: Borneo: 'Confrontation' with Indonesia.

1964-7: Aden (Radfan and port of Aden).

1970-98: SAS deployed in counter-terrorist role in Northern Ireland.

1970-76: Oman: Operation Storm (including Battle of Mirbat 19 July 1972).

1976-97: Northern Ireland: counter-terrorist operations.

1977: Mogadishu: Operation Fire-Magic (with German GSG-9).

1980: Prince's Gate, London: Operation Nimrod, Iranian Embassy hostage-rescue.

1981: Gambia: Restoration of President Jawara to power.

1982: Falklands Conflict (including Operation Paraquet to recapture South Georgia, and the Pebble Island Raid against Argentinian airbase in West Falkland.)

1987: Scotland: Peterhead prison siege.

1988: Gibraltar: Operation Flavius; SAS counter-terrorist team shoot and kill three IRA members.

1989: Colombia: anti-cocaine operation.

1990-1: Gulf War, including Operation Granby – behind-the-lines reconnaissance and sabotage – and Operation Victor, an assault on a Scud communications centre. General Schwarzkopf's assessment:

SUBJECT

Letter of Commendation for the 22d Special Air Service (SAS) Regiment.

1. I wish to officially commend the 22d Special Air Service (SAS) Regiment for their totally outstanding performance of military operations during Operation Desert Storm.

2. Shortly after the initiation of the strategic air campaign, it became apparent that the Coalition forces would be unable to eliminate Iraq's firing of Scud missiles from western Iraq into Israel. The continued firing of Scuds on Israel carried with it enormous unfavorable political ramifications and could, in fact, have resulted in the dismantling of the carefully crafted Coalition. Such a dismantling would have adversely affected in ways difficult to measure the ultimate outcome of the military campaign. It became apparent that the only way that the Coalition could succeed in reducing these Scud launches was by physically placing military forces on the ground in the vicinity of the western launch sites. At that time, the majority of available Coalition forces were committed to the forthcoming military campaign in the eastern portion of the theater of operations.

Further, none of these forces possessed the requisite skill and abilities required to conduct such a dangerous operation. The only force deemed qualified for this critical mission was the 22d Special Air Service (SAS) Regiment.

3. From the first day they were assigned their mission until the last day of the conflict, the performance of the 22d Special Air Service (SAS) Regiment was courageous and highly professional. The area in which they were committed proved to contain far more numerous enemy forces than had been predicted by every intelligence estimate, the terrain was much more difficult than expected and the weather conditions were unseasonably brutal. Despite these hazards, in a very short period of time the 22d Special Air Service (SAS) Regiment was successful in totally denying the central corridor of western Iraq to Iraqi Scud units. The result was that the principal areas used by the Iraqis to fire Scuds on Tel Aviv were no longer available to them. They were

required to move their Scud missile firing forces to the north-west portion of Iraq and from that location the firing of Scud missiles was essentially militarily ineffective.

4. When it became necessary to introduce United States Special Operations Forces into the area to attempt to close down the north-west Scud areas, the 22d Special Air Service (SAS) Regiment provided invaluable assistance to the US forces. They took every possible measure to ensure that US forces were thoroughly briefed and were able to profit from the valuable lessons that had been learned by earlier SAS deployments into Western Iraq. I am completely convinced that had US forces not received these thorough indoctrinations by SAS personnel US forces would have suffered a much higher rate of casualties than was ultimately the case. Further, the SAS and US joint forces the immediately merged into a combined fighting force where the synergetic effect of these fine units ultimately caused the enemy to be convinced that they were facing forces in Western Iraq that were more than tenfold the size of those they were actually facing. As a result, large numbers of enemy forces that might otherwise have been deployed in the eastern theater were tied down in western Iraq.

5. The performance of 22d Special Air Service (SAS) Regiment during Operation Desert Storm was in the highest traditions of the professional military service and in keeping with the proud history and tradition that has been established by that regiment. Please ensure that this commendation receives appropriate attention and is passed on to the unit and its members.

H. NORMAN SCHWARZKOPF
General, US Army Commander in Chief

1992-2004: Bosnia, as part of NATO intervention.

1993: Texas: the Waco siege.

2000: Sierra Leone, including Operation Barras, rescue of captured members of the Royal Irish Regiment.

2001-present: Afghanistan, including Operation Trent attack on Al-Qaeda opium plant, and attempt at Tora Bora to capture Bin Laden.

2003-present: Iraq, including joint 'black operations' with Delta Force (and others) as part of Task Force Black/Task Force Knight, reputed to have captured or killed 3,500 insurgents.

2011-present: Libya.

SBS (Special Boat Service)

Formed in 1942 from a marriage of SAS's D Squadron and the Commando Special Boat Sections, the SBS's main area of activity was the Aegean, but it also fought in the Mediterranean, Adriatic Sea and Atlantic (it was the SBS that made the legendary 1942 "Cockleshell Heroes" raid on Nazi-occupied Bordeaux). It was led by Major the Earl Jellicoe, an early member of David Stirling's 1 SAS.

The SBS was unorthodox in its dress (which consisted of any Allied uniform to hand), armament (the German MP38/40 was a favourite weapon) and parade-ground discipline. It was also pervaded by a very British sense of "dash", perfectly encapsulated in an incident where a junior officer, David Clark, landed on a German-occupied island, walked in to the officers' mess, and said, "It would be all so much easier if you would just raise your hands." Yet the appearance of casualness in the SBS was deceptive, and training for the unit at its specialist camp at Athlit in Palestine was gruelling, including many hours' instruction in the use of folboats and Greek caiques.

The Greek island of Simi, occupied by the Germans in 1941, was a favourite stomping-ground of the British Special Boat Squadron during the Second World War. The SBS raided Simi – even controlled it temporarily – on numerous occasions. As a result, the Wehrmacht was forced to strengthen the island's garrison with troops diverted from other fronts. It is estimated that as many as 181,000 German troops were tied down by the actions of the 250-strong SBS against Simi and the other Aegean islands. A memorable picture of the havoc the SBS wrought on Simi was left by SBS member John Lodwick, in his book *The Filibusters*:

The Simi operation had been considered for some time, but as long as the enemy possessed destroyers in the Aegean it had never looked practicable. Destroyers can interfere with landing operations, even at long range and at short notice. At the beginning of the year, there had been four destroyers in the Eastern Mediterranean. Only very gradually were they eliminated.

The German navy in those waters seldom put to sea. In March, one of these ships was damaged by a British submarine. Later, a second received a bomb amidships from a Beaufighter. Two remained lurking in Leros. In this emergency, Brigadier Turnbull requested London to send him out a small party of Royal Marine Boom Commando troops. A wise move, for though there were still many men in the SBS to whom folboating was second nature, the art of infiltration by canoe had undoubtedly declined since the days of "Tug" Wilson. Folboats, when used at all, were now used to land personnel, their role being no more aggressive than that of a gondola.

When Turnbull's marines first arrived in the Middle East the experts were inclined to scoff. Their attitude of condescension was abandoned when it was seen with what precision the newcomers handled their craft. In mid-June they went into Portolago Harbour, Leros, crossed two booms, sank the surviving destroyers with limpet charges and emerged without loss.

The way was now clear for Simi.

On 6 July Stewart Macbeth returned to base. He had made a personal reconnaissance of the island and pinpointed the enemy dispositions. Two days later the striking force, under Brigadier Turnbull himself, comprising ten motor launches, two schooners, 81 members of the SBS and 139 from the Greek Sacred Squadron, were concentrated in Penzik Bay, Turkey, under camouflage. Three parties were constituted: Main Force, under the Brigadier with Lapraik deputizing; West Force, under Captain Charles Clynes; and South Force, under Macbeth. On the night of 13 July the landings were made, and despite great enemy vigilance, passed everywhere unobserved. The only casualties suffered consisted of two Greek officers who fell into the water with heavy packs. They were drowned.

The approach marches were difficult, but all three forces were lying up and overlooking their targets before dawn. At first light a barrage was opened upon Simi Castle – the main Enemy stronghold – by mortars and multiple machine-guns. Two German "Ems" barges which had left harbour a few minutes before zero hour now came scuttling back. They had sighted the force of five British launches which was coming in to bombard the castle. Both motor launches and the SBS opened fire on these ships. Presently, large white flags could be seen waving from their bridges before they ran ashore and were captured in good working order.

"Stud" Stellin was clearing Molo Point. He had taken his first objective without opposition. Ahead of him, Germans were running up the hill to man their machine-gun posts. "I took a shot with my carbine," said "Stud", "but misfired. I therefore called upon Private Whalen to give them the works. We strolled in with grenades, and I think that everybody went a little mad. Soon, all the enemy were either down and dead, or up and waving their hands." Stellin locked these prisoners in a church, left a sentry outside it and moved on to his next objective.

Clynes, scheduled to attack gun positions, gave them three minutes softening from his Brens and then ordered his Greeks to charge. "All I can remember, then," he said, "is a general surge up the slope and two small and pathetic white handkerchiefs waving at the top of it. I ordered a 'Cease fire' all round, and began to count my prisoners."

By 0900 hours, Main Force Headquarters and the Vickers machine-gun and mortar troops had advanced to within 800 yards of the castle. Fire was intensified upon this target from all sides, mortar projectiles crashing on the battlements and nine-millimetre tracers searching every embrasure. The enemy reaction was spirited and indicated that they had by no means abandoned hope. Stellin, moving his patrol to clear some caique yards, received most of the attention. "The stuff started to whizz about. We had to cross a bridge. Somebody in the castle had a very accurate bead on that bridge. We doubled, but Lance-Corporal Roberts, Private Majury and Marine Kinghorn became pinned down under a low parapet, the slightest movement causing fire to be brought upon them. I told them to stay there . . ." They did.

They were not able to get up until the castle surrendered three hours later. Roberts, who attempted to while away the time by lighting a cigarette, raised his head an inch or two. He received a bullet graze from the temple to the neck.

Clynes had also been sent down to the caique yard with orders to clear it. On the way he met Lieutenant Betts-Gray, who throughout the action did excellent liaison work. Betts-Gray was hugging the rocks, pursued by a hail of fire. Clynes and his patrol were presently pinned down in their turn. Private Bromley was hit in the arm, and Betts-Gray, who had had miraculous escapes all day, in the buttocks once, and in the back twice, was assisted into a house and put to bed.

To the south, Macbeth and Bury, with their forces, had assaulted a monastery position after considerable mortar preparation. The surviving enemy were driven down a promontory towards the extremity of the island, where Macbeth called upon them to surrender. The first demand, written by Bob Bury, was rejected haughtily by the defenders as illegible. It was rewritten with the aid of a young Greek girl, who volunteered to carry it through the lines. This civilian armistice commission was successful and thirty-three more of the enemy laid down their arms.

Around the castle, the situation had developed into a stalemate, with mortar fire causing the garrison casualties and discomfort, but not sufficient in itself to bring about their surrender. Neither Brigadier Turnbull nor Lapraik considered that the position could be taken by direct assault. They decided to consolidate, make the maximum display of force at their disposal and institute surrender parleys. Accordingly, Brigadier Turnbull sent a German petty-officer, commanding one of the "Ems" barges, up under escort, with instructions to inform the enemy that they were completely surrounded, that the rest of the island was in British hands, and that further resistance on their part was as senseless as it was likely to prove costly.

The petty-officer returned an hour later. It appeared that the enemy were prepared to talk business. Lieutenant Kenneth Fox, a German speaker, now returned to the castle with the same man. A further hour elapsed during which the only incident was the emergence of a party of Italian carabinieri from the stronghold, weeping, and waving a Red Cross flag. "I thought I recognized one of these fellows," said Lapraik, "and sure enough it was the old rascal who had given us so much trouble during our previous occupation of Simi. He grew very pale when he saw me . . ."

Lieutenant-Commander Ramseyer, the naval liaison officer, was then sent up to expedite matters. He found Fox and the German Commander in agitated conference and himself in imminent danger from our mortar fire. At last, the capitulation was arranged and the garrison marched out. They had barely been collected and counted when three Messerschmitts flew over the port and dropped anti-personnel bombs.

"Too bad", the German Commander is reported to have said, shaking his head. "You see, that's what comes of being late. I thought they had forgotten about us. I radioed for them five hours ago." Prisoners taken in this action totalled 151, of whom seventeen were wounded. Twenty-one Germans and Italians had been killed. The SBS and Sacred Squadron losses were as usual microscopic, and, apart from the two Greek officers drowned, not a single man was killed. Six were wounded.

As soon as the Messerchmitts had disappeared, tea was taken by both armies in the caique yards. Sausages were fried and an ox, provided by the delighted population, roasted on a bowsprit. As for the prisoners, they were so delighted to find themselves treated deferentially instead of being shot out of hand, that they revealed the existence of many a cache of wine in their living-quarters. Bottles were transferred to the SBS packs, to be drunk at base.

Meanwhile, Lapraik, Macbeth, and Stellin, well known on the island, were borne to the town hall, where many speeches were made. The town jail was thrown open to the accompaniment of a furore which would have done credit to the storming of the Bastille. Unfortunately, only one prisoner was found inside and he, a Fascist, refused to be liberated.

"I admired these islanders," said Lapraik, "intensely; for they well knew that we could not remain and were rightly apprehensive of reprisals. But this did not diminish in any way their enthusiasm, though they were aware that hostile eyes were watching them, recording every incident. In the end, we caused them immense relief by taking the fifteen foremost quislings away with us."

General demolitions were begun by Bill Cumper and installations as varied as 75 mm gun emplacements, diesel fuel pumps and cable-heads, received generous charges. Ammunition and explosive dumps provided fireworks to suit the occasion. In the harbour, nineteen German caiques, some displacing as much as 150 tons, were sunk. At midnight the whole force sailed, the prisoners being crowded into the two "Ems" barges. Stellin, with his patrol and Captain Pyke, Civil Affairs Officer, remained behind as rear party, with instructions to report subsequent events on Simi, and to distribute nearly thirty tons of food which had been brought in for the relief of the civilian population.

The German reaction was as expected, and followed the traditional pattern of attempted intimidation preceding assault. On the following morning the town was heavily bombed. Stellin and his men sat tight in their slit trenches. When it was all over they emerged to find, as they had hoped, that two enemy motor launches were attempting to enter the harbour. Such accurate fire was opened on these ships that they withdrew, blazing. So did Stellin, whose keen ear had detected the approach of more bombers, and who knew that this was the prelude to re-occupation of the island. At three o'clock, from one of the more remote mountains, he watched the German flag hoisted over the citadel. But Stellin's adventures were not yet over; that night the launch re-embarking his party encountered an "E" boat on the return journey. So many and so various were Stellin's store of captured weapons that every man in his patrol was able to take a personal hand in the battle with a machine-gun. The "E" boat was left in a sinking condition.

The SBS – the inspiration for Alistair Maclean's novel, *The Guns of Navarone* – was disbanded in 1945, though elements were brought together under "Blondie" Hasler almost immediately at Fremington, Devon, as the School of Combined Operations, Beach and Boat Section (SCOBBS), which came under the control of the Royal Marines, who renamed SCOBBS the Special Boat Squadron. The SBS was among the first British units in action in the Korean War, attacking supply lines and communications. Despite being a maritime special force, the SBS has constantly been deployed in land warfare, from Borneo to Afghanistan. In 1987 the SBS was renamed Special Boat Service, and taken under the control of the UK Special Forces (along with the SAS, and 14th Intelligence Detachment) in the same year, the SBS formed M Squadron as a dedicated maritime counter-terrorist force.

The SBS, based at Poole in Dorset, is organised into four regular squadrons: C, X, M & Z; a reserve element augments the regulars.

Campaigns

1950-1: Korea.

1964-71: Borneo.

1972: Members of SBS (alongside SAS sergeant and bomb-disposal expert) parachute into Atlantic to board the cruise liner *QE2*, the subject of a bomb threat.

1970s: SBS deployed to Northern Ireland, mostly for covert surveillance.

1982: Falklands Conflict: among other actions, SBS leads re-taking of South Georgia and clearing on Fanning Head on Falklands.

1991: Operation Desert Storm: reconnaissance and sabotage missions in Kuwait and Iraq. In recognition of the SBS's efforts in the Gulf, the Regiment was sent a Letter of Commendation by the Commander-in-Chief, General H. Norman Schwarzkopf.

1999: SBS detachment sent to East Timor as part of UN peace-keeping mission.

2000: SBS troopers join SAS and Paras in Operation Barras, the rescue of British servicemen held hostage by the West Side Boys in Sierra Leone.

2001-present: Afghanistan: among other early actions SBS puts down rising at the ancient fort of Qala-i-Jangi; from 2006 the SBS was the primary UK Special Forces unit in theatre, and tasked with removing Taliban leaders.

2002-present: Counter-narcotics operations in the Caribbean.

2003-present: Iraq: at the commencement of the invasion SBS troops joined up with the US Navy Seals in diversionary raids on Al Faw Peninsula and the securing of the southern oil fields.

2009: SBS rescue British journalist from Taliban near Kunduz, Afghanistan.

2011: SBS evacuate British workers from Libya.

2012: In March a joint SBS-Nigerian force attempts to rescue two Western hostages from radical Islamic kidnappers in the Nigerian city of Sokoto. Both hostages, a British and Italian citizen, were killed by their captors during the operation.

UNITED STATES

US Navy SEALS
See p48.

US Naval Special Warfare Command is organized into the following configuration:

- Naval Special Warfare Group 1: SEAL Teams 1, 3, 5, 7
- Naval Special Warfare Group 2: SEAL Teams 2, 4, 8, 10
- Naval Special Warfare Group 3: SEAL Delivery Vehicle Team 1
- Naval Special Warfare Group 4: Special Boat Teams 12, 20, 22
- Naval Special Warfare Group 11: SEAL Teams 17, 18 (formerly *Operational Support Teams* 1, 2)

The total number of Navy SEALs assigned to Naval Special Warfare Command is approximately 2,000. About half of the SEALs are based at Little Creek Naval Amphibious Base and Dam Neck annex in Virginia (East Coast), and half at Naval Amphibious Base Coronado, California (West Coast). The Seal Delivery Vehicle (SDV) unit is based at Pearl Harbor, Hawaii.

Each SEAL Team is commanded by a Navy Commander. A SEAL Team has a Staff Headquarters element and three 40-man Troops. Each Troop consist of a Headquarters element consisting of a Troop Commander, typically a Lieutenant Commander. Each Troop can be task-organized for operational purposes into four squads, of eight 4–5-man fire teams.

The SEAL insignia is a winged trident, crossed with a rifle and anchor. The SEAL code reads:

Loyalty to country, team and team-mates. Serve with honor and integrity on and off the battlefield. Ready to lead. Ready to follow. Never quit. Take responsibility for your actions and the actions of your team-mates. Excel as warriors through discipline and innovation. Train for war. Fight to win. Defeat our nation's enemies. Earn your Trident every day.

The SEALs also have a Creed:

In times of war or uncertainty there is a special breed of warrior ready to answer our Nation's call. A common man with uncommon desire to succeed. Forged by adversity, he stands alongside America's finest special operations forces to serve his country, the American people, and protect their way of life. I am that man.

My Trident is a symbol of honor and heritage. Bestowed upon me by the heroes that have gone before, it embodies the trust of those I have sworn to protect. By wearing the Trident I accept the responsibility of my chosen profession and way of life. It is a privilege that I must earn every day.

My loyalty to Country and Team is beyond reproach. I humbly serve as a guardian to my fellow Americans, always ready to defend those who are unable to defend themselves. I do not advertise the nature of my work, nor seek recognition for my actions. I voluntarily accept the inherent hazards of my profession, placing the welfare and security of others before my own.

I serve with honor on and off the battlefield. The ability to control my emotions and my actions, regardless of circumstance, sets me apart from other men. Uncompromising integrity is my standard. My character and honor are steadfast. My word is my bond.

We expect to lead and be led. In the absence of orders I will take charge, lead my team-mates and accomplish the mission. I lead by example in all situations.

I will never quit. I persevere and thrive on adversity. My Nation expects me to be physically harder and mentally stronger than my enemies. If knocked down, I will get back up, every time. I will draw on every remaining ounce of strength to protect my team-mates and to accomplish our mission. I am never out of the fight.

We demand discipline. We expect innovation. The lives of my team-mates and the success of our mission depend on me – my technical skill, tactical proficiency, and attention to detail. My training is never complete.

We train for war and fight to win. I stand ready to bring the full spectrum of combat power to bear in order to achieve my mission and the goals established by my country. The execution of my duties will be swift and violent when required, yet guided by the very principles that I serve to defend.

Brave men have fought and died building the proud tradition and feared reputation that I am bound to uphold. In the worst of conditions, the legacy of my team-mates steadies my resolve and silently guides my every deed. I will not fail.

US Special Forces (Green Berets)

Formed in 1952, based at Smoke Bomb Hill, Fort Wragg, North Carolina. By 1958 the basic operational unit of Special Forces had become a twelve-man A-detachment or A-Team, comprising two officers, two operations and intelligence sergeants, two communications sergeants, two weapons sergeants, two engineers and two medics. Each detachment can also operate as two six-man teams, or 'split A-Teams'. Support is from a B-team, usually comprising of eleven men.

In honour of John F. Kennedy, who gave the Special Forces their post-Second World War lease of life, the Special Forces' psychological warfare training centre at Fort Wragg was named the John F Kennedy Special Warfare Center and School. In 1983 the Army authorized a Special Forces uniform tab showing a dagger crossed by three lightning flashes on the left shoulder. Due to the continued expansion of the Special Forces (current strength is upwards of 4,500 men), the seven Groups have HQs around the USA, each with a designated sphere of the world to watch over. The Green Berets operate under the auspices of the

Army Special Operations Command, which itself comes under the control of the United States Special Operations Command.

The Special Forces Creed is:

I am an American Special Forces soldier. A professional!

I will do all that my nation requires of me.

I am a volunteer, knowing well the hazards of my profession.

I serve with the memory of those who have gone before me: Roger's Rangers, Francis Marion, Mosby's Rangers, the first Special Service Forces and Ranger Battalions of World War II, the Airborne Ranger Companies of Korea.

I pledge to uphold the honor and integrity of all I am – in all I do.

I am a professional soldier.

I will teach and fight wherever my nation requires.

I will strive always, to excel in every art and artifice of war.

I know that I will be called upon to perform tasks in isolation, far from familiar faces and voices, with the help and guidance of my God.

I will keep my mind and body clean, alert and strong, for this is my debt to those who depend upon me.

I will not fail those with whom I serve.

I will not bring shame upon myself or the forces.

I will maintain myself, my arms, and my equipment in an immaculate state as befits a Special Forces soldier.

I will never surrender though I be the last.

If I am taken, I pray that I may have the strength to spit upon my enemy.

My goal is to succeed in any mission – and live to succeed again.

I am a member of my nation's chosen soldiery.

God grant that I may not be found wanting, that I will not fail this sacred trust.

"De Oppresso Liber"

Delta Force

Surprisingly, the Unites States of America was slow to establish a specialist anti-terrorist and hostage rescue unit, although all too often it is Americans who are the victims of attacks. It was not until November 1977 that the US Army's 1st Special Forces Operational Detachment Delta – Delta Force – came into being. The driving spirit behind Delta Force was Colonel Charles Beckwith, a Special Forces officer who had been extremely impressed by Britain's SAS during an exchange tour in 1962-3. For several years he badgered the Pentagon into setting up a similar unit in the US Army. Selection for the new unit was very much SAS-style, with hard physical, mental and psychological challenges weeding out nine out of ten applicants. Once selected, the successful candidate is sent on a five-month "Operators" course, where he is introduced to the many and varied skills that an anti-terrorist commando is expected to master. These include assault tactics, hostage management, communications, observation using the latest high-tech gear, climbing, small boat work and parachuting. Since the majority of Delta Force candidates are from Special Forces or Ranger units (about 70% from Ranger units in fact), they already possess many of these skills, but even so, they learn a lot before moving to their operational troop.

Delta Force is organised into operational squadrons; each squadron is broken down further into troops; the troops into four- or five-man teams. There is also a signals squadron and an aviation platoon, which operates AH-6 and MH-6 Little Bird helicopters. Delta's in-house intelligence section, unusually for a Special Forces unit, employs women. The overall strength of Delta Force, which is based at Fort Bragg, North Carolina, is around 2,500.

Marksmanship is a prime requirement in Delta Force, and Force members train up to four hours a day, five days a week. Such intensive training leads to very high shooting standards: Delta snipers are expected to make nine first-round hits out of ten at 1,000 yards, and score every time at 600 yards.

Like other elite counter-terrorist units, Delta Force has built its own Close Quarters Battle training facility (nicknamed "House of Horrors"), which simulates various kinds of combat situations, from hostage-taking to aircraft hijacks.

Just over a year after its foundation, the Force was alerted to a possible rescue mission as the US Embassy in Teheran was seized and the embassy staff held hostage. This was far from the mission they had trained for: penetrate hundreds of miles into hostile territory, making an assault in the middle of a major city and then get clear with 100 or more freed hostages.

Months of intensive training went into Operation Eagle Claw, as the rescue mission was called. It was to involve Delta Force (who are, after all, the US Army's "door-busters"), Special Forces units from Germany, US Marine Corps helicopter pilots, US Navy helicopters and ships and US Air Force air support.

The mission was a disaster, although through no real fault of the men who took part. The rescue plan developed was highly complicated: in phase one of the operation, the assault force was to fly to Masirah airfield in Oman in Lockheed C-141 Starlifters of the USAF. At Masirah they were to trans-ship to three MC-130E Hercules flown by USAF Special Operations Squadron crew, which would take them below radar level across the Gulf of Oman and land them at a remote spot in the Dasht-e Kavir salt desert in southern Iran. This landing site, codenamed "Desert One", was located some 300 miles south-east of Tehran. Thirty minutes after the Hercules landed at Desert One, the eight Sea Stallions were to land at the site. The Sea Stallions were minesweeping versions of the HH-53, selected because of their range and carrying capacity. The Sea Stallions were to be flown by USMC crews from the *Nimitz* in the Indian Ocean to Desert One, where they would refuel from EC-130E Hercules on the makeshift landing strip.

Major-General James Vaught, located at Wadi Qena airfield in Egypt, was in overall command of the rescue mission; Colonel Beckwith was commander of the rescue forces on the ground. Since Desert One was near a road, a twelve-man road-watch team, comprised of Delta men and Rangers, was included in the main party. In addition to the road-watch team, this comprised a thirteen-man Green Beret "A" Team tasked to assault the Foreign Ministry, and three Delta "elements": Blue Element (40 men) was

to secure the eastern sector of the Embassy compound; Red
Element (40 men) the western end; and White Element (13 men)
Roosevelt Avenue. After refuelling at Desert One, the eight Sea
Stallions were to fly the assault force to a forward landing-zone,
where the men would be dropped off; the Sea Stallions would then
hide in a wadi 14 miles to the north. Four Department of Defense
agents, already infiltrated into Tehran, would meet the assault
force's drivers and collect six Mercedes Benz trucks, which would
be used to ferry the assault force to their destinations.

At 8.30 p.m. the assault team would board the Merc trucks
and drive into Tehran. The rescue was timed to start at 11 p.m.
After "negotiating" the Embassy guards, the Delta elements were
to release the hostages and, if possible, clear the poles the students
had erected as anti-landing devices so the helicopters could come
in. If this was not possible, the Delta boys were to take the hostages
to a nearby football stadium, where the helicopters would pick
them up. Simultaneous with the Delta assault, the Green Beret
"A" Team was to storm the Foreign Ministry, grab the three
hostages, and take them to a nearby car park for "exfil" (extraction). Meanwhile, a Ranger company was to capture Manzariyeh
airfield 34 miles south of Tehran, where C-141s would fly in and
collect the assault force and hostages, who had all been flown
there from central Tehran by the indispensable Sea Stallions.

Such was the plan. And for a few tantalizing moments it
worked beautifully. At 10 p.m., right on schedule, the first
MC-130 landed at Desert One. The road watch team unloaded
and deployed – Colonel Beckwith de-planed with them, and
enjoyed some breaths of cool night air after the fug in the interior
of the Starlifter. Moments later, a bus came rolling along the
highway, right into the perimeter of Desert One. After shooting
the bus's tyres, the road-watch team herded the forty-five frightened passengers off and put them under guard. Only moments
later, to the dismay of the road-watch team, more vehicle lights
appeared through the darkness on what was meant to be a quiet
desert track. This time it was a petrol tanker. The road-watch
team launched an M72 Light Anti-tank Weapon, which set the
tanker alight. The driver leaped out, jumped into the cab of a
pick-up behind, and went off into the night. The flames from the

tanker reached 300 feet into the air. In this eerie hellish glare the assault force waited for the Sea Stallions. And waited, and waited.

Although the eight Sea Stallions took off at 7.30 p.m. local time, as scheduled from *Nimitz*, two hours into the 600-mile flight Number 6 had had to land due to "catastrophic blade failure". The crew burned any sensitive documents, and were picked by heli Number 8. Nearly an hour later the lead RH-53Ds flew into a sandstorm, with the pilots having to fly on instruments. Emerging from the whirling storm of dust, the pilots breathed a sigh of relief to see stars in a clear sky. The respite was brief: the Sea Stallions then flew into another, more violent dust storm, within the hour. Helicopter 5 then had a catastrophic electrical failure, lost use of its navigation and flight instruments, and was forced to return to the *Nimitz*. This left just six helicopters flying, the absolute minimum needed for the main phase of the rescue missions. Helicopter Number 3 was the first to clear the sandstorms, arriving at Desert One fifty minutes late. On getting out of the heli, the pilot, Major James Schaefer, told the waiting Beckwith, "It's been hell of a trip". Over the next thirty minutes, the remaining helicopters straggled in, their pilots to a man exhausted from battling the elements. The schedule was now eighty-five minutes over time. As the helicopters refuelled from the EC-130Es, Beckwith directed the emplaning of the assault force. Despite being behind time and down to six helicopters, the mission was still viable. Just.

Then came the mortal blow; it was discovered that helicopter Number 2 had hydraulic problems and needed to be counted out. The mission now had less than the minimum necessary number of helicopters. Colonel Beckwith was left with Hobson's choice: abort, and accept failure; or, try for success at impossible odds. The overall mission commander, General Vaught, was asked for his opinion over the sat comm. Vaught asked Beckwith "to consider going on with five". For agonising minutes Beckwith tussled over whether to go ahead, or go back. Then he announced, "Delta's going home". By radio link the President of the US, Jimmy Carter, concurred in the decision that the mission could not continue, and preparations began for withdrawal of the five operational helicopters, the C-130s, and the rescue force. Wearily the assault force got out of the choppers, and began loading onto the C-130s. It was nearly 2.40 a.m.

Something had to be done about the helicopters. Major Seiffert, the commander of the helicopter force, decided they would try to fly back to the *Nimitz*. Helicopter Number 4, however, had to refuel, since it had been on the ground longest, with engines idling. This meant that one of the Sea Stallions, Bluebeard 3, had to be moved from directly behind the required EC-130 to clear a space. Bluebeard 3 took off and banked to the left; due to the dust churned up by the rotor, the pilot was unable to see properly and struck the EC-130's vertical stabilizer with its main rotor, causing it to crash into the tanker aircraft. Both planes exploded, blasting debris in all directions. Ordinance on board the helicopter started popping, and Redeye missiles began "pinwheeling through the night like it was the Fourth of July". Eight members of the mission died in the explosion and subsequent fire: five USAF aircrew in the EC-130 (Major Richard L. Bakke, Navigator; Major Harold L Lewis Jr., Pilot & Aircraft Commander; TSgt Joel C. Mayo, Flight Engineer; Major Lyn D. McIntosh, Co-Pilot; and Captain Charles T. McMillan, Navigator); and three USMC in the Sea Stallion (TSgt John D. Harvey, Cpl George N. Holmes Jr., and SSgt Dewey L Johnson).

Somehow, the sixty-four Delta men in the C-130 managed to get out of the burning aircraft, rescuing its loadmaster in the process. With the heat from the burning C-130 and Bluebeard 3 about to set a chopper nearby alight, it was decided to abandon the Sea Stallions, others of which had been struck by shrapnel from the explosion or burning ammunition. The Marine helicopter pilots scrambled aboard the C-130s. In the haste to emplane, not all the helicopters were "sanitized", leaving the Iranians a gift of a cache of classified information, plus two working choppers. What began as a Special Forces mission became first a tragedy, then a farce. At almost 3 a.m., after being on the ground for four hours and fifty-six minutes, Delta left the desert.

The command and control of the many disparate parts of the rescue operation were shambolic. The big MH-53 helicopters could not cope with the desert sand, and there were not enough of them. After three had broken down the mission had to be scrubbed. To add a final capper to the whole affair, a collision at the "Desert One" airstrip deep inside Iran killed eight men and destroyed a C-130 and a helicopter.

Many lessons were learned from Operation Eagle Claw. The creation of the Joint Special Operations Command has given a single command body to clandestine operation units of all US services, and the formation of the Counter-Terrorist Joint Task Force (CTJTF) at Fort Bragg has significantly increased US capability in this specialised form of warfare.

Delta had much happier hunting in the second Gulf War, as part of Task Force, an Allied outfit comprising elements from Delta, US Navy DEVGRU, US Navy SEAL Team Three, and the 75th Ranger Regiment. The Force was approximately 1,500 strong. At the end of June 2003, an Iraqi building contractor told the 101st Airborne Division in Mosul that Saddam's sons Uday and Qusay were holed up in one of his houses in Baghdad's Falah district. With a $15 million bounty on the heads of HVTs One, Two and Three, such "tip-offs" were running at a dozen a day. So for three weeks Uday and Qusay remained in the house untroubled, with their feet up. Finally the information was relayed to Task Force (TF) 20, who investigated and decided that the intel was "hot".

On 22 July a TF 20 assault team was assembled and a cordon placed around the building by the 2nd Brigade of the 101st. An interpreter with a bullhorn shouted out to the two men to surrender. Their reply was a barrage of machine-gun fire. Using C-4 explosives, TF 20 operators stormed through the iron front gate into the walled compound. From there, some operators began clearing the first floor, while others climbed the back stairs. As TF 20's assault team began working its way into the building it came under fire from positions behind reinforced concrete on the first and second floors. They retired outside into the street where grenades were dropped on them, injuring three Special Forces operators and one of the paratroopers. An almighty firefight started up, with the 2nd Brigade pouring in covering fire from vehicle-mounted fifty-calibre machine-guns as TF 20 again tried to penetrate the building. However, return fire from the building kept them at bay. The TF operators discovered that the defenders had a strong position at the head of the stairs making any internal assault calamitous.

Colonel Joe Anderson, the CO of 2nd Brigade, decided that heavy weapons were called for, and ordered a strike on the building by Kiowa Warrior helicopters, which fired four 2.75-inch rockets at the target. While these missed, the bullets from the choppers' belt-fed .50-calibre machine-guns did not and shot up the building. Again, TF 20 attempted to assault the building, and again was repelled by small arms fire. At this, Colonel Anderson decided on his own mini-me version of "shock and awe", and ordered that Tube-launched Optically-tracked Wire-guided (TOW) missiles be fired at the house. Eighteen of them. Colonel Anderson later declared that his goal was "a combination of shocking them if they were still alive and damaging the building structurally so that it was unfeasible to fight in".

On finally entering the building, the operators from TF 20 found four bodies – three men and a fourteen-year-old boy. Two of the men were identified by their DNA and dental records as Uday and Qusay. The boy was Qusay's son. While the killing of Uday and Qusay Hussein demonstrated America's resolve in Iraq and removed two key figures around which insurgents might rally, it also destroyed a crucial lead to Number One HVT. The dead bodies of Uday and Qusay could hardly be interrogated as to their father's whereabouts.

The trail seemed to go cold. In the back rooms of Intelligence units, however, people were starting to have bright ideas. Hitherto, the main mindset was fixed on searching for Saddam and the other leading Ba'athists around the capital, Baghdad. Yet the Ba'ath regime had been a modern "Arab Socialist" crust on an old tribal society. Therefore, the best way of getting to Saddam was to piece together the network of tribal loyalties in the Tikrit area. Saddam's birthplace was in the village of Owja near the town of Tikrit, beside the Tigris, north-west of Baghdad. The area around Tikrit was where Saddam had his extended family, and where his tribe was based. Such was the Tikriti domination of Iraq that Saddam abolished the use of surnames to conceal the fact that so many of his key supporters bore the same surname – al-Tikriti – as did Saddam himself. He had hidden around Tikrit once before, in 1959, when on the run. Perhaps he had gone to ground there again? In which case, the focus of the piecing-to-gether of the tribal network should be Tikrit.

The US 4th Infantry Division, commanded by Colonel Hickey, took over the area around Tikrit, and almost immediately the Intelligence officer (S-2) of the 1st Brigade's Combat Team, Major Stan Murphy, begin developing an extended link diagram of the network of tribal figures who held any kind of position under Saddam, especially the men and boys who were his "enablers" – the yes men and the errand boys. Major Murphy's intel was fed to Task Force 20, which was renamed in July Task Force 121. "Hits" on suspected insurgents gradually brought more and more vital information. A raid on the farm of one of Saddam's bodyguards near Tikrit turned up jewellery worth $2 million belonging to Saddam's wife, Sajida Khairallah Talfah, and $8 million in US currency secreted away in two fireproof bank boxes. Better still, First Lieutenant Chris Morris's 1-22 platoon found the Saddam family photograph album. Captain Mark Stouffer's A Company, 1-22, captured one of Saddam's body-guards. A joint Task Force 121–1st Brigade raid on 16 June captured Abid Hamid Al-Tikriti (HVT Four).

Between July and December 2003 Task Force 121 made twelve unsuccessful raids to capture Saddam, together with 600 other operations against targets on the linked diagram. More than 300 interrogations were conducted. Again and again, the intel led to five extended families based in Tikrit. An important break came on 1 December, when a former driver divulged the name of Mohamed Ibrahim Omar al-Musslit. Ibrahim was Saddam's right-hand man, known to Task Force 121 as "the Source" or "the Fatman". Ibrahim was a regular face in the Saddam family photo album. Over the next two weeks nearly forty members of Ibrahim's family were interrogated in an attempt to track him down.

The turning-point came on 12 December 2003. During a raid on a house in Baghdad that functioned as an insurgency HQ, the Fatman was picked up and interrogated by Staff Sergeant Eric Maddox. By now it was 5 a.m. on 13 December, and Maddox was scheduled to leave Iraq at 8 a.m. on a C-17 for Doha. Just when Maddox was about to abandon hope, Ibrahim grudgingly gave up a location where Saddam might be found. On this intel, a 600-strong raiding force was assembled from 1st Brigade, Fourth Infantry Division. The raiding force, led by Colonel James Hickey, would isolate and secure the area. After this, Task Force 121 would go in and get Saddam. At precisely 8 p.m. on 13 December two sites, "Wolverine 1" and "Wolverine 2", outside the town of Ad-Dawr, were searched and cleared within minutes. There was no trace of Saddam. The searchers from Task Force 121 then moved in on a mud hut in a palm grove just to the north of Wolverine 1. Lieutenant-Colonel Steve Russell was the Commanding Officer of the 1st Battalion, 22nd Infantry of the 1st Brigade. He takes up the story:

Through their night vision goggles and thermal sights, soldiers of the 4th ID could see Special Operators moving soundlessly through the dark night to the target. Occasionally, the red beams of laser-aiming lights would reflect off trees and leaves, but it was deathly silent, save for the distant hum of OH-58 Little Birds and other Special Operations aircraft waiting for extraction, reinforcement, or attack. From his position, Saffeels could hear noises in the darkness. He and his fellow soldiers grew "a little jumpy", waiting for Saddam's forces. For Bocanegra the scene and all the activity became more intense. The assault force started clearing through the palm groves and came upon a little mud-hut structure with a courtyard. In that courtyard they heard a noise.

At 2010, with Hickey's troops sealing off the area, Special Operations forces burst into the hut, a simple construction behind a fence of dried palm leaves. It had been an orange picker's hut with one room and an open kitchen. They immediately seized one man trying to escape and another man in the hut. As it turned out, one was Saddam's cook; the other was the cook's brother and owner of the property. Inside, they found that the hut consisted of one room with two beds and a refrigerator containing a can of lemonade, a packet of hot dogs, a can of "Happy Brand" tuna, an opened box of Belgian chocolates, and a tube of ointment. A poster of Noah's Ark hung on the mud-brick wall. There were also two AK-47 assault rifles, various packages of new clothes, and a green footlocker containing $750,000 in American hundred-dollar bills. More telling: an orange and white Toyota Corolla taxi was parked outside. Rumors that Saddam had hidden in taxis and even masqueraded as a taxi driver appeared to be true.

Saddam was nowhere to be seen. It looked like yet another dry hole when, suddenly, one of the detainees broke away from the Special Operators and ran, telling them Saddam was hiding elsewhere and he would lead them to him. His sudden desire to co-operate and zeal to get them out of there further convinced the operators they were close. At the command vehicle, CW2 Gray stood next to Colonel Hickey, listening to the radio reports from the Special Operation forces. Those two individuals were exactly who the source stated would be at the farm. Things were going well. Reports continued to come in that Special Operations forces were still searching the area but had not found the tunnels that the source had said Saddam would be hiding in. Hickey calmly told them to take their time. Task Force Raider owned that portion of Iraq. He'd hold the cordon all night if necessary.

Another ten minutes went by. Still nothing. Outside the hut, the two dozen or so Special Operators were preparing to move off and expand their search. Something caught an operator's attention in the darkness of the moonless night, through the unearthly glow of his night-vision goggles. The ground just didn't look quite right. The sensation of an odd landscape was nothing unusual under the glow of a night-vision device, but it just didn't feel right, either. The closer the operator looked, the more it appeared to be out of place. The bricks and dirt were spread about too uniformly, as if someone were trying to conceal something. A thread of fabric protruded just slightly under the dirt. Strange.

At 2030 hours, the operators brushed away the debris, revealing a Styrofoam plug. True to his training, one of the Special Operators pulled the pin on a hand grenade while his colleagues prepared to remove the plug so he could drop it in. The remaining twenty or so soldiers prepared to fire their weapons, if engaged. The plug revealed a hole; the hole revealed a ratty-looking bearded man. The man raised his hands and announced: "I am Saddam Hussein. I am the President of Iraq, and I am willing to negotiate." The Task Force 121 commando covering the hole calmly replied: "President Bush sends his regards." Hickey's radio broke the silence as the Special Operator reported simply, "Sir, we may have the jackpot."

Hickey waited breathlessly. Back on the objective, several Special Operators yanked the dishevelled, disoriented man to the surface, unavoidably scratching his head in the tight confines of the hole. The operators quickly removed the 9mm pistol from his belt and checked him for the markings and other features that would preliminarily confirm they had their man. They began to prepare him for transportation with the standard, empty sandbag over his head and flex-cuffs on his hands. As they attempted to secure him, Saddam resisted – trying to shrug off the operators, acting belligerent, and even spitting in one soldier's face. In return, he was treated "just like any other prisoner", and forcefully subdued to the ground, where several operators held him down while others trussed him up.

Following his capture, Saddam was taken to the American base Camp Cropper near Baghdad. On 30 June 2004 Saddam was handed over to the interim Iraqi government to stand trial for crimes against humanity. The trial found Saddam Hussein guilty, and he was sentenced to death. Although the verdict and sentencing were both appealed, they were affirmed by Iraq's Supreme Court of Appeals. On 30 December 2006, Saddam was hanged.

Delta Force's structure is similar to the British 22 SAS, with 'Sabre Squadrons' containing around 80 "operators". Each sabre squadron is further broken down into three troops, two assault troops, and one sniper/recon troop. Based at Fort Bragg, Delta Force is thought to number around 800 personnel.

Major operations and missions

1977:	Operation Eagle Claw (Iran hostage crisis).
1983:	Invasion of Grenada.
1989:	Panama invasion.

1990-1:   Gulf War.
1993:   Battle of Mogadishu (Somalia).
2001-present: Afghanistan.
2001-present: Iraq.

SOURCES AND ACKNOWLEDGEMENTS

Bob Bennett, quoted in *SAS at War*, Anthony Kemp, Penguin, 2000. Copyright © 2000 Anthony Kemp

J. M. Calvert, quoted in A *History of the SAS Regiment*, J. Strawson, Secker & Warburg, 1985. Copyright © 1985 J. Strawson

Johnny Cooper, *One of the Originals: The Story of a Founder Member of the SAS*, Pan Books Ltd, 1991. Copyright © 1991 J. Murdoch Cooper

Peter de la Billière, *Looking for Trouble*, HarperCollins, 1995. Copyright © 1995 Peter de la Billière

Muki Betser (with R. Rosenberg), *Secret Soldier*, Simon & Schuster, 1996. Copyright © 1996 Muki Betser

Barry Davies, *Assault on LH181*, Bloomsbury, 1994. Copyright © 1994 Barry Davies

David Lloyd Owen, Imperial War Museum Sound Archive

John Lodwick, *The Filibusters*, Methuen, 1947. Copyright © 1947 John Lodwick

C. L. 'Dare' Newell, quoted in *History of the SAS Regiment*, J. Strawson, Secker & Warburg, 1985. Copyright © 1985 J. Strawson.

Steve Russell, *We Got Him!*, Pocket Books, 2012. Copyright © 2012 Steve Russell

David Stirling, quoted in *The Phantom Major*, by Virginia Cowles, Collins, 1958. Copyright © 1958 Virginia Cowles

Ron Yaw, quoted in *Seals*, T. L. Bosiljevac, Presidio Press, 1990. Copyright © 1990 T. L. Bosiljevac

BIBLIOGRAPHY

Baker, W.D., *Dare to Win: The Story of the New Zealand Special Air Service*, 1978

Beckwith, Charlie, *Delta Force*, 1984

Billière, General Sir Peter de la, *Looking for Trouble*, 1994

Bosiljevac, T.L., *SEALS*, 1990

Cole, Barbara, *Elite: The Story of the Rhodesian SAS*, 1984

Collins, John M., *Green Berets, SEALs & Spetsnaz*, 1987

Cowles, Virginia, *Phantom Major*, 1958

Crossland, Peter 'Yorky', *Victor Two*, 1996

Darman, Peter, *A-Z of the SAS*, 1992

Dickens, Peter, *SAS: The Jungle Frontier*, 1983

Farran, Roy, *Winged Dagger*, 1948

Operation Tombola, 1960

Flower, Ken, *Serving Secretly; Rhodesia into Zimbabwe 1964-1981*, 1987

Fowler, Will, *Weapons and Equipment of Special Forces*, 1996

Geraghty, Tony, *Who Dares Wins*, 1992

Harrison, Derrick, *These Men are Dangerous*, 1957

Hislop, J.H., *Anything But a Soldier*, 1965

Hoe, Alan, *David Stirling*, 1992

Horner, DM, *SAS Phantoms of the Jungle: A History of the Australian SAS*, 1989

Jeapes, Tony, *SAS Operation Oman*, 1980

Ladd, James, *Commandos and Rangers of World War II*, 1978

Lodwick, John, *The Filibusters*, 1957

Perkins, Roger, *Operation Paraquat: The Battle for South Georgia*, 1986

Robinson, Mike, *Fighting Skills of the SAS*, 1991

Simpson III, Charles M., *Inside the Green Berets*, 1983

Smiley, David, *Arabian Assignment*, 1965

Stanton, Shelby L., *Green Berets at War,* 1985
Sutherland, Lt-Col Ian, *Special Forces of the United States Army,*
    1990
Suvorov, Viktor, *Soviet Military Intelligence,* 1986
Warner, Philip, *Special Air Service,* 1971